Multi-Tiered Systems of Support for Young Children

Driving Change in Early Education

edited by

Judith J. Carta, Ph.D.
University of Kansas
Kansas City

and

Robin Miller Young, Ed.D.
Northern Illinois University
Dekalb

with invited contributors

Baltimore • London • Sydney

Paul H. Brookes Publishing Co.
Post Office Box 10624
Baltimore, Maryland 21285-0624
USA
www.brookespublishing.com

Copyright © 2019 by Paul H. Brookes Publishing Co., Inc.
All rights reserved.

"Paul H. Brookes Publishing Co." is a registered trademark of
Paul H. Brookes Publishing Co., Inc.

Story Friends™, Ages & Stages Questionnaires®, and AEPS® are registered trademarks of
Paul H. Brookes Publishing Co., Inc.

Typeset by Absolute Service, Inc., Towson, Maryland.
Manufactured in the United States of America by Sheridan Books, Inc., Chelsea, Michigan.

All examples in this book are composites. Any similarity to actual individuals or circumstances is coincidental, and no implications should be inferred.

Purchasers of *Multi-Tiered Systems of Support for Young Children: Driving Change in Early Education* are granted permission to download, print, and photocopy the forms in the text for educational purposes. These forms may not be reproduced to generate revenue for any program or individual. Photocopies may only be made from an original book. *Unauthorized use beyond this privilege may be prosecutable under federal law.* You will see the copyright protection notice at the bottom of each photocopiable page.

Library of Congress Cataloging-in-Publication Data

Names: Carta, Judith J., editor. | Young, Robin Miller, editor.
Title: Multi-tiered systems of support for young children : driving change in early education / edited by Judith J. Carta and Robin Miller Young.
Description: Baltimore, Maryland : Paul H. Brookes Publishing Co., 2019. | Includes bibliographical references and index.
Identifiers: LCCN 2018010774 (print) | LCCN 2018026703 (ebook) | ISBN 9781681253060 (epub) | ISBN 9781681253077 (pdf) | ISBN 9781681251943 (paperback)
Subjects: LCSH: Early childhood education. | Early childhood special education. | Student assistance programs. | Academic achievement. | BISAC: EDUCATION / Preschool & Kindergarten. | EDUCATION / Special Education / General.
Classification: LCC LB1139.23 (ebook) | LCC LB1139.23 .M86 2019 (print) | DDC 371.9–dc23
LC record available at https://lccn.loc.gov/2018010774
British Library Cataloguing in Publication data are available from the British Library.

2022   2021   2020   2019   2018

10   9   8   7   6   5   4   3   2   1

Table of Contents

About the Videos and Downloads v
About the Editors vii
About the Contributors ix
Preface xvii
Acknowledgments xx

1 Introduction to Multi-Tiered Systems of Support in
  Early Education 1
  Judith J. Carta

2 Leadership Practices to Design and Operationalize
  MTSS Frameworks for Young Children 15
  Robin Miller Young

3 Employing Implementation Science to Transition Early
  Childhood Systems into MTSS 41
  Allison J. Metz, Jennifer Schroeder, and Robin Miller Young

  Appendix 3A: A Stage-Based Active Implementation
  Planning Tool 63

  Appendix 3B: Multi-Tiered Systems of Support in Early Childhood:
  Stages of Implementation Analysis 68

4 Using Data-Based Decision Making to Improve Learning
  Outcomes for All Children 73
  Robin L. Hojnoski and Joy C. Polignano

5 Developing and Sustaining High-Quality Tier 1 Early
  Literacy and Language Practices 97
  Judith J. Carta, Charles R. Greenwood, and Mary Abbott

  Appendix 5A: Tune-Up Checklist 111

6 Designing and Implementing Tier 2 Instructional Support in
   Early Literacy and Language.. 113
   *Arnold Olszewski, Christa D. Haring, Xigrid T. Soto,
   Lindsey Peters-Sanders, and Howard Goldstein*

7 Designing and Implementing Tier 2 Instructional Supports to
   Promote Social-Emotional Outcomes... 131
   *Mary Louise Hemmeter, Lise Fox, Phillip S. Strain,
   Jessica K. Hardy, and Jaclyn D. Joseph*

8 Creating and Providing Tier 3 Instructional Support..................................... 153
   *Ruth A. Kaminski, Kelly A. Powell-Smith, and
   Katherine Bravo Aguayo*

9 Meeting the Needs of Young Dual Language Learners in
   Multi-Tiered Systems of Support 171
   Lillian K. Durán and Alisha Wackerle-Hollman

   Appendix 9A: Language Exposure Evaluation Report (LEER).................. 191

10 Meeting the Needs of Young Children With Disabilities in a
   Blended ECE and ECSE Multi-Tiered System of Support.............................. 193
   Robin Miller Young, Lynette K. Chandler, and Judith J. Carta

11 Scaling Up Multi-Tiered Systems of Support 215
   Lise Fox, Barbara J. Smith, and Deanna Pearce Law

12 Engaging Families in Multi-Tiered Systems of Support................................ 235
   Lisa L. Knoche and Susan M. Sheridan

   Appendix 12A: Self-Assessment of Family Engagement Practices........... 249

   Appendix 12B: Home–School Plan.. 251

13 The Path Forward for Multi-Tiered Systems of Support in
   Early Education.. 253
   Scott R. McConnell

Index 269

About the Videos and Downloads

Purchasers of this book may download, print, and/or photocopy the forms for educational use. Purchasers of this book may access accompanying video content that illustrates key concepts discussed throughout the chapters. The forms are included with the print book and are also available online with the video links at **www.brookespublishing.com/carta/materials**

About the Editors

Judith J. Carta, Ph.D., Juniper Gardens Children's Project, University of Kansas, 444 Minnesota Avenue, Suite 300, Kansas City, KS 66101

Dr. Carta is a senior scientist in the Institute for Life Span Studies and professor of special education at the University of Kansas. She has directed a number of federally funded research centers and projects focused on developing practices that teachers and parents can use to promote children's early learning, particularly in vulnerable populations. Her key research and policy interests include tiered intervention models for advancing children's language, early literacy, and social-emotional development; methods for monitoring children's progress; and communitywide interventions for promoting early learning. She was the co-director of the Center for Response to Intervention in Early Childhood. She currently co-directs the Bridging the Word Gap Research Network, a collaborative of over 150 researchers, program implementers, civic leaders, and policymakers seeking to find better ways to enhance young children's language-learning environments. She was formerly a teacher of young children with special needs, a member of the Federal Advisory Panel on Head Start Research and Evaluation, a commissioner on the Division for Early Childhood's Commission on Recommended Practices, and the editor of *Topics in Early Childhood Special Education*.

Robin Miller Young, Ed.D., NCSP, Early Childhood Education Program, Department of Special and Early Education (SEED), Gabel Hall 162-E, Northern Illinois University, Dekalb, IL 60115

Dr. Young is currently an assistant professor of early childhood education at Northern Illinois University where she prepares future teacher leaders to employ evidence-based practices to identify assets and provide services to meet the needs of children and families. Prior to her present position, Dr. Young guided development of MTSS frameworks while serving on classroom and administrative leadership teams at Prairie Children Preschool (Aurora, IL). The community preschool has operated as an ECE/ECSE blended program since 1998 and has won awards for developing and operating systemwide practices that effectively integrate early learning and social-emotional tiered-instructional models. Her professional partnership work includes direct services, consultative supports, and coaching strategies for moving programs into MTSS frameworks. Additionally, she ensures that professional preservice and in-service training and licensure efforts to create a workforce prepared to provide effective and efficient services in this framework. Dr. Young's scholarship includes grant-funded work resulting in numerous presentations, published curricula, book chapters, and data-based and practitioner-oriented articles. She is currently examining methods to prepare early childhood educators to design and deliver multi-week, interdisciplinary instructional units that develop children's vocabulary skills within proactive social-emotional settings. Dr. Young is also examining preparation of directors/principals and teacher-leaders who can engage in leadership behaviors that will continue moving early learning programs into effective and efficient MTSS frameworks.

About the Contributors

Mary Abbott, Ph.D., Dynamic Measurement Group, 859 Willamette Street, Suite 320, Eugene, Oregon
Dr. Mary Abbott is a research scientist focusing in areas of literacy instruction. Her research areas of interest include preschool, K–12, adult literacy instruction and implementation, literacy assessment, Response to Intervention/multi-tiered systems of support (RTI/MTSS), and teacher professional development.

Katherine Bravo Aguayo, Professional Development Specialist and Senior Research Assistant, Dynamic Measurement Group, 859 Willamette Street, Suite 320, Eugene, Oregon
Katherine Bravo Aguayo is a professional development specialist and senior research assistant with Dynamic Measurement Group. She has worked with students in grades pre-K through high school in a variety of research and educational settings for the past decade and is co-author of the Preschool Early Literacy Indicators (PELI), a measure of early literacy skills. She earned her master's degree in special education with an emphasis in early intervention from the University of Oregon where her research interests included dual language development and educational supports for children with autism spectrum disorder.

Lynette K. Chandler, Ph.D., Consultant, California
Dr. Lynette K. Chandler retired from Northern Illinois University, where she taught courses in early intervention (EI) and early childhood special education (ECSE) and served as the program coordinator for special education. She currently works as a consultant for a variety of EI/ECSE grant-funded projects. She is a past president of the Division for Early Childhood and serves as a member of the editorial board for several EI/ECSE focused journals.

Lillian K. Durán, Ph.D., University of Oregon, Special Education and Clinical Sciences, 5261 University of Oregon, Eugene, Oregon
Dr. Lillian K. Durán has a doctoral degree in educational psychology from the University of Minnesota and is currently an associate professor in the Department of Special Education and Clinical Sciences at the University of Oregon. Her research focuses on improving instructional and assessment practices with preschool-age dual language learners (DLLs). She is currently a co-principal investigator on an IES Goal 5 measurement grant to develop a Spanish version of the Individual Growth and Development Indicators (S-IGDIs), an early language and literacy general outcome measure for screening and progress monitoring in preschool.

Lise Fox, Ph.D., University of South Florida, 13301 Bruce B. Downs Boulevard, Tampa, Florida
Dr. Lise Fox is a professor in the Department of Child and Family Studies at the University of South Florida. She is one of the developers of the Pyramid Model for Promoting Social Emotional Competence in Infants and Young Children and is engaged in national training and technical assistance for implementation of the approach. Her research areas include: Positive behavior support, classroom coaching of early educators, data-based decision-making, and program-wide implementation and scale-up.

Howard Goldstein, Ph.D., University of South Florida, 13301 Bruce B. Downs Boulevard, Tampa, Florida
Dr. Howard Goldstein is Associate Dean for Research and Professor of Communication Sciences and Disorders at University of South Florida. He is a nationally known scholar for his research in the field of child language intervention. His recent research has sought to enhance the language and literacy development of students in high-poverty schools who are at high risk for language and reading disabilities. Dr. Goldstein's contributions to the field were recognized through honors of the American Speech-Language-Hearing Association in 2016.

Charles R. Greenwood, Ph.D., University of Kansas, Juniper Gardens Children's Project, 444 Minnesota Avenue, Suite 300, Kansas City, Kansas
Dr. Charles R. Greenwood is a doctoral graduate of the University of Utah. Former director of the Juniper Gardens Children's Project, he is an accomplished researcher and author of behavioral and educational research and practice focused on children and families in low-income communities. His current research is focused on early childhood applications and issues of the MTSS/RTI approach to instruction and services.

Jessica K. Hardy, Ph.D., University of Louisville, Department of Special Education, Louisville, Kentucky
Dr. Jessica K. Hardy is currently Assistant Professor of Special Education, and her primary research interests including evidence-based instructional practices and early childhood coaching. She also has extensive experience working with teachers and coaches in using the Pyramid Model in early childhood classrooms to support young children's social-emotional development and address their behavioral needs. She was formerly a Head Start teacher and a preschool special education teacher.

Christa D. Haring, Ph.D., CCC-SLP, University of South Florida, 13301 Bruce B. Downs Boulevard, Tampa, Florida
Dr. Christa D. Haring served as a special educator, speech-language pathologist, and teacher educator for 10 years in public schools, spurring her interest in identifying ways to measure and improve outcomes for low-performing teachers and students. Currently, she teaches educator preparation courses centered on instructional practices to improve reading skills for students with dyslexia. Her research focuses on language and literacy interventions for parents and teachers, and innovative community programs supporting children from high-poverty areas.

Mary Louise Hemmeter, Ph.D., Vanderbilt University, Department of Special Education, 304D One Magnolia Circle, Nashville, Tennessee
Dr. Mary Louise Hemmeter is Professor of Special Education at Vanderbilt University. Her research focuses on effective instruction, supporting social emotional development and addressing challenging behavior, and coaching teachers. She has been a principal investigator (PI) or Co-PI on numerous projects funded by the U.S. Departments of Education and Health and Human Services. Through her work on the National Center on the Social Emotional Foundations for Early Learning and funded research projects, she was involved in the development of the Pyramid Model for Supporting Social Emotional Competence in Young Children and a model for coaching teachers to implement effective practices known as Practice Based Coaching.

Robin L. Hojnoski, Ph.D., Lehigh University, 111 Research Drive, Bethlehem, Pennsylvania
Dr. Robin L. Hojnoski is an associate professor in school psychology at Lehigh University. Her research centers on applying school psychology principles and practices to support trajectories for early school success. She has conducted work specifically in the areas of assessment and intervention in early mathematics.

Jaclyn (Jackie) D. Joseph, Ph.D., BCBA, University of Denver, Denver, Colorado
Dr. Jaclyn D. Joseph is an assistant research professor at the University of Denver where she works at the Positive Early Learning Experiences Center. Dr. Joseph is involved in a number of projects at the PELE Center that involve research and technical assistance on the LEAP Model, Pyramid Model, Prevent Teach Reinforce for Young Children, and Prevent Teach Reinforce for Families. Dr. Joseph's professional and research interests include young children with challenging behavior and interventions for improving their social-emotional competence. She is also dedicated to promoting and advocating for high-quality inclusive early care and education opportunities for all young children and especially for her determined, strong, and amazing little girl who has a rare genetic disorder.

Ruth A. Kaminski, Ph.D., Dynamic Measurement Group, 859 Willamette Street, Suite 320, Eugene, Oregon
Dr. Ruth A. Kaminski is Director of Research and Development for Dynamic Measurement Group. Dr. Kaminski's academic background includes degrees in speech pathology, early intervention, and school psychology. For more than 20 years she has conducted research on assessment and preventative interventions for preschool and early elementary-age children. Dr. Kaminski is a co-author of *Dynamic Indicators of Basic Early Literacy Skills* (DIBELS) and of *Reading Ready*, a Tier-3 intervention for early literacy skills in preschool.

Lisa L. Knoche, Ph.D., University of Nebraska-Lincoln, 238 Teachers College Hall, Lincoln, Nebraska
Dr. Lisa L. Knoche is an applied developmental psychologist with expertise in the design, development, and evaluation of early childhood intervention and prevention programs implemented to support healthy development in young children and support family engagement in early learning. Dr. Knoche is particularly experienced

in issues of implementation science and is interested in identifying and supporting effective professional development strategies for early childhood professionals serving children birth through age 5 years in home- and center-based settings. She has extensive experience in implementing collaborative research programs with community partners.

Deanna Pearce Law, M.Ed., Omaha, Nebraska
Deanna Pearce Law has served as a school psychologist since 2005 in a number of schools across Canada and in the United States. She completed her master's degree in education at the University of British Colombia in Vancouver, Canada. Deanna continued her studies in early childhood at the University of Colorado Denver, where she completed her doctorate in education leadership for educational equity. Her dissertation research focused on multi-level systems implementation of evidence-based practices in early childhood education and the Pyramid Model for Supporting Social Emotional Competence in Infants and Young Children. She is currently working as an independent consultant in Omaha, Nebraska, and enjoys time with her 18-month-old daughter, Laya Faye, and husband, Derek Law.

Scott R. McConnell, Ph.D., University of Minnesota, 56 East River Parkway, Minneapolis, Minnesota
Dr. Scott R. McConnell is Professor of Educational Psychology and Fesler-Lampert Chair in Urban and Regional Affairs at the University of Minnesota. His research focuses primarily on preschool-age children and the skills and competencies that will enable them to learn and participate in school and other settings. He and his colleagues at IGDILab are developing and testing applications for Individual Growth and Development Indicators of language and early literacy development for preschoolers. He also is involved in several efforts, locally and nationally, to eliminate the word gap—language disparities that occur early in young children's lives.

Allison J. Metz, Ph.D., Frank Porter Graham Child Development Institute at The University of North Carolina at Chapel Hill, 105 Smith Level Road, Chapel Hill, North Carolina
Dr. Allison J. Metz is a developmental psychologist, Director of the National Implementation Research Network (NIRN), and Senior Implementation Specialist at the Frank Porter Graham Child Development Institute at The University of North Carolina at Chapel Hill. Dr. Metz specializes in the implementation, mainstreaming, and scaling of evidence to achieve social impact for children and families in a range of human service and education areas, with an emphasis on child welfare and early childhood service contexts. Her work focuses in several key areas including the development of evidence-informed practice models; the use of effective implementation and scaling strategies to improve the application of evidence in service delivery systems; and the development of coaching, continuous quality improvement, and sustainability strategies. She is Co-Chair for the Global Implementation Conference, a part of the Global Implementation Initiative. Dr. Metz is co-editor of *Applying Implementation Science in Early Childhood Programs and Systems* (with T. Halle & I. Martinez-Beck; Paul H., Brookes Publishing Co., 2013).

Arnold Olszewski, Ph.D., Miami University, 301 South Patterson Avenue, Oxford, Ohio
Dr. Arnold Olszewski is an assistant professor and speech-language pathologist in the Department of Speech Pathology and Audiology at Miami University. His research focuses on developing feasible, evidence-based language and literacy interventions for young children. Dr. Olszewski's research has been published in various journals and presented at national conferences.

Lindsey Peters-Sanders, M.A.T., University of South Florida, 13301 Bruce B. Downs Boulevard, Tampa, Florida
Lindsey Peters-Sanders is a doctoral candidate in the Department of Communication Sciences and Disorders at the University of South Florida. Her research focuses on implementing supplemental language and early literacy instruction that applies a multi-tiered systems of support framework in preschools serving at-risk children.

Joy C. Polignano, Ph.D., NCSP, Berks County Intermediate Unit, Reading Pennsylvania
Joy C. Polignano, Ph.D., NCSP, earned her doctoral degree and national certification in school psychology from Lehigh University before completing a U.S. Department of Education Institute of Education Sciences (IES) postdoctoral fellowship with the Anita Zucker Center for Excellence in Early Childhood Studies at the University of Florida. She has worked as an early care and education teacher and has been actively involved in the implementation of four, large-scale IES randomized-controlled efficacy studies designed to promote the social-emotional competence and pre-academic skill development of young children with or at risk for disabilities. She currently serves as an early intervention school psychologist in Pennsylvania.

Kelly A. Powell-Smith, Ph.D., NCSP, Dynamic Measurement Group, 859 Willamette Street, Suite 320, Eugene, Oregon
Dr. Kelly A. Powell-Smith is Vice President and Associate Director of Research and Development at Dynamic Measurement Group. Dr. Powell-Smith, a nationally certified school psychologist, obtained her doctorate in school psychology from the University of Oregon. She is a former associate professor of school psychology at the University of South Florida. She was a faculty associate of the Florida Center for Reading Research (FCRR) and a consultant with the Eastern Regional Reading First Technical Assistance Center (ERFTAC). She has provided training in formative assessment and academic interventions in 22 states and Canada. Over the past 25 years, Dr. Powell-Smith has conducted research related to children with various learning and behavioral difficulties and has conducted over 225 national, state, and regional workshops and presentations.

Jennifer Schroeder, Ph.D., The Implementation Group, Boulder, Colorado
Dr. Jennifer Schroeder is a clinical child psychologist with over 15 years of experience consulting to nonprofit, education, government, and philanthropic organizations to improve and sustain effective programs and services for children, youth, and families. She is the founder and president of The Implementation Group, a strategic planning and evaluation firm that supports effective implementation

practices in human services and education. She holds a doctorate in clinical child psychology from Bowling Green State University and completed pre- and postdoctoral fellowships at Yale University.

Susan M. Sheridan, Ph.D., University of Nebraska-Lincoln, 216 Mabel Lee Hall, Lincoln, Nebraska
Dr. Susan M. Sheridan is Director of the Nebraska Center for Research on Children, Youth, Families and Schools (CYFS) and a George Holmes University professor of educational psychology at the University of Nebraska-Lincoln. Dr. Sheridan's research is focused on parent–teacher relationships; the development of meaningful home–school partnerships; early childhood education and interventions; rural education; and interventions promoting children's social skills, social-emotional development, and behavioral competencies. Dr. Sheridan has published more than 100 books and chapters and has refereed journal articles on these and related topics. Noteworthy awards include the American Psychological Association's Division 16 (School Psychology) Lightner Witmer Award (1993) for early career accomplishments, the Senior Scientist Award (2015) for distinguished career-long scholarship, the 2005 Presidential Award from the National Association of School Psychologists, and the 2014 University of Nebraska's Outstanding Research and Creativity Award.

Barbara J. Smith, Ph.D., University of Colorado, 1380 Lawrence Street, Denver, Colorado
Dr. Barbara Smith is Research Professor and one of the original developers of the Pyramid Model and the associated statewide implementation approach. Her areas of interest are early childhood policy and implementation supports of evidence based practices.

Xigrid T. Soto, M.S., University of South Florida, 13301 Bruce B. Downs Boulevard, Tampa, Florida
Xigrid T. Soto is a doctoral candidate in the Department of Communication Sciences and Disorders at the University of South Florida. She works under the mentorship of Dr. Howard Goldstein, whose area of specialty includes the provision of preventative early literacy and language interventions to at-risk preschoolers living in poverty. Her research focuses on the delivery of early literacy interventions for Latino preschoolers who are dual language learners.

Phillip S. Strain, Ph.D., University of Denver, 1380 Lawrence Street, Denver, Colorado
Dr. Phillip S. Strain is the James C. Kennedy Endowed Chair in Urban Education at the University of Denver. Dr. Strain has worked in the field of early intervention since 1974, is the author of over 300 scientific papers and serves on the editorial boards of over a dozen professional journals. His primary research interests include: 1) intervention for young children with early onset conduct disorders; 2) remediation of social behavior deficits in young children with autism; 3) design and delivery of community-based, comprehensive early intervention for children with autism; and 4) analysis of individual and systemic variables affecting the adoption and sustained use of evidence-based practices for children with severe behavior disorders.

Alisha Wackerle-Hollman, Ph.D., University of Minnesota, 2001 Plymouth Avenue North, Minneapolis, Minnesota
Dr. Alisha Wackerle-Hollman is an educational psychologist whose research addresses both development of English, Spanish, and Hmong early literacy and language measures for preschool-age students as well as the design and evaluation of parent education programs. She is the co-director of the IGDIlab, a research lab at the University of Minnesota where she has secured over 5 million dollars in funding since 2012. Dr. Wackerle-Hollman's work focuses on measurement systems designed to evaluate progress on language and literacy in English- and Spanish-speaking preschoolers and the adaptation of these measures for use on tablet devices. She is specifically interested in using data from these measurement platforms to support effective data-based decision making in the context of multi-tiered systems of support.

Preface

The last 20 years have witnessed several changes in the landscape of early education. Policymakers and the general public are increasingly aware of the importance of the early years and the need to provide young children with high quality learning experiences. Early education programs are seeking to support children in achieving developmental milestones, prepare them with skills and motivation to engage successfully in the early elementary school curriculum, and give them the foundation they need for lifelong learning. Greater percentages of young children are attending early education programs whether they are state-funded preschool programs, other community-based child care programs, Head Start programs, or faith-based programs for young children. In addition, with demographic shifts, early educational programs are serving greater numbers of children from immigrant families. Thus, issues of home language, culture, and second-language learning are becoming increasingly pressing. Moreover, as more children with special needs and behavior challenges participate in early childhood settings, teachers require more sophisticated skills to provide all children with appropriate levels of instructional support to help them achieve essential outcomes and to prevent more serious learning problems.

National organizations for early educators have laid out the principles and practices for meeting the learning needs of all children (Copple & Bredekamp, 2009; DEC/NAEYC, 2009). Among these are specific strategies for assessing children's growth in learning to identify children who would benefit from greater amounts of instructional support, interventions that increase children's learning opportunities and add greater instructional intensity, and approaches for using data on children's learning to evaluate how well instruction is changing children's learning trajectories. Multi-tiered systems of support (MTSS) is a framework that uses a systematic problem-solving model and data-based decision-making process across all levels of an educational system to ensure that every child receives the level of academic and behavioral support needed to be successful (Batsche et al., 2005). The intent of MTSS is to provide every child with an educational program founded on evidence-based instruction and progress-monitoring practices to help them learn the early academic skills and developmental competencies needed to promote their readiness for school. The expectation is that when MTSS strategies are implemented in early education settings, preschool-age children will be less likely to need special education or other remedial services when they enter the elementary grades (Greenwood, Bradfield, Kaminski, Linas, Carta, & Nylander, 2011).

The purpose of this book is to define and describe each of the components necessary to implement MTSS at the individual child and classroom levels and to illustrate how the components work together within a larger MTSS framework within a program. Although both general and special early education embrace the notion of preventing academic and social problems for children at risk for developmental delays, the evidence base for practices for closing the school readiness gap is just emerging. In this volume, we identify how many of those practices can be implemented within a tiered model and how this information can be used to improve the academic proficiency and social-emotional growth of all children.

This book is written for all who are striving to organize early education programs into systems that provide preschool children with carefully designed instruction that matches their level of need. We realize that before programs dive into an educational reform or new set of practices, achieving consensus among their team members for this new direction will be a necessary first step. We hope this book and its accompanying videos will help individuals understand the components of MTSS and see how a team can work together to take on a new framework like MTSS and how team members can contribute to implementing this approach in their setting. We hope that the vignettes will help to personalize the context for each chapter's content and will help the reader appreciate the perspective of the practitioner who is learning about MTSS and its implementation.

We think this book is unique in a number of respects. First, it goes beyond the conceptual or theoretical aspects of MTSS. It describes each of the components of MTSS: the use of evidence-based instruction in the core curriculum or foundation, the use of measures and a decision-making framework for identifying children needing additional support, the implementation of enhanced tiers of instruction to meet the needs of all children, and the frequent monitoring of children's growth in response to enhanced instruction. Second, it describes how professionals should engage families in MTSS, and it puts a clear focus on ways children who are dual-language learners and/or who have special instructional needs would be included in a program implementing MTSS. Finally, it helps school, district, and regional educational leaders understand how Implementation Science can be used to guide the systematic integration of MTSS into their programs, and then, once that is in place, to scale-up MTSS more broadly.

Although this volume provides direction for how MTSS can be implemented at this writing, we acknowledge that this framework and how it is operationalized is evolving. MTSS continues to be modified in response to new research, new policies, and knowledge generated through its implementation. Our hope is that this text will illustrate to program leaders and practitioners that MTSS can be used to deliver instruction that meets the needs of each child, that it will offer the decision-making tools to make instructional adjustments as necessary, and that the resulting programs will be stronger and more effective.

REFERENCES

Batsche, G., Elliott, J., Graden, J., Grimes, J., Kovaleski, J., Prasse, D., et al. (2005). Response to intervention: Policy considerations and implementation. Alexandria, VA: National Association of State Directors of Special Education.

Copple, C., & Bredekamp, S. (2009). Developmentally appropriate practice in early childhood programs serving children from birth through age 8 (3rd ed.). Washington, DC: NAEYC.

Division for Early Childhood (DEC), National Association for the Education of Young Children (NAEYC). (2009). *Early childhood inclusion: A joint position statement of the Division for Early Childhood (DEC) and the National Association for the Education of Young Children (NAEYC)*. Retrieved from http://www.dec-sped.org/position-statements

Division for Early Childhood (DEC), National Association for the Education of Young Children (NAEYC), & National Head Start Association (NHSA). (2013). *Frameworks for Response to Intervention in early childhood: Description and implications*. Missoula, MT: Author. Retrieved from http://www.dec-sped.org/position-statements

Greenwood, C. R., Bradfield, T. Kaminski, R., Linas, M., Carta, J. J, & Nylander, D. (2011). The Response to Intervention (RTI) approach in early childhood. *Focus on Exceptional Children. 43*, (9), 1-22.

Acknowledgments

A project of this scope depends on a host of collaborators. To everyone who provided us with your wisdom, expertise, time, energy, and financial support, we want to convey our sincere gratitude. In particular, we would like to thank:

- The contributing authors whose wisdom and dedication to improving the outcomes of young children shined through each chapter.

- The editorial and production teams at Brookes (Johanna Schmitter, Melissa Solarz, Shannon McClellan, Lynda Phung Wheeler, and Mary Beth Winkler) whose expertise was instrumental in bringing this book into print.

- April Fleming, whose editorial assistance and recommendations gave each chapter its special polish.

- Annivar Salgado and his Infinitec Team, whose skill and expertise created video products that will show our readers how MTSS really works.

- Mikey Mullen at the Center for Professional Studies at Towson University who provided the finishing touches to our video material.

- Superintendent Dr. Karen Sullivan, Indian Prairie School District (IPSD) 204, a visionary early childhood educator, who led development of one of the first inclusive/blended community preschools in the country and served as its first principal where all children could achieve essential schooling outcomes with their community peers. Her kindness and generosity allowed filming to take place at the Crouse Education Center, IPSD's administrative center and the location of Prairie Children Preschool (PCP).

- Dr. Kristine Black, Tammy Cain, Cathleen Czaplewski, Latia Johnson, and Natalie Phillips, exemplary early childhood educators and specialists at PCP, whose time and talents as actresses in our videos allowed us to showcase authentic teamwork in an MTSS framework.

- Sally Osborne, PCP Principal, the PCP Office Team, and PCP Custodial Staff for their generous welcome, support, and local arrangements that allowed us to film on site at their school for this project.

- Esteemed IPSD 204 colleagues who served at PCP and in Early Childhood Education before PCP opened in 1998, whose service to the young children and families of IPSD 204 informed, and continues to inform, our understandings of the MTSS framework and inclusive/blended schools and classrooms.
- Collaborators from the Center for RTI in Early Childhood (Charles Greenwood, Scott R. McConnell, Howard Goldstein, Ruth Kaminski, Jane Atwater and their teams) who were pioneers in developing some of the necessary ingredients for RTI.
- The National Center for Special Education Research within the Institute of Educational Sciences, which had the vision to provide the funding for CRTIEC and other research projects that have provided the empirical support for MTSS.

*I would like to thank my husband, Charlie Greenwood,
for being a constant source of knowledge, inspiration, joy, and love for
these many years. Thanks also go to my daughter, Amelia,
who keeps me grounded in searching for ways to promote meaningful
outcomes for all children.*
— *Judith J. Carta*

*To my parents, Bob and Ann Miller, thanks for the gifts
of rousing encouragement and steadfast support; every child should
experience the unconditional love I have experienced throughout
my lifetime. To my children, Matthew and Meagan, thank you for the
boundless joy you have brought to my life, and the future blessings yet
to be experienced. Finally, endless thanks to my husband, Rich Young,
for your unwavering strength and support of my various professional
projects throughout the years to improve the lives of young children and
their families. You are a fabulous life partner, and I love you!
With family and faith, all things are possible.*
— *Robin Miller Young*

1

Introduction to Multi-Tiered Systems of Support in Early Education

Judith J. Carta

Despite the increasing availability of quality early education programs in recent years, a sizable portion of young children leave preschool lacking many of the skills needed to engage in and benefit from instruction in quality kindergarten classes. Some children have limited vocabularies, whereas others lack social-emotional skills and have difficulties with self-regulation (Child Trends Databank, 2015). Some may not have acquired skills in early literacy, math, or science that pave the way to academic success. The reasons for these challenges are many. Some children have come from homes with limited opportunities to learn these skills and behaviors that will be needed in kindergarten (Blair, 2010). Many may not have received the necessary support for language and social-emotional development from their teachers, caregivers, or family members. In addition, some may not have had opportunities to attend high-quality preschool and been able to learn school readiness skills. Other children may have delays in acquiring these skills in spite of ample opportunities to learn them.

The learning needs of students entering preschool programs are complex and growing in number. Early education programs are increasingly aware that higher proportions of their students may be at risk for later learning and behavior problems and are seeking ways to provide more timely interventions. While programs face growing challenges of providing children with instruction of varying levels of intensity to match their needs, new evidence-based practices can reduce the achievement gap while children are still in early education settings. If children's delays are identified early, and they receive an appropriate level of instructional intervention in a timely manner, many children will acquire the skills they need to be successful in kindergarten and beyond. Multi-tiered systems of support (MTSS) offer programs and a framework of evidence-based practices to ensure that children receive the support they need without having to demonstrate failure first.

MTSS offers a new paradigm that shifts the ways programs respond to students—a shift from trying to fit students into specific programs and services to a new approach focused on designing services and support around the needs of the individual student. In this way, programs employing MTSS have a quicker way of identifying students showing the first signs of delay and addressing these delays with individualized supports, therefore preventing problems and improving the likelihood that students will be ready to succeed in kindergarten.

We, the authors, have written and organized this book to help those who are striving to organize early education programs into systems that provide preschool children with carefully designed instruction that matches their level of need. MTSS offers a framework with useful tools that helps educators address children's diverse learning needs through a set of practices for identifying children who need more instructional support, implementing those practices, and quickly determining whether the practices are working. The purpose of this book is to describe each of the components of MTSS and to illustrate for practitioners how the practices work together within a larger MTSS framework within a school, program, or state. Our goal is to help practitioners, program administrators, and researchers alike understand those practices, learn about the evidence supporting them, and provide information to guide the implementation of MTSS, resulting in improved learning proficiency of all children. We hope this book will help readers to understand the many practices of MTSS, comprehend how the components of MTSS work together, and recognize how team members can work together to support their implementation.

We also have designed this book for use in graduate and undergraduate teacher education programs in early childhood education (ECE) and early childhood special education (ECSE). We realize that students who go on to teach young children will be working in programs that are addressing the needs of children with and without disabilities. The information presented in this book should be relevant to teachers in ECE or ECSE programs and should help them apply evidence-based practices to all children. Although the content in this book should be relevant to the entire early childhood age range (birth to age 8), it will be most applicable for programs serving preschool-aged children. We think that the information in this text will be most relevant to program directors and practitioners within center-based settings such as state-funded prekindergarten classes, Head Start, or other center-based programs (including private, tuition-based programs).

Programs that implement MTSS use a systematic problem-solving model and data-based decision-making process that can be applied at any number of educational grade levels or to programs serving students varying in ability levels. This book describes the application of MTSS to early education. Depending on the specific early education setting, the key players that form the leadership team that drives the MTSS initiative in preschool programs will vary. In a state-funded prekindergarten program, for example, the players may include individuals such as the speech therapist, school psychologist, school social worker, early childhood coordinator, literacy specialist, positive behavior support specialist, and school principal. In a Head Start program, individuals involved may include the Head Start director, disabilities coordinator, coaches, or teachers. In all cases, programs must choose the most appropriate staff members to design the system, select screeners and interventions, carry out the universal screening, engage in data-based decision making to determine how children are identified for higher tiers of intervention, implement each tier of intervention, and monitor children's progress in response to intervention.

The fundamental promise of MTSS is that all students will be engaged in educational programs founded on evidenced-based instruction and progress-monitoring practices to increase the likelihood that they will master early academic and developmental competencies. When these systems are implemented in early education settings, children will more quickly receive the level of instructional support that meets their needs. The promise of this approach is *prevention*. More timely, efficient, and individualized support to young children through MTSS means children will be less likely to need special education services when they enter elementary school (Greenwood et al., 2011).

WHAT IS MTSS?

MTSS is a "whole-school, data-driven, prevention-based framework for improving learning outcomes for every student through a layered continuum of evidence-based practices and systems" (Colorado Department of Education, 2015a, p. 1). The goal of MTSS is to organize the resources available in a system or program to meet the needs of all students. At the core of MTSS is a data-based, decision-making problem-solving process that guides differentiated instructional supports to students based on their demonstrated need (Batsche et al., 2005; Colorado Department of Education, 2015b; Deno, 2016; Stoiber & Gettinger, 2016). MTSS is based on the following core principles:

1. All children can learn and achieve when they are provided with high-quality supports to match their needs.

2. Instruction should focus on both academic and behavioral goals.

3. Children showing signs of delay should be identified as early as possible and provided with a level of instructional intensity to match their needs.

4. Interventions to address children's needs should be designed by collaborative teams that include parents, administrators, teachers, and other instructional staff, and should be guided by student data and informed by evidence-based practices.

5. Children's responses to intervention should be continuously monitored, and explicit data-based decision rules should be in place for making adjustments in intervention.

6. All intervention should be based on evidence-based practice implemented with fidelity.

MTSS is based on an earlier instructional framework, Response to Intervention (RtI), and both approaches have focused on identifying and addressing students' learning needs at the earliest possible time. RtI paved the way for MTSS and incorporates many of the same principles as MTSS, including high-quality, research-based instruction of all students, universal screening of all students to identify those showing the earliest signs of learning difficulties, evidence-based interventions that increase the intensity of instruction to address students' problem areas, frequent progress monitoring for tracking students' response to targeted interventions, and decision making based on progress-monitoring data. In most past approaches to RtI, the focus was primarily on providing support for struggling learners in the academic areas—primarily in literacy, language, and sometimes mathematics. In contrast, MTSS moves beyond RtI in that it focuses on creating a continuum of systemwide strategies and structures that aim to address barriers to student learning in both academic and behavior areas. Thus, MTSS offers the potential to create systemic change resulting in improved academic and social outcomes for all learners. In addition, MTSS puts a greater focus on systemwide support for teachers' delivery of instruction that will benefit all students. In school districts, this systemwide support means that practices, programs, and policies are aligned at the classroom, school, and district levels. This typically means that teachers, administrators, and instructional support personnel often change the way they work together and shift to a more collaborative and cohesive culture.

Core Components of MTSS

A number of MTSS models exist across states and school districts, and these vary somewhat in their content and manner of delivery. The following core set of components outlines the basic features of MTSS that can be found across most models.

1. *Evidence-based instruction and intervention practices:* The foundation of MTSS is its use of research-based instructional and intervention practices that have been proven effective in improving outcomes for students. The use of scientifically based interventions within RtI was originally stipulated within the Elementary and Secondary Education Act of 1965 (PL 89-10). In MTSS, the assumption is that evidence-based practices (EBPs) will be implemented within both academic and behavioral domains. EBPs are defined as "instructional techniques that meet prescribed criteria related to the research design, quality, quantity, and effect size of supporting research, which have the potential to help bridge the research-to-practice gap and improve student outcomes" (Cook & Cook, 2011, p. 73). Whereas some interventions and instructional practices may have been validated as effective, the number of practices that have been validated for use in early education settings is still quite limited. However, EBPs can also include those for which demonstrated outcomes have been obtained by practitioners using progress monitoring or program evaluation data (Stoiber & Gettinger, 2016). An important caveat about EBPs is that they will not necessarily be effective for all students or in all contexts. One important aspect of the effectiveness of a practice will depend on the quality or fidelity of its implementation. Thus, programs should be sure to gather ongoing fidelity data on their selected instructional interventions to be sure that these strategies are implemented as designed and intended (Gresham, MacMillan, Beebe-Frankenberger, & Bocian, 2000). (More information about EPBs can be found in Chapter 5.)

2. *Emphasis on ensuring implementation fidelity:* When instructional practices are implemented with fidelity, it means that the essential components of the practice are being implemented as designed. The validity of MTSS depends on the effective implementation of each aspect of the system: the universal screening, intervention at each of the available tiers, progress monitoring, and data-based decision making. When each aspect of the system is implemented

as designed, the entire system should be self-correcting and continuously improving based on the cycle of data gathering, action, further data gathering, reappraisal, and refinement (Mercier Smith, Fien, Basaraba, & Travers, 2009). When a practice is not implemented as designed or with the frequency or consistency needed, students are less likely to show improvements in targeted skills. Measuring intervention fidelity is critical in determining if a student's progress is traceable to the intervention used in a multi-tiered system. Failure to examine how well an intervention is delivered can lead to a potentially erroneous conclusion that a student's lack of progress is a result of the student's disability or delay when in fact the intervention was not implemented with fidelity. (More information about implementation fidelity can be found in Chapter 8.)

3. *Universal screening and progress monitoring:* A unique feature of MTSS and RtI is ongoing universal screening and progress monitoring on multiple occasions throughout the school year. Review of these data may be useful for two purposes; first, they may reflect the effectiveness and efficiency of the core instruction being provided to all children. If a high percentage of children are not meeting benchmarks on universal screening measures or showing inadequate growth on progress monitoring measures in response to the core curriculum, then the program leadership teams might use these data to justify modifying the core curriculum to enhance the likelihood of success for all learners. Second, universal screening of all children on an ongoing basis provides a means of identifying those children who may need additional instructional supports to acquire academic skills or address behavioral challenges. Once additional interventions are implemented, progress monitoring is used to determine whether children have demonstrated growth on targeted skills in response to the additional instructional support. (More information about universal screening and problem solving can be found in Chapter 4.)

4. *Layered continuum of supports:* A common feature of MTSS or RtI is the provision of multiple levels or tiers of instructional support to meet the needs of all students—from those making adequate progress in response to the core curriculum to those who may be struggling to master skills. Tier 1 encompasses effective core curriculum and intentional teaching to all students. This ensures that all students have access to a purposefully organized educational environment, a curriculum with evidence-based scope and sequence, and instruction that provides opportunities to learn essential skills in developmentally appropriate activities. Tier 2 typically provides targeted instruction, often in small groups, to those children needing additional academic or behavioral support to help overcome specific learning gaps. Within an MTSS framework, the school/program leaders can determine the type of Tier 2 supports needed for various groups of children. For example, analysis of student performance data might reveal that a significant number of children would benefit from supplemental instruction in phonological awareness skills beyond that provided in the Tier 1 curriculum. Rather than creating multiple individual tutoring plans, the school/program may decide to create a standard Tier 2 phonological awareness intervention or acquire a commercially available intervention that focuses

on this domain, both of which can be implemented in small groups for effective and efficient delivery of the necessary instruction. Tier 3 is more intensive and is typically individually designed and often, though not exclusively, provided in one-to-one interactions between adults and children with significant learning needs. With this type of continuum, instructional or behavioral supports are arranged from least to most intensive, and children are matched to the tier most closely aligned with their needs.

Several other aspects of the tiered model include the following:

- The tiers are *additive*, meaning that learners who need the most intensive intervention receive Tier 1 interventions whenever possible plus those that are appropriate at upper tiers
- The boundaries between tiers are seamless so that the provision and removal of supports is fluid, depending on children's needs
- A learner does *not* have to progress from less-intensive tiers through more-intensive tiers in order to receive highly intensive interventions.

The MTSS framework is not a "wait to fail" model (DEC/NAEYC/NHSA, 2013); instead, interventions and supports of the appropriate intensity are provided whenever the need for such intensive intervention is determined. Consequently, some children may start at the highest tier (most intensive) and move to lower tiers (less intensive) as their needs dictate (see Figure 1.1).

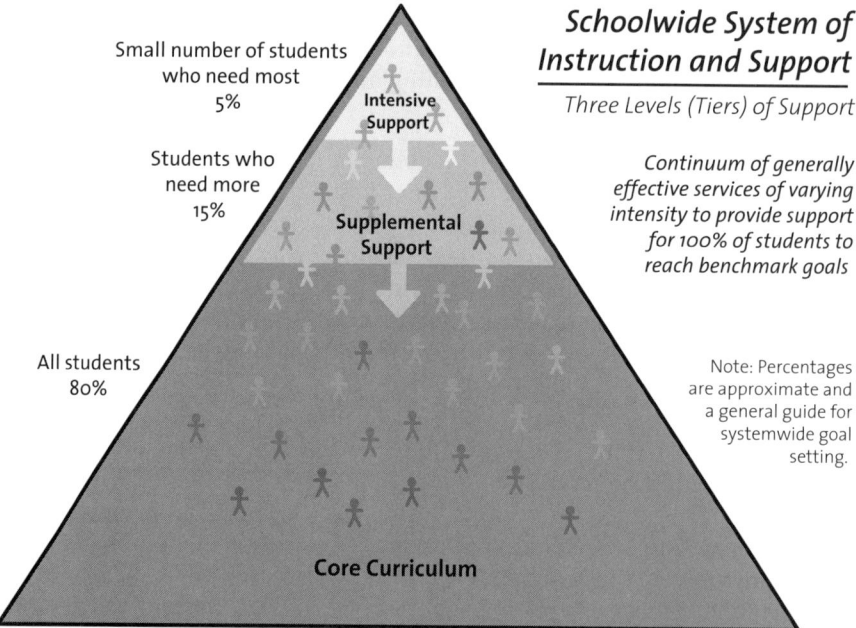

Figure 1.1. Schoolwide system of instruction and support: Three levels (tiers) of support. Reprinted with permission from Dynamic Measurement Group (2009) in Kaminski, R. (2009, September). Center for Response to Intervention in Early Childhood. Presentation at the RTI Innovations Conference, Salt Lake City, UT.

5. *Data-based problem solving and decision making:* A fundamental component of MTSS is the use of the problem-solving process by instructional teams to determine student's needs (Brown-Chidsey & Steege, 2010). The problem-solving process was first introduced with the early implementation of the early RtI models (Marston, 2002; Reschly & Tilly, 1999). The problem-solving process typically includes four steps, beginning with *Problem Identification*, in which what a student should be able to know and do are clearly defined and the problem or discrepancy is laid out between these behavioral/academic expectations and what is actually occurring. During the second step, *Problem Analysis*, hypotheses are developed by the instructional team and multiple sources of data are gathered to confirm or refute the hypotheses. In the third step, *Intervention Plan Development and Implementation*, intervention strategies or interventions are proposed to match the student's need identified in Step 1. Practitioners implement the intervention and receive appropriate support to ensure that the intervention is implemented with fidelity. In the fourth step, *Evaluation of Response to Intervention*, data on the student's progress are examined and evaluated after the intervention has been implemented with fidelity for an adequate amount of time. The instructional team uses the data to determine whether the student's current intervention should be modified, continued, or terminated. (More information about data-based problem solving and decision making can be found in Chapter 4.)

6. *Shared leadership:* A key feature of MTSS is the notion that leadership teams are necessary at both the district and school levels. While some early education programs may not function within school districts, the need for leadership teams at levels beyond the "building" or immediate program level is important. The purpose of these teams is to ensure effective implementation across the multiple levels of the system, which in local education agencies are the district, school, classroom, and individual student. The data-based, problem-solving, and decision-making processes use school–level progress data to identify system support needs such as how best to allocate available resources and funding and how best to target professional development. (More information about leadership teams can be found in Chapter 2.)

7. *Family, school, and community partnering:* An important feature of MTSS models is the development of strategies to encourage family involvement in their child's learning. Parents are critical to the child's success in school and successful MTSS models include parents on their child's instructional team. Programs should have clear protocols for obtaining families' input and involvement in each of the tiers of instructional support and should carry out professional development focused on approaches to promote the engagement of families from diverse cultural and linguistic backgrounds. (More information about engaging families in MTSS can be found in Chapter 12.)

MTSS IN EARLY CHILDHOOD EDUCATION

Most current approaches to educating young children in preschool programs assume that students are benefiting from the core curriculum. If parents or teachers suspect a child may need additional support, it often is not until the student is showing significant problems with learning or behavior—and then the student must go through a process to determine his or her eligibility for special education services. Once the student is determined to be eligible, an instructional team and the parent will design an individualized education program (IEP) that outlines the student's instructional goals and objectives. Specialized interventions to address those goals may or may not be implemented in the general classroom environment.

In contrast to that more traditional framework based on a response to students' lack of adequate progress or "failure" to grow in skills or fluency of performance, MTSS focuses on preventing and providing support for all students, with a more rapid intervention for individual students based on their demonstrated need (Gersten et al., 2008). MTSS employs a unique measurement approach based on universal screening of all children on multiple occasions across the school year. Data from these screenings help identify students not demonstrating expected rates of growth on progress monitoring measures and who might benefit from more intensive instruction. Interventions of increasing intensity (or tiers of instruction) are used to provide an appropriate level of intensity to match individual students' level of need. Students receiving higher tiers of instruction also receive frequent monitoring to ascertain whether the increased level of instruction results in increases in their growth. In this way, programs employing MTSS have a quicker way of identifying students showing the first signs of delay and addressing these delays with individualized supports, therefore preventing problems and improving the likelihood that students will be ready to succeed in kindergarten.

While MTSS may seem a novel concept to many early educators or other professionals who serve preschool students, some principles underlying the MTSS framework should be relatively familiar to early educators (Greenwood et al., 2011). First, early education is founded on the importance of early intervention as a means of preventing or reducing delay. Through universal screening, MTSS attempts to find children who are showing the first signs of learning difficulties instead of waiting for them to demonstrate a significant delay before providing them with additional instructional supports. Second, many early education programs attempt to individualize children's instruction to address the diversity of children they serve. MTSS provides a systematic approach to identifying struggling learners and providing them with a level of instructional intensity to match their needs. Third, the use of progress monitoring has been an important feature across early education settings as programs attempt to determine whether children are making growth in response to the instruction being delivered. Similarly, in MTSS, programs use progress monitoring to examine children's responses to intervention to determine whether changes are necessary in the instruction targeted to a specific child or children within a classroom or program.

Tiered models have been developed for young children and increasingly are being adopted by programs, districts, and states. One of the most popular tiered models, the Pyramid Model, a framework that outlines a set of practices for promoting the social-emotional competence of all young children including children with persistent challenging behavior, is currently being used by hundreds of programs across several states (see Chapters 7 and 11). The practices in the Pyramid Model are defined in tiers to highlight the universal supports necessary for promoting the social-emotional outcomes of all children, the prevention practices designed to provide additional instruction and support to children at risk of challenging behavior or social-emotional delays, and the intervention practices targeted for children with persistent challenging behavior or social-emotional delays. Worth noting is the fact that this popular tiered approach is being implemented by the wide variety of programs serving young children, including community-based child programs, Head Start programs, and Part B and Part C programs, as well as family child care. Studies of implementation of the Pyramid Model have documented its effectiveness in changing teachers' practices for preventing and intervening in children's challenging behavior and improving children's social skills (Hemmeter, Snyder, Fox, & Algina, 2016).

Tiered models have also been developed and shown to enhance young children's early academic skills. The Recognition and Response Model (Buysse & Peisner-Feinberg, 2010) is an example of a tiered instructional model focused on language/early literacy and numeracy skills. Like other tiered models, Recognition and Response is organized around four components:

1. *Recognition* of children needing additional support using screening, assessment, and progress monitoring

2. Research-based instruction for all children and validated instruction for specific children who need additional supports *(Response)*

3. A hierarchy of interventions

4. A collaborative problem-solving approach involving the instructional team and parents working together

Two studies have recently confirmed the effectiveness of Recognition and Response for improving children's outcomes in the areas of language and early literacy (Buysse, Peisner-Feinberg, Soukakou, Fettig, Schaaf & Burchinal, 2016).

Finally, some of the necessary individual components of MTSS systems have been developed specifically for preschool-aged children. Universal screening and progress measures are now available that have been specifically designed for use in guiding data-based decision making in MTSS systems in early childhood. Chapter 4 describes some of the My-IGDI measures that have been designed specifically to identify children who might be most likely to benefit from Tier 2 and 3 interventions in early literacy and language (Wackerle-Holman, Rodriguez, McConnell, Bradfield, & Rodriguez, 2015). Similar measures are available to identify dual language learners who might need additional support (see Chapter 9) or those needing more intensity of instruction in mathematics (Hojnoski, Silberglitt, & Floyd, 2009). These tools will help early education programs easily identify those students needing support and quickly provide them with intervention aligned to their level of need.

Another critical component of MTSS now available to programs serving young children are interventions specifically designed to promote short-term growth that ultimately leads to improved school readiness. A number of these interventions for children needing Tier 2 and Tier 3 support in early literacy and language have been designed and proven to be effective (see Chapters 6 and 8; Goldstein, 2016; Goldstein & Kelley, 2016; Goldstein, Kelley, et al., 2016; Goldstein & Olszewski, 2015; Kaminski & Powell-Smith, 2017). These interventions have been designed to increase children's opportunities to respond and practice important skills. Moreover, these interventions have been designed to address some of the challenges of early childhood settings—they are inexpensive and relatively easy to implement.

Current Challenges to Implementation of MTSS in Early Education

While many advances have taken place to provide early education programs with the knowledge and tools they need to implement tiered models, a variety of barriers still remain as administrators, teachers, and instructional teams seek to implement MTSS to support young children and their families. It is important for programs to consider these as they strive to put these tiered approaches into place.

Lack of a Trained Workforce   Although a number of new tools are now available to support MTSS in early education, there remain a number of challenges to successfully implementing this approach in programs for young children. One of the most significant challenges is the training and expertise of the workforce in many early education settings. In a recent national survey, state directors of early education programs indicated that the major challenge to carrying out RtI, a forerunner to MTSS, in settings for young children was the lack of a trained workforce who could implement the essential components of RtI (Linas, Greenwood, & Carta, 2012). Programs that are serious about adopting MTSS will have to commit to providing the sustained professional development that will be necessary to promote the high-fidelity implementation of MTSS components. They will need to appreciate that more than one-day workshops are necessary for meaningful change to occur in their programs that will result in high-quality instruction. Programs will also need to create the infrastructure necessary to carry out ongoing coaching and supports to build the capacity to sustain an MTSS model.

Knowledge and Appreciation of Evidence-Based Instruction   Another challenge to implementing MTSS in early education is the scarcity of evidence-based instruction in all tiers. While research is available that describes evidence-based instruction in areas such as language, literacy, and social-emotional behaviors (e.g., Bierman & Motamedi, 2015; Powell & Dunlap, 2009; Wasik, Bond, & Hindman, 2006), many early education teachers may not have received systematic instruction on how to implement these powerful interventions within their own classrooms (Justice, Mashburn, Hamre, & Pianta, 2008). As a result, the types of explicit instructional strategies known to promote children's growth in learning are frequently missing in typical early education programs. Many individuals in programs for young children will need to adjust their thinking about implementing the types of intentional instructional strategies necessary to support children's early learning and change children's trajectories to put them on a track toward success. Moreover, a greater awareness among early education professionals will be necessary to understand that they can shape children's growth in academic skills and social behavior by increasing children's opportunities for learning and that this intentional instruction can be carried out in developmentally appropriate ways.

State and Federal Influences on MTSS in Early Education   An additional challenge to the implementation and scaling up of MTSS in early education is having support at federal and state levels. While MTSS approaches continue to evolve and take shape in various forms across the states, multiple factors influence what MTSS looks like in each state and locale. Because ultimately public education in the United States is driven by the states, they will be the entities that determine how MTSS in early education is operationalized. Nonetheless, the federal government provides funding and guidance that supports initiatives like MTSS and quality education.

For example, the Individuals with Disabilities Education Improvement Act (IDEA) of 2004 (PL 108-446) and Every Student Succeeds Act (ESSA) of 2015 (PL 114-95) both have provided funds to compensate states for meeting certain mandates and adhering to certain restrictions.

Professional organizations also act as major influences on the way MTSS is developed and implemented. For example, in 2013 three prominent national organizations—the Council for Exceptional Children's Division for Early Childhood (DEC), the National Association for the Education of Young Children (NAEYC), and the National Head Start Association (NHSA)—collaborated to create a joint paper on RtI. Although the purpose of the paper was primarily to define and describe RtI, it provided an opportunity for early childhood professionals across general and special education to hear from professional organizations in a way that de-mythologized RtI. It offered all early educators a common ground that has proven useful to begin conversations about the possibility of moving toward RtI. A next iteration of a joint paper across national early education organizations will help states and the federal government develop policies to guide programs in establishing successful MTSS models.

Administrative Support and Resources   One final challenge to mounting successful MTSS initiatives in early education is leadership for carrying out and maintaining MTSS. Programs that are undertaking the shift to MTSS must have the administrative support and leadership to guide them through the essential steps of systems change that will result in a successful shift into full implementation and sustainability of MTSS. Many early education administrators have not had the opportunity to learn about strategies for leading their programs toward this new way of individualizing for all children. Successful leaders must have the skills to create a vision, the knowledge about how to allocate time and staff to design the system, and the means to acquire the resources to carry out and evaluate the new system. These leadership assets are often limited, so systems must focus on enhancing these leadership resources to enhance programs' capacities to grow and change.

ABOUT THIS BOOK

This book provides the reader with an introduction to each of the critical components necessary to implement MTSS at the individual child and classroom levels, and to illustrate for practitioners how the components work together within a larger MTSS framework. The book brings together some of the best experts in the field of intervention to promote language, early literacy, and social-emotional development. Chapter authors have extensive experience carrying out research on intervention strategies to promote learning and development, developing tools for identifying children who need more instructional support, guiding teams in using data to make instructional decisions and monitor children's progress, and scaling up these practices through evidence-based professional development within states and programs. Often, authors have included in their chapters many items that can help the reader more easily apply the concepts about MTSS to classroom practice. These items include useful tools such as measures, checklists, data collection sheets, and examples of graphs and reports. In addition, each chapter includes resources and links to online material where readers can access the most current information about MTSS and material that supports its implementation. Each of the chapters also includes vignettes to help personalize the content of the chapter and integrate the practitioner's perspective with that of the MTSS expert.

Finally, an added feature of the book are videos that help illustrate some of the important steps a program might take as it moves through the process of adopting MTSS. The videos will allow viewers to get a close-hand look at the following:

1. How the various members of a program come together to consider MTSS and, with a principal's leadership, achieve consensus about trying out MTSS in their program
2. How the program team uses Implementation Science to guide them in the process of considering adoption of MTSS and obtaining commitment from the classroom teams
3. How the team members study program-level data to examine how well the program is meeting the needs of all children and what they can do to enhance the quality of their curriculum and instruction
4. How they discuss and use class-level data to evaluate areas of strengths and needs in instructional areas and provide strategic instruction to those students needing additional support beyond the core curriculum
5. How they use data-based decision making to examine how to individualize instruction for a child who is showing signs of learning difficulties, and how they use data to evaluate how well their more intensified instruction works over time.

Throughout the book, several chapters include callouts for relevant videos that demonstrate content covered in that chapter. To access the videos, please visit www.brookespublishing.com/carta/materials.

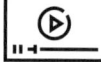

We hope that the videos will help bring MTSS to life and illustrate the staff dispositions, attitudes, and values that will increase the success and sustainability of MTSS. We know that MTSS will only work well when program staff work together from the very beginning as they think through the process of adoption of this new approach, gather data to see how they will integrate MTSS into their existing ways of operating, and use data to inform their practices at the program, classroom, and individual-child levels. The Introductory Video will help you learn about this book and its accompanying video series. We hope that seeing teams in action will be helpful to instructional teams who are considering MTSS for the first time as well as veteran MTSS implementers. Moreover, we hope the videos that show the various members of the team working together will be useful to school/program administrators as well as practitioners who may be teachers, school psychologists, speech and language therapists, social workers, family members, or other members of a school instructional team.

RESOURCES

Buysse, V., & Peisner-Feinberg, E. S. (Eds.). *Handbook of Response to Intervention in early childhood.* Baltimore, MD: Paul H. Brookes Publishing Co.

Division for Early Childhood (DEC), National Association for the Education of Young Children (NAEYC), & National Head Start Association (NHSA). (2013). *Frameworks for Response to Intervention in early childhood: Description and implications.* Missoula, MT: Author. Retrieved from http://www.dec-sped.org/position-statements

Greenwood, C. R., Bradfield, T., Kaminski, R., Linas, M., Carta, J. J., & Nylander, D. (2011). The Response to Intervention (RTI) approach in early childhood. *Focus on Exceptional Children, 43*(9), 1–22.

Jimerson, S. R., Burns, M. K., & VanDerHeyden, A. (Eds.). (2016). *Handbook of Response to Intervention: The science and practice of multi-tiered systems of support* (2nd ed.). New York, NY: Springer.

McElhattan, T., Carta, J., & Young, R. M. (2015). *Annotated resources: MTSS/RTI in early childhood.* Retrieved from http://www.crtiec.dept.ku.edu/wp-content/uploads/2015/10/MTSS-Annotated-Resource-List-10-20-15.pdf.

National Association for the Education of Young Children (NAEYC), & National Head Start Association (NHSA). (2013). *Frameworks for Response to Intervention in early childhood: Description and implications.* Missoula, MT: Author. Retrieved from http://www.dec-sped.org/position-statements

REFERENCES

Batsche, G., Elliott, J., Graden, J., Grimes, J., Kovaleski, J., Prasse, D., Tilley, W. (2005). *Response to Intervention: Policy considerations and implementation.* Alexandria, VA: National Association of State Directors of Special Education.

Bierman, K. L., & Motamedi, M. (2015). SEL programs for preschool children. In J. A. Durlak, C. E. Domitrovich, R. P. Weissberg, & T. P. Gullotta (Eds.), *Handbook on social and emotional learning: Research and practice* (pp. 135–150). New York, NY: Guilford.

Blair, C. (2010). Stress and the development of self-regulation in context. *Child Development Perspectives, 4*(3), 181–188. http://doi.org/10.1111/j.1750-8606.2010.00145.x

Brown-Chidsey, R., & Steege, M. W. (2010). *Response to Intervention: Principles and strategies for effective practice.* New York, NY: Guilford Press.

Buysse, V., & Peisner-Feinberg, E. (2010). Recognition and response: Response to Intervention for pre-k. *Young Exceptional Children, 13*(4), 2–13.

Buysse, V., Peisner-Feinberg, E., Soukakou, E., Fettig, A., Schaaf, J., & Burchinal, M. (2016). Using recognition and response (R&R) to improve children's language and literacy skills: Findings from two studies. *Early Childhood Research Quarterly, 36,* 11–20. doi:http://dx.doi.org/10.1016/j.ecresq.2015.11.005

Child Trends Databank. (2015). *Early school readiness.* Retrieved from https://www.childtrends.org/?indicators=early-school-readiness

Colorado Department of Education. (2015a, May). *What is MTSS?* Retrieved from https://www.cde.state.co.us/mtss/whatismtss

Colorado Department of Education. (2015b, September). *Multi-Tiered System of Support (MTSS).* Retrieved from https://www.cde.state.co.us/mtss

Cook, B. G., & Cook, S. C. (2011). Unraveling evidence-based practices in special education. *Journal of Special Education, 47*(2), 71–82.

Deno, S. (2016). Data-based decision-making. In S. Jimerson, M. Burns, & A. VanDerHeyden (Eds.), *Handbook of Response to Intervention: The science and practice of multi-tiered systems of support* (pp. 9–28). New York, NY: Springer.

Division for Early Childhood (DEC), National Association for the Education of Young Children (NAEYC), & National Head Start Association (NHSA). (2013). *Frameworks for Response to Intervention in early childhood: Description and implications.* Missoula, MT: Author. Retrieved from http://www.dec-sped.org/position-statements

Elementary and Secondary Education Act of 1965, PL 89-10, 20 U.S.C. §§ 241 *et seq.*

Every Student Succeeds Act (ESSA) of 2015, PL 114-95, 20 U.S.C. §§ 1400 *et seq.*

Gersten, R., Compton, D., Connor, C. M., Dimino, J., Santoro, L., Linan-Thompson, S., & Tilly, W. D. (2008). *Assisting students struggling with reading: Response to Intervention and multi-tier intervention for reading in the primary grades. A practice guide (NCEE 2009–4045).* U.S. Department of Education, National Center for Education Evaluation and Regional Assistance, Institute of Education Sciences; Washington, DC. Retrieved from http://ies.ed.gov/ncee/wwc/publications/practiceguides

Goldstein, H. (2016). *PAth to literacy.* Baltimore, MD: Paul H. Brookes Publishing Co.

Goldstein, H., & Kelley, E. S. (2016). *Story friends storybook set.* Baltimore, MD: Paul H. Brookes Publishing Co.

Goldstein, H., Kelley, E. S., Greenwood, C. R., McCune, L., Carta, J. J., Atwater, J., . . . Spencer, T. (2016). Embedded instruction improved vocabulary learning using automated storybook reading among high risk preschoolers. *Journal of Speech, Language, and Hearing Research, 59,* 484–500. doi:10.1044/2015_JSLHR-L-15-0227

Goldstein, H., & Olszewski, A. (2015). Developing a phonological awareness curriculum: Reflections on an implementation science framework. *Journal of Speech, Language, and Hearing Research, 58,* 1837–1850.

Greenwood, C. R., Bradfield, T., Kaminski, R., Linas, M., Carta, J. J., & Nylander, D. (2011). The Response to Intervention (RTI) approach in early childhood. *Focus on Exceptional Children, 43*(9), 1–22.

Gresham, F. M., MacMillan, D. L., Beebe-Frankenberger, M. E., & Bocian, K. M. (2000). Treatment integrity in learning disabilities intervention research: Do we really know how treatments are implemented? *Learning Disabilities Research and Practice, 15,* 198–205.

Hemmeter, M. L., Snyder, P. A., Fox, L., & Algina, J. (2016). Evaluating the implementation of the Pyramid Model for promoting social-emotional competence in early childhood classrooms. *Topics in Early Childhood Special Education.* Advance online publication. doi:10.1177/0271121416653386

Hojnoski, R. L., Silberglitt, B., Floyd, R. G. (2009). Sensitivity to growth over time of the preschool numeracy with a sample of preschoolers in Head Start. *School Psychology Review, 38,* 402–418.

Individuals with Disabilities Education Improvement Act (IDEA) of 2004, PL 108-446, 20 U.S.C. §§ 1400 *et seq.*

Justice, L. M., Mashburn, A., Hamre, B., & Pianta, R. (2008). Quality of language and literacy instruction in preschool classrooms serving at-risk pupils. *Early Childhood Research Quarterly, 23*(1), 51–68. http://doi.org/10.1016/j.ecresq.2007.09.004

Kaminski, R. A., & Powell-Smith, K. A. (2017). Early literacy intervention for preschoolers who need Tier 3 support. *Topics in Early Childhood Special Education, 36,* 205–217. doi:10.1177/0271121416642454

Linas, M., Greenwood, C. R., & Carta, J. (2012). *Taking a snapshot of early childhood Response to Intervention across the United States: 2009–2012.* Poster presented at the Head Start National Research Conference, Washington, DC.

Marston, D. (2002). A functional and intervention-based assessment approach to establishing discrepancy for students with learning disabilities. In R. Bradley, L. Donaldson, & D. Hallahan (Eds.), *Identification of learning disabilities* (pp. 437–447). Mahwah, NJ: Erlbaum.

Mercier Smith, J. L., Fien, H., Basaraba, D., & Travers, P. (2009). Planning, evaluating, and improving tiers of support in beginning reading. *Teaching Exceptional Children, 41*(5), 16–22.

Powell, D., & Dunlap, G. (2009). *Evidence-based social-emotional curricula and intervention packages for children 0–5 years and their families (Roadmap to effective intervention practices).* Tampa: University of South Florida, Technical Assistance Center on Social Emotional Intervention for Young Children.

Reschly, D., & Tilly, W. D. III (1999). Reform trends and system design alternatives. In D. Reschly, W. D. Tilly III, & J. Grimes (Eds.), *Special education in transition: Functional assessment and noncategorical programming* (pp. 19–48). Longmont, CO: Sopris West.

Stoiber, K. C., & Gettinger, M. (2016). Multi-tiered systems of support and evidence-based practices. In S. Jimerson, M. Burns, & A. VanDerHeyden (Eds.), *Handbook of Response to Intervention: The science and practice of multi-tiered systems of support* (pp. 121–142). New York, NY: Springer.

Wackerle-Hollman, A., Rodriguez, M. I., McConnell, S., Bradfield, T., & Rodriguez, M.C. (2015). Redefining individual growth and development indicators: Comprehension. *Assessment for Effective Intervention, 40*(2), 89–85. doi:10.1177/1534508414551404

Wasik, B.A., Bond, M.A., & Hindman, A. (2006). The effects of a language and literacy intervention on Head Start children and teachers. *Journal of Educational Psychology, 98,* 63–74.

2

Leadership Practices to Design and Operationalize MTSS Frameworks for Young Children

Robin Miller Young

Linda Rizzuto, Meadowlark Preschool's newly hired principal, and Barb Mueller, the assistant principal, met to plan a Instructional Leadership Team (ILT) summer institute arranged by the school district. Linda knew that Meadowlark's staff had started to examine the rationale for shifting into a multi-tiered systems of support (MTSS) framework before their previous principal retired as the school board had decided to shift all the programs/schools into an MTSS framework. Linda also knew that shifting into an MTSS framework would present leadership challenges for her and the ILT, as she had engaged in this change process as an early childhood education/early childhood special education (ECE/ECSE) teacher in her previous setting. Yet, the benefits of providing services in an MTSS framework to staff, parents, and children would make the process worthwhile. The MTSS practices include delivering a strong core curriculum, conducting universal screening, using a collaborative, team- and data-based decision-making process to match children's needs to interventions of appropriate intensity, and providing interventions in a tiered model to ensure that children and families gain targeted skills, knowledge, and dispositions. As a prelude to planning for their summer institute, Barb described the work that the ILT had carried out thus far to move into an MTSS framework.

During the last few months of the previous school year, the ILT engaged in several consensus-building activities around the MTSS framework. First, the ILT arranged staff members into small, interdisciplinary Professional Learning Community groups (PLCs) to allow them to learn more about MTSS frameworks in early childhood settings. As PLCs, the group members met once a month to read a short article or watch a short video on MTSS and then discuss the content and possible implications for their program. The ILT also arranged visits to a nearby preschool operating in an MTSS framework to better learn the pros and cons of such a shift in practices from those colleagues who had been doing it. The summer institute's goal was to examine student performance data for the last few years and to identify strengths and areas needing improvement. Then, the team could look at their delivery system components and processes and target system changes that would result in improved outcomes for children and families. As Barb pulled up the program data on her computer, Linda started brainstorming ways to use the ILT summer institute to give staff a voice and ownership in the nuts and bolts of the change process, including how to create a trusting culture with these new team members.

INTRODUCTION

Effective and efficient, differentiated, developmentally appropriate services are delivered to young children and their families through early childhood systems (Division for Early Childhood [DEC], 2014; Kagan & Kauerz, 2012; Metz, Halle, Bartley, & Blasberg, 2013). Systems are typically defined by two features: 1) their specific infrastructures, also called *elements* or *components*, that articulate the "what" of the system; and 2) all of the *processes* or *operational procedures* that allow the system to function consistently, effectively, and efficiently across time—in other words, the "how" of the system. In summary, the system components and processes affect one another reciprocally to create stimulating environments where children and families acquire essential skills and dispositions through interactions with well-prepared service providers. Furthermore, continuous improvement cycles ensure that the system results in achievement of targeted developmental and educational outcomes.

System components and processes in early childhood systems are often aligned vertically through the various system levels. For example, the "assessment" system component impacts how IDEA (Individuals with Disabilities Education Act) Child Find activities are conducted in early childhood education classrooms (e.g., knowledge of screening procedures), at the school/program level (e.g., coordinating screening across multiple classrooms), through local and regional communities (e.g., local public school district or county-level agency conducts screening activities and/or ensures compliance at local level), through statewide networks (e.g., data reported to state departments of education), or finally, at the national level (e.g., data reported to federal government; see Figure 2.1).

Essential system functions also need to be aligned horizontally; that is, coordinated and aligned across schools, agencies, and institutions that provide services concurrently to children and families at that same system level (e.g., the local public-school administration and/or regional agency coordinates preschool screenings across multiple public school systems, for-profit and not-for-profit early care and education providers). Well-prepared leaders are needed to arrange system components and processes vertically and horizontally; moreover, they need to know how to operate the system component and process interactions at their assigned levels so that children and families can achieve strong intervention outcomes (Young, Chandler, Hood, & Kennedy, 2012; see Figure 2.2).

This chapter focuses on school/program leaders who serve as catalysts for moving local schools and programs from current service delivery system models into MTSS frameworks. School and program leaders are designated as the focus for MTSS systems change for three reasons: 1) they are accountable for achieving the targeted outcomes that stakeholders identify, 2) they are the legitimate authority to create and institute system changes, and 3) their actions can have a great impact on the organizational culture that is crucial to the success of the movement.

MTSS Frameworks for Young Children   17

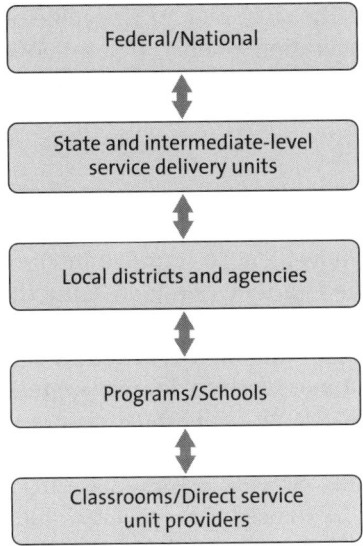

Figure 2.1. Vertical system hierarchy.

This chapter discusses leadership preparation and competencies, with a specific focus on the preparation of public school principals. It also describes the work conducted by school/program leadership teams who serve as the change process engine. Strategies employed by leaders and their leadership teams to move into MTSS practices are shared throughout the chapter and highlighted in the essential Resources section. Finally, the accompanying video series includes three videos illustrating an early childhood education program's ILT engaging in practices to support an MTSS service delivery model. Video 1 illustrates consensus-building

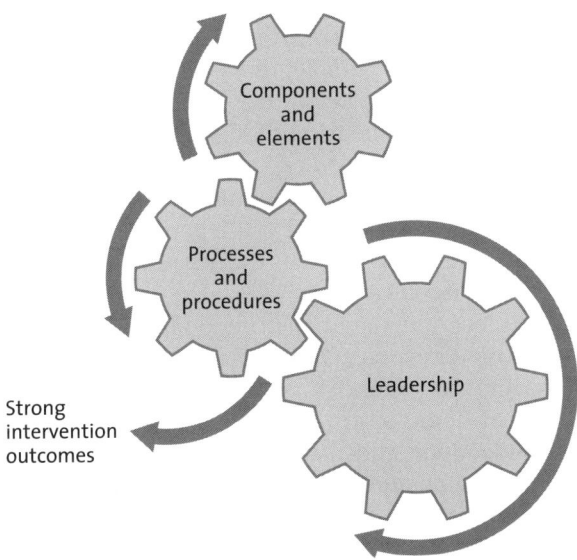

Figure 2.2. Leadership interactions with system structural components and processes.

that the MTSS initiative is the right one for a specific program; Video 2 illustrates the team's use of Implementation Science (IS) to move into these practices (see also Chapter 3); and Video 3 illustrates the team employing data-based decision making to ensure the core curriculum is effectively meeting all children's needs (see also Chapters 4 and 5).

A SYSTEM'S FOCUS WITHIN AN MTSS

At the very heart of the movement to improve intervention outcomes for young children and their families is a focus on increasing the organizational effectiveness and efficiency of early childhood systems (Kagan & Kauerz, 2012). Achieving targeted outcomes for families and their children can be difficult, even impossible, if practitioners fail to examine a service delivery system's purpose, infrastructure, and operating procedures. Practitioners must ensure that systems are intentionally arranged and operated to achieve desired ends, goals, or objectives (Duda, Fixsen, & Blase, 2013; Young, Shields, & Chandler, 2011).

Kauerz and Kagan (2012) stated that an early childhood system is "an orderly and comprehensive assemblage of interrelated elements that creates equitable, accessible, comprehensive, and quality services for young children" (p. 88). Regarding school systems, the component parts are organized and arranged to interact and produce academic achievement (Castillo & Curtis, 2014); in the case of early education systems, achievement of targeted developmental and early learning outcomes is the desired goal. Furthermore, the system components or elements are coordinated and aligned with one another and serve as an infrastructure or internal working structure (e.g., the "what" of a system). In early education systems, these include the learners ("who" will benefit from service receipt, such as children and/or family members), curriculum ("what" will they learn), instruction ("what" methods will be used to transmit knowledge and skills and develop dispositions), the environment ("where" will they learn), and outcomes assessment ("what" has been learned, gained, improved). A system's second defining feature includes the processes and operational procedures (e.g., the "how" of a system) that enable a system to operate effectively and efficiently to achieve its stated purpose. In early education systems, these include activating communication protocols, engaging in decision-making processes, ensuring that staff members complete designated responsibilities, enforcing relevant rules and laws, holding staff accountable for achieving results, and developing and sustaining a desired organizational culture. Effective MTSS models for children and youth across the age continuum need to include system components and processes that result in children, youths, and families achieving essential outcomes.

Early efforts to describe tiered instructional and intervention models for young children were titled Response to Intervention (RtI; Carta, 2009; Greenwood et al., 2008). This occurred primarily as the early childhood initiative had deep roots with the types of tiered instructional and intervention models, called RtI, that were being developed for students in the K–12 age/grade span (Batsche et al., 2005). It was not until the position statement titled *Frameworks for Response to Intervention in Early Childhood: Description and Implications* (DEC, National Association for the Education of Young Children [NAEYC], & National Head Start Association [NHSA], 2013) was adopted that the field started to acknowledge that this initiative would result in significant system-level changes.

Consider again the name of this movement: *multi-tiered system of support*. The premier noun in the name, the focus of this movement, is "system." The initiative is a call for system change in general (Castillo & Curtis, 2014), and specifically, to change the systems for identifying and ultimately meeting these children's developmental and educational needs (Buysse & Peisner-Feinberg, 2013). Simultaneously, in the field of early childhood education, several other concurrent movements' primary aims are also system improvements. These initiatives include efforts to define how children and families should be brought together in programs and schools, such as the inclusion and blending movements (DEC & NAEYC, 2009; Pretti-Frontczak, Grisham-Brown, & Sullivan, 2014), to clarify the professional parameters of those who provide services, such as professionalizing the early care and education workforce (Goffin, 2015), and to implement specific curricular and instructional practices, such as a play-based or academically focused kindergarten program (Bassok, Latham, & Rorem, 2016; Brown, Feger, & Mowry, 2015). One of the common themes in these movements to improve our early learning systems is the need to determine where in the system to target the change efforts.

DIRECTING EFFORTS AT THE SCHOOL/PROGRAM SYSTEMS LEVEL

In the following section, rationale for targeting the school/program to start shifting into MTSS practices is provided. Consequently, effective program/school leaders are described, as well as leadership strategies they may employ, to change the system infrastructure (components) and processes into those aligned with the MTSS framework.

Focus on Schools and Programs

School buildings are the organizational unit targeted for movement into MTSS practices in the K–12 MTSS arena (Batsche, n.d.; Kurns & Tilly, 2007). As stated by Castillo and Curtis (2014), "Delivery of the services that will have an impact on student outcomes ultimately occurs at the school level, necessitating a focus on changing the practices of teachers, principals, instructional support personnel, and other school-level leaders" (p. 13). When the MTSS model/framework is modified for implementation into many different early childhood settings, the word *school* can be replaced with the word *program* to designate the primary organizational target for change. Indeed, consideration of the number of early care and education systems and their unique characteristics (Institute of Medicine [IOM] and National Research Council [NRC], 2015) mandates that each school/program customize the MTSS framework and principles to meet the needs of their particular children and families given their local resources and challenges.

For example, when MTSS will be implemented in early education settings, the "school" may be a dedicated early childhood learning center operated by a local school district responsible, in part, to serve the needs of children with identified delays and disabilities (Brown & Tom, 2012; Chandler & Young, 2009; Nylander, 2009). One of the strengths of early learning centers affiliated with school districts is the capacity to align programming between the early childhood and K–12 levels to meet the needs of all children, including those with learning challenges, identified delays, and disabilities. This includes the organization's articulated vision ("What kind of organization do we want to be?", "What are our long-term goals for our children?"), mission ("How will we get there?", "How will we see our vision come to fruition?"), purpose ("Why do we exist?"), and values ("By which rules shall we play?") (Knoff, 2014; Shields, Laubenstein, & Young, 2009; Shields & Young, 2010) so that the children and families have a cohesive experience along the age continuum (Young et al., 2012). Leaders of preschools affiliated with local districts also may have distinct advantages to tap into financial and personnel resources to engage in sustainable initiatives, such as Positive Behavioral Interventions and Support (PBIS; Stormont, Lewis, Beckner & Johnson, 2008; Young, Snow, Frech, & Shields, 2011) and PLCs (Dufour, Dufour, Eaker, & Many, 2010).

A second organizational configuration might be an early learning program operated by an intermediate unit of school governance, such as a county, that exists between state and local levels to provide highly specialized services and technical assistance to the local district, or a consortium of districts. These may be special education cooperative or "joint agreement" agencies (Illinois), or intermediate school districts (Michigan), and so forth. In many cases, the program might include children who are considered at risk of developing delays and disabilities (statewide pre-K at-risk grant) as well as those with already identified delays and disabilities (ECSE; Peter, Mervyn, & Mannes, 2012; Rathburn & Hanke, 2015). Intermediate governance service delivery may be deemed equally effective but more efficient than services provided by local districts. For example, a program leader at the intermediate level may not need to oversee school facilities operations; however, the leader will need to attend to specific consensus-building challenges and horizontal-level program-building efforts because the stakeholders and initiative implementers may be spread across a variety of individual school districts who are geographically disparate or have competing programmatic priorities.

A similar though not identical organizational structure may be in place for Head Start programs administered at the county level (Lemmer, 2016; Urshel, 2014). Although not an intermediate level of a public-school system, county-level Head Start programs do exist as a part of the vertical hierarchy of a multileveled system. As such, they enhance the local and regional early childhood community's capacity to meet the needs of children who meet income eligibility criteria and are at risk of developing delays and disabilities. Head Start leaders have many resources and mandates that are different from those of the public-school programs, allowing them the flexibility to use their program's strengths to meet unique and specific challenges.

Focus on Program and School Leaders

To lead the diverse programs described in the previous section, individuals must be prepared to engage in leadership and managerial behaviors at their system level. Focusing on leaders is particularly appropriate when examining system change efforts, as ultimately the system leaders are likely to be held accountable for whether the system achieves targeted outcomes identified by the stakeholders (Castillo & Curtis, 2014). Stakeholders meet semi-regularly to gauge progress toward actualization of the vision, achievement of the mission, allocation, and distribution of resources (e.g., money, personnel); thus, the stakeholder group holds the lead administrator accountable for whether organizational goals are achieved. For example, if a school principal or preschool director is hired to ensure that children reach predetermined early language and literacy standards and acquire certain prosocial skill competencies, the principal/director will engage in strategic leadership behaviors to create the strongest likelihood that children will gain these essential skills. Typically, stakeholders have a vested interest in ensuring that the system effectively and efficiently meets its goals, so careful consideration should be given to stakeholder group membership. Stakeholders may include: 1) front line service providers such as educators, teaching assistants, speech pathologists, school psychologists, and other specialists; 2) members of the other system levels (e.g., central office staff); 3) parents who receive services and/or the parents of children who receive services; and 4) members of the broad school community who stand to gain or lose if the program does well or poorly. The stakeholder group should arrange policies, financial supports, and organizational cultural supports so the program/school leaders can move successfully into MTSS practices.

In addition to being accountable for the results, the school/program leaders typically have legitimate authority to create and institute system changes at their level. Building principals and directors who serve in site-based management positions will need to propose system changes that are approved by, or at least coordinated with, upper levels of the district/organization administrative hierarchy. Nonetheless, most site-based managers can enact system changes that fall within their jurisdiction. This seems to be particularly true of early childhood education programs (Koralek & Ramey, 2015), as compared to K–12 programs. The school/program leader can generally work on his or her own or with a leadership team to modify system components or elements, such as core curriculum implementation and application of preferred formative assessment tools. Leaders can also change system processes and procedures, such as changing the meeting agenda and format within teaming processes and engaging in data-based decision making to determine the need for supplemental curricula as long as the school/program maintains its accreditation and adheres to local, state, and federal program requirements and laws. Although upper-level administrators are increasingly becoming more sophisticated regarding the delivery of high-quality early childhood education services (Brown, Squires, Connors-Tadros, & Horowitz, 2014), they still rely on the expertise of their early childhood school and program leaders to lead the way on these decisions (Koralek & Ramey, 2015).

Finally, school/program leaders have a great impact on shifting the setting's organizational culture, and being able to accomplish this cultural shift is critical to the success of the movement. Organizational culture includes the shared values, assumptions, and collective beliefs regarding elements, processes, and outcomes that are important; it also includes explicit and implicit rules for how individuals and groups of people within the organization will treat and interact with one another, and the customary practices that distinguish each setting from one another (Bloom & Abel, 2015). The school/program leaders, through their completion of specific administrative and leadership tasks and the purposeful, intentional interactions with supervisors, staff, and stakeholders, can shift the culture into one that embraces engaging in a change process to better meet children's and families' needs.

An effective leader must be able to skillfully support staff through the change process. This starts with acknowledging that leaving one set of familiar practices and moving into a set of less familiar practices can be difficult. The leader who has a reputation of being trustworthy, has given staff a voice in the transition process, and can facilitate development and execution of a transition plan into the new way of doing business will be well rewarded (Shields, 2011). Second, the leader will need to articulate effectively the legitimate needs of those at the grass-roots level to those at upper levels of the hierarchy ("bottom up"). He or she will also need to eloquently describe and profess support for the strategic vision, organizational values, and governing board priorities to those who are at the lower levels of the hierarchy ("top down"). Few, if any, initiatives will be successful if they do not include consideration of both kinds of communication and problem-solving efforts (Shields et al., 2009). Other proven strategies for shifting the culture include the following:

1. Acknowledging current staff members' philosophies and beliefs about how children grow and learn (e.g., constructivist approach in an emergent curriculum) while continuing to press for an increasingly scientific basis for decision making (e.g., published studies attesting to the effectiveness of an intervention that employs explicit instruction)

2. Respecting divergent values and priorities while still seeking synergistic solutions to the challenges (e.g., comparing proposed field trip expenses with those for an on-site activity that has a comparable outcome without the larger expense)

3. "Ramping up" excitement and anticipation for engaging in a new venture (e.g., providing inspirational quotes in a dramatic or comedic way in regular announcements, at the beginning of meetings, on print agendas and newsletters, or on a display board as staff enter the building to generate enthusiasm)

4. Providing plenty of reinforcement to meet staff members' wants and needs and to keep the momentum going (e.g., descriptive feedback delivered in person, a special PBIS teacher parking spot)

5. Initiating new traditions that celebrate small and large accomplishments that acknowledge effort and taking "calculated risks" (e.g., end-of-year staff success celebration and karaoke party)

In summary, the successful movement of early childhood systems into MTSS service delivery models can only be accomplished with leaders who are strategically positioned in the system, have the right tools to address the challenges and rewards of systemwide change efforts, and employ sound judgment on how and when to apply those tools.

PREPARING TO LEAD AN MTSS SYSTEM FOR YOUNG CHILDREN

Early education program leaders who want to spearhead the movement into MTSS practices must have the necessary knowledge, skills, and dispositions to lead the specific change process from current service delivery models into MTSS frameworks (Shields et al., 2009). For public school preschools and early childhood programs, several resources are available that provide direction for the competencies these leaders must demonstrate.

In 2005, the National Association of Elementary School Principals (NAESP) created a list of recommended practices for leading an early childhood program and advised principals to obtain in-service professional development to acquire the recommended skills. However, more recently, The National Governors' Association (NGA; Szekely, 2013) and other organizations have suggested that preparing strong and capable leaders for early learning systems ought to start at the preservice level. Specifically, elementary school principal preservice preparation programs should include early childhood education content to increase school principals' capacity to lead high-quality and effective early learning programs. Indeed, many states revised their principal preparation program requirements so that candidates engage in rigorous course content and field experiences to be effective leaders of "school communities and programs that address student learning and school improvement for young children (i.e., students in early childhood programs), English Language Learners (ELLs), and students with disabilities (i.e., have an individualized education program—IEP)" (Young, Hunt & Hood, 2013, p. 1).

One Illinois principal preparation program (Loyola University of Chicago) revised its course content and field experiences to support developing principals who can lead early learning programs that embrace an MTSS framework (Israel, Fine, Sostak, & Young, 2013; Young, Morrison, Kennedy, & Bohanon, 2014). The Loyola faculty addressed the principal preparation standards applicable to all candidates noted previously and then ensured that the specific skills and competencies recommended to lead an MTSS framework were also included in the principal preparation program of study. These leadership recommendations, originally generated for K–12 MTSS framework leaders, include the following:

1. Set a vision for the problem-solving process
2. Support development of staff performance expectations specific to MTSS
3. Exercise responsibility for resource allocation for the MTSS framework
4. Facilitate a priority-setting process
5. Ensure follow-up and satisfactory completion of designated activities
6. Support program evaluation
7. Monitor staff support and climate (Batsche, n.d.)

Future efforts to create an evidence base for successfully leading in an MTSS service delivery framework for young children will need to reference the revised DEC (2014) recommended practices (RPs) with a focus on the leadership practices added to the revision. Specifically, the DEC Leadership RPs "address the responsibilities of those in positions of program authority and leadership related to providing services to young children who have or are at-risk for developmental delays/disabilities and their families" (DEC, 2014, p. 4). The DEC leadership position statement (DEC, 2015) and published examples of authentic leadership strategies applied in early learning settings (LaRocco & Bruns, 2013) should also be referenced as MTSS school/program leaders' need to master the specific competencies required to meet the needs of these children and their families.

Emerging work being conducted regarding early childhood leadership will need to be reviewed and integrated into future MTSS in early childhood leadership competencies. These sources are likely to include the following:

- The NAEYC-led initiative titled *Power to the Profession* (NAEYC, http://www.naeyc.org/our-work/initiatives/profession/naeyc-announces-new-national-collaboration)

- Print publications on leadership development such as *Leadership: Supporting a New Generation of Early Childhood Professionals* (Koralek & Ramey, 2015)
- Work conducted by leadership institutes such as the McCormick Center's *Whole Leadership* initiative (https://mccormickcenter.nl.edu/library/whole-leadership-a-framework-for-early-childhood-programs)
- Early childhood program director credentials (http://mccormickcenter.nl.edu/professional-development/national-director-credential/).

We will also need to stay apprised of leadership development efforts to refine K–12 MTSS models, such as comprehensive and long-standing state-wide initiatives in Michigan (https://miblsi.org) and Florida (http://www.floridarti.usf.edu/), to find applications for leading early childhood programs.

In addition, IS application to system-building in early childhood settings (Chapters 3 and 11; Metz, Naoom, Halle, & Bartley, 2015) has significant implications for developing leaders who can lead programwide initiatives, such as MTSS. Leaders will need to create an IS team and serve as integral team members. Leadership is also one of the three "drivers" that operationalize the initiative (competency and organization are the other two); thus, school/program leaders will need to have "willingness to allocate the necessary time and resources for training, ongoing technical assistance, and monitoring of early childhood educators in the use of the new innovation" (Metz et al., 2015, p. 9).

This final section on preparing leaders for MTSS service delivery models for young children examines the most recent NAESP principal competencies to lead pre-K to grade 3 Learning Communities (NAESP, 2014). The competencies are presented next, accompanied by several applied illustrations of how school/program leaders can link that competency with leadership strategies for an MTSS service delivery system appropriate for young learners.

Competency 1: Embrace the Pre-K–Grade 3 Learning Continuum

Bring ECE and early elementary-level leaders together on a regular basis to engage in joint professional development and to create synergistic solutions to common problems. These might include options such as allocating Title I funds for pre-K and elementary programs so gains that children achieve in early learning programs can be extended into the elementary years.

Competency 2: Ensure Developmentally Appropriate Teaching/Practices

Create and conduct PLCs (Dufour et al., 2010) with ECE and early elementary-level educators grouped heterogeneously to share developmentally appropriate practices (DAPs) in assessment and educational strategies. For example, in a PLC group, assessment data across both settings might be reviewed and then educators might collaboratively develop procedures to implement highly effective multi-week instructional units that focus on vocabulary development with categorical and interdisciplinary connections, building on active and multi-modal student engagement practices that meet DAP guidelines for both settings (Neuman & Wright, 2013).

Competency 3: Provide a Personalized Blended Learning Environment

Develop and implement a strategic plan with stakeholders to move instructional programs into inclusive (DEC/NAEYC, 2009)/blended (Pretti-Frontczak et al., 2014) models so that proper differentiation to support children's individual growth can be put into place. "One strategy principals use to help tailor instruction to a child's individual needs is a response to intervention (RtI) framework" (NAESP, 2014, p. 41).

Competency 4: Use Multiple Measures of Assessments to Guide Student Growth

Conduct evaluations of the core (universal or Tier 1) curriculum's effectiveness with multiple measures aligned across domains (social-emotional) and/or early academic disciplines (early language and literacy, early math and numeracy) along the age–grade continuum; share data and decision-making processes with stakeholders to facilitate program improvement (Young et al., 2014).

Competency 5: Build Professional Capacity Across the Learning Community

Connect with other school/program leaders in other districts and agencies and at other system levels (Elliott & Morrison, 2008) to learn more about leading in an MTSS framework specifically and other evidence-based tiered instructional practices that will support achievement of pre-K–grade 3 outcomes. Create a leadership succession plan so that aspiring leaders are regularly being prepared to step into leadership roles when opportunities arise.

Competency 6: Make Your School a Pre-K–Grade 3 Learning Hub for Families and Communities

Arrange for children and families to experience a successful entry and engagement as they transition from local infant and toddler programs into programs for preschoolers, and then into early elementary experiences; create out-of-school and summer learning options, conduct special celebrations (e.g., NAEYC "Week of the Young Child"), and cultivate open-door policies that engage all members of the pre-K–grade 3 community.

Future research regarding leadership for moving early childhood service delivery systems into MTSS frameworks, and then sustaining these frameworks over time, may move forward most quickly by examining the work conducted by the school/program leaders who are specifically prepared to perform the competencies noted above.

LEADING THROUGH MTSS COLLABORATIVE TEAMING PROCESSES TO ACHIEVE TARGETED OUTCOMES

This chapter's final topic is leading the MTSS initiative through development and use of collaborative teaming processes to achieve various system and constituent goals. Goals should reflect input from stakeholders, described previously, and include program objectives that lead to achievement of essential outcomes. The four team processes discussed here include: 1) the administrative leadership team, or "LEAD" team, that included the principal and the three program coordinators who had formal authority to operate the program/school), 2) the ILT, 3) PLCs (Dufour et al., 2010; Minnesota Department of Education, 2006), and 4) the IS team.

The first team addressed is the school/program-level administrative team (LEAD team). In public-school programs, there may be a principal and then other subordinated leaders, such as assistant or associate principals, lead teachers, program coordinators, and others, who assist in completing specific program functions. Likewise, in some agencies/organizations, there may be a director and other managerial staff who complete specific organization or program functions. The primary leader must create a strong administrative leadership team whose members can work cohesively to accomplish formal administrative and managerial responsibilities such as hiring and evaluating staff, overseeing budgets, maintaining the facility, addressing union issues, and more, while also creating a trusting and productive climate in which system change activities can take place successfully. The LEAD team members share responsibilities for successful operation of the entire school/program, and moving into an MTSS framework is one of many important tasks.

The second team is the ILT, whose sole purpose is to ensure that the instructional and intervention delivery system results in verifiable gains for young children and their families. This school/program-level group gathers once or twice a month to do strengths-based problem-solving and data-based decision making to ensure that progress is being made toward meeting accountability goals. The ILT also ensures that a continuous improvement process is being employed that results in changes in the system components and processes when necessary. In some system change frameworks, one of the first steps an ILT takes is to build consensus that MTSS is the right initiative for a particular program. The ILT drives the process of moving into an MTSS framework by knowing components (e.g., the learners, the curriculum, the instructional methods, the assessment procedures) as well as the processes (e.g., communication procedures, decision-making processes, relevant rules and laws) and having the authority to change them. A hypothetical ILT membership grid, aligned with the chapter's opening vignette, is provided in Figure 2.3 to illustrate how the ILT members represent various program constituents. Note in particular that every campus, classroom, disciplinary group, and PLC small group is represented. This allows for effective "bottom-up" communication of ideas from the staff to be shared in ILT decision making and "top-down" communication of information and decisions from the program/school leadership team to staff essential for shared leadership (Shields, 2011).

See Video 1 for an illustration of an ILT engaging in the consensus-building process.

As noted earlier in the chapter, the school/program leader needs to articulate a vision, a mission, and core values that are unique to his or her early learning program. In addition, each leader needs to create an organizational culture that includes explicit and implicit rules about how the culture members will treat one another. In high-performing programs/schools, the designated leader accomplishes these tasks in a shared leadership style with the ILT. Examples of a vision, mission, core values, guiding practices, and standard operating procedures developed by an ILT for an early childhood education program are provided in Figure 2.4. An organizational culture that contains these elements, developed in a collegial manner with representative input from the staff and stakeholders, stands the best chance of serving as a strong foundation for moving into MTSS and shifting into new infrastructures and practices.

So, how does a school/program leader set an agenda and use the ILT meeting time to drive the change process and move into an MTSS framework? The most

	Name	Title/Role	Campus	Team	PLC #	Disc	Gender	Years	Notes
1	Linda	Principal (parallel to elementary principal)	Main	LEAD	NA	T	F	10	Liaison with central office; leads strategic planning; staff development through PLC processes, coaching, evaluations
2	Barb	Assistant principal and assessment coordinator	Main	LEAD	NA	Psy	F	12	Leads social-emotional initiatives (Pyramid Model and PBIS); schedules annual reviews, oversees Child Find
3	Carla	Educator: blended ECE/ECSE/"at risk"	Main	Bison	1	T	F	7	Hispanic woman; native Spanish speaker; takes lead with multicultural, art, music, drama, and field trip initiatives
4	Nihar	Educator: ECE Title I in elementary school building	Elementary school	Lion	2	T	F	2	Asian-American woman who was previously a teacher's assistant in the program; takes lead with school–business partnerships
5	Susan	Educator: ECSE self-contained	Ancillary	Zebra	3	T	F	15	Veteran employee, teacher union representative; takes lead with professional development on technology
6	Mark	Educator: blended ECE/ECSE/"at risk"	Ancillary	Panda	4	T	M	13	Lead teacher at the ancillary campus; takes lead with parent-teacher association (PTA) activities; often requested as student teaching mentor
7	Gwen	Speech-language pathologist (SLP)	Ancillary	Panda/Lynx	4	SLP	F	1	Newest program faculty member; proficient in newest adaptive communication devices
8	Aaron	School psychologist (Psy)	Main	Multiple; + Bison	1	Psy	M	17	Previous Head Start teacher; takes lead with data collection and analysis; trained as problem-solving coach
9	Joyce	Occupational therapist (OT)	Ancillary	Multiple; + Whale	5	OT	F	9	Innovative practitioner; leads OT disciplinary meetings; leads writing winning grant proposals
10	Mateo	ELL/DLL specialist; social worker (SSW)	Main	Multiple; + Gecko	6	ELL/DLLSSW	M	5	Native Spanish speaker; links to central office ELL/DLL services; provides direct services; supports staff and families

Figure 2.3. Example of early childhood program/school Instructional Leadership Team membership.

(continued)

Figure 2.3. *(continued)*

Key: Early childhood education/early childhood special education (ECE/ECSE), Professional Learning Community (PLC), Not applicable (NA)	
Notes: The following program elements are represented:	

Children:	Representative of district-wide demographics:
	  Typically developing children
	  Children deemed "at risk" of developing delays and disabilities
	  Children with identified delays and disabilities
	  Children from families of various income levels
	  Children from families of various self-identified racial and ethnic backgrounds
	  Children from families with various languages spoken
	  All geographic parts of the attendance area

Title/Role:	Instructional program responsibilities; not always same as "Discipline"
Classroom types:	Blended ECE/ECSE "at risk" ECSE self-contained ECE Title 1
Campus:	Three locations where programs are housed (e.g., main, ancillary, and elementary school)
Team:	Assigned classroom team(s) identified by animal, bird, or insect mascot
Professional Learning Community (PLC):	Each of the six PLC groups to which that staff member is assigned. Typically, each person is assigned to just one PLC, but some classroom specialists are assigned to two PLCs to facilitate teaming.
Disciplines (Disc)	Teacher (T) Speech-language pathologist (SLP) School psychologist (Psy) Occupational therapist (OT) English language learner (ELL)/dual language learner (DLL) specialist Social worker (SSW)
Classroom team members on same PLC	Group 1 = Educator and Psychologist Group 4 = Educator and Speech-language pathologist
Unique qualities:	Gender: male (M) or female (F) Years of experiences (Years) Leadership responsibilities with various initiatives, program components, and processes

effective ILTs start with conceptualizing themselves as a large PLC group with all staff assigned to smaller PLCs; that is, they become "collaborative teams whose members work interdependently to achieve common goals for which members are mutually accountable" (Dufour et al., 2010, p. 11). As noted in the ILT composition chart in Figure 2.3, the ILT is composed of representatives from each of the smaller PLCs. Typically, each staff member is assigned to just one PLC group; however, some staff members, such as specialists who are assigned to provide direct and consultative services in more than one classroom (e.g., speech-language pathologist), may be assigned to more than one PLC to support collaborative classroom team and PLC small group dynamics. The PLC vertical alignment from program small groups, through the ILT, through district-level PLCs allows all staff to "embrace high levels of learning for students as both the reason the organization exists and the fundamental responsibility of those who work in it" (Dufour et al., 2010, p. 11). The PLC orientation is a general means of achieving school improvement that can pave the way for movement into a specific system's change initiative such as MTSS. When the PLC team members ask questions such as, "What is it we want our students to learn?," "How will we know if each student has learned it?," "How will we respond when some students do not learn it?," and "How can we extend and enrich the learning for students who have demonstrated proficiency?" (Dufour et al., 2010, p. 119), they create a culture where eventual use of a specific four-step problem-solving model can be implemented; when team members say they want

Vision ("What are our long-term goals for children?") All students will obtain foundational skills and knowledge for future success.		Mission ("How will we see our vision come to fruition?") Staff, family, and community members will work together to provide positive learning experiences.
Core values →	**Guiding practices** →	**Standard operating procedures (SOP)** Embedding our core values and guiding practices into daily routines/activities
Innovation Accountability Collaboration Communication	1. Strive for excellence: Challenge yourself, apply new concepts, and share lessons learned.	• Incorporate new strategies as evidence-based practices emerge. • Use current research-based curricula, interventions, and assessments. • Build relationships and gain knowledge by sharing lessons learned. • Use data-based problem solving to enhance student outcomes.
Communication Respect Collaboration	2. Create positive relationships: Initiate and respond to create positive and productive working relationships with fellow staff members, displaying considerate and cooperative behavior in professional relationships.	• Actively listen to everyone with respect—seeking first to understand. • Communicate openly and honestly to the right person about the right issues. • Develop and adhere to ground rules and norms for collaborative meetings. • Paraphrase to ensure accurate comprehension and understanding. • Gather all of the facts before deciding on a course of action. • Trust that everyone is doing their job.
Communication Respect Collaboration	3. Full participatory decision making: Involve all team members in the decision-making process.	• Invite others to share perspectives and/or express their feelings and ideas. • Acknowledge everyone's ideas and expertise in working toward solutions. • Offer suggestions and provide input through appropriate channels.
Communication Accountability	4. Be accountable for our actions: See it, own it, solve it, do it.	• Be on time for work and meetings. • Model professional appearance. • Request a substitute teacher with enough notice for sub to be obtained. • Participate in drop-off/pick-up duties.
Accountability	5. Safety first for one and all: Adhere to safety guidelines for children, visitors, and self.	• Bring attendance to the office at the start of each session. • Maintain and activate classroom door alarms. • Close and secure building doors when entering and exiting. • Work together: We are all responsible for every student's safety.
Communication Collaboration Respect Accountability	6. Communicate effectively: Share information with all involved staff (certified and classified) and parents emphasizing confidentiality in relationship to staff, kids, and families.	• Establish processes to keep team members informed. • Inform specialists via e-mail when they need to attend a team meeting. • Allow 24-hour notice on time-sensitive issues (e.g., meeting time changes). • Respond to e-mails, phone calls, and other communication within 24 hours. • Keep confidential information that someone shares with you confidentially. • Maintain team meeting notes in electronic format on the server.

Figure 2.4. Example vision, mission, core values, guiding practices, and standard operating procedures. (Adapted from "Prairie Children Preschool Core Values: Revised Core Values Committee—Indian Prairie #204, Prairie Children Preschool, October 2010." Indian Prairie School District #204, Prairie Children Preschool Instructional Leadership Team, unpublished internal document, 2010. Reprinted with permission.)

to achieve SMART goals (*S*pecific, *M*easurable, *A*ttainable, *R*esults-oriented, and *T*ime-bound), they open the door to identifying specific program outcomes that can be linked to participation in professional development activities that are delivered through PLCs. See the Minnesota Department of Education (2006) guide in the Resources section for more information about the intersection of ILTs and PLCs. See also Table 2.1 that includes example end-of-year reflections of three smaller PLC groups aligned with the chapter vignette regarding their progress in achieving their SMART goals and their first-time experiences working in a PLC.

The last team type to be presented is an implementation team, based on an active framework within the IS field (Duda et al., 2013; Metz et al., 2015; see Chapter 3). School/program leaders will need to find ways to embed the IS implementation team's purpose and function into the existing ILT, or to create a separate team. Given the realities of limited resources to operate two similar, though not identical teams, the ILT will likely take on functions of the IS implementation team, described in more detail in Chapter 3. Regarding the specific MTSS initiative for early learning systems, embedding the IS implementation team functions into the ILT would be critical for ensuring that all of the MTSS components "are fully developed within the site, that the infrastructure is supported for continuous improvement of all staff, and that positive outcomes are being achieved" (Duda et al., 2013, p. 403). The team has three functions: 1) assisting service providers to implement specific new practices, 2) accepting responsibility for results in successful implementation of these practices, and 3) creating preparedness for staff and systems to engage in the new practices. Essentially, an ILT that is going to take on the IS implementation team function for a school/program wanting to shift into MTSS frameworks needs time, expertise, and latitude to accomplish this weighty task in the short and long term.

See Video 2 for illustration of an ILT examining the Implementation Science Active Frameworks to assist their move into MTSS practices.

In addition to functioning as a PLC and an IS implementation team, the ILT has several other functions that can help establish use of evidence-based practices in an early childhood MTSS framework. Examples of these functions include the following:

1. *State outcomes:* Determine essential student learning targets that should be achieved by the end of the school year. Outcomes need to be observable and measurable, linked to state early learning standards, and linked to upper- (e.g., local school board) and lower- (e.g., classroom) system levels (SMART goals are one goal format; visit https://go.solution-tree.com/PLCbooks for examples).

2. *Convey expectations:* Clarify staff performance expectations, including decision-making practices such as which decisions will be made by the school/program leader, the ILT, classroom teams, and individual staff members, as well as how decisions will be made (e.g., voting or consensus arrangements). Communicating performance expectations explicitly, embedding them into your organizational culture, and ensuring that adhering to them will be honored and reinforced are also important.

3. *Arrange planning time:* Create a year-long calendar that includes meeting time for staff aligned with your program's teaming processes, including the teams described previously, disciplinary teams (e.g., all speech-language pathologists), and classroom teams (e.g., in the vignette, each classroom team

Table 2.1. Example of Professional Learning Communities (PLCs): Collaborative Teams' SMART Goal End-of-Year Reflections

PLC group number	SMART goal progress	Accomplishments	Challenges and strategies	Comments/ Discussions
PLC Group 2 Two teachers of blended ECE/ ECSE class, Title I class, and physical therapist (PT) assigned to provide direct services and consultative support to those specific classrooms.	Our literacy SMART goal was met through measured student performance. Student growth was positively impacted by creating and using adapted materials to scaffold curriculum, instruction, and student skill demonstration for three books.	We are proud of the efficiency and effectiveness of our product and the improved focus on instruction and improved student outcomes.	We used PLC time wisely and efficiently, but this project required much more time than was allocated for it. We will scaffold remaining project books.	We all feel lucky to have a good team that is very cohesive and passionate about collaborating and data-based decision making to meet children's needs.
PLC Group 3 Three teachers of self-contained ECSE classes plus school psychologist (psy) and speech-language pathologist (SLP) assigned to provide direct services and consultative support to those specific classrooms	Goal: Use the Verbal Behavior MAPP assessment (VB–MAPP; Sundberg, 2008) to monitor development of targeted social skills and pragmatic language skills. Use natural environment with same-age peers to teach students to play games requiring verbal turn-taking and prosocial skills. Student performance of targeted outcomes increased.	Students were taught specific interactive skills to play various games requiring those skills (e.g., pretaught playground games). VB–MAPP was used to monitor progress and determine teaching focus. Team members increased skills for using technology in small groups and 1:1 teaching.	We need to generate an agenda for the next meeting at the current meeting. Our collaborative team involved staff from various disciplines and ability-diverse classrooms; as a result, our goal was more narrowly focused on meeting needs of children with common prosocial and pragmatic challenges.	Team reflected upon the school-wide process for transitioning students from self-contained into ECE/ECSE blended settings. Team feels process needs to be more standardized while keeping individualized framework as well. We want to increase sharing of research-based curricular and instructional practices.
PLC Group 4 Three teachers of blended ECE/ECSE classrooms plus SLP and school social worker (SSW) assigned to provide direct services and consultative support to those specific classrooms.	Literacy SMART goal: Individual Growth and Development Indicators (IGDIs; McConnell & Greenwood, 2013) data reveal effective Tier 2 vocabulary intervention titled Sound Start (McCormick, Throneburg, & Smitley, 2002). Data-based fine motor small-group scores increased.	We created a strong organizational process, and we adhered to our meeting norms. Meetings were very productive due in large part to our agenda format that keeps us on target. (We always know what's next!)	Team meeting dates need to coincide with data collection as a whole using MyIGDIs for Early Literacy (EL; McConnell, Bradfield, Wackerle-Hollman, & Rodriquez, 2012) and MyIGDIs for Early Numeracy (EN; Hojnoski & Floyd, 2013), curriculum-based assessment (common end-of-instructional-unit, student-generated learning artifacts judged by a common rubric), and so forth.	Please keep our group together! We have some great interventions, and everyone is invested and actively participates. Next year we will plan units together, including use of Smartboard technology, therapists' schedules, Sound Start, PATHS, and fine motor intervention groups.

(continued)

Table 2.1. (continued)

PLC group number	SMART goal progress	Accomplishments	Challenges and strategies	Comments/ Discussions
	Promoting Alternative Thinking Strategies (PATHS; Domitrovich, Greenberg, Kusche, & Cortes, 2004) pretest and positive behavior intervention and supports (PBIS; Stormont, Lewis, Beckner, & Johnson, 2008) data used to create PATHS small group; scores moved in targeted direction.	Data-based decision making helped us to ensure all students were making progress toward learning targets.	Meet every 3 weeks (consistent time frame between meetings) to better share materials and plan together.	Allow time for job-alike observation of peers matched by roles (teacher-with-teacher) in other classrooms/ settings, so we can learn new performance responsibilities from those who are putting them into practice.

Key: ECE/ECSE, Early childhood education/early childhood special education; SMART, Specific, Measurable, Attainable, Results-oriented, and Time-bound.

Sources: Domitrovich, Greenberg, Kusche, and Cortes (2004); Hojnoski and Floyd (2013); McConnell, Bradfield, Wackerle-Hollman, and Rodriquez (2012); McConnell and Greenwood (2013); McCormick, Throneburg, and Smitley (2002); Stormont, Lewis, Beckner, and Johnson (2008); Sundberg, (2008).

is identified by an animal, bird, or insect mascot, so the team in the vignette was the Panda classroom team). Tasks may include curricular planning, planning for individual children, PLCs to learn new skills, and so forth. Hold people accountable for meeting, adhering to an agenda to complete the purpose, and sharing meeting results with others in a timely fashion.

4. *Choose assessments:* Examine current tools and assessment processes to ensure the right amount of data from reliable and valid sources is collected and used for decision making. Design common assessment processes to gather data for decision making at the program, class, and individual student levels. A program/schoolwide time frame for regular data collection and decision making across an entire school year also needs to be developed; an example timeframe is available in Figure 2.5.

See Video 3 for a demonstration of data-based problem solving at the program/school level, Video 4 for an example at the classroom level, and Video 5 for an illustration at the individual-child level.

5. *Deploy core curriculum:* Examine core curriculum, as well as supplemental curricula and student performance data, to ensure a match to students' needs. Reaffirm choices or engage in a process to adopt curricula that better match your learners' needs. Ensure curricula are implemented with fidelity and proper dosage; develop and align multiweek instructional units that are standards based, include evidence-based curricular choices, and are linked to other systems-level curricula (vertical and horizontal).

6. *Implement teaching strategies:* Ensure that core instructional methods, and those provided in other tiers, are matched to learners' needs and curricular

Dates/tasks	Fall dates		Winter dates		Spring dates	
myIGDIs (EL and EN)	9/3 to 9/17		1/5 to 1/21		4/29 to 5/13	
CBA	9/18 to 10/10		1/22 to 2/6		4/13 to 5/1	
Portfolio items	10/10		2/6		5/1	
Teaching Strategies (TS) GOLD® (Heroman & Tabors, 2010) checklists; focused objectives	First data point to be completed within the first 6 weeks of a child with IEP or at-risk status starting classes.				Second data point completed 2 weeks prior to AR for AR between 1/55 and 5/15. Students with at-risk status also due 5/15.	
ELL (ELL students only)	Complete TS GOLD English acquisition objectives 37, 38 by 10/31.				Complete TS GOLD English acquisition objectives 37, 38 by 5/15.	
ECO progress rating	• ECO entry rating is to be completed by diagnostic team or classroom team completes ECO entry rating on move-in students. • ECO progress rating will be done at each child's AR.					
IEP goal updates	Go home 10/31		Go home 1/23		Go home 4/10	Go home 1/29
Report cards	Send 10/23		Send 2/19			Send 5/28
PATHS pretest	Complete PATHS pretest on ALL students.				Complete PATHS posttest only on students needing SE intervention based on pretest.	

Key: EL, early literacy; EN, early numeracy; CBA, curriculum-based assessment; AR, annual review is a yearly meeting required for a student with an IEP (individualized education program); ELL, English language learner; ECO, Early Childhood Outcomes are progress ratings of each child with an IEP that are completed yearly; PATHS, Promoting Alternative Thinking Strategies (Domitrovich, Greenberg, Kusche, & Cortes, 2004); TS GOLD®, Teaching Strategies GOLD: Birth through Kindergarten Assessment Toolkit.

Figure 2.5. Example schoolwide academic year data-collection and decision-making calendar. Adapted from *Prairie Children Preschool Core Values: Revised Core Values Committee—Indian Prairie #204, Prairie Children Preschool, October 2010*. Indian Prairie School District #204, Prairie Children Preschool Instructional Leadership Team, unpublished internal document, 2010. Reprinted with permission.

objectives. Conduct treatment integrity checks and check delivery of proper dosage. Ensure availability of a model with more- and less-intensive tiers and scaffolds, plus access and training for technology.

7. *Create environments:* Ensure that the cultural (e.g., beliefs about young children and their families, values promoted, implicit and explicit rules, focus on equity, use of traditions and celebrations), physical (e.g., space, equipment, materials), social (e.g., interactions with peers, siblings, and family members), and temporal (e.g., sequence and length of routines and activities) environments are intentionally designed to ensure success for all students and staff, including parents (DEC, 2014); inclusive and blended practices are celebrated (DEC/NAEYC, 2009; Pretti-Frontczak et al., 2014).

8. *Establish communication protocols:* Clarify how you will communicate—how often you will initiate communication, how long before you reply; use of e-mail, public address system, classroom versus program newsletters, print or electronic formats, use of web site; and what types of information will be communicated by various means. For meetings, decide how agendas will be set, when to conduct meetings in person or electronically, and where to save minutes.

9. *Employ strengths-based problem solving:* Set the expectation that staff and parents will focus on each child's and family's personal, familial, community, and cultural assets while engaging in strengths-based problem solving at all systems' levels. Employ a collaborative, team-based, and data-based process, such as that described in Chapter 4.

10. *Conduct professional development (PD):* Ensure that all PD activities are planned and conducted with evidence-based staff development protocols, and provide high-quality initial training and ongoing embedded training, such as coaching, for practitioners, indirect support staff, and leaders at all system levels.

11. *Craft partnerships:* Collaborate with university faculty (Chandler, 2012), agency staff, and consultants from other fields (e.g., business, health services) who have skills and knowledge that can support visionary thinking and creative, innovative ways to reshape the MTSS initiative to meet the needs of young children and their families.

CONCLUSION

This chapter has addressed the broad topic of leadership in the development, delivery, and evaluation of effective and efficient, differentiated, developmentally appropriate services to young children and their families. A case was made for examining the service delivery system because shifting effectively and efficiently into an MTSS framework for young children will require understanding system components and processes, arranging the organizational culture to support moving through a change process, as well as creating a process for shifting into the new system, such as IS. School/program leaders are the key to shifting into MTSS frameworks because they are accountable for achieving desirable outcomes for children and families, they have formal authority to make system changes, and they have a significant impact on the school/program's culture to engage successfully in the change process. The chapter concludes with information about how to prepare school/program leaders who have the knowledge, skills, and dispositions to lead MTSS frameworks for young children.

Examining leadership theory and its application to MTSS frameworks for young children is a relatively new endeavor in the fields of school administration, early childhood, early childhood special education, and education reform movements such as MTSS. By necessity, the bulk of references on leadership applicable to developing, operationalizing, evaluating, and re-visioning MTSS frameworks for young children have been drawn from blog entries, anecdotal essays, practitioner journals, conference presentations, and newsletter accounts from those who are pioneers and innovators in this work. Other more scholarly citations were drawn from related fields (e.g., school psychology, early childhood special education) to provide a wider scope of reference for this emerging body of work. Excitement is building within the pioneers and innovators of the MTSS frameworks for young children, and across partners in the related fields, to engage in more rigorous program descriptions, and quantitative and qualitative studies to better inform the next wave of framework revisions. Many potential questions must be asked and answered; two seem especially pertinent, given the chapter's system's perspective. First, researchers will need to evaluate various aspects of the framework from a system's perspective (Castillo, 2014), taking cues from Charles Greenwood's

(Young, Carta, & Greenwood, 2014) proposals to examine service delivery outcomes experienced by young children and their families. Second, a systems change paradigm described by George Batsche and colleagues (Batsche, George, & Little, 2008) for K–12 MTSS models suggests that "entrepreneurial" system change efforts, described as site-specific, driven by core visionary people, based on local strengths and opportunities as well as internal motivations, are not as likely to be as successful as those described as "sustainable," characterized as site generic, driven by policy, and guided by blueprints and external motivations. Careful attention to these types of system change efforts, as well as other emerging work on system change (Castillo & Curtis, 2014), will surely position the MTSS frameworks for young children on a firm foundation to be more completely embedded in early childhood service delivery systems in the future.

At the beginning of the summer institute, Linda and Barb engaged the Meadowlark ILT members in PLC team-building activities so the team members could experience Linda's shared leadership style; it also allowed the team to reset the vision, mission, core values, and guiding practices for the program. With those program development processes successfully under way, the ILT members examined the program-level early language and literacy data from student portfolios. During the May assessment, only 65% of the students were rated by their teachers as meeting proficiency criteria. Mark, the lead teacher, explained that they had come to consensus on moving into MTSS practices to improve student outcomes, but they had not changed any of their infrastructure or processes. So, the ILT's first decision was to locate and start administering an appropriate early language and literacy universal screener that would better meet their needs. The ILT members agreed that once the new universal screener was administered in early September, they would be able to determine how much they needed to enhance their core curriculum (Tier 1) and who might need supplemental, strategic instruction (Tier 2) and intensive instruction (Tier 3). Several team members had recently attended districtwide training on Neuman and Wright's (2013) vocabulary development strategies and were now considered early literacy coaches. They were enthusiastic about piloting the evidence-based vocabulary strategies but agreed that the ILT needed to have better data on which to make these decisions. The ILT members agreed that these were wonderful aspects of MTSS practices to put into place, and the day ended with a plan for team members to share the results of the ILT meeting with their small PLC groups, classroom teams, and discipline team members. With the productive and trusting organizational culture being cultivated through the LEAD team, the actively engaged ILT, the PLC teaming processes, and disciplinary and classroom teams, plus support from Meadowlark's district's central office, Linda felt confident that moving into an MTSS framework would result in the Meadowlark Preschool children achieving essential developmental and educational outcomes.

RESOURCES

Division for Early Childhood (DEC), National Association for the Education of Young Children (NAEYC), & National Head Start Association (NHSA). (2013). *Frameworks for Response to Intervention in early childhood: Description and implications.* Missoula, MT: Author. Retrieved from http://www.dec-sped.org/position-statements

Dufour, R., Dufour, R., Eaker, R., & Many, T. (2010). *Learning by doing: A handbook for Professional Learning Communities at Work™* (2nd ed.). Bloomington, IN: Solution Tree Press. An invaluable resource for school teams who want to engage in PLCs. Visit http://go.solution-tree.com/PLCbooks to download reproducibles in the book.

Hafer, M. (2011, March). *A teacher's perspective on RTI in EC/preschool settings* [Web log post]. Retrieved from http://www.rtinetwork.org/rti-blog/entry/1/119. An ECE/ECSE licensed educator describes participation in districtwide training to operate her inclusive/blended classroom in a school/programwide MTSS framework; the educator also describes school/program ILT efforts to shift into an MTSS model.

Minnesota Department of Education. (2016). *Principal action resource: The instructional leadership team and Professional Learning Communities*. Roseville, MN: Author. http://mnstem.com/mdeprod/groups/communications/documents/basic/bwrl/mdu5/~edisp/mde059560.pdf

RtI Action Network (Producer). (2012, October). *Prairie Children Preschool: A virtual visit*. A 14-minute video to illustrate Prairie Children Preschool's implementation of MTSS practices. http://rtinetwork.org/professional/videos/virtualvisits

Shields, L. (2011). *The leader's role: RTI in early childhood settings* [Web log post]. Retrieved from http://www.rtinetwork.org/rti-blog/entry/1/152. Former principal of an award-winning early childhood program/school (PBIS and RtI) describes how she and the ILT worked in a PLC format to move into MTSS practices.

Young, R.M. (2012, June). *Response to Intervention in Early Childhood (RTI-EC) Discussion* [Web log post]. Invited blog entry on professional development to support transitioning into MTSS/RtI practices. Retrieved from http://npdci.fpg.unc.edu/blogs/response-intervention-early-childhood-rti-ec

Young, R.M., Snow, L.M., Frech, C., & Shields, L. (2011). *Developing socially competent and emotionally resilient young children through an early childhood RTI framework*. Retrieved from http://www.rtinetwork.org/learn/rti-in-prekindergarten/developing-socially-competent-and-emotionally-resilient-young-children. Invited article posted on the RtI Action Network's website. A multi-year, collaborative process is described to shift into a tiered intervention model to build children's prosocial skills, including DAP PBIS strategies.

REFERENCES

Bassok, D., Latham, S., & Rorem, A. (2016). Is kindergarten the new first grade? *AERA Open, 1*(4), 1–31. doi:10.1177/2332858415616358

Batsche, G. (n.d.). *Building support*. Retrieved from http://www.rtinetwork.org/getstarted/buildsupport/buildingsupport

Batsche, G., Elliott, J., Graden, J. L., Grimes, J., Kovaleski, J. F., Prasse, D., . . . Tilly III, W. D. (2005). *Response to intervention: Policy considerations and implementation*. Alexandria, VA: NASDSE.

Batsche, G., George, H. P., & Little, M. (2008, September). *Scaling up response to intervention*. Invited presentation at the Administrators' Management Meeting (AMM) sponsored by the Florida Department of Education, Bureau of Exceptional Education and Student Services, St. Petersburg, Florida.

Bloom, P. J., & Abel, M. B. (2015, May). Expanding the lens—leadership as an organizational asset. *Young Children, 70*(2), 10–17.

Brown, C. P., Feger, B. S., & Mowry, B. (2015, September). Helping others understand academic rigor in teachers' developmentally appropriate practices. *Young Children, 71*(4), 62–69.

Brown, K. C., Squires, J., Connors-Tadros, L., & Horowitz, M. (2014, July). *Preparing principals to support early childhood teachers (CEELO FastFact)*. New Brunswick, NJ: Center on Enhancing Early Learning Outcomes (CEELO).

Brown, M., & Tom, K. (2012, February). *Addressing social emotional learning through RTI in early childhood settings*. Paper presented at the annual convention of the National Association of School Psychologists (NASP), Philadelphia, PA.

Buysse, V., & Peisner-Feinberg, E. S. (2013). Response to Intervention: Conceptual foundations for the early childhood field. In V. Buysse & E. S. Peisner-Feinberg (Eds.), *Handbook of Response to Intervention in early childhood* (pp. 3–23). Baltimore, MD: Paul H. Brookes Publishing Co.

Carta, J. (2009, October). *Opening comments*. Keynote conducted at the 2009 Center for Response to Intervention (RtI) in Early Childhood (CRTIEC) First Annual RtI Early Childhood Summit, Albuquerque, NM.

Castillo, J. M. (2014). Best practices in program evaluation in a model of response to intervention/multitiered system of supports. In P. L. Harrison & A. Thomas (Eds.), *Best practices in school psychology: Foundations* (pp. 329–342). Bethesda, MD: NASP.

Castillo, J. M., & Curtis, M. J. (2014). Best practices in systems-level change. In P.L. Harrison & A. Thomas (Eds.), *Best practices in school psychology: System-level services* (pp. 11–28). Bethesda, MD: National Association of School Psychologists (NASP).

Chandler, L. K. (2012, February). *The benefits of collaboration: University faculty and preschool-based professionals working together* [Web log post]. Retrieved from http://www.rtinetwork.org/rti-blog/entry/1/180

Chandler, L. K., & Young, R. M. (2009, October). *Leadership skills for implementing preschool RtI and problem-solving*. Paper presented at the meeting of the 25th annual conference of the Division for Early Childhood (DEC), Albuquerque, NM.

Division for Early Childhood (DEC). (2014). *DEC recommended practices in early intervention/early childhood special education*. Retrieved from http://www.dec-sped.org/dec-recommended-practices

Division for Early Childhood (DEC). (2015). *DEC position statement on leadership in early intervention and early childhood special education*. Retrieved from http://www.dec-sped.org/position-statements

Division for Early Childhood (DEC), National Association for the Education of Young Children (NAEYC). (2009). *Early childhood inclusion: A joint position statement of the Division for Early Childhood (DEC) and the National Association for the Education of Young Children (NAEYC)*. Retrieved from http://www.dec-sped.org/position-statements

Division for Early Childhood (DEC), National Association for the Education of Young Children (NAEYC), & National Head Start Association (NHSA). (2013). *Frameworks for Response to Intervention in early childhood: Description and implications*. Missoula, MT: Author. Retrieved from http://www.dec-sped.org/position-statements

Domitrovich, C., Greenberg, M., Kusche, C., & Cortes, R. (2004). *PATHS (Promoting Alternative Thinking Strategies) preschool program*. South Deerfield, MA: Channing Bete.

Duda, M. A., Fixsen, D. L., & Blase, K. A. (2013). Setting the stage for sustainability: Building the infrastructure for implementation capacity. In V. Buysse & E. S. Peisner-Feinberg (Eds.), *Handbook of Response to Intervention in early childhood* (pp. 397–417). Baltimore, MD: Paul H. Brookes Publishing Co.

Dufour, R., Dufour, R., Eaker, R., & Many, T. (2010). *Learning by doing: A handbook for Professional Learning Communities at Work* (2nd ed.). Bloomington, IN: Solution Tree Press.

Elliott, J., & Morrison, D. (2008). *Response to Intervention blueprints for implementation: District level edition*. Alexandria, VA: NASDSE.

Goffin, S. G. (2015). *Professionalizing early childhood education as a field of practice: A guide to the next era*. Minneapolis: Redleaf Press.

Greenwood, C. R., Carta, J. J., Baggett, K., Buzhardt, J., Walker, D., & Terry, B. (2008). Best practices integrating progress monitoring and response-to-intervention concepts into early childhood. In A. Thomas, J. Grimes, & J. Gruba (Eds.), *Best practices in school psychology V* (pp. 535–548). Washington, DC: NASP.

Heroman, C., & Tabors. P.O. (2010). *Teaching strategies GOLD®: Birth through kindergarten assessment toolkit.* Washington, DC: Teaching Strategies.

Hojnoski, R., & Floyd, R. (2013). *Individual Growth and Development Indicators of Early Numeracy (IGDIs-EN).* Saint Paul, MN: Early Learning Labs.

Institute of Medicine (IOM) and National Research Council (NRC). (2015). *Transforming the workforce for children birth through age 8: A unifying foundation.* Washington, DC: The National Academies Press. doi:10.17226/19401

Israel, M., Fine, J., Sostak, S., & Young, R. M. (2013). The Loyola University (Chicago) redesign of the principal preparation program. In R. M. Young, E. L. Hunt, & L. Hood (Eds.), *The Leadership to Integrate the Learning Continuum (LINC) tool kit: Redesigning principal preparation programs across four Illinois institutions* (pp. 67–80). Normal, IL: Center for the Study of Education Policy, Illinois State University.

Kagan, S. L., & Kauerz, K. (2012). *Early childhood systems.* New York, NY: Teachers College Press.

Kauerz, K. & Kagan, S.L. (2012). Governance and early childhood systems. In S. L. Kagan & K. Kauerz (Eds.), *Early childhood systems* (pp. 87–103). New York, NY: Teachers College Press.

Knoff, H. M. (2014). Best practices in strategic planning, organizational development, and school effectiveness. In P. L. Harrison & A. Thomas (Eds.), *Best practices in school psychology: System-level services* (pp. 29–41). Bethesda, MD: National Association of School Psychologists (NASP).

Koralek, D., & Ramey, M. D. (Eds.). (2015, May/June). Leadership: Supporting a new generation of early childhood professionals [Special Issue]. *Young Children, 70*(2).

Kurns, S., & Tilly, D. W. (2007). *Response to intervention blueprints: School building level edition.* Alexandria, VA: NASDSE.

LaRocco, D. J., & Bruns, D. A. (2013). It's not the "what," it's the "how": Four key behaviors for authentic leadership in early intervention. *Young Exceptional Children, 16*(2), 1–12.

Lemmer, S. (2016, January). *Using data-based decision making to drive program quality in pre K: The story of one Head Start program* [Web log post]. Invited blog entry to describe RTI employed in a Head Start program. Retrieved from http://www.schoolreadinessblog.com/author/stephanie_lemmer

Metz, A., Halle, T., Bartley, L., & Blasberg, A. (2013). The key components of successful implementation. In T. Halle, A. Metz, & I. Martinez-Beck (Eds.), *Applying implementation science in early childhood programs and systems* (pp. 21–42). Baltimore, MD: Paul H. Brookes Publishing Co.

Metz, A., Naoom, S. F., Halle, T., & Bartley, L. (2015). *An integrated stage-based framework for implementation of early childhood programs and systems (OPRE Research Brief OPRE 2015-48).* Washington, DC: U.S. Department of HHS, Office of Planning, Research and Evaluation, Administration for Children and Families.

McConnell, S., Bradfield, T., Wackerle-Hollman, A., & Rodriguez, M. (2012). *Individual Growth and Development Indicators of Early Literacy (IGDIs-EL).* Saint Paul, MN: Early Learning Labs.

McConnell, S. R., & Greenwood, C. R. (2013). General outcome measures in early childhood and the Individual Growth and Development Indicators (IGDIs). In V. Buysse & E. Peisner-Feinberg (Eds.), *Handbook of Response to Intervention (RTI) in early childhood* (pp. 143–154). Baltimore, MD: Paul H. Brookes Publishing Co.

McCormick, C. E., Throneburg, R. N., & Smitley, J. M. (2002). *A Sound start: Phonemic awareness lessons for reading success.* New York, NY: The Guildford Press.

Minnesota Department of Education. (2016). *Principal action resource: The instructional leadership team and Professional Learning Communities.* Roseville, MN: Author.

National Association for the Education of Young Children. (2016, May 25). *NAEYC announces a new national collaboration to set professional guidelines for all early childhood educators (Power to the Profession).* Washington, DC: Author. Retrieved from https://www.naeyc.org/our-work/initiatives/profession/naeyc-announces-new-national-collaboration

National Association of Elementary School Principals (NAESP). (2005). *Leading early childhood learning communities: What principals should know and be able to do.* Alexandria, VA: Author.

National Association of Elementary School Principals (NAESP). (2014). *Leading pre-K-3 learning communities: Competencies for effective principal practice.* Alexandria, VA: Author.

Neuman, S. B., & Wright, T. S. (2013*). All about words: Increasing vocabulary in the common core classroom, Pre-2– Grade 2.* New York, NY: Teachers College Press.

Nylander, D. (2009, October). *Navigating through RTI with a compass and a lifeboat. Early Childhood RTI Summit.* Retrieved from http://www.crtiec.org/rti_summit/documents/NylanderNavigatingthroughRTIwithaCompass-NMSummitt10-09.pdf

Peter, C., Mervyn, C., & Mannes, T. (2012, March). *Preschool Response to Intervention.* Paper presented at the Michigan Integrated Behavior and Learning Support Initiative [MiBLSi]) state conference, Lansing, MI.

Pretti-Frontczak, K., Grisham-Brown, J., & Sullivan, L. (Eds.). (2014). *Blending practices for all children* (Young Exceptional Children Monograph Series No. 16). Los Angeles: Division for Early Childhood of the Council for Exceptional Children.

Rathburn, K., & Hanke, M. (2015, September). *Assessment, curriculum, and team collaboration.* Paper presented at the Illinois State-wide Collaborative Early Childhood Conference—SharingAVision, Springfield, IL.

Shields, L. (2011, June). The leader's role: RTI in early childhood settings [Web log post]. Retrieved from http://www.rtinetwork.org/rti-blog/entry/1/152

Shields, L., Laubenstein, P., & Young, R. M. (2009, August). *Shared leadership. . . Opportunities discovered: Leadership that benefits ALL young learners.* Paper presented at the meeting of the Illinois State Board of Education (ISBE) Special Education Directors' Conference, Peoria, IL.

Shields, L., & Young, R. M. (2010, October). *Linking principals across the early childhood and elementary levels to create a seamless learning continuum.* Paper presented at the Illinois Principals Association (IPA) annual conference, Peoria, IL.

Stormont, M., Lewis, T. J., Beckner, R., & Johnson, N. W. (2008). *Implementing positive behavior support systems in early childhood and elementary settings.* Thousand Oaks, CA: Corwin Press.

Sundberg, M.L. (2008). *Verbal Behavior Milestones Assessment and Placement Program (VB – MAPP). A language and social skills assessment program for children with autism or other developmental disabilities.* Concord, CA: Advancements in Verbal Behavior Press (AVB Press).

Szekely, A. (2013, May). *Leading for early success: Building school principals' capacity to lead high-quality early education.* Washington, DC: NGA.

Urshel, C. (2014, June). Supplementing the preschool core: Applying a mulitiered system of support to a county Head Start program. *NASP Communique', 42*(8), 10–11.

Young, R. M., Carta, J. J., & Greenwood, C. (2014, October). *Leading MTSS/RTI in EC: Preparing to launch and lifting off!* Invited full-day workshop to the 17th Annual RTI Innovations Conference, Salt Lake City, Utah.

Young, R. M., Chandler, L. K., Hood, L., & Kennedy, A. (2012, October). *Leadership for developing a seamless learning continuum: Birth through early elementary years.* Paper presented at the Division for Early Childhood 28th Annual International Conference, Minneapolis, MN.

Young, R. M., Hunt, E. L., & Hood, L. (Eds.). (2013). (Eds.), *The Leadership to Integrate the Learning Continuum (LINC) tool kit: Redesigning principal preparation programs across four Illinois institutions.* Normal, IL: CSEP, Illinois State University.

Young, R. M., Morrison, D., Kennedy, A., & Bohanon, H. (2014, February). *School psychology faculty preparing principals to lead pre-K–12 MTSS/RTI schools.* Symposium conducted at the 2014 NASP Annual Convention, Washington, DC.

Young, R. M., Shields, L., & Chandler, L. K. (2011). The emerging early childhood (EC) RTI movement: Promoting early schooling successes for three- to five-year-olds. [Monograph Lucky 21 #4]. *Response to Intervention (RTI): 21 questions and answers; just what is RTI?* (pp. 12–16). Warner Robins, GA: CASE.

Young, R. M., Snow, L. M., Frech, C., & Shields, L. (2011). *Developing socially competent and emotionally resilient young children through an early childhood RTI framework.* Retrieved from http://www.rtinetwork.org/learn/rti-in-pre-kindergarten/developing-socially-competent-and-emotionally-resilient-young-children

3

Employing Implementation Science to Transition Early Childhood Systems Into MTSS

Allison Metz, Jennifer Schroeder, and Robin Miller Young

The new executive director of early childhood programming at the Lincoln Intermediate School District (LISD), Nate Johnson, was hired to improve student outcomes and address growing concerns of parental dissatisfaction across the LISD's five member districts. Currently, the LISD operates an early childhood special education (ECSE) program that includes self-contained preschool classrooms housed in five different sites with limited opportunities for children with disabilities to access the general education curriculum and to be educated with peers who do not have identified disabilities. Nate has to ensure that the resulting program educates all of the learners well and with clearly defined stewardship of the LISD and local school district resources. He believes that an early learning system built on the defining features of the multi-tiered systems of support (MTSS) framework will be the best way to accomplish this objective. The MTSS framework employed in a neighboring school district's early childhood inclusive preschool program is comprised of high-quality curricula for all children, data-based decision making within a collaborative problem-solving process, and the provision of instruction and interventions of varying intensities matched to children's and families' needs. According to Nate's colleague in the nearby district, shifting into an MTSS framework from the former way of operating has resulted in strong achievement of essential student developmental and educational outcomes, increased parent satisfaction, and resource accountability.

    Nate knows he will need to create and lead an Early Childhood Leadership Team (ECLT) that can determine if the MTSS framework is the right innovation for their particular community. The leadership team will also have to consider options to provide more inclusive programming, and Nate is excited to think about ways in which that might be accomplished. His colleague in the nearby school district has invited Nate to visit the MTSS program in action, and suggested that Nate learn about Implementation Science (IS) beforehand. Nate starts to read about IS and the accompanying Active Implementation Frameworks (AIFs) so he can prepare for his visit and anticipate how to use these tools with his own leadership team. Nate wants to see how the IS AIFs of Stages, Teams, Drivers, and Improvement Cycles can be used by his team to transition their program into a service delivery framework that will result in improved outcomes for children and families in his school district.

INTRODUCTION

When communities want to improve their ability to meet the needs of young children and families, community stakeholders must start by conducting a needs assessment to identify unmet service needs and community assets. Then, based on their findings, stakeholders consider options for meeting community needs. Community stakeholders may decide to work from a "clean slate" and install a new program or school. Alternately, stakeholders may take an existing program or school and make changes to achieve targeted results. Most, although not all, communities have some early learning programs in place, even if the services are not well coordinated and some service gaps exist (Kauerz & Kagan, 2012).

The majority of communities do not start with a clean slate. In the early care and education field, only a limited number of early learning programs are created in this manner. Rather, stakeholders of a particular early learning program or school examine how well they are actualizing their vision, meeting their mission, adhering to their cultural values and, ultimately, meeting their community members' needs. Once stakeholders engage in this self-evaluation process, they identify and employ strategies that are likely to improve system functioning and achieve essential outcomes for community members. Sometimes these changes are small, and change happens gradually over time. Sometimes stakeholders decide to make systemwide changes. In this case stakeholders may either 1) create a conceptual framework that includes the essential features, program development guidelines, and defining parameters of a proposed service delivery system; or 2) work within an existing service delivery system and adapt it to better meet their own needs.

Once stakeholders have decided to either create their own model or install an existing model, the next step is to operationalize the model (e.g., get the model up and running) so the services are received by the community members.

Stakeholders opting to work within an existing service delivery system may choose to customize the MTSS framework as their new way of serving community needs. This is the situation in which Nate from our opening vignette finds himself: as the leader of a program that needs to change, he is considering MTSS as a potential solution. From the viewpoint of a home-building analogy, Nate is planning to complete a major renovation on his habitable two-story bungalow, which does not include modernized, effective, and efficient structures and services. The process of updating Nate's current home (e.g., his current service delivery model) to a more effective and efficient home (e.g., MTSS service delivery framework) requires a long-term plan, a renovation team, a checklist of what will be changed or retained, and an evaluation process to assess work quality, timeliness of task completion, and data to inform any necessary adjustments.

Nate looks to IS to facilitate changing his current program into an evidence-based program. IS is "the scientific study of variables and conditions that impact changes at practice, organization, and system levels" (Duda, Fixsen, & Blase, 2013, p. 398). Basically, IS guides the change process over the long term from a current

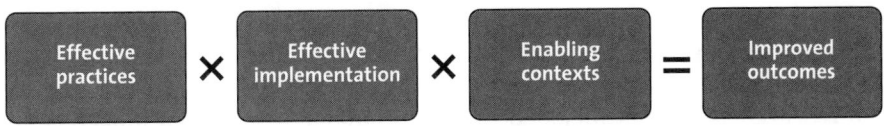

Figure 3.1. Active Implementation Formula. From The National Implementation Research Network, Frank Porter Graham Child Development Center, University of North Carolina, Chapel Hill (2017). Reprinted by permission.

way of delivering services into an evidence-based framework, model, or practice in order to achieve essential outcomes for children and families. IS helps to put evidence-based frameworks, models, and practices into place across a wide range of service delivery settings through purposeful and strategic transition activities. Activities may occur sequentially or simultaneously to promote the start-up, sustainability, and ultimately the effectiveness of frameworks, models, and practices.

IS can be summarized by the formula depicted in Figure 3.1 and includes effective practices, effective implementation, and the enabling context, which together lead to improved outcomes. This equation, also known as the Active Implementation Formula, emerged from an iterative, research-based process to develop recommended practices for bringing evidence-based practices to scale (Fixsen, Blase, Metz, & Van Dyke, 2013; Metz, Halle, Bartley, & Blasberg, 2013).

The three factors on the left side of the Active Implementation Formula refer to *what* is implemented (effective practices), *how* it is implemented (effective implementation) and *where* it is implemented (enabling contexts), respectively. Effective practices need to be research-based and matched to program goals, put into place in a deliberate and adaptive manner, and supported by a hospitable environment and intentional learning processes. *Effective implementation* refers to the strategies put into place to support those effective practices, and the *enabling context* refers to the environmental conditions that support new practices. Each variable within the formula is essential—if any one of the variables is not present, positive child outcomes are unlikely to be achieved and sustained. Thus, achievement of positive outcomes for children in programs requires a combination of effective interventions or practices, proven implementation strategies, and enabling contexts.

IS provides a systematic process for selecting an evidence-based framework or model (such as MTSS), supporting effective implementation and scaling-up, and ensuring that the organization's context, or environment, can sustain the new model over time. The purpose of this chapter is to describe how IS can support the effective implementation and scaling-up of the MTSS framework in early childhood settings. Video 2 of our accompanying video series illustrates an early childhood education program's Instructional Leadership Team's (ILT) use of IS to move into an MTSS service delivery model. Chapter 11 also examines the use of IS to scale-up the Pyramid Model.

 See Video 2 for illustration of an ILT's use of IS to assist their move into MTSS practices.

Active Implementation Frameworks

The AIFs are lenses for viewing the processes of applying IS to bring evidence-based practices to education and other social service settings; that is, to close the research-to-practice gap. These lenses lead to specific and coordinated action steps for facilitating the change process from a current way of providing services to an evidence-based service delivery model. The AIFs were first conceptualized by Fixsen, Naoom, Blase, Friedman, and Wallace (2005) while they were conducting a research study that included interviews and a synthesis of implementation evaluation literature. The original four AIFs included Stages of Implementation, Implementation Teams, Implementation Drivers, and Improvement Cycles. Each AIF was built around one specific concept and its underpinnings that, when activated or put into motion, purposefully transitions a human or social service delivery program, model, or practice over time into evidence-based practices.

Consider the AIFS in the context of the home improvement analogy. For Nate to transition from his two-story bungalow (e.g., current way of meeting children's needs) into a more modern, effective, and efficient house (e.g., MTSS service delivery system), the Stages of Implementation would serve as the overall construction plan, reflecting decisions on what demolition, construction, or evaluation activities would take place on each day of a long-range plan (2–4 years for most social service reform efforts, according to Duda et al., 2013). The Implementation Team might include the architect, banker, and general contractor who would work with Nate and his stakeholders from the beginning until project fruition. The Implementation Drivers would represent the physical properties of the home (plumbing, appliances, electricity, single-pane windows, window AC unit) that would undergo gradual and incremental changes, keeping some of physical properties of the home (2 × 4-inch wooden studs or frame), getting rid of others, and adding some new ones. The improvement cycles would delineate that Nate, construction supervisors, and municipal code enforcement officers assess the work quality in a timely manner to ensure all parts of the process are on course toward building completion.

Since 2005, AIFs have been employed in the field, analyzed, and refined to represent the best available evidence gathered from implementation evaluation literature and best practices. AIFs have been used to bring about changes in a wide range of human and social services delivery systems across several states in the United States and abroad (e.g., Canada) to improve programs in education, generally, and early childhood, specifically (e.g., Head Start, K–3 Formative Assessment project in North Carolina, home visiting programs; see the National Implementation Research Network [NIRN] web site: http://nirn.fpg.unc.edu). In refining and revising the AIFs, an additional AIF emerged, providing a more robust conceptual framework to the process of defining *what* should be implemented. That is, the end-product, evidence-based program, model, or practice needs to be clearly described so stakeholders and front-line service providers can articulate the innovation's required features as well as the rationale for that particular end-product. Originally called an *implementation prerequisite* (Duda et al., 2013; Metz et al., 2013), it now serves as AIF #1: Selecting a Usable Innovation.

Active Implementation Framework #1: Selecting a Usable Innovation AIF #1 includes four criteria that must be articulated in assessing a usable innovation:

1. Philosophy, values, and principles
2. Essential functions
3. Operational definitions
4. Practical performance assessments

The process of Selecting a Usable Innovation (AIF #1) requires program changers to screen a variety of potential evidence-based, innovative frameworks, models, or practices that are highly likely to result in achievement of essential outcomes (Fixsen et al., 2013). As a result of the screening process, one evidence-based innovation is chosen for closer scrutiny within AIF #2: Stages of Implementation. The decision on whether to select a given evidence-based innovation as the targeted framework, model, or practice is not made until the Exploration stage activities (described in the Stages section to come) are underway and the innovation under scrutiny is deemed to be a good match for a specific program's needs.

MTSS as a Usable Innovation The MTSS service delivery framework promotes using evidence-based practices incorporated within early childhood systems to ensure that young children receive the appropriate level of services that match their needs (Buysse & Peisner-Feinberg, 2010; Greenwood et al., 2011). Thus, it holds merit as a potential service delivery framework to which current practitioners might aspire. The MTSS service delivery model is, in many ways, more effective and efficient than current mechanisms for offering educational opportunities. Specifically, in many early learning programs, system infrastructure decisions (e.g., elements and components) such as curriculum (*what to teach*), intervention materials (*how to teach/intervene*), environmental arrangements (*how to arrange to teach/intervene*), and assessment tools (*how to monitor progress toward goals*) are not made at a systems level—they are made arbitrarily and result in limited accountability for achieving results.

In contrast, in an MTSS service delivery model, the system infrastructures are redesigned at the system level in a systematic fashion to include high-quality curriculum, proven intervention materials, evidence-based environmental arrangements, and valid and reliable assessment tools with accountability for achieving results. Therefore, the entire process for educating children is likely to be enhanced. A one-size-fits-all approach to providing all children with common classroom experiences might result in mismatches between children's needs and the instruction provided. A better use of resources is research-based instruction that is matched to children's needs and implemented with fidelity with appropriate intensity and length of time (e.g., dosage) to promote children's growth. Moreover, dynamic system processes at the classroom level and school/program level include use of an ongoing decision-making process based on student performance data. Teams make time-sensitive decisions based on performance data to better align resources with children's needs. MTSS is a better use of resources than the "just-wait-until-the-child-matures" approach embraced by many current programs that may limit children's access to needed interventions until a problem is significantly entrenched.

The use of active implementation strategies can help programs and schools realize the potential of the MTSS service delivery framework in improving outcomes for young children. Key recommendations based on AIFs include:

- Building the capacity of schools and programs so they are ready to use MTSS strategies and practices and participate in rigorous quality improvement processes

- Engaging in identification, installation, and improvement of implementation infrastructure to achieve competency, alignment, and sustainability of MTSS practices

- Utilizing stage-based work that aligns implementation activities to the developmental phase of implementation efforts
- Practicing intentional use of data to drive decision making and continuous quality improvement

To be implementable in practice, the local school/program Leadership Team must define the MTSS framework according to the four criteria of a usable innovation (Fixsen et al., 2013; Metz, Bartley, Blase, & Fixsen, 2011), enumerated below and with key words in italics.

1. The *philosophy, values, and principles* of the MTSS service delivery framework: The early childhood practitioner's decisions are guided by the philosophy, values, and principles embedded into the framework, which ensures consistency, integrity, and sustainable effort across all practitioners. Within the MTSS framework, this criterion should be aligned with the identified goals for the local early childhood community. Such locally defined goals might include: 1) bringing young children together at one site, such as a dedicated early childhood center so the district's financial and personnel resources can be expended more efficiently; 2) evaluating the effectiveness of the Tier 1 curriculum through child performance outcome measures rather than more subjective, indirect measures; 3) educating children with diverse abilities and circumstances together through the creation of a blended program (early childhood education [ECE] and ECSE practices integrated into classrooms, programs, and community settings for children with and without identified disabilities; Pretti-Frontczak, Grisham-Brown, & Sullivan, 2014); and 4) meeting children's needs early by providing differentiated instruction as soon as the need is documented and not waiting until formal identification of a disability has taken place.

2. The *essential functions* that define all of the team members' roles: A clear description of the essential functions that clarify and delineate the role of educators, paraprofessionals, therapists, and other team members and inform their day-to-day activities provides an unmistakable identification of the MTSS defining features. Essential functions are also sometimes referred to as core components or practice elements. These functions may include: 1) developing and conducting a common multiweek instructional unit planning process with designated roles for each team member; 2) coordinating and conducting delivery of related services, such as speech therapy, within blended classrooms to identified children; and 3) operating a four-step, data-based decision-making process to ensure children are progressing satisfactorily with the provided interventions.

3. The *operational definitions* for the essential functions that allow MTSS to be *teachable, learnable, doable, and assessable:* The essential functions need to be defined operationally with clear descriptions of core activities that allow MTSS to be *teachable, learnable, doable, and assessable* across a range of contexts. Operational definitions promote consistency in how educators function at the level of service delivery. From an MTSS perspective in early learning settings, the core activities might include: 1) designing and delivering instruction within the larger multiweek unit plan, such as large-group dialogic

reading lessons and small-group explicit vocabulary instruction; 2) collecting data weekly to monitor children's progress toward essential benchmarks; and 3) setting team meeting agendas and ensuring that team members adhere to them within each phase of the problem-solving process.

4. The *practical performance assessments* of implementation integrity: Stakeholders and team members need to assess whether MTSS is implemented as intended by early childhood professionals. Practitioner adherence to targeted procedures and processes is known as procedural integrity. Performance assessments are used to improve practitioner competency through processes of procedural integrity self-assessment, peer or coach assessment, and in some cases supervisor assessment. Once these assessments are conducted, then professional development supports, such as training and coaching, can be provided to improve performance of the targeted skills. From an MTSS perspective in early learning settings, this would involve utilizing a performance assessment process to match services to children's needs across tiers, which could be a simple checklist completed in the "intervention implementation" plan evaluation stage of the problem-solving process. A second performance assessment would measure adherence to all steps of each identified evidence-based practice or program. See Chapters 4 and 8 for examples of integrity checklists for evidence-based assessment processes and interventions.

The MTSS service delivery framework has several benefits for implementation and scaling of this approach in early childhood systems. This framework

- *Provides a fully operationalized practice model for consistent implementation of an MTSS approach.* Well-defined frameworks improve the likelihood that educators can implement essential functions as well as understand the philosophy, purpose, and values of a multi-tiered approach and how each practice works in tandem within the system.

- *Facilitates the development of effective training protocols, coaching strategies, and fidelity assessments.* A well-operationalized framework allows for the development of competency-based hiring, training, coaching, and performance assessments that are "in service to" the MTSS essential functions. Since the MTSS approach is essentially a coordinated system of individual programs or practices layered in a tiered approach, it is essential that the necessary competency-based supports and assessments for all levels of the approach be clearly outlined. Without this level of definition and common understanding of how the specific components will work in synchronization with one another, programs will be unable to develop the right supports and infrastructure for ensuring MTSS is implemented effectively and improved over time.

- *Refines the organizational and systems supports to facilitate consistent MTSS practice across educators and other direct service providers.* A well-operationalized framework will allow programs to develop decision-support data systems, administrative practices, and systems partnerships aligned with the expectations for the new way of work. The MTSS approach is a system strategy, so the system leaders will need to assess the necessary systemwide components (essential infrastructure elements) and processes (how those structures work together) to determine needed changes to ensure effective framework implementation at all system levels. In addition, MTSS is a programwide strategy, so examining the program/school level components and processes will need to be done to ensure effective implementation at the classroom/practitioner level as well.

- *Promotes the use of continuous improvement strategies as essential functions.* Activities of MTSS are continually tested in interactions with children and families as programs and systems can only improve innovations that are well defined.

- *Ensures that outcomes linked to MTSS implementation can be accurately interpreted.* Outcomes are challenging to interpret when there is a lack of clarity in "what" was implemented. If expected outcomes are not achieved, fidelity assessment data related to the practice components can provide an explanation and facilitate action planning. This is true whether the fidelity assessment data are related to a specific program or to a process, as in the case of effectively matching services to need.

As noted earlier, one of the key factors in the Active Implementation Formula is *what* is implemented. When practices lack specification, it is challenging for educators to figure out *what* they should be implementing, which results in impediments to implementation with good outcomes for communities (e.g., Hall & Hord, 2015). Practice profile methodology can be used to identify and describe the core components of a practice so that they are teachable, learnable, and doable. Practice profiles are a promising method for operationalizing, assessing, and improving practices developed through practitioner engagement and rigorous preparation methods (Metz, 2016; Metz & Easterling, 2016). In addition, practice profiles describe in detail the guiding principles and essential functions that operationalize a usable innovation. A working draft of a Global Implementation Specialist Practice Profile (Metz, Louison, Ward, & Burke, 2017) is an example practice profile. Interested readers should check the Resources section at the chapter's end to learn how to download the practice profile from the National Research Implementation Network (NIRN) web site. Once a strategy or practice is described in sufficient detail, effective implementation methods can be applied to build the educators' competencies to work in a new way, to use data to continuously improve the innovation, and to ensure that leadership and administrative practices are in service to new expectations.

Moving Programs/Schools Into an MTSS Framework: Supporting the "How"

Previous syntheses of implementation research (Damschroder et al., 2009, Durlak & DuPre, 2008; Fixsen et al., 2005; Meyers, Durlak, & Wanderman, 2012) have yielded active ingredients for successful implementation of evidence-based practices. There are four key ingredients or strategies that can be used to support programs to implement MTSS practices: Stages (it takes time), Teams (it takes a village), Drivers (it takes support), and Improvement Cycles (it takes data). These key ingredients are described and linked to IS constructs in Figure 3.2. The first AIF is selecting a Usable Innovation which, for the purpose of this book, is MTSS. Once a Usable Innovation is selected, these four AIFs bring the innovation to Full Implementation.

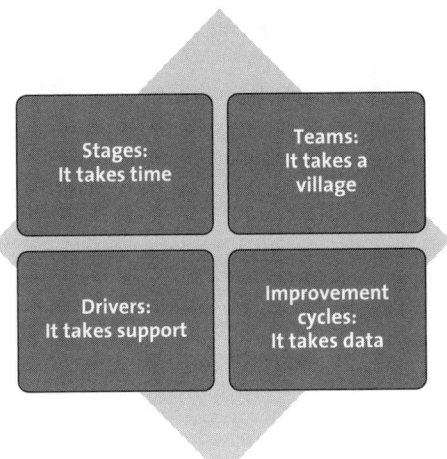

Figure 3.2. Active Implementation Frameworks. From The National Implementation Research Network, Frank Porter Graham Child Development Center, University of North Carolina, Chapel Hill (2017). Reprinted by permission.

Active Implementation Framework #2: Implementation Stages (It Takes Time)
Educators, direct care providers, therapists, related service providers, supervisors, principals, program directors, and agency executives and school superintendents need support to implement MTSS strategies and practices. The first ingredient of active implementation is related to Stages of Implementation, and the time and process it takes to shift approaches and practices in programs. There is accumulating evidence on purposeful, active, and effective implementation approaches for supporting the use of evidence-based practices in early childhood contexts. The IS literature confirms that implementation occurs in four discernable stages or phases with common elements present throughout each stage (Aarons, Hurlburt, & Horowitz, 2011; Fixsen et al., 2005; Meyers et al., 2012):

Stage 1: Exploration

Stage 2: Installation

Stage 3: Initial Implementation

Stage 4: Full Implementation

Activities of each of the remaining AIFs—Teams, Drivers, and Improvement Cycles—are accomplished as the transition process moves through these four Stages of Implementation. Although four primary Stages of Implementation are identified, implementation may not always move in a linear fashion through such phases (Aarons et al., 2011; Fixsen et al., 2005), and the stages are often messy, overlapping, and iterative. Often, strategies or practices may advance to one stage, then revisit a previous stage based on implementation needs. There also may be instances in which one aspect of a strategy or practice is in Initial Implementation, while another aspect of a strategy or practice is in Exploration and working to assess needs and identify infrastructure elements. Figure 3.3 depicts the purpose and activities for MTSS Teams, Drivers, and Improvement Cycles in the four implementation stages.

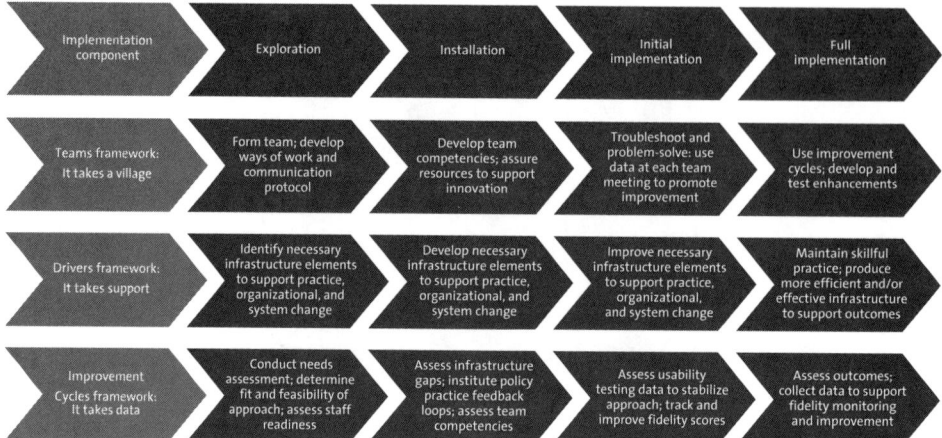

Figure 3.3. Active Implementation Framework #2: Stages of Implementation: It takes time. From The National Implementation Research Network, Frank Porter Graham Child Development Center, University of North Carolina, Chapel Hill (2017). Reprinted by permission.

Stage 1: Exploration The first stage of implementation is *Exploration*. It occurs well before the strategies or practices identified within an MTSS framework are put in place "on the ground," or, alternatively, is the first stage of reassessing whether what is currently in place is the best fit for the needs of the target population or community. Activities of this stage include assessing the needs of children and families, judging the fit and feasibility of MTSS to meet identified needs, developing a team and communication processes to support the work as it progresses through stages, and deciding on an action plan and resources needed to enact the plan.

Seasoned and novice practitioners have stated that this stage is a particularly important one, as many want to move into specific MTSS practices (e.g., adoption of a "universal screener" to monitor student progress, provision of a standard protocol approach for a Tier-2 intervention, employment of a systematic, data-based process to determine student response to an intervention) but lack the guidance and knowledge to make systemic program changes that would support new practices. To that end, Exploration stage activities aligned to the MTSS initiative for young children are being delineated, piloted, and evaluated so that a stronger, more evidence-based exploratory process is available for early childhood practitioners.

Stage 2: Installation The second stage of implementation, *Installation*, is about securing and developing the support needed to put MTSS into place. At this stage, MTSS strategies and practices are usually not yet being delivered, but the necessary individual and organizational competencies and supporting infrastructure (e.g., training and coaching protocols, data dashboards, and administrative supports) are being established so that MTSS strategies and practices can be successfully put in place in the very near future. For many programs/schools, this stage involves preparing to "shift" current practices into MTSS practices, so planning organizational culture changes and preparing staff to move through a change process are especially important.

Stage 3: Initial Implementation   During the third stage, *Initial Implementation*, MTSS practices are put in place for children and families, as are strategies to promote continuous improvement. In this stage, program staff members are checking to see if colleagues are working through the change process well. They are also gathering data to assess implementation fidelity and developing improvement strategies or adjustments based on the data.

Stage 4: Full Implementation   Lastly, *Full Implementation* is achieved when the new practice or approach has stabilized, and the consistent use of MTSS results in improved outcomes for children and programs/schools, and at the system level. Strategies and practices also demonstrate highly functioning improvement cycles, whereby information is routinely collected on how the services are being delivered and the extent to which MTSS processes (e.g., training, coaching, and leadership) are fully functioning. Full implementation is defined as more than 50% of practitioners implementing the innovation with fidelity and achieving expected outcomes; full implementation of any new strategy or practice, including MTSS, can take 2–4 years (Duda et al., 2013).

Two appendices are included at the chapter's end to assist leadership teams in employing the AIF stages. Appendix 3A, titled *Stage-Based Active Implementation Planning Tool* is an excerpted appendix from an OPRE research brief created to offer an integrated stage-based framework to be used by change-makers to plan their stage-based change process (Metz et al., 2015). The *Stage-Based Active Implementation Planning Tool* includes four matrices, one for each stage of the AIF (Exploration, Installation, Initial Implementation, and Full Implementation). Within each matrix, common implementation elements are listed as column headings, and "key questions" that ECE program leadership teams need to review and subsequently answer are provided within each column. The key questions require the Leadership Team to examine their current status in moving into the chosen usable innovation and the steps they may want to take next. Using the *Stage-Based Active Implementation Planning Tool* to initiate a change process and monitor movement during the process has several merits, including that 1) it has been specifically designed for use in early childhood programs, 2) it includes all four phases of the AIF stages and core implementation elements, and 3) the question format of the discrete components make it user-friendly for ILT use. One drawback is that it does not specifically address MTSS in early childhood programs as a usable innovation.

A second AIF planning tool has been provided in Appendix 3B. Titled *MTSS in Early Childhood (EC): Stages of Implementation Analysis* (Young, n.d.), it is an adaptation of the *Stages of Implementation Analysis: Where Are We?* tool developed by Blase, van Dyke, and Fixsen (2013) at The State Implementation and Scaling-up of Evidence-based Practices Center (SISEP). It has been used in three pilot studies of early childhood educators (pilot 1), school principals (pilot 2), and Early Childhood ILT members (pilot 3) whose programs were thinking about moving into MTSS practices or whose programs had already started to shift into these practice (Young, n.d.). The original *Stages of Implementation* document included analyses of all four phases of the AIF (Exploration, Installation, Initial Implementation, Full Implementation); however, the *MTSS in EC: Stages of Implementation Analysis* planning tool provided in the appendix only addresses the Exploration phase at this time. Completion of the described activities may help leadership teams determine if the MTSS initiative for young children is the right fit for a specific school/program or agency; also, feasibility and stakeholder readiness for moving into MTSS practices for young children, as well as initial installation steps, may be determined from completing the checklist.

Active Implementation Framework #3: Teams (It Takes a Village)   The next active implementation ingredient is related to what we call the Implementation Team. As noted earlier, the ILT may function as the MTSS Implementation Team, or in some cases, there may a separate Implementation Team. See Figure 2.3 for an example composition chart for an ILT that will function as an Implementation Team.

Implementation Teams have been called a "new lever" for organization change in education (Higgins, Weiner, & Young, 2012). Implementation Teams are described as accountable and sustainable because teams can tolerate individual staff turnover, and knowledge is shared among individuals. As individuals leave, remaining team members can carry on while new members are brought on and learn the complex, required skill sets required of members.

Implementation Teams are groups of individuals who have the task of intentionally designing, monitoring, and supporting the implementation processes. Teams may include key personnel (i.e., program administrators, practitioners) and key stakeholders (i.e., program developers, funders, recipients of program services, or community members). Ideally, teams should be established at every level of a program or system, or should target different aspects of an initiative. For example, for a complex initiative such as a statewide implementation of the MTSS service delivery framework, separate Implementation Teams may be necessary to fully support the scale and scope of a statewide initiative. That is, although a statewide initiative might call for tiered models, one team might take on tiered supports for social-emotional functioning, such as the Pyramid Model (e.g., Fox, Dunlap, Hemmeter, Joseph, & Strain, 2003), while another team addresses tiered early academic models, such as early literacy development (e.g., Buysse & Peisner-Feinberg, 2010). Implementation Teams at each of these levels, or aligned with different aspects of the MTSS service delivery framework, should represent different perspectives, including practice, supervision, administrative leadership, and policy perspectives. These different perspectives can be present within a single Implementation Team or be represented through a linked teaming structure across levels of a program or system.

Research has found that there are varying levels of support for putting a new practice into place (Greenhalgh, Robert, MacFarlane, Bate, & Kyriakidou, 2004). There is "letting it happen," which is when no supports are put into place and teachers or home visitors are left to figure it out on their own. There is "helping it happen" where some supports are put into place, but there is not a commitment to ongoing capacity for the new practice to be sustained. Then there are AIF strategies that create accountable structures to support the needs of the educators and programs in using MTSS practices. In order to realize outcomes for children, programs need to "making it happen." Implementation Teams are a mechanism that programs can use to make implementation of MTSS happen. The group of key stakeholders that is formed to support the MTSS approach can be thought of as an Implementation Team that is tasked with both identifying the needs of a community and the associated strategies and practices to meet those needs as well as monitoring and supporting the ongoing quality improvement process. As is discussed in more detail next, there can be more than one coordinated Implementation Team depending on the size and scope of the MTSS approach in a community or region.

How Do Implementation Teams Support Shifting Into an MTSS Service Delivery Framework? Initially and continuing over time, Implementation Teams become fluent in using good implementation practices to support MTSS. Teams then engage in stage-based work to help identify and build upon current system strengths, help manage expectations, highlight systems change success, and focus on creating communication pathways among and across stakeholders. Using an MTSS approach, the Implementation Team(s) may initially focus their efforts on identifying the community's needs for young children and their families, identify the needed strategies and practices to meet those needs, support the development of data-driven quality improvement processes, and shepherd needed systems' changes to ensure that support is provided, that the community is engaged in the process, and that the enabling context supporting all levels of the system is developed and improved over time.

The role of ensuring support includes assessing and creating ongoing "buy in" and readiness. Implementation Teams provide information about the reasons for change, the new practice or approach, and the implementation supports and commitment of leaders to make changes in the system that will facilitate the effective use of innovations in classrooms, centers, and regions. Ensuring support also includes ensuring that educators and administrators have the support needed to be competent and to implement MTSS strategies and practices well. Teams also monitor implementation fidelity of MTSS practice and related outcomes and conduct action planning to solve challenges, build sustainability, and align system functions.

Another critical role and function of an MTSS Implementation Team is to engage the program's community. This is an area where many programs have great expertise, so it may be the easiest component of the Implementation Team's work. Involving stakeholders in a meaningful way creates opportunities to share information, address concerns, "mine" the expertise they bring, and build support for decisions. Because the philosophy and values of an MTSS approach are to ensure that young children's needs are being met in "real time" *and* are able to evolve over time using a multi-tiered approach, it would be imperative to engage community stakeholders for input on the needs of its youngest members over time and for feedback on how well the MTSS approach seems to be working.

Finally, Implementation Teams actively create hospitable environments to ensure that an enabling context exists to support MTSS strategies and practices. Any given Implementation Team has authority to improve areas for creating a more hospitable environment (e.g., scheduling, resources, curriculum choices, professional development resource allocation). Other areas are beyond their sphere of influence. This means that each Implementation Team needs to systematically and transparently communicate with other teams who can positively influence the policy, regulatory, and funding environments at their system level.

Active Implementation Framework #4: Implementation Driver (It Takes Support)
Educators, supervisors, and program leaders need support to implement MTSS strategies and practices. The next ingredient of active implementation, the *Implementation Driver* AIF, includes the core components or building blocks of the infrastructure needed to support practice, organizational, and systems change

(Metz & Bartley, 2012). The implementation drivers emerged on the basis of the commonalities among successfully implemented programs and practices (Fixsen et al., 2005; Fixsen, Blase, Duda, Naoom, & Wallace, 2009), and the structural components and activities that make up each implementation driver contribute to the successful and sustainable implementation of strategies and practices. There are three types of implementation drivers and when used collectively, they ensure optimal and sustainable implementation of MTSS strategies and practices: competency drivers, organization drivers, and leadership drivers.

Competency drivers are mechanisms to develop, improve, and sustain educators' ability to implement MTSS to benefit young children and their families. The four competency drivers include selection, training, coaching, and fidelity assessment (Metz & Bartley, 2012). The competency drivers are described here and illustrated in Figure 3.4.

- Selection—Effective implementation of MTSS requires the specification of skills, abilities, and other characteristics that support a practitioners' competence in implementing MTSS strategies and practices. Once these prerequisites have been identified, practitioners who possess such skills and abilities can be recruited. Leaders are increasingly looking to bring on board individuals who will support the MTSS framework in disposition and in practice.

- Training—Training should provide knowledge related to the theory and underlying values of MTSS, introduce the components and rationales of key strategies and practices, and provide opportunities to practice new skills to meet fidelity criteria and receive feedback in a safe and supportive training environment.

- Coaching—Most new skills can be introduced in training but must be practiced and mastered on the job with coaching to achieve fidelity to the strategy or practice model.

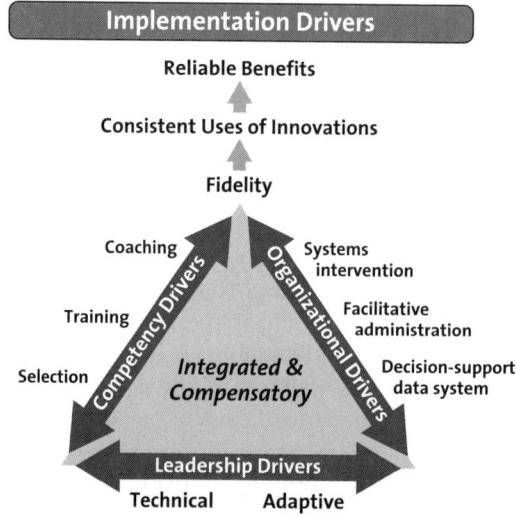

Figure 3.4. Active Implementation Framework #4: Implementation Drivers: It takes support. From The National Implementation Research Network, Frank Porter Graham Child Development Center, University of North Carolina, Chapel Hill (2017). Reprinted by permission.

- Fidelity assessment—Fidelity assessments are designed to assess skill application and outcomes reflected in selection criteria, taught in training, and reinforced in coaching.

Organization drivers intentionally develop the organizational supports and systems interventions needed to create a hospitable environment for a MTSS service delivery framework. Organization drivers ensure that competency drivers are accessible, effective, and that data are used for continuous improvement. The three organization drivers are described below.

- Decision-support data systems—Data are used to assess key aspects of overall organization performance and support decision making to ensure continued implementation over time. Decision-support data systems include quality assurance data, fidelity data, and outcome data. Data need to be reliable, reported frequently, built into practice routines, accessible at actionable levels, and used to make decisions.

- Facilitative administration—Early childhood program leaders supporting an MTSS service delivery framework will need to make use of a wide range of data to inform decision making and keep practitioners organized and focused on the desired outcomes. Leadership must be committed to MTSS strategies and practices and be available to address challenges and create solutions, develop clear communication protocols and feedback loops, adjust and develop policies and procedures to support the new way of work, and reduce administrative barriers.

- Systems interventions—These are strategies to work collaboratively with external systems to ensure availability of financial, organizational, and human resources required to support MTSS service delivery at the program level. Examples might include ensuring that systems and agencies who provide services to young children and families at both ends of the age continuum on either side of the preschool years (e.g., early intervention Part C service system providers and early elementary school staff) understand how the MTSS model is aligned to identification and service provision to various children. The external system alignment is a critical aspect of implementation efforts.

Leadership drivers ensure that leaders use appropriate strategies to address different types of challenges and that diversified leadership is built throughout an organization at every level of the system. The drivers serve both integrative and compensatory functions in such a way that weaknesses in one driver can be compensated by strengths in other drivers.

Active Implementation Framework #5: Improvement Cycles (It Takes Data)

Continuous improvement cycles are necessary because new practices or innovations do not fare well in existing organizational structures and systems. In order to operate the continuous improvement cycle, quantitative and qualitative data on system operations and outcomes must be gathered and shared for decision-making purposes. Unfortunately, without effective feedback loops within and across levels of an organizational system, effective strategies and practices, such as those used in an MTSS approach, are often changed to fit the existing systems, as opposed to existing systems changing to support the effective practices.

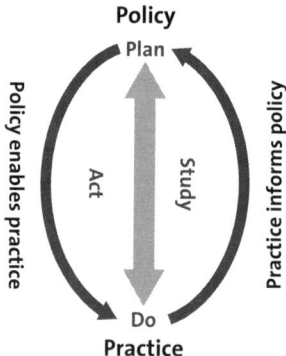

Figure 3.5. Practice–Policy Communication Cycle: Feedback loops. From The National Implementation Research Network, Frank Porter Graham Child Development Center, University of North Carolina, Chapel Hill (2017). Reprinted by permission.

IS emphasizes the need for continuous quality improvement through the systematic assessment and feedback of information and data related to planning, implementation, and outcomes (Chinman, Imm, & Wandersman, 2004). Damschroder and colleagues (2009) noted that reflecting and evaluating is an essential implementation process, referring to the use of feedback loops about the progress and quality of implementation accompanied with regular Implementation Team debriefing about progress and experience: "Dedicating time for reflecting or debriefing before, during, and after implementation is one way to promote shared learning and improvements along the way" (p. 11).

Data are used to drive decision making as well as to support effective communication and feedback loops across multiple levels of the system. AIF #5 highlights the importance of feedback loops and emphasizes that connecting policy to practice is a key aspect of reducing early learning systems' barriers to high-fidelity implementation. The practice-to-policy communication loop, as illustrated in Figure 3.5, seems to be a critical feature of successful efforts to implement practice models on a scale significant to affect child outcomes. In successful system change efforts, leadership teams frequently (at least monthly) receive information about what is helping or hindering the efforts to make full and effective use of innovations at the practice level (Khatri & Frieden, 2002). This is illustrated by the vertical words *practice informs policy* part of the graphic. The information may consist of descriptions of practitioner experiences or more precise data (e.g., administrative, fidelity, survey, or focus group data). Based on the information from practitioners, leadership can reduce systems barriers to implementation and strengthen the facilitators to achieve the desired outcomes for children and families (Fixsen et al., 2013). This is illustrated by the vertical words *policy enables practice* part of the graphic.

Practice–policy feedback loops are an example of a continuous improvement cycle, typically signified as the Plan, Do, Study, Act cycle (Deming, 1986). As noted in Figure 3.6, the four pieces of a continuous improvement cycle include 1) specifying the plan that helps move service and interventions forward, 2) focusing on facilitating the implementation of the plan, 3) developing assessments to understand

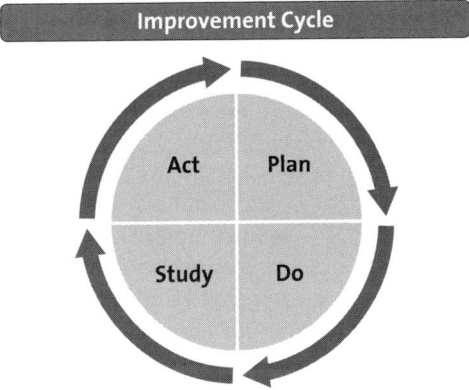

Figure 3.6. Active Implementation Framework #5: Improvement Cycle: It takes data, plus communication and learning. Plan, Do, Study, Act. From The National Implementation Research Network, Frank Porter Graham Child Development Center, University of North Carolina, Chapel Hill (2017). Reprinted by permission.

how the plan is working, and 4) making changes to the next iteration of the plan to improve implementation.

A hallmark of early implementation is using data to identify solutions to problems that arise and to drive decision making. It is critical to address barriers and develop solutions quickly rather than allowing problems to re-emerge and reoccur (Metz & Albers, 2014). The Implementation Teams use improvement cycles to troubleshoot and problem-solve barriers to implementation and improve the implementation infrastructure.

The Enabling Context: Stakeholders Supporting MTSS Implementation

Collaboration has been found to be critical to the implementation of evidence-based practices in early childhood systems. Interpersonal contacts within and between stakeholder groups have been demonstrated to be important influences on the adoption of new practices (Palinkas et al., 2011). As individual stakeholders self-organize through interactions, these interactions produce opportunities for co-learning and collaborative problem solving of complex systems challenges. As Implementation Teams form, part of their work is to focus on opportunities to collaborate and to identify the best way to communicate, share ideas, and develop solutions. Co-creation takes place through the active involvement of stakeholders in all stages of the production and implementation process, resulting in service models, approaches, and practices that are contextualized and tailored to settings (Metz & Albers, 2014; Metz & Bartley, 2017). Bringing the MTSS service delivery framework to scale in programs/schools requires the commitment of important actors (e.g., policymakers, funders, researchers, ECE and ECSE educators, SLPs, school psychologists, school social workers, OTs, PTs) to a common agenda that includes striving for the infrastructure needed to support and sustain MTSS strategies and practices.

The development of an aligned, sustainable infrastructure is vital for effective implementation of evidence-based practices. The infrastructure is often invisible to policymakers and funders, program developers, and educators who work to implement evidence-based practices and innovations. Both transformative and incremental changes will need to be made by each major stakeholder group (i.e., policymakers and funders, MTSS consultants, and schools/programs leaders and direct service providers) in order to co-create a visible infrastructure in service to evidence-based practices such as MTSS in education (Metz & Albers, 2014). Examples of such collaborative processes are provided next.

Building Practitioner Competency Implementation Teams need to consider the roles of policymakers and funders, program/school leaders and direct service providers, researchers and MTSS experts, higher education partners, and parents in building the capacity and competency of educators to use the MTSS framework with fidelity. For example, funders and policymakers can incentivize the use of MTSS practices by providing adequate timeframes and resources for skill-based training and coaching and consultation of educators, as well as mandating regular fidelity assessments and reporting requirements. MTSS experts can identify prerequisites for doing the work and ensuring that educators' needed supports are well defined for programs seeking to use MTSS frameworks. Programs can build educator competency by providing staff with essential training, developing and implementing coaching service delivery plans, and using fidelity data for improvement purposes rather than for compliance purposes.

Developing Enabling Contexts The roles of policymakers and funders, programs and schools, researchers and MTSS experts, higher education, and parents in developing hospitable organization and systems context to support the use of an MTSS framework cannot be overstated. Funders can provide resources for the creation, testing, and maintenance of decision-support data systems, the ongoing engagement of leadership, and the creation of enabling cross-systems partnerships to aid in service delivery. MTSS experts can support organizational and systems change by reaching out to key stakeholders systemwide to address barriers to successful service delivery. Programs and schools can work with external systems to ensure the availability of financial, organizational, and human resources required to support the work of practitioners. The alignment of external systems to support the work is a critical aspect of implementation.

CONCLUSION

As described in this chapter, the emerging field of IS provides a strong organizational schema and dynamic processes for supporting the effective implementation and scaling-up of an MTSS framework for meeting the educational and developmental needs of young children and their families. In order to achieve strong, positive outcomes from early childhood programs, ILTs need to shift their programs into a system of MTSS where data-based decision making ensures that children's and families' needs are matched to effective and efficient instruction and interventions. Choosing MTSS as a usable innovation is the first of five AIFs serving as tools and strategic guides for practitioners, leaders, and stakeholders who want to implement an evidence-based service delivery model and bring it to scale. Subsequently, the four remaining AIFs, including stages, teams, drivers, and improvement cycles, facilitate the development and deployment of a multiyear process to create consensus on the need for MTSS, to shift the infrastructure and program culture to achieve successful implementation, and to ensure operation of a data-based, continuous improvement cyclical process to keep everyone accountable for desirable results.

Nate Johnson, the LISD early childhood executive director, warmly greeted all those who came to celebrate the completion of Lincoln Prairie Preschool's (LPP) first year of operation. As he shook hands, he reflected on the process to transition the ECSE program, existing previously as self-contained classes spread across five schools, into an MTSS service delivery model designed to serve all kinds of children and families, including young children with delays and disabilities, housed in a newly built early childhood center (LPP).

The ECLT chose the MTSS service delivery framework as the Usable Innovation (AIF #1) and then ensured it would be a "good match" for meeting their needs as part of the Exploration activities in the AIF #2 (Stages of Implementation). Once the ECLT decided to make this transition, the ECLT members also decided to take on the Implementation Team (AIF #3) responsibilities themselves rather than create a separate team. With those decisions behind them, they moved forward and created a multiyear plan using the AIF stages as their guide to accomplish the shift into an MTSS service delivery model. Early on, they realized that their vision was to create a community-based, inclusive (also known as ECE/ECSE "blended") instructional program. This type of program model would meet the needs of all young children and families from their neighborhoods and community, including those with delays and disabilities, who were the focus of their original mission. Subsequently, the ECLT used the Implementation Drivers (AIF #4) to identify needed shifts from the former system infrastructure elements and processes for delivering instructional services into revised MTSS elements and processes to accomplish this objective. The team also used Improvement Cycles (AIF #5) to ensure services provided to children and families always resulted in achievement of essential outcomes and to check on the timely accomplishments of the transition process.

The five AIFs facilitated the transition into an MTSS service delivery model. As a result, the LPP was created and built to offer a tuition-based community preschool experience, linked to the state's accreditation process, to all of the young children and families in the neighborhoods and community. LPP's classrooms and school settings are composed of children whose parents pay tuition for them to be educated there, children from low-income families whose enrollment is supported with state and federal grant assistance, and children with identified delays and disabilities who receive ECSE services with their neighborhood and community peers. Nate looked at the faces of the children who were moving on to kindergarten and reflected on the children who would take their places and experience the high quality programming the LPP offers to all children in their community.

RESOURCES

Division for Early Childhood (DEC), National Association for the Education of Young Children (NAEYC), & National Head Start Association (NHSA). (2013). *Frameworks for Response to Intervention in early childhood: Description and implications*. Missoula, MT: Author. Retrieved from http://www.dec-sped.org/position-statements

Elliott, J., Batsche, G, & Tilly, W. D. (2011). *Response to Intervention blueprints for implementation: State level edition*. Alexandria, VA: National Association of State Directors of Special Education (NASDSE). Retrieved from http://www.nasdse.org/publications-t577/rti-blueprints-for-implementation-state-level.aspx

Elliott, J. & Morrison, D. (2008). *Response to Intervention blueprints for implementation: District level edition*. Alexandria, VA: National Association of State Directors of Special Education (NASDSE). Retrieved from: http://www.nasdse.org/publications-t577/rti-blueprints-for-implementation-district-level.aspx

Kurns, S., & Tilly, D. W. (2008). *Response to Intervention blueprints: School building level edition*. Alexandria, VA: National Association of State Directors of Special Education (NASDSE). Retrieved from http://www.nasdse.org/publications-t577/rti-blueprints-for-implementation-school-building.aspx

Metz, A., Halle, T., Bartley, L., & Blasberg, A. (2013). The key components of successful implementation. In T. Halle, A. Metz, & I. Martinez-Beck (Eds.), *Applying implementation science in early childhood programs and systems* (pp. 21–42). Baltimore, MD: Paul H. Brookes Publishing Co.

Metz, A., Louison, L., Ward, C., & Burke, K. (2017). *Global implementation specialist practice profiles: Skills and competencies for implementation practitioners*. Chapel Hill, NC: National Implementation Research Network and Centre for Effective Services. Retrieved from https://nirn.fpg.unc.edu/resources/is-practice-profileandhttp://fpg.unc.edu/resources/global-implementation-specialist-practice-profile

Metz, A., Naoom, S. F., Halle, T., & Bartley, L. (2015). *An integrated stage-based framework for implementation of early childhood programs and systems (OPRE Research Brief OPRE 2015-48)*. Washington, DC: Office of Planning, Research, and Evaluation, Administration for Children and Families, U.S. Department of Health and Human Services.

The National Implementation Research Network's Active Implementation Hub. http://implementation.fpg.unc.edu. A web site developed and maintained by the State Implementation and Scaling-up of Evidence-based Practices Center (SISEP) and the National Implementation Research Network (NIRN). It includes resources for individuals and teams who want to get started using IS to make systemic program changes and materials for those individuals and teams who want to dive deeper into active implementation.

REFERENCES

Aarons, G. A., Hurlburt, M., & Horowitz, S. M. (2011). Advancing a conceptual model for evidence-based practice implementation in public service sectors. *Administration and Policy in Mental Health, 38*, 4–23.

Blase, K., van Dyke, M., & Fixsen, D. (2013). *Stages of implementation analysis: Where are we?* The State Implementation and Scaling-up of Evidence-based Practices Center (SISEP). Chapel Hill, NC: Frank Porter Graham Child Development Institute, University of North Carolina, Chapel Hill. http://implementation.fpg.unc.edu/sites/implementation.fpg.unc.edu/files/NIRN-Education-StagesOfImplementationAnalysisWhereAreWe.pdf

Buysse, V., & Peisner-Feinberg, E. (2010). Recognition and response: Response to Intervention for pre-k. *Young Exceptional Children, 13*(4), 2–13.

Chinman, M., Imm, P., & Wandersman, A. (2004). *Getting to outcomes 2004: Promoting accountability through methods and tools for planning, implementation, and evaluation.* Santa Monica, CA: RAND Corporation Technical Report. Retrieved from https://www.rand.org/pubs/technical_reports/TR101.html

Damschroder, L. J., Aron, D. C., Keith, R. E., Kirsh, S. R., Alexander, J. A., et al. (2009). Fostering implementation of health services research findings into practice: A consolidated framework for advancing implementation science. *Implementation Science, 4*(50). Retreived from http://www.implementationscience.com/content/4/1/50

Deming, W. E. (1986). *Out of the crisis.* Cambridge, MA: MIT Press.

Duda, M. A., Fixsen, D. L., & Blase, K. A. (2013). Setting the stage for sustainability: Building the infrastructure for implementation capacity. In V. Buysse & E. S. Peisner-Feinberg (Eds.), *Handbook of Response to Intervention in early childhood* (pp. 397–414). Baltimore, MD: Paul H. Brookes Publishing Co.

Durlak, J. A., & DuPre, E. P. (2008). Implementation matters: A review of research on the influence of implementation on program outcomes and the factors affecting implementation. *American Journal of Community Psychology, 41,* 327–350.

Fixsen, D. L., Blase, K., Duda, M., Naoom, S., & Wallace, F. (2009). Core implementation components. *Research on Social Work Practice, 19,* 531–540.

Fixsen, D., Blase, K., Metz, A., & Van Dyke, M. (2013). Statewide implementation of evidence-based programs. *Exceptional Children, 79*(2), 213–230.

Fixsen, D. L., Naoom, S. F., Blase, K. A., Friedman, R. M., & Wallace, F. (2005). *Implementation research: A synthesis of the literature.* (FMHI Publication No. 231). Tampa, FL: University of South Florida, Louis de la Parte Florida Mental Health Institute, National Implementation Research Network.

Fox, L., Dunlap, G., Hemmeter, M. L., Joseph, G. E., & Strain, P.S. (2003). The Teaching Pyramid: A model for supporting social competence and preventing challenging behavior in young children. *Young Children, 58*(4), 48–52.

Greenhalgh, T., Robert, G., MacFarlane, F., Bate, P., & Kyriakidou, O. (2004). Diffusion of innovations in service organizations: Systematic review and recommendations. *The Milbank Quarterly, 82*(4), 581–629.

Greenwood, C. R., Bradfield, T., Kaminski, R., Linas, M., Carta, J. J., & Nylander, D. (2011). The Response to Intervention (RTI) approach in early childhood. *Focus on Exceptional Children, 43*(9), 1–22.

Hall, G. E., & Hord, S. M. (2011). *Implementing change: Patterns, principles and potholes* (3rd ed.). Boston, MA: Allyn and Bacon.

Hall, G. E., & Hord, S. M. (2015). *Implementing change: Patterns, principles, and potholes* (4th ed.). Boston, MA: Pearson.

Higgins, M. C., Weiner, J., & Young, L. (2012). Implementation teams: A new lever for organizational change. *Journal of Organizational Behavior, 33*(3), 366–388.

Kauerz, K., & Kagan, S. L. (2012). Governance and early childhood systems. In S. L. Kagan & K. Kauerz (Eds.), *Early childhood systems* (pp. 87–103). New York, NY: Teachers College Press.

Khatri, G. R., & Frieden, T. R. (2002). Rapid DOTS expansion in India. *Bulletin of the World Health Organization, 80*(6), 457–463.

Kurns, S., & Tilly, D. W. (2008). *Response to Intervention blueprints: School building level edition.* Alexandria, VA: National Association of State Directors of Special Education (NASDSE).

Metz. A. (2016). *Practice profiles: A process for capturing evidence and operationalizing innovations.* (White paper published by the National Implementation Research Network). Retrieved from http://nirn.fpg.unc.edu/sites/nirn.fpg.unc.edu/files/resources/NIRN-Metz-WhitePaper-PracticeProfiles.pdf?o=implenet

Metz, A., & Albers, B. (2014). What does it take? How federal initiatives can support the implementation of evidence-based programs to improve outcomes for adolescents. *Journal of Adolescent Health, 54*(3), 92–96.

Metz, A., & Bartley, L. (2012). Active Implementation Frameworks for program success: How to use implementation science to improve outcomes for children. *Zero to Three Journal, 32*(4), 11–18.

Metz, A., & Bartley, L. (2017). Co-creating the conditions to sustain the use of research evidence in public child welfare. *Child Welfare, 94*(2), 115–139.

Metz, A., Bartley, L., Blase, K., & Fixsen, D. (November 2011). *Practice profiles: Implementing, coaching, and evaluating new practices.* Washington, DC: Permanency Innovations Initiative Grantees Meetings, Children's Bureau.

Metz, A., & Easterling, D. (2016). Using implementation science to translate foundation strategy *Foundation Review. 8*(2), 116–137. doi:10.9707/1944-5660.1302

Metz, A., Halle, T., Bartley, L., & Blasberg, A. (2013). The key components of successful implementation. In T. Halle, A. Metz, & I. Martinez-Beck (Eds.), *Applying Implementation Science in early childhood programs and systems* (pp. 21–42). Baltimore, MD: Paul H. Brookes Publishing Co.

Metz, A., Louison, L., Ward, C., & Burke, K. (2017). *Global implementation specialist practice profiles: Skills and competencies for implementation practitioners.* Chapel Hill, NC: National Implementation Research Network and Centre for Effective Services. http://fpg.unc.edu/resources/global-implementation-specialist-practice-profile and http://nirn.fpg.unc.edu/sites/nirn.fpg.unc.edu/files/resources/NIRN-ISPracticeProfile-06-05-2017.pdf

Metz, A., Naoom, S. F., Halle, T., & Bartley, L. (2015). *An integrated stage-based framework for implementation of early childhood programs and systems* (OPRE Research Brief OPRE 2015-48). Washington, DC: Office of Planning, Research, and Evaluation; Administration for Children and Families; U.S. Department of Health and Human Services.

Meyers, D. C., Durlak, J. A., & Wandersman, A. (2012). The quality implementation framework: A synthesis of critical steps in the implementation process. *American Journal of Community Psychology.* doi: 10.1007/s10464-012-9522-x

Palinkas, L. A., Holloway, I. W., Rice, E., Fuentes, D., Wu, Q., & Chamberlain, P. (2011). Social networks and implementation of evidence-based practices in public youth-serving systems: A mixed-methods study. *Implementation Science, 6*(1), 1.

Pretti-Frontczak, K., Grisham-Brown, J., & Sullivan, L. (Eds.). (2014). *Blending practices for all children* (Young Exceptional Children Monograph Series No. 16). Los Angeles, CA: Division for Early Childhood of the Council for Exceptional Children.

Young, R. M. (n.d.). *MTSS in Early Childhood (EC): Stages of implementation analysis: Trends among three innovation pilots to shift ECE programs into MTSS service delivery models.* Manuscript in preparation.

Appendix 3A

A Stage-Based Active Implementation Planning Tool

The following matrix outlines key questions to ask for each of the core elements (implementation teams, data and feedback loops, and infrastructure) throughout the four stages of implementation and serves as a stage-based planning tool. At each stage of implementation, implementation teams are conducting activities, using data and feedback loops to guide their decision-making and ongoing improvement, and developing, improving, and sustaining infrastructure components to support implementation. These common elements of implementation serve different roles and functions at each stage. The purpose of this guide is to present an integrated stage-based framework that can be used by practitioners and administrators to plan their stage-based change process, by researchers to formulate implementation questions and develop formative and summative testing plans for different stages of implementation, and by policymakers to clarify what it takes to fund an effective implementation process.

Table 1. Integrated Stage-Based Planning Tool
for Implementation of Early Childhood Programs and Systems

Exploration		
Core Features and Activities of Implementation Teams	**Core Uses of Data and Feedback Loops for Decision Making and Continuous Improvement**	**Core Activities to Develop Implementation Infrastructure** (General and Innovation-Specific Capacity)
Selection and Membership: • Has a team been formed to serve as an accountable structure for facilitating stage-based implementation? • Were team members mutually selected into their roles by volunteering for roles they were encouraged to apply for? • Does each team contain one or more members who are knowledgeable about the intervention or change strategy, implementation infrastructure, use of data for decision-making and improvement, and systems change? • Do members represent practice, supervisory, leadership, and policy perspectives either on a single team or through a linked teaming structure? • Does the team include program developers or intermediary organizations?	Need Assessment and Fit and Feasibility Assessment: • Needs: What are the needs of our target population? • Fit: Does this initiative fit (or fight) with current projects, context, organizational, and systems values and philosophies? • Resources: What resources will be available to our early childhood program? What system should we choose to implement this new strategy or intervention? • Evidence: What is the evidence that a potential strategy will work? Under what circumstances and with what target populations was this evidence generated? What outcomes can we expect if we implement this strategy well? • Readiness for replication: How well defined is this strategy? Do we know the core components that make this strategy "work?" Will program development be necessary? How involved will the developer or intermediary organization be?	Planning for the Implementation Infrastructure: Implementation Teams ask, "How are we planning for the infrastructure?" Infrastructure to Support Practice: • Are early childhood practitioners open to the new innovation? • Are the organizational mission, leadership, and climate aligned with the new innovation? • Will staff with the necessary prerequisites be available? • Is training available and affordable? Does training meet best practices for skill development? • Who will provide coaching and supervision? What steps will we need to take to ensure a coaching plan is in place? • How will staff performance be assessed? What steps are needed to ensure a performance assessment system is in place?

(continued)

Appendix 3A *(continued)*

Exploration		
Core Features and Activities of Implementation Teams	**Core Uses of Data and Feedback Loops for Decision Making and Continuous Improvement**	**Core Activities to Develop Implementation Infrastructure** (General and Innovation-Specific Capacity)
Development of a Team Charter: • Does the team have a charter or "Terms of Reference" (internal memorandum of understanding) that describes how it functions, communicates, makes decisions, and moves forward with its mission and objectives? Development of Linked Communication Protocol: • Has the team developed "linked communication protocols" to provide accountability for making decisions and providing feedback? Frequency of Meeting: • Does the core Implementation Team convene twice a month at a minimum (weekly recommended) at this stage? • How often do ancillary teams (e.g., leadership team, community advisory board) meet?	• Capacity: Will early childhood practitioners meet minimum qualifications for implementation? Can we make the necessary structural, instrumental, and financial changes necessary? • Sustainability: Are there sufficient resources and capacity to sustain this innovation through full implementation and beyond? Decisions Teams Make During Exploration: • Will the proposed strategy meet our needs? • Do we have "what it takes" to move forward? Is moving forward both desirable and feasible? • How will we communicate these decisions to others?	Infrastructure to Support Organization and Systems: • Are there the necessary community connections and resources to move forward with the innovation? • What questions will we need to answer to ensure that implementation is happening as planned? Where will we get this data? What technology needs do we have? • What administrative practices may need to change to support implementation? What policies, procedures, or processes need to be developed or revised? • What systems alignment issues will need to be addressed to facilitate implementation?
Installation		
Core Features and Activities of Implementation Teams	**Core Uses of Data and Feedback Loops for Decision Making and Continuous Improvement**	**Core Activities to Develop Implementation Infrastructure** (General and Innovation-Specific Capacity)

Development or Team Competencies to Support Implementation:
 	
Does the core Implementation Team …
• Know and apply the innovation of approach?
• Know and apply the implementation infrastructure?
• Know and apply Improvement cycles?
• Know and apply systems change?
 	
Development or Policy Practice Feedback Loops:
 	
• Has the team developed active processes to gather practice-level information (e.g., barriers to implementation) from practitioners and supervisors implementing the new way of work and feed the information up the system to leadership?
	Troubleshooting and Continuous Improvement:
	
	Are the linked communication protocols developed during exploration in place and happening as planned? How can communication be improved? Are we effectively engaging leadership in the process?
	• In the event that team membership or structure changes, how can we ensure that team competencies are maintained?
	• What changes might we need to make before we initiate new ways of work?
	   ○ Are changes to the innovation necessary?
	   ○ Are changes to implementation supports (e.g., training, coaching, leadership strategies) necessary?
		Installing the Implementation Infrastructure:
		
		Implementations Teams ask, "How are we developing and installing the infrastructure?"
		
		Infrastructure to Support Practice:
		
		• Have readiness plans for practitioners increased openness to the innovation?
		• Has the first cohort of staff been selected?
		• Has initial training occurred?
		• Have coaching plans been developed to support practitioners in the new way of work?

(continued)

Installation		
Core Features and Activities of Implementation Teams	**Core Uses of Data and Feedback Loops for Decision Making and Continuous Improvement**	**Core Activities to Develop Implementation Infrastructure** (General and Innovation-Specific Capacity)
• Has the team developed active processes to ensure that leadership decisions are fed back down the system to those carrying out the new way of work? Frequency of Meetings: • Does the core implementation team convene weekly? • Does the core implementation team meet with leadership bi-weekly? • How often do ancillary teams meet? Is this often enough to support implementation?	○ Are changes to data collection processes needed? Has the implementation infrastructure we planned for during the exploration stage been developed and installed during this current stage of implementation? • Are general capacities in place? • Are innovation specific capacities in place? Decisions Teams Make During Installation: • Is the implementation infrastructure installed (good enough) to move into initial implementation when service delivery starts? • How might we improve the implementation infrastructure before we initiate the new way of work?	Infrastructure to Support Organizations and Systems: • Has leadership expressed commitment to the new way of work? How has this been demonstrated? • Have agreements with community partners been established? Are partner expectations clear? • Have data systems been assessed and determined to be ready (or developed to be ready)? • Have policies, procedures, and processes been revised or developed to support the new way of work? • Have systems partners been engaged?
Initial Implementation		
Core Features and Activities of Implementation Teams	**Core Uses of Data and Feedback Loops for Decision Making and Continuous Improvement**	**Core Activities to Develop Implementation Infrastructure** (General and Innovation-Specific Capacity)
Improvement Cycles: Have teams engaged in different types of improvement cycles? Examples include: • Usability testing to stabilize the model • Rapid cycle problem solving to detect strengthens and gaps and develop solutions quickly • Policy practice feedback loops to ensure effective and efficient communication between policy and practice levels Frequency of Meetings: • Does the core implementation team convene monthly or less often? If less often, has this affected implementation negatively or is the innovation stable enough for less frequent meetings? • Does the core implementation team meet with leadership bi-weekly or at least monthly?	Troubleshooting Practitioner Competency: • How satisfied are practitioners with the support they have received to implement the new way of work? • What are data telling us about what is working or not working regarding practitioner selection, training, and coaching? • What changes might we need to make to strengthen practitioner competency? • What are early fidelity or staff performance assessment data telling us about the strength of implementation? Troubleshooting Organizational Supports: • What are the data telling us about what is working or not working regarding organizational and systems supports?	Implementations Teams ask, "How are we supporting the infrastructure?" Infrastructure to Support Practice: • What is being done to support ongoing readiness of practitioners, supervisors, and administrators? • Has there been staff turnover? How has this been addressed? • Has follow-up or booster training occurred? Is this needed? • Are practitioners receiving coaching as planned? Infrastructure to Support Organizations and Systems: • Does leadership continue to support the new way of work? How is this demonstrated? • Are community partnerships facilitative of implementation goals?

Appendix 3A *(continued)* (page 4 of 5)

Initial Implementation		
Core Features and Activities of Implementation Teams	**Core Uses of Data and Feedback Loops for Decision Making and Continuous Improvement**	**Core Activities to Develop Implementation Infrastructure** (General and Innovation-Specific Capacity)
• Are rapid cycle problem-solving teams convened as needed? When they are convened, do they meet at least once a week to address the challenge quickly and then disband? Development of Team Charter: • Does the team need to revisit their team charter? • Has there been turnover? How are new members on-boarded? Linked Communication Protocols: • With whom (specific names, roles) in leadership, management, and the community is the implementation team meeting and communicating? Has this been effective?	• What changes might we need to make to strengthen organizational alignment? • What are early outcomes telling us about the potential efficacy of the new innovation? Decisions Teams Make During Initial Implementation: • How can we continue to support the implementation infrastructure? • How can we more effectively problem-solve? • Are we asking the right questions? • Are we collecting the data we need to guide our decision making? • What changes might we need to make to the innovation, implementation supports, or data collection processes? • Are we ready to move to an outcome study?	• Are data systems operable? Are data reports usable? Is data entry and review built into regular practice routines? • Are there policy–practice alignment or misalignment issues? How are they being addressed? • Are additional systems interventions needed (e.g., policy, legislative, funding, community partners)?
Full Implementation		
Core Features and Activities of Implementation Teams	**Core Uses of Data and Feedback Loops for Decision Making and Continuous Improvement**	**Core Activities to Develop Implementation Infrastructure** (General and Innovation-Specific Capacity)
Improvement Cycles: • Does the team continue to use data and feedback mechanisms to support and improve the functioning of implementation Infrastructure components? Please note that it is recommended the infrastructure is formally assessed every 6 months (minimum of annually). Develop and Test Enhancements: Now that the implementation supports are routinized and integrated into the system … • Has the core implementation team assessed whether enhancements to the innovation or implementation infrastructure may reduce the burden of implementation or increase efficiency of implementation with similar outcomes?	Questions Implementation Teams Answer: Improving Practitioner Competency: • Are practitioners implementing the innovation with fidelity? • How might the innovation or implementation infrastructure be enhanced to reduce burden of implementation or increase efficiency of developing practitioner competency without compromising outcomes (enhancements)? • How might the innovation or implementation infrastructure be enhanced to improve outcomes for children further (enhancements)?	Implementations Teams ask, "How are we improving and sustaining the infrastructure?" Infrastructure to Support Practice: • Can readiness be sustained and extended to new cohorts of practitioners? • Are there more efficient or effective ways to train and coach staff? • If the model is scaled, would training or coaching components need to be redesigned? Infrastructure to Support Organizations and Systems: • What role can leadership play in replicating or scaling the initiative if outcomes are achieved?

(continued)

Appendix 3A *(continued)*

Full Implementation		
Core Features and Activities of Implementation Teams	**Core Uses of Data and Feedback Loops for Decision Making and Continuous Improvement**	**Core Activities to Develop Implementation Infrastructure** (General and Innovation-Specific Capacity)
• Has the core implementation team assessed whether enhancements to the innovation or implementation infrastructure might improve outcomes? Frequency of Meetings: • Does the core implementation team convene monthly or at least bi-monthly? • Would implementation benefit from the team meeting more frequently? • Does the core implementation team meet with leadership bi-monthly or quarterly? Development of Team Charter: • Does the team need to revisit their Team Charter? • Has there been turnover? How are new members on-boarded? Linked Communication Protocols: • What are workers, supervisors, leadership, and community partners saying about the kinds of supports in place for implementation? • How are feedback loops functioning? Do workers feel like they are heard? Is leadership getting the information they need?	Improving Organizational Supports: • Are we getting the intended outcomes? • How might the innovation or implementation infrastructure be enhanced to improve outcomes for children further (enhancements)? Decisions Teams Make During Full Implementation: • How will this model be sustained? • Is this model ready for large-scale implementation and/or scale up? • Can we scale the innovation? • Should we develop and test an enhancement to the model? • What data will we collect to assess the enhancement? • What results will we need to make the enhancement permanent?	• Are community partnerships facilitative of current and future goals related to implementation (e.g., replication or scaling)? • How can data systems become more efficient and practical for helping to solve implementation challenges? • If the model is scaled, would the data system need to be altered to support more robust analysis or information sharing? • What contextual changes have happened that can affect systems alignment? How can we continue to monitor and improve alignment? • Are additional systems interventions needed (e.g., policy, legislative, funding, community partners)?

Appendix 3A Stage-Based Active Implementation Planning Tool. From Metz, A., Naoom, S. F., Halle, T., & Bartley, L. (2015). *An Integrated Stage-Based Framework for Implementation of Early Childhood Programs and Systems*. Office of Planning Research and Evaluation (OPRE), U.S. Department of Health and Human Services, 20–23. Reprinted by permission.

Appendix 3B

Multi-Tiered Systems of Support in Early Childhood:
Stages of Implementation Analysis

State, Region, District, or School: _____ Date: _____

Implementation team members completing this analysis: _____

"Is the multi-tiered systems of support (MTSS) in early childhood (EC) framework the right system initiative for a specific program/school or agency? If so, how do we get started?" These are important questions to ask as program/school and agency leaders evaluate different ways to provide effective and efficient early care and education services to young children and their families who also have demonstrable outcomes. Completion of the Exploration Stage activities in this document may help programs/schools and agencies determine if the MTSS in EC initiative is the right fit for a specific school/program or agency. It may also help determine feasibility and staff readiness for shifting into MTSS in EC practices, as well as the beginning steps of Installation. A school/program or agency leadership team should complete the document. For activities scored as "Not Yet In Place" or "Initiated or Partially In Place," the Implementation Team may wish to:

a. Examine the importance of the activity in relationship to achieving success.
b. Identify and address barriers to completion of the activity.
c. Ensure that an action plan related to the item(s) is developed (sub-activities, accountable people identified, timeline, evidence of completion) and monitored.

Scoring Key

A strength of stage score can be computed for each stage to help guide action planning. Award points for each element (e.g., 1–10) and for each sub-element where those are available (e.g., 2 a–g) to arrive at a total possible of 46 (2 × 23).

- Each element/sub-element identified as **In Place** = 2 Points
- Each element/sub-element identified as **Initiated or Partially In Place** = 1 Point
- Each element/sub-element identified as **Not Yet In Place** = 0 Points

Documentation

For each element that is identified as "In Place" or "Initiated or Partially in Place" please briefly describe or reference the evidence and/or data sources that demonstrate that that element is observable or measureable (e.g., needs assessment document, fidelity reports, training plan). One data source may serve to document several items. Use the back of the document or attach relevant evidence and/or data sources as supplemental pages to this document.

Appendix 3B *(continued)*

Adaptation of Stages Analysis Developed Specifically for MTSS in Early Childhood

	EXPLORATION Stage-Related Activities for: MTSS in Early Childhood	In Place (2 points)	Partially in Place or Initiated (1 point)	Not Yet in Place (0 points)	Evidence for "In Place" or "Initiated or Partially in Place" Components. Use back of page if necessary.
1.	**Form Implementation Team:** This might be an Instructional Leadership Team with a focus on MTSS in EC implementation (repurpose/expand a current team) or create a specifically dedicated MTSS in EC Team.				
2.	**Engage in Exploration Process:** Explore activities, timeline, benefits, and risks, and communicate activities to key stakeholder groups, including families. Consider activities aligned with MTSS in EC defining components and processes, 2a through 2g.				
	a) *Ensure alignment:* For example, teaching (curricula, instructional practices), staffing (hire, train, PD, evaluate) and decision making (data, teams, communication) are aligned vertically (across the age/grade continuum) and horizontally (at any one age/grade level) so all participants are engaged in a consistent, holistic learning experience.				
	b) *Use universal screener(s):* Tools are needed that are reliable and valid, sensitive to instructional effects, have benchmarks of adequate progress, are low cost and efficient, and have accurate indicator(s) of children's performance on future essential outcomes.				
	c) *Develop a tiered instructional model:* Develop differentiated curricula, instructional and environmental arrangements, and aligned assessment tools and processes of varying intensity (Tiers 1, 2, and 3); Tier 1 is top priority.				
	d) *Use tools that are research-based, scientifically validated practices:* Curricula, instructional tools, environmental tools, assessment tools, and decision-making processes are evidence based.				
	e) *Ensure treatment integrity:* Ensure that a high quality, comprehensive curriculum addressing developmental, early academic, and social-emotional competencies is employed with integrity at each level; each person adheres to plan.				
	f) *Create teams:* Configure membership so that high performing, collaborative teams engage in a four-step, strengths-based, problem-solving process (Problem Identification, Problem Analysis, Intervention Development and Implementation, and Plan Evaluation) to ensure student needs are matched with instruction of the correct intensity.				
	g) *Expect accountability:* School-wide accountability is needed to achieve an observable and measurable goal for student growth; Continuous Quality Improvement (CQI) is in place, coaching and Professional Learning Community members assist program improvement.				

(continued)

Appendix 3B *(continued)*

	EXPLORATION Stage-Related Activities for: MTSS in Early Childhood	In Place (2 points)	Partially in Place or Initiated (1 point)	Not Yet in Place (0 points)	Evidence for "In Place" or "Initiated or Partially in Place" Components. Use back of page if necessary.
3.	**Analyze Data:** Determine need and prevalence. Example: Do you have a Universal Screener in place? If yes, examine universal screening data at district, organization, and/or school/program level to determine how effectively and efficiently school/program goals are being achieved. Change Tier 1 if it is not effective before adding other tiers.				
4.	**Select Targeted Areas:** Address needs (e.g., student, teacher, family outcomes): (a) academic and socially significant issues, (b) parent and community perception of need, (c) data indicating need.				
5.	**Review:** Identify how MTSS in EC might match your target areas and address needs.				
6.	**Review and Discuss MTSS in EC model:** Use the Hexagon Tool: Exploring Context (http://implementation.fpg.unc.edu/resources/hexagon-tool-exploring-context) to look at 6a through 6f below.				
	a) Needs of Students: How well would the MTSS in EC model meet the needs of families and children? Example: How might it close the achievement gap of students who are low performers? How can data-based decision making assist in matching instruction of the right intensity to meet children's needs at various tiers, including children with Individualized Education Programs (children moving from Tier 1 to Tier 2 to Tier 3 and moving from Tier 3 to Tier 2 to Tier 1)? *Needs of Teachers and Staff:* How would the MTSS in EC model impact staff efficiency and use of human, financial, and natural resources? Would there be a positive impact on school climate and culture?				
	b) Fit: How well would MTSS in EC fit with current initiatives, priorities, structures and supports, and parent/community values? Example: It fits well with initiatives to support "Inclusionary/Blended" practices, "Birth to Grade Three Seamless Learning Continuum," Intentional Teaching, strategies for ELLs, newer teacher evaluation models (e.g., Danielson), alignment of the CCSS from Pre-K to Elementary, state early learning standards, and so forth. It is supported by Division for Early Childhood (DEC)/National Association for the Education of Young Children (NAEYC)/National Head Start Association (NHSA).				
	c) Resource availability: What resources are available for training, staffing, technology supports, curricula, data systems, and administration? Example: Can you access problem-solving training through statewide PD/coaching resources, local special education cooperative or joint agreement?				

(continued)

Appendix 3B *(continued)*

EXPLORATION Stage-Related Activities for: MTSS in Early Childhood	In Place (2 points)	Partially in Place or Initiated (1 point)	Not Yet in Place (0 points)	Evidence for "In Place" or "Initiated or Partially in Place" Components. Use back of page if necessary.
d) **Outcome evidence:** What outcomes might be expected if the program or practices are implemented well? What do those who are experienced in MTSS in EC say about the outcomes they have achieved? What is their evidence?				
e) **Readiness for replication:** Who else at the local, regional, state, and national level has been successful? Where do you find expert assistance? Where can you see good MTSS in EC models?				
f) **Capacity to implement:** Can you implement MTSS in EC as intended and sustain and improve implementation over time? Example: Is there a long-term commitment from the school board? Do you have a low rate of staff turnover? Do you have a leadership plan of succession? **Productive discussion:** Schedule time and conduct a productive discussion of a thorough exploration process focused on the MTSS in EC model. Implementation Team(s) need to consider six areas listed above (6a through 6f)				
7. **Determine match:** Determine match of MTSS in EC for your program needs based on assessment results above. Would a different initiative meet your needs better?				
8. **Methods:** Develop methods to promote exploration and assess "consensus and commitment" for range of impacted stakeholders.				
9. **Analyze:** Conduct analysis of information and results of exploration activities.				
10. **Implementation Team:** Recommendation made to select or not MTSS in EC; forward to appropriate level (e.g., next leadership level team, best practices groups, local partners, alliance, District leadership) for final decision.				
Total points				
Average % in each category— Strength of Exploration score				
Overall Score: (23 items × 2 = Maximum of 46 points possible)				

Adapted by Young (2014) from *Stages of implementation analysis: Where are we?* (pp. 1–5) by Blasé, K., van Dyke, M., & Fixsen, D. (2013). The State Implementation & Scaling-up of Evidence-based Practices Center (SISEP). Chapel Hill, NC: Frank Porter Graham Child Development Institute, University of North Carolina Chapel Hill. Adapted and used with permission of SISEP. No endorsement from the SISEP or NIRN is implied nor should it be assumed for this adaptation.

4

Using Data-Based Decision Making to Improve Learning Outcomes for All Children

Robin L. Hojnoski and Joy C. Polignano

When Maplewood School District's elementary schools shifted into a multi-tiered systems of support (MTSS) model, they successfully implemented a data-based decision-making approach to increase children's language and literacy skills. Because improving language and literacy skills has been a districtwide focus, the Early Childhood Instructional Leadership Team (ILT) decided to adopt a similar approach to promote achievement of early learning outcomes for the district's preschoolers. Maggie Ronan, the district's early childhood coordinator, is taking the lead in preparing preschool staff members to collect and use data to make curricular and instructional decisions. To do this, she will need to identify appropriate assessment tools that will generate data everyone can use to ensure that a rigorous curriculum is employed, effective teaching strategies are implemented, and children who are struggling to gain language and early literacy skills receive supports matched to their needs. The process of matching children's needs with appropriate supports in a team-based decision-making process occurs in the elementary MTSS framework, and Maggie feels it can be done in MTSS for early childhood programs as well. She also will need to prepare administrators and teachers to lead program- and classroom-level data-based decision-making teams, ensure everyone is trained, and coordinate a regular schedule for reviewing data and making decisions, providing classroom coverage as necessary so teachers can participate.

Maggie's colleagues at the elementary level have stated that the language and literacy data are useful in decision making at the program/school, classroom, and individual-child levels, and Maggie feels that they will also be useful at these three levels in the preschool program. Although the specific questions to be addressed at each level are somewhat different, they all focus on evaluating data in relation to a standard (e.g., local norms, national norms, curricular goals), determining whether growth rates are sufficient to meet specified goals (e.g., expected rates of improvement), identifying potential programmatic supports to accelerate performance (e.g., instruction and intervention selection), and assessing the effects of changes that occur. Maggie realizes moving into an MTSS framework will be a challenging task for everyone involved, but she feels that she and the program staff are up to the task, knowing that the young children and families will benefit from a more systematic data-based decision-making process that results in better alignment of supports to meet needs at multiple levels. She pulls out her laptop and starts listing tasks she will need to do and a proposed time frame to get these tasks started, to get the program shifting into these practices.

INTRODUCTION

Broadly speaking, assessment may be thought of as a process for gathering information to make informed instructional decisions (National Research Council, 2008). There are several distinct purposes of assessment, including screening, diagnostic and eligibility determinations, individualized planning and monitoring of progress, and program evaluation (National Research Council, 2008). When conceptualizing an assessment system, educators must ask themselves three questions: 1) What is the purpose of the assessment? 2) What is the decision to be made on the basis of the assessment data? and 3) What data need to be collected to make the decision?

The purpose of assessment informs the instructional decisions that can be made and guides the choice of data to collect. This chapter will describe the ways in which a systematic process of data-based decision making increases the quality of the decisions to be made and ultimately improves learning outcomes for all children. This chapter also provides guidance on how to plan for and begin implementing data-based decision making on a practical level with consideration for the different levels at which decision making can occur (i.e., program, classroom, individual). The video series that accompanies this book includes three videos that illustrate application of the problem-solving process at the school/program level (Video 3), the classroom level (Video 4), and at the individual-child level (Video 5).

THE PROBLEM-SOLVING MODEL

The problem-solving model conceptualized by Deno and Mirkin in 1977 and since elaborated upon (e.g., Deno, 1989, 2002, 2005; Pluymert, 2014; Shinn, 1995) serves as an effective framework for data-based decision making. The problem-solving model was developed to help educators monitor the effectiveness of interventions and determine the appropriate intensity of services needed by a student (Deno & Mirkin, 1977), much like in MTSS. Bransford and Stein (1984) termed the steps in a problem-solving model IDEAL: *I*dentify the problem, *D*efine the problem, *E*xplore solutions, *A*pply a solution, and *L*ook at the effects of the solution. While slight variations exist, the general model consists of four steps, each with its own data collection requirements and decision to be made: 1) problem identification, 2) problem analysis, 3) intervention implementation, and 4) plan evaluation. Although the problem-solving model is described sequentially, as illustrated in Figure 4.1, it is a recursive approach whereby a team may return to any previous step based on data collected throughout the process.

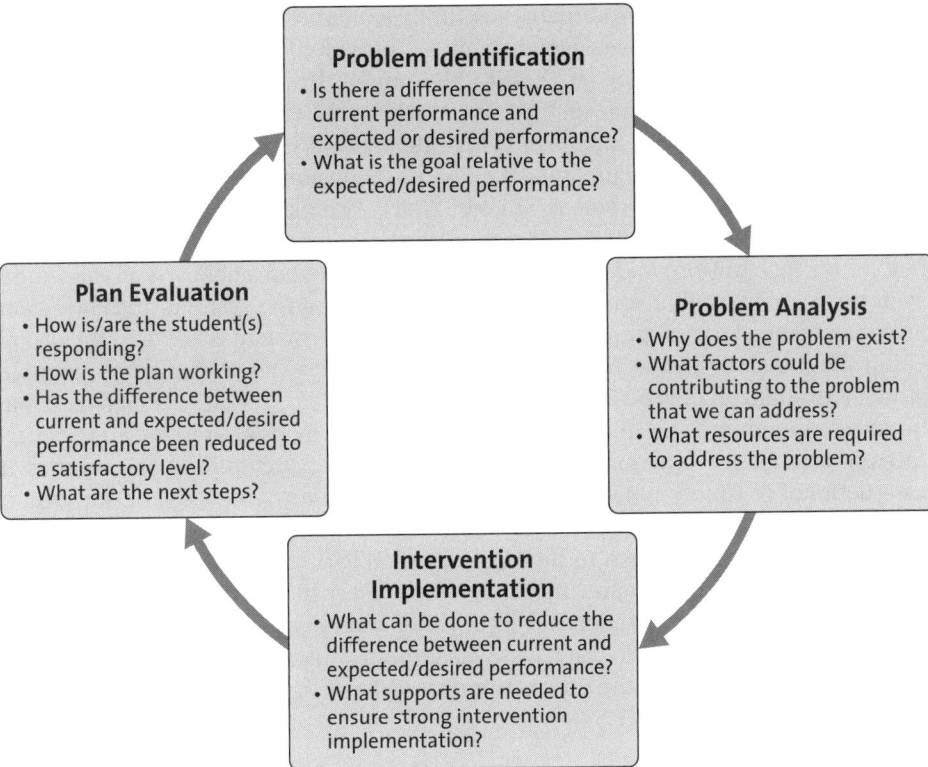

Figure 4.1. Steps of the problem-solving model. *Source:* Batsche, G. et al., 2005.

Problem Identification

The decision to be made in the first phase of the problem-solving model centers on identifying the problem and selecting the data to be used to define the problem. Within a problem-solving framework, a problem is defined as a discrepancy between *what is occurring* and *what is expected or desired* within a specific ecological context (Deno, 1989), and problem-solving is conceptualized as efforts to reduce this discrepancy (Deno, 1995). The problem can occur across a range of domains (i.e., academic, behavioral, adaptive skills) and levels (i.e., program, classroom, and individual student). Assessment data are gathered about current performance and the desired or expected levels of performance; consideration is given to the magnitude of the discrepancy between the two, or simply, the size of the problem (see Figure 4.1 for questions to answer in this phase). The domain of interest (e.g., academic or social behaviors) and level of decision making (i.e., program, classroom, or individual student) are key considerations in selecting assessment tools, procedures, and standards for evaluating the discrepancy. Using data gathered about current levels of performance and expected or desired levels of performance, the problem is defined in measurable and observable terms with the context of the problem clearly delineated (e.g., the conditions or circumstances under which the problem occurs). At a program level, data collection may include the use of a universal screening tool that targets skills considered instrumental to educational success. These may be commercially available assessments, such as Individual Growth and Development Indicators of Early Literacy (IGDIs-EL; McConnell, Bradfield, Wackerle-Hollman, & Rodriguez, 2012), or other district or program data that are routinely collected in a standardized manner, such as Positive Behavioral Interventions and Supports (PBIS), classwide targeted prosocial behaviors (Stormont, Lewis, Beckner, & Johnson, 2008; Young, Snow, Frech, & Shields, 2011). At a classroom level, data collection may involve data teachers routinely collect on student academic performance (e.g., letter recognition) and behavior (e.g., points earned in a behavior management system). At an individual student level, data collected at the systems and classroom level can be used to compare individual student performance relative to the group. Other data specific to the presenting problem may also be relevant; for example, student attendance may be identified as a target problem, and attendance data may be used to examine the discrepancy between an individual student and average rates of attendance. The magnitude of the difference, such as the discrepancy in instructional or functional skill levels or in the frequency, intensity, or duration of behaviors, provides an indication of the severity of the problem and may be used to determine the level at which to intervene in an MTSS, with more significant problems addressed with a greater intensity of services. In addition, consideration is given to strengths at the student level (i.e., skills and performance) and contextual level (i.e., curriculum, teacher behavior, classroom activities) that may be leveraged in developing instruction and intervention to address the identified problem.

Problem Analysis

Once a problem has been identified and defined, the next step is to generate potential hypotheses, or explanations, for *why* a problem is occurring. Problem analysis has been defined as "the systematic process of assessment and evaluation aimed at understanding the causal and maintaining variable associated with an undesirable discrepancy" (Christ, 2008, p. 159). The decision to be made in this phase involves determining the factor or set of factors that seem most related to the problem, using data collected to explore the hypotheses generated (see Figure 4.1 for questions to answer in this phase). When exploring hypotheses, educators consider a variety of possible individual and environmental factors that may influence student performance, such as those presented in Figure 4.2. To the extent possible, instructional teams use a low-level inference approach to evaluating hypotheses, relying on objectively collected data, and focusing on contextual and alterable variables (e.g., amount of instructional time, arrangement of the classroom environment) versus using a high inference approach that emphasizes within-child (e.g., intelligence, physical impairment) and inalterable variables (Christ, 2008). For example, teams might use information gathered through record reviews, additional assessments, interviews with teachers and caregivers, or direct observation data to supplement the data used to define the problem. These additional sources of data can provide valuable information about factors that may be contributing to the identified problem. Early identification of factors contributing to the problem minimizes the use of resources on interventions unlikely to result in skill or behavior change. In addition, identification of individual and contextual strengths can be used to develop potential solutions, supporting efficiency in decision making and intervention.

Student factors
- Does the student have a medical condition?
- Has the student been taught the expected/desired skill?
- Does the student possess necessary prerequisite skills?
- What are the student's strengths?

Teacher and classroom factors
- Has the teacher been provided sufficient resources to support the student?
- Does the teacher consistently implement reinforcement strategies?
- Are there sufficient opportunities for practice across activities/routines?
- In what activities/routines is the student successful?

Curricular factors
- Is the curriculum evidence-based?
- Is the curriculum implemented with fidelity?
- Is support provided for curriculum implementation?
- Is the curricular focus aligned with students' learning targets?

Social-contextual factors
- Are expectations consistent across home and school settings?
- How do peers react to the student in problematic and nonproblematic times?
- Can the physical arrangement of the classroom, including materials, be a factor?

Figure 4.2. Example factors to consider when analyzing the problem.

Intervention Development and Implementation

Once the team has identified the most probable hypothesis, or likely factor(s) contributing to the problem, and identified individual and contextual strengths, the intervention development and implementation phase begins. The decision to be made in this phase is what intervention or set of instructional practices will best meet the identified needs and address the problem while leveraging individual and contextual strengths as much as possible. When hypotheses are developed that use a low-level inference approach and focus on alterable variables, the link between assessment and intervention is stronger (Batsche, Castillo, Dixon, & Forde, 2008). Furthermore, incorporating student and contextual strengths is likely to lead to a better fit between the identified need and the intervention, increasing the ecological validity of the process. Several factors must be considered by the instructional team in selecting an intervention, including its evidence base, the resources needed for implementation, and data collection requirements for monitoring progress (see Figure 4.1).

To promote evidence-based practice, research supporting the effectiveness of an intervention should be identified, and interventions with a strong evidence base should be selected when possible. Instructional teams may decide to select interventions using a standard protocol approach or problem-solving approach. With a standard protocol approach, the same evidence-based intervention is provided to all students who exhibit similar problems within a specified domain (Fuchs, Mock, Morgan, & Young, 2003). Standard protocol approaches have advantages with regard to integrity; all educators in a program can be trained to implement the intervention to promote consistency across staff, which can be monitored using a uniform system (Fuchs et al., 2003). Examples include Tier 2 curricula targeting language and early literacy development, such as the *Story Friends*™ and *PAth to Literacy* programs (see Kelley, Goldstein, Spencer, & Sherman, 2015; Noe, Spencer, Kruse, & Goldstein, 2014; Spencer et al., 2012; see also Chapter 6). In contrast to a standard protocol approach, a problem-solving approach to intervention accounts for individual student differences by selecting interventions that correspond to the specific hypothesized function or cause of a problem behavior or skill deficit as identified by the data collected (Fuchs et al., 2003). In developing individualized interventions, consideration should be given to the theoretical or conceptual basis for individualized intervention supports. For example, teachers may design an intervention founded on evidence-based behavioral principles or big ideas in early numeracy even though the intervention itself has not been empirically evaluated as a unified set of intervention practices.

Regardless of which approach to intervention selection is used, resources needed for implementation and acceptability of the intervention by individuals involved must be considered. It is critical that the instructional team ensure those responsible for implementation and monitoring an intervention have the supports and resources needed prior to implementation, including training on the intervention and corresponding data collection requirements. Attending to individual and contextual strengths may be particularly useful in considering implementation. For example, if a teacher already has a classwide behavior management system in place, then designing an individualized system that connects to the classwide system may increase the implementation fidelity and acceptability by reducing the demands on the teacher to implement very different systems. Similarly, if small-group instructional time is already organized, leveraging this time to provide more intensive targeted instruction for a small group of students may reduce the need to find additional time in the daily schedule.

To facilitate plan evaluation during the intervention development and implementation phase, the team determines how data will be gathered on an ongoing basis. Key issues in selecting any assessment method include evaluating the technical adequacy (i.e., reliability and validity) of the method, the match between the target problem and the method, and the feasibility of data collection within the given context and over an extended period of time. When an appropriate assessment method is selected, goals are then established using baseline performance, and a time line for evaluation is developed. In addition, the team outlines a process for monitoring adherence to an intervention protocol, or the degree to which it is implemented accurately. Finally, the team identifies the goal of an intervention and the criterion for success. In some cases, the goal may be set using the discrepancy data collected in the problem identification phase; for example, the goal may be to increase average student skill level in a classroom to that of the average skill level in higher performing classrooms. In other cases, the goal may be set using a criterion identified by the team; for example, the goal may be to increase an individual child's engagement to the level of comparison peers. In both cases, data are collected during the intervention period to monitor student progress toward the specified goal. In addition, in both cases, the team evaluates intervention integrity. This process may involve direct observation of intervention implementation and/or self-monitoring using a checklist. A sample treatment integrity checklist for a mathematical instructional activity is shown in Figure 4.3. This activity uses a Five Frame, a set of equal-sized boxes in a 1×5 array (see Figure 4.3, line 3), to help students visualize numbers up to 5. Moving the counters, such as plastic chips, into and out of the Five Frame helps students form visual images of the numbers represented. This form is meant to be completed by an independent observer but also could be adapted as a self-monitoring tool.

Treatment Integrity Checklist

Lesson 1: Counting with one-to-one correspondence (moving counters)

Intervention agent: _____

Date: _____ Time: _____ Evaluator: _____

Intervention components	Completed? Yes	Completed? No	Comments
Warm-up activity: Verbal counting			
1. Instructed students to verbally count to 5			
2. Counted aloud and clapped with students			
Learning activity 1: Introducing Five Frame and counters			
3. Five Frame and counters displayed ☐☐☐☐☐			
4. Asked students to describe Five Frame and counters			
5. Introduced Five Frame and allowed students to repeat "Five Frame"			
6. Described Five Frame			
7. Introduced counters and allowed students to repeat "counters"			
8. Asked students to identify Five Frame			
9. Asked students to identify number of boxes on Five Frame			
10. Encouraged student responses and provided positive feedback			
Learning activity 2: Moving counters into Five Frame			
11. Displayed Five Frame with five counters below it			
12. Narrated process of lining up counters below Five Frame			
13. Narrated process of moving first two counters into Five Frame			
14. Asked students where to place third counter			
15. Asked students where to place fourth counter			
16. Asked students where to place fifth counter			
17. Moved the counters out of the Five Frame			
18. Instructed students to watch the process of lining up counters underneath the Five Frame			
19. Called on student to place the first counter			
20. Called on student to place the second counter			
21. Called on student to place the third counter			
22. Called on student to place the fourth counter			
23. Called on student to place the fifth counter			
24. Introduced independent practice activity			
25. Disseminated materials			
26. Watched student responses and provided feedback			
Review			
27. Asked students to identify the Five Frame			
28. Asked students to identify the number of boxes on the Five Frame			
29. Asked students to identify how many counters go in each box of the Five Frame			
30. Provided positive reinforcement			

Figure 4.3. Treatment Integrity Checklist.

Multi-Tiered Systems of Support for Young Children: Driving Change in Early Education
by Judith J. Carta and Robin Miller Young.
Copyright © 2019 by Paul H. Brookes Publishing Co., Inc. All rights reserved.

Plan Evaluation

Ongoing evaluation is necessary to determine whether an intervention is successfully meeting students' needs. In MTSS, this is generally considered as evaluating the student's (or students') response to intervention. The decision to be made in this phase is multi-pronged: 1) Has an intervention been effective, and is the problem being addressed adequately? 2) Is an intervention ineffective and thus, the problem has not been addressed? and 3) What is the next step in addressing the identified problem? (See Figure 4.1.) To evaluate the effect of an intervention and implementation plan, student outcome and intervention integrity data are used to determine if the discrepancy between actual performance levels and expected or desired performance levels is decreasing. In practical terms, data are examined to determine whether the student is making adequate gains in the targeted area. If an intervention is evaluated as successful (i.e., the student demonstrates gains consistent with the established goal), then the team decides whether to continue the intervention so the student can meet progressively higher criterion levels, lessen the intervention intensity, or discontinue the intervention if mastery is achieved. If an intervention is viewed as unsuccessful, the instructional team first considers implementation integrity. Were all of the intervention steps followed as planned? If yes, the team considers alternative explanations for the lack of desired gains (e.g., What was the student's level of engagement during implementation? Did the student have high absence rates during the intervention phase?). The team cycles through the phases of the problem-solving model again, considering whether the correct problem was identified, most probable hypothesis selected, and most appropriate intervention implemented. The team may decide to intensify the intervention, add additional components, reconsider the appropriateness of the goals that had been set, or change the intervention altogether.

CONSIDERATIONS FOR PROBLEM-SOLVING IN EARLY EDUCATION SETTINGS

The problem-solving model provides an important framework for data-based decision making both within MTSS models and in the absence of those models. As a general way of thinking, the problem-solving model prompts educators to clearly define goals, collect data on an ongoing basis, and evaluate data to determine whether goals are being met. This framework can be applied to both academic and behavioral domains with several advantages. In the problem-solving model, a systematic process that promotes a more organized approach to collecting, analyzing, and using data is emphasized. Use of data at each step facilitates a more objective and measurable system for making decisions. The recursive process promotes more thoughtful and intentional instructional decision making that ends only when the problem is resolved or the discrepancy is reduced to satisfactory levels. In applying the problem-solving model in early education settings, there are several unique considerations.

Selecting Target Skills or Behaviors

According to the National Research Council (2008), early childhood outcomes should 1) reflect valued societal domains, 2) be linked to important later outcomes, and 3) be a common target of intervention, given that outcomes must be responsive to changes in environmental conditions. In addition, to be used in data-based decision making, outcomes should be defined in measurable and observable terms. A number of skills and behaviors could meet these criteria, and to some degree, targets selected will depend on the needs and goals of specific settings or programs. Broadly, targets may include early literacy and numeracy skills that have been found to be linked to later academic success (e.g., Duncan et al., 2007), as well as social-emotional skills that have an impact on school adjustment, self-regulation, and prosocial behavior (e.g., Denham & Burton, 2003). Given that all states have adopted early learning standards (Barnett, Carolan, Squires, Clarke Brown, & Horowitz, 2015), these standards may provide a basis for determining what to assess, for interpreting student performance on assessments, and for reporting results to the public (National Research Council, 2008).

Gathering Data on Target Skills or Behaviors

Once a target has been selected, consideration is given to the method and tools for gathering data. First, consideration is given to the purpose of assessment (e.g., screening, eligibility determination, program planning) because the type of data gathered and the data collection method must align with the purpose (Schwartz & Olswang, 1996). Second, the specific skills or behaviors targeted for assessment determine the type of data that are gathered. Some skills lend themselves more to direct assessment whereas other skills may be better assessed through authentic assessment procedures including direct observations and portfolios. Finally, some targets may be better suited for judgment-based methods such as checklists and rating scales.

Direct assessments include published, norm-referenced tests and curriculum-based models that require students to respond to assessment prompts. Although norm-referenced assessments are generally useful in eligibility determinations, many are difficult to translate into intervention strategies because of their broad focus. Furthermore, norm-referenced tests yield standard scores that may not be sensitive to growth over short periods of time, and the multiple forms needed for progress monitoring are largely unavailable (Hintze, 2009); thus, these approaches may be less useful in data-based decision making within MTSS (McLean, Hemmeter, & Snyder, 2014). Curriculum-based assessment (CBA) models may be more useful within MTSS, given the link between assessment and instruction. CBA typically takes two forms. *Specific skills mastery assessment* assesses student performance on specific subskills that are systematically sampled from the local curriculum and ordered hierarchically as short-term objectives (Fuchs & Deno, 1991). In contrast, *general outcome measures* (GOM) are used to assess global outcomes across a variety of skills linked to the curriculum (Shapiro, 2011). Measurement targets are a subset of skills selected from the universe of possible skills based on their representativeness of a valued global outcome (Fuchs & Deno, 1991). The availability of general outcome measures for young children is increasing in a number of important domains, and these tools show promise for use in MTSS models.

Whereas direct assessments involve standardized procedures typically used outside of classroom routines and activities, authentic assessment refers to assessments that occur in naturally occurring activities, routines, and settings by familiar individuals (Bagnato & Simeonsson, 2008). Examples of authentic assessment include systematic observations to quantify a student's behavior, documentation of performance through portfolios, and sampling of permanent products in which various information sources are organized to summarize a student's skill level and progress (McLean et al., 2014). These types of assessment methods can provide information about student mastery of curricular goals and are effective in communicating with and involving parents in the assessment process (Brassard & Boehm, 2007). Some research suggests these methods may also better capture student strengths (Campbell, Milbourne, & Silverman, 2001). Checklists and rating scales can represent both direct assessment approaches when accompanied by a normative comparison group or reflect student mastery of specific skills in a task analysis, for example. Figure 4.4 provides examples of considerations in selecting an assessment method.

Each method of assessment has advantages and disadvantages that need to be considered relative to the purpose of the assessment, the skills being assessed, the decision to be made, and who is collecting the data. One challenge in early education is the limited number of published and available measures that can be used in data-based decision making. As such, in general, a multi-method, multi-informant approach to assessment is recommended. That is, multiple methods of gathering quantitative and qualitative data should be used with multiple individuals who interact with the student to formulate a greater understanding of the student's strengths, needs, and goals. Instructional teams think carefully about defining the problem in measurable terms and using objective measurement approaches. Assessment methods are selected that best capture the target behavior and its salient dimensions. In all cases, consideration for the purpose of the assessment and the alignment between the purpose and the method will strengthen the comprehensiveness and quality of the decision-making process.

Domain- or skill-specific screening
- Is the assessment efficient to use with large numbers of students?
- Can educators easily administer the assessment, interpret the results, and apply the findings?
- Does the assessment have evidence of sensitivity and specificity; that is, does it correctly detect students who need further problem solving or intervention and weed out those who do not?

Eligibility determination
- What necessary information has yet to be captured by existing assessment data?
- How should this additional information be gathered (direct observations, authentic assessments, direct assessments, judgment-based rating scales, interviews, portfolio products)?
- What is the incremental validity of each proposed method; that is, how will the data generated contribute to a greater understanding of a student's strengths and needs?
- Does the proposed method meet state requirements for eligibility determination?

Intervention development
- Does the assessment provide information that has utility for evaluating intervention effectiveness (e.g., For a student with pre-academic needs, does the assessment provide information about his or her current skills and areas in need of further development? For a child with behavioral needs, does the assessment provide information about antecedents and consequences across settings?)?
- Does the assessment include an evaluation of learning contexts (e.g., school and home settings)?

Figure 4.4. Considerations when selecting an assessment method.

COMPARISONS IN DATA-BASED DECISION MAKING

Because the problem-solving model can be used for different decisions at multiple levels, consideration is given to the type of comparison (i.e., data gathered at one point in time or data gathered over time), the point of comparison (i.e., interindividual and intraindividual), and the level of the data-based decision-making process (i.e., program, classroom, and individual). Early educators have long made one-point-in-time decisions regarding individual student eligibility for special education using interindividual comparisons, or comparisons between students (e.g., How does the student's performance compare to that of a national sample of students?). They also have extensive experience making intraindividual decisions about a student's progress using observational data collected on the student's performance over time (e.g., Has the student's problem behavior decreased?; McConnell, 2000). However, some decisions to be made within a problem-solving framework may require new approaches that continue to emerge from research.

Comparison of Static Scores

Data comparisons at one point in time typically consist of interindividual comparisons, either individually or as a group. Interindividual comparisons can be made using normative samples, benchmark data, or local norms. Normative data that accompany standardized, commercially available assessments are typically representative of the larger population of interest (e.g., a national sample of 4-year-olds) and provide an indication of how the performance of an individual student or a group of students compares to that of other same-age students. Benchmarks, or cut scores, are empirically derived to predict future outcomes and typically accompany CBA tools (Shapiro, 2011). These scores are often used to categorize student performance according to levels of risk (i.e., low risk, some risk, at risk) and can be used to determine the tier of intervention that a student might receive. Finally, locally gathered data, a local norm, provide information about a particular student within the local educational context (i.e., curriculum, classroom size) and can be useful in reducing bias in educational decision making because students are compared to a similar population (Stewart & Silberglitt, 2008).

In some cases, both benchmark data and local norms can be used to gain a more nuanced understanding of student performance. For example, performance data may suggest that all students are meeting the benchmark criterion for success or, conversely, that no students are meeting the benchmark. Assessment results that indicate all students are meeting the benchmark may occur in programs where local norms exceed national norms. In such cases, local norms may be more useful for identifying students who are performing below locally derived expectations. A program may elect to provide further support to the lowest performing 20% of students, even though the students met the nationally derived benchmark. When data indicate no students are meeting the benchmark criterion, the local standard of performance may be much lower than that which is expected based on other sources of normative data. A greater number of students in need of higher quality instruction or targeted intervention, combined with limited resources, necessitates long-term problem solving at the program level (e.g., How can we strengthen universal instruction?) and may also require a short-term focus on those students demonstrating the greatest level of need on the basis of local norms. Within early education, the use of benchmarks and cut scores is a relatively new development, and as such, their use in a problem-solving data-based decision-making model requires careful consideration and critical thinking, especially given the tremendous variability in skill development in early childhood and differences in students' exposure to formal learning experiences.

Comparison of Scores Across Time

Comparison of data over time focuses on changes in performance that occur from one time point to another time point. When data are collected on a few occasions (e.g., administering benchmark assessments at fall, winter, and spring time points), there are several different graphing options. One option is to use a column graph that depicts the percentage of children scoring above, at, or below a criterion. In Figure 4.5, data are organized around a criterion score from a standardized universal screening tool. Column graphs were made for each assessment occasion, and the percentages of students who met criterion were compared to evaluate whether more children were scoring below, above, or at the criterion over time. Figure 4.5 is used for discussion by the ILT in Video 3 that illustrates school/program-level problem solving.

Box plots also may be used (see Figure 4.6) to represent performance at the systems or classroom level. Plotting an individual student's score directly on the box plot highlights performance at the individual level within the context of the system or the classroom. The box represents scores between the 25th and 75th percentiles with a line drawn at the median, or the 50th percentile. The lines over the top and bottom of the boxes represent the entire range of scores from 0 to 100 percent (e.g., 0–15 pictures named correctly). Collectively, these areas represent the quartiles. Students scoring in the dark gray shaded area in Figure 4.6 represent the 25th–50th percentile whereas students scoring in the light gray shaded area represent the 50th–75th percentile. Students scoring below or above the box are considered below the 25th or above the 75th percentile, respectively. Those students scoring below the box may be considered as most in need of intervention.

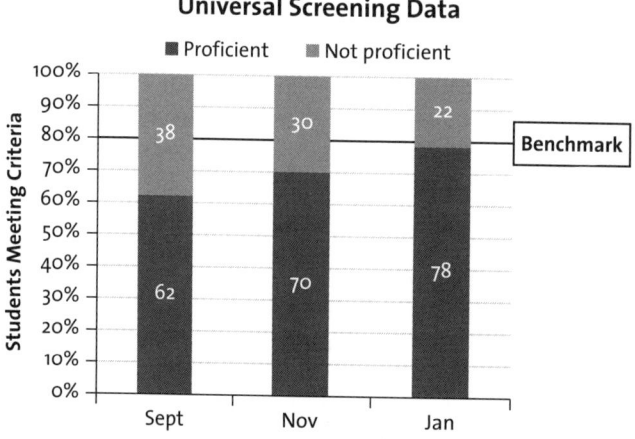

Figure 4.5. Data organized around a criterion score depicted over time.

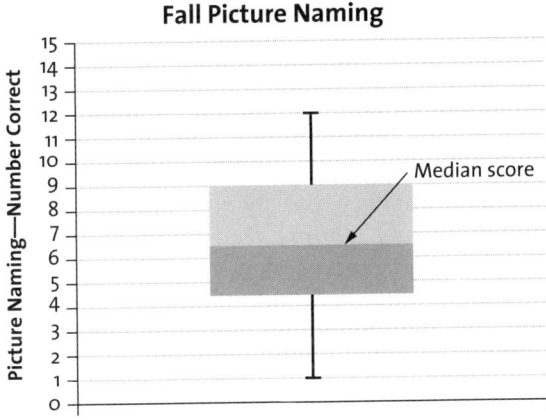

Figure 4.6. Box plot of Picture Naming scores at one point in time for a group.

In looking at the box plot from one point in time to another at a systems or classroom level, consideration is given to whether the entire range of scores has moved in the desired direction and to the dispersion among the scores (e.g., Are differences in student performance widening over time or is variation in performance minimizing over time?). Similarly, to assess growth over time at the classroom or program level, the number of children meeting or exceeding benchmark scores can be compared from one time point to another. Finally, at a basic level, the mean, or average, score can be compared from one time point to another. At an individual level, continued plotting of individual data against system- or classroom-level data allows for evaluation of student progress as compared to a reference group.

This is illustrated in Figure 4.7 when Miriam's scores on one of the IGDIs 1.0 measures, Pictures Naming Fluency (PNF), is graphed with box plots over the fall,

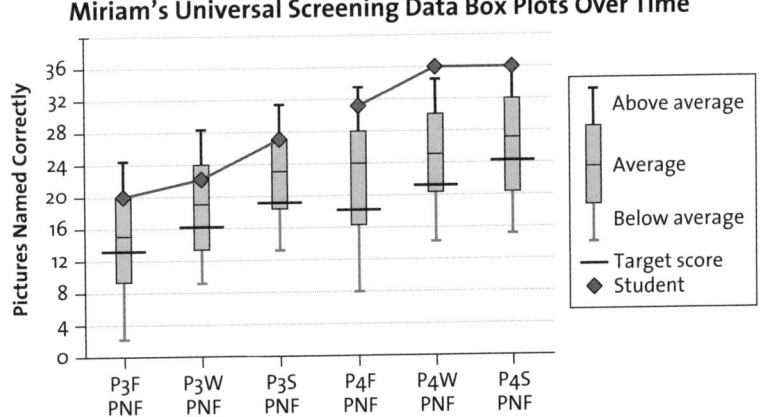

Figure 4.7. Box plot of IGDIs 1.0 Picture Naming Fluency (PNF) data over time. (*Key:* Units = number of pictures correctly named in one minute; average = 25th to the 75th percentile of students assessed in fall [F], winter [W], and spring [S] of 3-year-old [P3] and 4-year-old [P4] preschool years; target score = benchmark derived from locally developed norms.) AIMSweb. Copyright © 2008 NCS Pearson, Inc. Figures reproduced with permission. All rights reserved.

winter, and spring of her 3-year-old (P3) and her 4-year-old (P4) preschool years. The comparison groups included all children across the entire program (approximately 300 for each P3 and P4 age group). Four conclusions are offered from visual inspection of the graphed data. First, Miriam demonstrated proficient vocabulary knowledge during each assessment period, earning scores that were significantly above the target/benchmark score derived from locally developed norms. Thus, program staff could feel confident that she was gaining the necessary early language skills necessary for later reading success. Second, she earned scores that were at the top of the average range of her peers during the 3-year-old preschool year and exceeding the average range during her 4-year-old preschool year, suggesting that she was among the most proficient children for her age in the program in terms of vocabulary development throughout her enrollment. Third, Miriam started as a proficient student with a score of 20 (fall of P3 year), and she continued to make gains, earning scores of 36 during the winter and spring of her P4 year. She may have reached a ceiling and could not produce the names of more than 36 pictures in one minute. Finally, in terms of the peer group, the average ranges of each assessment time period continued to move upward over time, indicating that as a group, the students' overall vocabulary proficiency increased over time. Interestingly, the target/benchmark score fell between the spring of the P3 year and fall of the P4 year; however, the average range expanded, and the average score increased slightly. For the winter and spring P4 year, the target/benchmark score increased to above P3 levels, the average range climbed higher, and the average score increased to above P3 levels.

When data are collected more continuously over time, for example, when student progress is monitored to evaluate response to intervention, data can be analyzed using principles of single-case design in which performance during a baseline phase without intervention is compared to performance during an intervention phase when targeted supports are provided (see Gast, 2010; Riley-Tillman & Burns, 2009). Figure 4.8 provides an illustration of a single-case design. In this type of design, several features of the data are of interest. First, variability of the

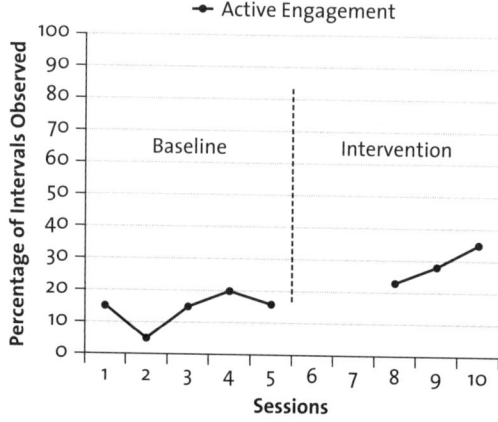

Figure 4.8. Sample single-case design graph for engagement.

data is important to consider. Data that are extremely variable decrease our confidence in making decisions about the effect of an intervention, and when data are variable, attempts should be made to identify what might be causing the variability. For example, conducting observations at different times of day or in different settings may lead to variability in engagement data. Further understanding how these sources of variability contribute to the identified problem can increase intervention effectiveness. For example, engagement may be higher in settings with frequent opportunities for active participation versus settings that do not include frequent opportunities for active participation. This knowledge may lead educators to increase opportunities for active participation in order to increase engagement. Second, the average or mean difference in performance may be of interest in comparing phases. This involves calculating the average score, or rate of behavior across sessions, within the baseline phase and the intervention phase and comparing the two values. For example, across three observations of peer initiations, a child initiated an average of 3 interactions per session prior to intervention. After the intervention was implemented, the child initiated an average of 7 interactions per session. This type of comparison is useful for evaluating changes in social skills or behavioral occurrences over time. For early learning skills, rate of growth, or slope, is also of interest and can be calculated using most web-based graphing systems (e.g., Chart Dog).

A challenge when examining change over time in early education settings is that the expected rate of growth for any given skill is largely unknown. Although research has generated expected rates of growth for later developing skills such as oral reading fluency, similar rates of growth are not yet available for skills targeted in early education, though research is continuing in this area (e.g., Greenwood, Buzhardt, Walker, McCune, & Howard, 2013). In the absence of an empirically derived growth rate, educators can consider the rate of growth in terms of goal achievement. This can be done by creating an aimline that provides a visual estimate of the student's expected rate of growth to achieve a goal within a specified time period for either academic or behavioral targets. Educators can create an aimline by graphing a student's baseline performance and plotting the desired performance at a later point in time and drawing a line to connect these two scores. Then, data collected continuously over time can be evaluated relative to the aimline.

A four-step process for instructional decisions, labeled IDEA, can be applied to most graphed data; each of the letters in IDEA stands for the first word in each step: 1) Inspect the last four data points; 2) Decide what the scores look like (e.g., Are scores moving in the desired direction?); 3) Evaluate why the scores are this way (e.g., Are changes the result of the intervention?); and 4) Apply a decision relative to achievement (e.g., Should we continue the intervention, increase the goal, or make a change?) (Shapiro, 2011). In evaluating change over time, the use of both interindividual (i.e., between individuals) and intraindividual (i.e., within one individual over time) comparisons may be important to establish a more comprehensive understanding of student performance. For example, a student may have made significant gains in skill acquisition relative to his or her previously measured performance (intraindividual comparison); however, when compared to his or her peer group or a national normative sample (interindividual comparison), the student's performance may still be low enough to warrant concern and the need for additional intervention.

LEVELS OF DATA-BASED DECISION MAKING

Data play a central role in improving instructional practices across program, classroom, and individual student levels. Program-level analysis is essential for evaluating the effectiveness of the core curriculum in meeting early learning goals and standards. Administrators may examine how students enrolled in a program compare to a national normative standard at one point in time (e.g., the number of students meeting or exceeding benchmark standards). Administrators may also evaluate whether subgroups of students within the same program show differences in performance (e.g., Are there differences in performance between students who do or do not receive special education services?). At the intra-individual level, administrators may use data to examine growth over time of students enrolled in the program, addressing the question of whether students as a group made progress from one point in time to another.

At the classroom level of analysis, problem solving centers on evaluating the effectiveness of the core curriculum in helping children achieve specific goals in the context of planning instruction for groups of students. Interindividual comparisons may be made using a national normative standard, asking questions regarding performance at one point in time as well as growth over time (e.g., Which students in the classroom are meeting or exceeding benchmark standards at this point in time? Which students may need additional supports?). Over time, teachers and administrators may be interested in whether the number of students meeting or exceeding benchmark standards grows. With regard to intraindividual comparisons, whether a local standard in the form of classroom comparisons or a national normative standard is used, questions center on whether students as a group are making adequate progress toward important goals or whether there is a need to adjust instructional strategies.

At the individual-student level, interindividual comparisons involve evaluating a target student's performance relative to his or her peers using a local or national normative group or a benchmark standard. Teachers might ask how this student's performance compares to the performance of others (i.e., one point in time or growth over time). Intra-individual comparison involves evaluating the target student's performance relative to his or her performance at a prior point in time to determine whether the student is making progress. A combination of both interindividual and intraindividual comparisons is recommended when instructional teams are deciding whether an individual student needs additional supports to accelerate progress.

PROBLEM SOLVING AS APPLIED TO EARLY LEARNING

Numerous obstacles/opportunities need to be considered in using the problem-solving model in early childhood. As opportunities, these considerations promote critical thinking, innovation, and adaptation to ensure that a systematic process is used to improve outcomes for young children and promote early school success.

Problem Identification

In the case of Maplewood School District, Maggie, the early childhood coordinator, along with a school psychologist and speech-language pathologist, collected language and early literacy data using the IGDIs-EL (McConnell et al., 2012) on all students enrolled in the district's preschool classrooms. Maggie, the classroom teachers, the building principal, the school psychologist, and the speech-language pathologist met to review the data following the first data collection period in the fall (see Figure 4.5, "Sept" column data). Using data from this one point in time, the team identified two problems. The first problem was identified at the program level. Using criteria provided by IGDIs-EL developers, large numbers of children were performing below what was desired at that point in the school year on the IGDIs-EL task represented by the graphed "universal screening data." The use of this benchmark standard allowed the district to define the problem as the discrepancy between the students' current scores and the benchmark score indicating success. In addition to using IGDIs-EL benchmarks, the team discussed student performance relative to state- and district-identified early learning standards and curricular goals. The team decided that because so many of the students were scoring below what was expected, instructional decision making should occur at Tier 1 or core/universal level. This type of decision making is further illustrated in Video 3 of the accompanying video series.

The second problem the team identified was at the individual student level. Some students' scores indicated relatively low vocabulary proficiency compared to IGDIs-EL norms on the Picture Naming Fluency (PNF) measure and also relative to their peers in the program. Thus, the problem was expressed as a discrepancy between the students' scores at a national and local norm level. To further understand this problem, the team considered additional existing data. Teacher observations indicated these students did not participate in classroom activities or engage with their peers to the same extent as other students, although they did not present with behavioral challenges. Portfolio data consisting of drawings with labels added by the teacher suggested that the students generated limited content during such activities. All of these pieces of data were used to conclude that the vocabulary development of these students was indeed a concern to be addressed.

Problem Analysis

To support problem analysis at the program/school level, the team discussed the core curriculum used for language and early literacy, the training that had been provided to implement the curriculum, and the need for ongoing support. In reviewing the data gathered, one consideration was the amount of time devoted to literacy instruction. A review of teacher planning materials indicated that instruction was limited to a short period of the day. In addition, some of the literacy activities outlined in the curriculum were not very explicit in their focus on early literacy skills. Furthermore, although the curriculum seemed to adequately address beginning sounds, there was less emphasis on pairing letters with sounds to support development of the alphabetic principle. The team also discussed performance differences between classrooms by looking at the number of students in each classroom who were meeting or exceeding benchmarks. Based on the data, in some classrooms, more students were entering school with fewer skills than in other classrooms. This suggested the need for additional support in those classrooms along with supplementing the curricula with specific activities to support letter–sound correspondence skills and rhyming.

To support problem analysis at the individual-child level, additional information was collected on overall development, school attendance, classroom engagement, language status, and home literacy environment. When this information was discussed further, several children with low performance were identified as dual language learners, and in the case of two additional children, a review of records indicated overall developmental concerns. Although a decision was made to address the universal level of core instruction for language and early literacy overall, the team decided the discrepancy between these students' scores and what was expected was significant enough to warrant additional efforts consistent with a Tier 2 intervention to address language skills in addition to classroom engagement.

Intervention Development and Implementation

At the program/school level, based on the data collected during the problem analysis phase, the team decided to increase the amount of instructional time devoted to language and early literacy at the universal level by planning several activities throughout the day that targeted specific early literacy skills. In planning activities, Maggie, the teachers, and the teacher assistants ensured that the focus on literacy was explicit and intentional. Specific steps for implementing the activities were identified, and checklists were created to guide the use of each step. In addition, Maggie agreed to visit each classroom to provide assistance as needed to ensure the activities were going smoothly. The school psychologist also planned to observe in the classroom using the Classroom Code for Interactive Recording of Children's Literacy Environments (CIRCLE; Atwater et al., 2012), an early literacy classroom observation checklist to provide feedback on the classroom literacy focus. The team decided that teacher planning forms would be used to document the changes in literacy instruction and the winter assessment data would be reviewed to evaluate students' response to these changes.

To address the second problem of the needs of individual children, the team decided to strategically use small-group time and best practices in shared book reading to target vocabulary development. The team worked together to identify books and corresponding vocabulary and then created a script for each of the books to ensure students had multiple exposures to targeted words. They decided that expressive measures of vocabulary may prove too difficult for these students, so they created a receptive measure that allowed students to select the correct response from a set of three options. This measure would be administered prior to beginning a new book and at the end of the week following the scheduled reading sessions.

To target engagement, the team decided to use picture response cards at circle time whenever possible. For example, instead of having one child label the weather each day, students were given two cards with weather pictures and were asked to hold one up in response to the prompt, "What is our weather today?" To increase engagement during center activities, teachers would pair target students with verbally skilled peers and provide a structured activity in which they could engage together. To assess the effect of these strategies, the team decided to use single-case design methodology. The school psychologist agreed to conduct baseline observations on each student's level of engagement across activities and on several occasions before the strategies were implemented. While the strategies were being implemented, the school psychologist would continue to collect observational data and graph these data. The team agreed that after a period of 6 weeks, they would review the data. Figure 4.8 shows a graph depicting percentage of time the student was engaged during five baseline observations and then in three sessions after intervention was implemented. The team could use those data to decide whether the change from baseline to intervention in the target behavior was in the desired direction and sufficient.

Plan Evaluation

At the program/school level, when the winter assessment data were collected, the team reviewed the progress that students made as a group. In examining growth over time, the team compared the number of students meeting or exceeding the IGDIs-EL benchmarks in the winter with the same data collected in the fall. Maggie created box plots so the team could evaluate progress through intraindividual comparison (i.e., fall to winter). They were pleased to see that many students made gains in their early literacy skills and agreed to continue using the strategic literacy activities. In addition to the IGDIs-EL data, the team discussed the observational data teachers collected to monitor progress toward state and district standards and curricular goals. Overall, teachers reported increased engagement in literacy activities and more accurate responding during literacy circle-time activities.

For the individual-child level, the team met to review the data collected on individual students following 6 weeks of the strategic use of shared book reading and engagement strategies. As was evident in the graphed data, most students were more actively engaged in shared book reading. In terms of vocabulary development, some students made positive gains, learning several of the targeted words each week. Based on students' rates of progress, the instructional team decided that some students no longer needed the more intensive strategic shared book reading intervention. Other students did not make as much progress, however, and the team decided to investigate additional strategies to use with these students moving forward, cycling back to the problem analysis phase.

CONCLUSION

In summary, early childhood educators need to increase the quality of the curricular, instructional, and environmental decisions that determine how they will intervene with young children and their families to improve their developmental and learning outcomes. The first action to take is to ensure that all stakeholders and team members agree on the type of decision that has to be made. This is essential as different decision types (e.g., developmental screening, progress monitoring, development of individualized education program [IEP] goals) may be best matched to different types of data. Once agreement is made on the decision type, then the data-collection process is arranged and conducted so the collected data are aligned with the decision type.

The formative use of data is central to effectively supporting student outcomes, and a specific, evidence-based problem-solving process was conceptualized and has been used since the late 1970s as an effective framework for data-based decision making. The steps of the problem-solving model move in a sequential fashion; however, it is a recursive model allowing a team to return to any previous step as needed to arrive at a defensible decision. The steps include a problem identification phase where problems are defined as discrepancies between current levels of performance and a desired criterion, using data collected on important student outcomes. Next, team members employ a problem analysis step in which factors contributing to the discrepancy are identified for possible intervention development; subsequently, intervention implementation occurs when a plan is developed and put into place. The last step is to plan evaluation where the impact of interventions on student outcomes is evaluated to determine whether goals are met or additional supports are needed.

As illustrated in an applied example, the data-based, problem-solving process can be used to address problems that may be present at various levels of MTSS service delivery. These problems may include those at the program/school level, such as determining if the Tier 1 (e.g., core or universal) curriculum is meeting the needs of all children enrolled in the program. Teams who work at this level can also determine what to do and how to monitor implementation of a program/schoolwide curricular change. This data-based process may also be used at the classroom level to examine problems that might occur across whole classrooms of students to ensure strong achievement of targeted outcomes. Finally, the growth and progress of individual children can be monitored in an evidence-based, problem-solving process to ensure that effective and efficient interventions are put into place and the children are achieving essential developmental and early academic outcomes.

Maggie reflected on the changes that had taken place throughout the last year, as the early childhood program staff started to shift into an MTSS framework, which included the use of a data-based decision-making process to ensure they were identifying students' needs and matching those needs with appropriate supports. Although the ILT and classroom teams experienced challenges in implementing the problem-solving model and data-based decision making in early education, they noted many benefits of this structured process in their year-end faculty meeting. Maggie coached the team in implementing a system of effective assessment procedures that facilitated identification of problems. When problems were expressed in terms of a discrepancy, she and the ILT worked through a series of problem-solving steps to reduce discrepancies through effective instruction and intervention. Continued assessment and dialogue allowed for formative evaluation of student progress to ensure that time was not lost when instructional changes were needed. For Maplewood School District, extending this part of their elementary MTSS model into their early education program, with modifications to address developmentally appropriate practices for young learners, led to a systematic approach to improving outcomes for all students at the program/school, classroom, and individual levels.

RESOURCES

Akers, L., Del Grosso, P., Atkins-Burnett, S., Monahan, S., Boller, K., Carta, J., & Wasik, B. A. (2015). *Tailored teaching: The need for stronger evidence about early childhood teachers' use of ongoing assessment to individualize instruction.* Research Brief OPRE Report #2015-59. Washington, DC: Mathematica Policy Research. Retrieved from https://www.acf.hhs.gov/sites/default/files/opre/tailored_teaching_the_need_for_stronger_evidence_about_early.pdf

Carta, J. J., Greenwood, C. R., Walker, D., & Buzhardt, J. (2010). *Using IGDIs: Monitoring progress and improving intervention for infants and young children.* Baltimore, MD: Paul H. Brookes Publishing Co.

ChartDog. ChartDog Graph Maker is a "featured tool" on the Intervention Central web site that provides teachers, schools, and districts with free resources to help struggling learners and implement Response to Intervention and attain the Common Core State Standards. Users can enter their own data and then the web site will generate charts and graphs of the data. http://www.interventioncentral.org/teacher-resources/graph-maker-free-online

Coffee, G., Ray-Subramanian, C., Schanding, T., & Feeney-Kettler, K. (2013). *Early childhood education: A practical guide to evidence-based, multi-tiered service delivery.* New York, NY: Routledge.

Division for Early Childhood (DEC), National Association for the Education of Young Children (NAEYC), & National Head Start Association (NHSA). (2013). *Frameworks for Response to Intervention in early childhood: Description and implications.* Missoula, MT: Author. Retrieved from http://www.dec-sped.org/position-statements

Greenwood, C. R., Carta, J. C., & McConnell, S. R. (2011). Advances in measurement for universal screening and progress monitoring of young children. *Journal of Early Intervention, 33,* 254–267.

National Association of School Psychologists. (2015). *Early childhood services: Promoting positive outcomes for young children* (Position statement). Bethesda, MD: Author.

REFERENCES

Atwater, J. B., Reynolds, L. H., Schiefelbusch, J., Lee, Y., Montagna, D., & Tapia, Y. (2012). *Classroom CIRCLE: Classroom Code for Interactive Recording of Children's Learning Environments* (version 2.0). Kansas City: Juniper Gardens Children's Project, University of Kansas.

Bagnato, S. J., & Simeonsson, R. J. (2008). *Authentic assessment for early childhood intervention: Best practices.* New York, NY: Guilford.

Barnett, W. S., Carolan, M. E., Squires, J. H., Clarke Brown, K., & Horowitz, M. (2015). *The state of preschool 2014: State preschool yearbook.* New Brunswick, NJ: National Institute for Early Education Research.

Batsche, G., Elliott, J., Graden, J. L., Grimes, J., Kovaleski, J. F., Prasse, D., . . . Tilly III, W. D. (2005). *Response to intervention: Policy considerations and implementation.* Alexandria, VA: NASDSE.

Batsche, G. M., Castillo, J. M., Dixon, D. N., & Forde, S. (2008). Best practices in linking assessment to intervention. In A. Thomas & J. Grimes (Eds.), *Best practices in school psychology IV: Vol. 1* (pp. 177–193). Washington, DC: National Association of School Psychologists.

Bransford, J. D., & Stein, B. S. (1984). *The IDEAL problem solver.* New York, NY: W. H. Freeman.

Brassard, M. R., & Boehm, A. E. (2007). *Preschool assessment: Principles and practices.* New York, NY: Guilford.

Campbell, P. H., Milbourne, S. A., & Silverman, C. (2001). Strengths-based child portfolios: A processional development activity to alter perspectives of children with special needs. *Topics in Early Childhood Special Education, 21,* 152–161.

Christ, T. J. (2008). Best practices in problem analysis. In A. Thomas & J. Grimes (Eds.), *Best practices in school psychology IV: Vol. 1* (pp. 159–176). Washington, DC: National Association of School Psychologists.

Denham, S. A., & Burton, R. (2003). *Social and emotional prevention and intervention programming for preschoolers.* New York, NY: Kluwer-Plenum.

Deno, S. L. (1989). Curriculum-based measurement and alternative special education services: A fundamental and direct relationship. In M. R. Shinn (Ed.), *Curriculum-based measurement: Assessing special children* (pp. 1–17). New York, NY: Guilford Press.

Deno, S. L. (1995). School psychologist as problem solver. In A. Thomas & J. Grimes (Eds.) *Best practices in school psychology III* (pp. 471–484). Washington, DC: National Association of School Psychologists.

Deno, S. L. (2002) Problem-solving as best practice. In A. Thomas & J. Grimes (Eds.), *Best practices in school psychology IV: Vol. 1* (pp. 37–56). Washington, DC: National Association of School Psychologists.

Deno, S. L. (2005). Problem-solving assessment. In R. Brown-Chidsey (Ed.), *Assessment for intervention: A problem-solving approach.* (pp. 10–40). New York, NY: Guilford Press.

Deno, S. L., & Mirkin, P. K. (1977). *Data-based program modification: A manual.* Reston, VA: Council for Exceptional Children.

Duncan, G. J., Dowsett, C. J., Claessens, A., Magnuson, K., Huston, A. C., Klebanov, P., . . . Japel, C. (2007). School readiness and later achievement. *Developmental Psychology, 43,* 1428–1446.

Fuchs, D., Mock, D., Morgan, P. L., & Young, C. L. (2003). Responsiveness-to-intervention: Definitions, evidence, and implications for the learning disabilities construct. *Learning Disabilities Research & Practice, 18,* 157–171.

Fuchs, L. S., & Deno, S. L. (1991). Paradigmatic distinctions between instructionally relevant measurement models. *Exceptional Children, 57,* 488–500.

Gast, D. L. (2010). *Single subject research methodology in behavioral sciences.* New York, NY: Routledge.

Greenwood, C. R., Buzhardt, J., Walker, D., McCune, L., & Howard, W. (2013). Advancing the construct validity of the Early Communication Indicator (ECI) for infants and toddlers: Equivalence of growth trajectories across two early head start samples. *Early Childhood Research Quarterly, 28,* 743–758.

Hintze, J. M. (2009). Curriculum-based assessment. In T. Gutkin & C. Reynolds (Eds.), *The handbook of school psychology* (4th ed., pp. 397–409). Hoboken, NJ: Wiley.

Kelley, E. S., Goldstein, H., Spencer, T. D., & Sherman, A. (2015). Effects of an automated Tier 2 storybook intervention on vocabulary and comprehension learning in preschool children with limited oral language skills. *Early Childhood Research Quarterly, 31,* 47–61.

McConnell, S. R. (2000). Assessment in early intervention and early childhood special education: Building on the past to project into our future. *Topics in Early Childhood Special Education, 20,* 43–48.

McConnell, S., Bradfield, T., Wackerle-Hollman, A., & Rodriguez, M. (2012). *Individual Growth and Development Indicators of Early Literacy (IGDIs-EL).* Saint Paul, MN: Early Learning Labs.

McLean, M., Hemmeter, M. L., & Snyder, P. (2014). *Essential elements for assessing infants and preschoolers with special needs.* Upper Saddle River, NJ: Pearson.

National Research Council. (2008). *Early childhood assessment: Why, what, and how?* Washington, DC: The National Academies Press. doi:10.17226/12446

Noe, S., Spencer, T. D., Kruse, L., & Goldstein, H. (2014). Effects of a Tier 3 phonological awareness intervention on preschoolers' emergent literacy. *Topics in Early Childhood Special Education, 34,* 27–39.

Pluymert K. (2014). Problem-solving foundations for school psychological services. In P. L. Harrison & A. Thomas (Eds.), *Best practices in school psychology: Data-based and collaborative decision making* (pp. 25–40). Bethesda, MD: National Association of School Psychologists.

Riley-Tillman, T. C., & Burns, M. K. (2009). *Evaluating educational interventions: Single-case design for measuring response to intervention.* New York, NY: Guilford.

Schwartz, I. S., & Olswang, L. B. (1996). Evaluating child behavior change in natural settings: Exploring alternative strategies for data collection. *Topics in Early Childhood Special Education, 16,* 82–101.

Shapiro, E. S. (2011). *Academic skills problems: Direct assessment and intervention* (4th ed.). New York, NY: Guilford Press.

Shinn, M. (1995). Best practices in curriculum-based measurement and its use in a problem-solving model. In J. Grimes & A. Thomas (Eds.), *Best practices in school psychology III* (pp. 547–568). Silver Spring, MD: National Association of School Psychologists.

Spencer, E., Goldstein, H., Sherman, A., Noe, S., Tabbah, R., Ziolkowski, R., & Schneider, N. (2012). Effects of an automated vocabulary and comprehension intervention: An early efficacy study. *Journal of Early Intervention, 34*, 195–221.

Stewart, L. H., & Silberglitt, B. (2008). Best practices in developing academic local norms. In A. Thomas & J. Grimes (Eds.), *Best practices in school psychology IV: Vol. 1* (pp. 225–242). Washington, DC: National Association of School Psychologists.

Stormont, M., Lewis, T. J., Beckner, R., & Johnson, N. W. (2008). *Implementing positive behavior support systems in early childhood and elementary settings*. Thousand Oaks, CA: Corwin Press.

Young, R. M., Snow, L. M., Frech, C., & Shields, L. (2011). *Developing socially competent and emotionally resilient young children through an early childhood RtI framework*. Invited article posted on the RtI Action Network's web site. Retrieved from http://www.rtinetwork.org/learn/rti-in-pre-kindergarten/developing-socially-competent-and-emotionally-resilient-young-children

5

Developing and Sustaining High-Quality Tier 1 Early Literacy and Language Practices

Judith J. Carta, Charles R. Greenwood, and Mary Abbott

As the leadership team members of the prekindergarten program at Maplewood School began to plan how they would build their multi-tiered systems of support (MTSS) program, their first step was to take stock of the strengths on which they would build their tiered model as well as to identify some of the challenges they needed to address. They realized that they needed to examine multiple aspects of the Tier 1 foundation that they provided to support all children. The centerpiece of Tier 1 is their curriculum for teaching language and literacy to all children. In order to design a plan for MTSS, they determined that they needed to ask several questions about their curriculum: Is it covering the complete content and skills that their program had earlier identified as instructional goals for their children? Does the content covered in the curriculum also align with their state early learning standards? If not, what is missing? Is the curriculum "evidence-based"—does it have a proven track record of producing the results they are looking for?

The team realized that they would need to gather some information to answer these questions. For example, how well does their selected curriculum compare to others that target early literacy and language goals? To answer this question, they would need to review the available research evidence about their curriculum. They also realized that other important questions included whether their staff was implementing the curriculum as it was designed to be implemented (i.e., with fidelity) and whether it was being implemented at the recommended frequency. To take a closer look at the curriculum and the way it was actually being implemented in each of the classrooms, they opted to carry out classroom observations during times devoted to early literacy and language to determine whether children were getting sufficient instructional opportunities in these two domains throughout the day. They also would need to see whether all of the children were adequately engaged in classroom activities so that each of them would be able to profit from the available instructional opportunities offered in each activity. They decided as a team to divide up these Tier 1 questions and to assign individual team members to gather specific sources of data to answer these questions. Then, as a team, they could develop a course of action to shore up any areas of weakness in Tier 1 and move ahead on designing MTSS for their program.

INTRODUCTION

Leadership teams from prekindergarten always face the ever-present challenge of the wide variation in the language and early literacy experiences that children in their programs encounter prior to entering their programs. While preschool is considered a time to provide all children with the education and skills needed to benefit their later academic instruction, most program leaders understand that a one-size-fits-all education will not address the diversity of needs reflected in the children they serve. To address this diversity, many programs have embraced MTSS as a potential solution because it provides supports that are able to meet different children's needs.

At the very heart of MTSS is Tier 1: core instruction for all children. A fundamental principle of tiered systems is that Tier 1 is the cornerstone for the entire framework. MTSS will only succeed if Tier 1 is founded on high-quality instruction based on an evidence-based core curriculum implemented with fidelity. Research shows that when programs use evidence-based Tier 1 curricula implemented with fidelity, they typically have fewer children who may need greater levels of instructional intensity (Foorman, Francis, Fletcher, Schatschneider, & Mehta, 1998).

A study of multiple early education programs and classrooms by the Center for Response to Intervention in Early Childhood (CRTIEC) has helped identify some critical steps that programs can follow when designing their own effective Tier 1 (Carta et al., 2016). These steps help a leadership team examine features of their Tier 1 such as their core curriculum, the instructional procedures used in implementing the curriculum, the fidelity with which those procedures are implemented, and the dosage or amount of instruction taking place. The steps for implementing Tier 1 are similar to the steps one might take in making a favorite family recipe, such as spaghetti sauce!

How does one go about making spaghetti sauce that fills the home with an irresistible aroma and brings everyone into the kitchen before food is even on the table? The key is to start with a great recipe—one that lists the ingredients, the equipment needed, and how the ingredients will be combined to make the sauce. Similarly, the recipe or starting point for Tier 1 is a research-based core curriculum; that is, a proven winner—a recipe for success that is results based. The second step is following the recipe. To ensure success, one cannot deviate too much from the recipe. Similarly, to maximize success and help children learn the critical skills outlined in the curriculum, educators need to implement the curriculum using evidence-based instructional procedures carried out with fidelity. A third crucial step to making great spaghetti sauce is adding enough of the right ingredients. Without the critical ingredients, such as ripe San Marzano tomatoes and fresh garlic, the sauce won't be as tasty as the recipe promises. Similarly, when implementing Tier 1, professionals have to make sure that children are getting the correct quantity or dosage of the curriculum—meaning that the curriculum needs to be implemented with adequate frequency (as prescribed) so that it affords children adequate instructional opportunities that promote active engagement and learning. One final step in preparing the sauce is making sure that it meets expectations. Tasting the sauce regularly as it cooks and adjusting the seasoning are important steps in order to be pleased with the final result. Similarly, when implementing Tier 1, children need to show the expected growth in response to the instruction provided. Regular monitoring of each child's progress is a way to ensure that children are benefiting from instruction. If their progress does not meet expectations, then adjustments need to be made to instruction.

In short, the steps to implementing an effective Tier 1 include 1) starting out with an evidence-based curriculum and instructional practices, 2) making sure the curriculum and instruction practices are implemented with fidelity, 3) providing adequate dosage in terms of the frequency and duration of implementation ensuring that children receive adequate instructional opportunities and maintain adequate levels of active engagement, and 4) carrying out regular progress monitoring of children to be sure they are demonstrating adequate growth, and if not, adjusting instruction in response to data when necessary. In this chapter, we describe the research basis for these important features of Tier 1 and provide greater detail about how programs should go about implementing each of these steps as they evaluate Tier 1.

WHAT IS THE CURRENT STATE OF TIER 1 WITHIN EARLY EDUCATION PROGRAMS?

A small but growing research literature provides strong evidence that the quality of language and early literacy instruction provided to children in prekindergarten programs is often in the low to moderate range (Guo, Sawyer, Justice, & Kaderavek, 2013; Justice, Mashburn, Hamre & Pianta, 2008). Unfortunately, this appears to hold true across all types of programs, including those focused on children who are at risk who attend state-funded pre-K programs, Head Start, Title 1 programs, and tuition-based programs as well as those that include children with special needs (Maxwell et al., 2009).

Instructional Support for Early Literacy

Research about quality of instruction has focused on what teachers are doing to support learning in general and specifically how instruction has been designed to foster literacy and language and how instruction has affected child engagement. Observational studies using the CLASS Pre-K (Pianta, La Paro, & Hamre, 2008) have reported that instructional support levels are often well below the midpoint on a 7-point subscale (e.g., Cabell, Justice, Konold, & McGinty, 2011). In a study carried out by the Center for Response to Intervention in Early Childhood (CRTIEC) across 65 classrooms in 4 states, the observed levels of instructional support for programs with language and early literacy goals averaged only 2.5, a full point below the midpoint on this CLASS subscale (Carta et al., 2016). This means that, on average, teachers often failed to provide opportunities to develop children's more complex language, to promote children's thinking and problem solving, and to use feedback to deepen children's knowledge and skills.

Research also has revealed that too often teachers spend very little classroom time providing children with language and literacy experiences. Some studies have attempted to quantify the amount of teacher-provided language and literacy instruction with a construct called Teacher Literacy Focus (TLF; e.g., Powell & Diamond, 2011).

TLF in prekindergarten programs can be defined by the occurrence of teacher talk about the names of things (vocabulary), letters (alphabet), sounds in words (phonological awareness), reading of letters and words, and concepts such as categories and comparisons (comprehension). In the CRTIEC observational study described previously, the Classroom Code for Interactive Recording of Children's Literacy Environments (CIRCLE; Atwater et al., 2012) was used to assess the actual time teachers spent implementing activities with a specific focus on literacy and language. Across the 65 classrooms in the CRTIEC study, the average observed time in activities with TLF was surprisingly low—only 16% of total observed time (Greenwood et al., 2013). This finding of limited exposure to early literacy/language in preschool is concerning because research has clearly demonstrated that classroom time devoted to quality language and literacy instruction is highly related to children's growth on critical skills for later academic success: comprehension, phonological awareness, and alphabet knowledge (Justice, Chow, Capellini, Flanigan, & Colton, 2003; van Kleeck, Vander Woude, & Hammett, 2006).

Children's Academic Engagement

In addition to instructional support and TLF, another important indicator of Tier 1 quality is the level of children's academic engagement in response to instruction. Academic engagement is participation in learning and academic-related tasks and involves active behaviors such as talking with the teacher about a literacy activity in a center, asking questions, reading or looking at books, carrying out science-related activities, and doing a counting game with a peer, among other behaviors. (Finn & Zimmer, 2012; Fredricks, Blumenfeld, & Paris, 2004). Clearly, if children are to learn the language and preacademic skills being taught, then they need to interact with and practice using those skills within activities. Research documents that children who spend more time actively engaged in literacy-focused activities such as learning letters and sounds, oral language development, and shared book reading realized better academic outcomes compared to children who were observed engaging in free play (Powell & Diamond, 2011). When teachers increase the amount of TLF instruction, children's active academic engagement increases and this results in greater growth in their literacy outcomes (Greenwood, Abbott, Beecher, Atwater, & Petersen, 2016).

Some research has shown that children's engagement varies widely depending on how teachers arrange classroom activities within settings. Downer, Rimm-Kaufman, and Pianta (2007) reported that children were more likely to be engaged when in small-group instruction compared to large-group activities, individualized work settings, and basic skills instruction. The CRTIEC observational study discovered that in many classrooms, the largest proportion of the classroom daily schedule was taken up with activities that were the least likely to set the stage for children's engagement. For example, center time took up an average of 45% of the observed prime time for instruction, but within this very common activity, children were actively engaged only 15% of the time. On the other hand, during storytime (which on average took up only 7% of the observation time), children were engaged 87% of the time.

What accounts for these differences in TLF and children's active engagement can be explained by the interactions that teachers plan, initiate, and maintain with children in the classroom (Chien et al., 2010; Downer et al., 2007; Mashburn, 2008; McGinty, Breit-Smith, Justice, Kaderavek, & Fan, 2012; McGinty, Justice, Piasta, &

Kaderavek, 2011). More research is clearly needed on ways teachers can arrange classroom activities and their instructional interactions to optimize children's engagement in ways that promote children's acquisition of critical skills (Burchinal et al., 2008; Diamond, Justice, Siegler, & Snyder, 2013). Similarly, programs need to study how well their Tier 1 instructional practices are setting the stage for children's active responding and paving the way to their success in literacy.

WHAT OBSTACLES DO PROGRAMS FACE IN IMPLEMENTING HIGH-QUALITY TIER 1?

If knowledge about the important ingredients for promoting children's school readiness in Tier 1 are readily available, why aren't those ingredients being implemented more consistently and more frequently in America's preschools? Consider the following two reasons: First, programs have difficulty finding evidence-based curricula to support children's early literacy and language skills. Second, even when programs have strong curricula, they often lack the resources for the type of intensive professional development that will lead to high-fidelity implementation of the instructional practices that will promote learning and children's engagement. Each of these challenges will be discussed below.

Curriculum: Making Sure the Content of Instruction Is Sound

The cornerstone of Tier 1 is the curriculum—the substance of what teachers will teach and the content that children are expected to learn. In spite of the fundamental importance of curriculum, knowledge about which curricula are most effective and how to select from those available are still elusive to most programs. Important considerations a program might ask in choosing a curriculum include: 1) Does it align with our values, goals, and learning standards? 2) Does it mesh with sociocultural and individual characteristics of our student population? 3) Is it comprehensive in covering the goals and standards? 4) Does it square with the values and wishes of families and the communities we serve? and 5) Does it address the most important predictors of learning and development? (National Association for the Education of Young Children [NAEYC] & National Association of Early Childhood Specialists in State Departments of Education [NAECS-SDE], 2003).

While the first of these considerations will need to be addressed through programs' self-assessment and reflection, the last consideration can be addressed through knowledge of what the research says are the most important skills that predict later academic success. The literature points to the skills that most clearly predict later reading outcomes (Diamond et al., 2013; Dickinson, 2011; Shanahan & Lonigan, 2008). Phonological awareness, phonological memory, rapid automatic naming (of letters, digits, objects, and colors), alphabet knowledge, and writing are all strong predictors of reading in the early elementary grades (Eunice Kennedy Shriver National Institute of Child Health and Human Development, 2010). These and other skills related to later reading ability, such as concepts about print, print knowledge, oral language, and visual processing, all are critical aspects of children's early literacy experiences in preschool. The extent that these are an explicit focus in preschool curricula has been quite variable and often limited (Powell & Diamond, 2011). Therefore, when programs assess the quality of Tier 1 in their programs, they should assess whether these skills are a focus of the curriculum and whether children receive adequate opportunity to learn and practice these skills.

Some good resources exist to help programs learn about the strength of research evidence behind various curricula. Among these resources are the Preschool Curriculum Evaluation Research Initiative (Preschool Curriculum Evaluation Research Consortium, 2008) and the What Works Clearinghouse web site (2016). In each of these resources, comparative information is provided about the amount and strength of the evidence behind many curricula aimed at prekindergarten children.

One more recent guide, developed by the National Center on Quality Teaching and Learning (NCQTL; 2015), provides a comprehensive approach to evaluating and comparing curricula. The approach taken by this guide allows a program to compare whether it has clearly defined learning goals, is evidence-based and has demonstrated effects on child outcomes, follows an organized scope and sequence (i.e., whether it covers each critical domain in a sequenced progressive manner), includes well-designed and engaging activities, provides teachers with guidance on how to engage in high-quality interactions, and gives teachers supports for individualizing instruction as well as other considerations. Each of these resources will provide programs with helpful guides for making informed decisions when making curriculum choices.

Implementing Evidence-Based Instructional Practices

While a sound curriculum provides the content of instruction, the instructional practices define how the teaching of that content will take place. Teams that are evaluating Tier 1 in their programs need to attend to both aspects of instruction. Although many early education programs may have the goal of helping children become actively engaged in learning new concepts and skills, they often fail to check on whether teachers are implementing the types of instructional practices that result in children's active engagement in learning. Programs seeking to build a high-quality Tier 1 should be aware that some instructional strategies are more likely to promote children's engagement and learning than others, and teachers may need systematic coaching in learning these effective instructional practices.

How does a program identify which instructional practices will actually work in its setting and result in meaningful change? A few key principles are helpful in identifying potent instructional strategies for young children: 1) they should be research-based or demonstrated to promote learning, 2) they should be engaging and developmentally appropriate, 3) they should be easy for teachers to implement and acceptable to them, and 4) they should be embedded throughout the classroom day and thus increase children's learning opportunities.

Instructional practices that adhere to these principles are those referred to as "explicit instruction" (Archer & Hughes, 2011). Explicit instruction makes it clear to students what they are being asked to do within a lesson and what it looks like when accomplished (Phillips, Menchetti, & Lonigan, 2008). For example, when teaching the concept of compound words, explicit instruction might first *define* the concept (e.g., "compound words are made up of two words that you put together to make a new word"); then *model and explain* (e.g., when I put "butter" and "fly" together, they make the word "butterfly"); and finally provide *guided practice* with feedback, followed with supported practice, then independent practice (Archer & Hughes, 2011). Specific feedback, one of the components of guided practice, is most effective when it occurs immediately after the child produces the desired behavior and helps the child know what he or she is doing right. Explicit instructional procedures that incorporate these features have been found to result in more growth than implicit instruction when applied to phonological awareness (Bailet, Repper, Murphy, Piasta, & Zetter-Greeley, 2013; Koutsoftas, Harmon, & Gray, 2009) and vocabulary (Marulis & Neuman, 2010).

Other aspects of explicit teaching critical for promoting learning include careful sequencing of instruction, pacing, and delivery of intervention. Also, narrowing the focus of instruction within sessions by limiting the instruction to one or two specific skills makes the learning task easier for children and reduces memory demands. One final aspect of explicit teaching is the incorporation of planned redundancy or systematic review (Phillips et al., 2008). Children need many opportunities to practice newly acquired skills to gain mastery in them. When teachers plan to teach a specific skill, concept, or vocabulary word, they need to be sure to plan instruction on those elements so that they occur at various times of the day as well as within an ongoing cycle across the year and across multiple settings. In that way, children are much more likely to generalize and become fluent in the targeted skill.

Ensuring That Effective Practices Are Implemented With Fidelity

Although teachers may plan to implement specific effective instructional practices throughout the classroom day, the likelihood that they will be consistently implemented with the intended frequency as indicated on a lesson plan is not very high. If instructional practices are truly going to make a difference in promoting children's learning, teachers need to carry through and implement them, and programs need to ascertain whether this happens. There are a variety of ways programs can gather information related to how well practices are being implemented. First, using a self-assessment measure, teachers can reflect on and report whether they implemented the practices they had planned. An example of this is the Tune-Up Checklist (Appendix 5.A; Abbott, Knoche, Petersen, & Payette, 2012). The Tune-Up-Checklist is a list of questions that prompts teachers to self-assess how they have engaged in a set of instructional practices that maximize children's early literacy and language skills such as arranging the content of instruction, maximizing opportunities to learn specific skills, grouping children for instruction, and providing accommodations for children who have special needs or who are dual language learners. The Tune-Up Checklist can be the basis for teachers' self-reflection or can be the basis for targeting goals for coaching.

Besides using a tool that allows teachers to report on their use of instructional practices, programs need an objective means of measuring how well teachers implement these practices or adhere to the instructional practices as designed. For example, one specific intervention for promoting language, called IDEAS (Abbott, Greenwood, Beecher, Petersen, & Payette, 2012), incorporates five specific steps for giving children explicit instruction, modeling, and feedback. IDEAS is an acronym for each of the five steps: 1) *Identify* the word using "I do it" (modeling), "We do it" (guided practice), and "You do it"; 2) *Define* the word; 3) *Explain* the word further and give examples; 4) *Ask* a comprehension question such as "When do you use a _____?"; and 5) *Say* it again (have the child repeat the word). Implementation coaches would use a strategy-specific checklist with each of the five steps scored as being either *not implemented* (scored 0), *partially implemented* (scored 1), or *fully implemented* (scored 2). Using a checklist like this, a coach could calculate a fidelity score for each observed IDEAS instructional session (representing the percentage of implementation) by adding the total number of points for each session, dividing that number by the total possible, and dividing the total possible by 100. Higher levels of fidelity of instructional strategies, or "adherence," are usually associated with better student outcomes (e.g., Durlak & DuPre, 2008). Doing occasional spot checks on fidelity of implementation of specific instructional strategies would give programs some assurances that children are receiving high-quality instructional practices. See Video 3 for an example of a leadership team discussing IDEAS.

One additional related factor that may pose a barrier to providing children with effective Tier 1 instruction has to do with the dosage or amount of evidence-based practices a child receives. Even with the best of intentions, the amount of instruction that is planned is not always delivered. Unforeseen, real-world events, such as field trips, holiday parties, special interventions needed for addressing children's challenging behaviors, and so forth, are likely to occur even in well-organized classrooms. Therefore, another factor that should be considered related to dosage of instruction received by individual children has to do with their attendance or presence in the classroom to receive the evidence-based practice (Wasik, Mattera, Lloyd, & Boller, 2013). For example, if a child has a chronic illness and misses class on 30% of the scheduled class days, his or her optimal amount of exposure or dosage to the instructional practices may only be 70%.

**Universal Screening and Progress Monitoring:
Checking to See if Children Are Responding to Effective Instruction**

Even when a classroom or a child receives the prescribed dosage of evidence-based curriculum using explicit instructional practices with fidelity, it may not be effective. Some children may need to be taught some other skills prior to engaging in the curriculum (e.g., they may need to learn some behavioral expectations regarding sitting in one's chair and attending to the teacher; McElhattan, 2014). For this reason, implementation of evidence-based instruction should always be accompanied by ongoing assessment or progress monitoring to see whether a child (or a class) is responding to the instruction.

Ongoing progress monitoring of all children in the class allows teachers to determine whether instruction has resulted in student learning or growth. Having some system to regularly monitor children's progress is a means of determining on a frequent basis whether children are acquiring key skills. Conducting regular progress monitoring like this allows for "mid-course corrections," or changes, in how and what is taught to the class as well as how instruction is implemented with individual students to maximize learning. This type of frequent assessment calls for measures that are quick and easy for teachers to carry out. These ongoing progress checks can also be opportunities for children to practice skills and obtain corrective feedback on skills being targeted during lessons.

As mentioned in Chapter 4, various types of data should be collected to examine whether the curriculum and instruction being provided is making a difference at the program, classroom, and individual child levels. At the program level, universal screening data should be gathered to indicate how well students are performing relative to national or local norms. This information will provide the program with clues about how to adjust its core curriculum in Tier 1. Programwide or classwide data on universal screening measures can indicate the percentage of students who are meeting national norms in specific domains (e.g., language, phonological awareness, numeracy, social-emotional skills). This information can help provide a leadership team with information on whether the planned core curriculum is adequate. See Video 3 for an example of how a leadership team uses programwide universal screening data to see how well Tier 1 is working.

Programs may need to decide whether their entire curriculum needs supplementing in certain areas to strengthen universal instruction. For instance, does more time need to be devoted to instruction or does more opportunity for explicit instruction need to be provided over and above what the core curriculum prescribes? Baseline universal screening data may also indicate that a few children in each classroom are not meeting local or national norms. Information such as this can help a team decide that supplemental Tier 2 or Tier 3 interventions are needed for small groups of children or individuals. Measures useful for this purpose in areas such as early literacy and language are Individual Growth and Development Indicators (IGDIs; McConnell & Missall, 2008) and the Preschool Early Literacy Indicators (PELI; Kaminski et al., 2014). These measures can help a program determine whether the majority of children are not showing progress in Tier 1 or whether a few children in each class are not demonstrating growth in response to the core curriculum being provided. If the data reveal a widespread lack of growth on progress-monitoring measures, the program leadership team should take a careful look at how to enhance their Tier 1. If a few children are failing to respond to Tier 1, extra support should be given to them in the form of a Tier 2 intervention to help increase their rates of growth. When changes like this are made either programwide or with individual children, progress-monitoring measures should continue to be used so that changes in rates of growth can be documented that result from these changes.

HOW CAN PROGRAMS SUPPORT THE HIGH-QUALITY IMPLEMENTATION OF TIER 1?

A critical aspect of ensuring and maintaining high-quality implementation of Tier 1 is the use of evidence-based approaches to professional development for enhancing teachers' skills. If teachers are to learn and implement Tier 1 curriculum and instructional practices with fidelity, the program needs to commit to coaching on content-specific skills or practices. Coaching can be carried out in a number of different ways: through the use of experts or consultants, peers or fellow learners, or even through one's self (self-reflection). Coaching strategies known to promote active learning include role playing, modeling, providing detailed action plans for carrying out lessons, observing teachers and providing specific feedback on practices, and providing scaffolding that builds on teachers' strengths and current knowledge.

Practice-based coaching (PBC) is "a cyclical process for supporting effective teaching practices that lead to positive outcomes for children" (Snyder, Hemmeter, & Fox, 2015, p. 134). PBC occurs within the context of a partnership between teacher and coach and aims to provide support for a teacher's implementation of evidence-based practice. PBC involves three specific components: "shared goals and action planning, focused observation, and reflection and feedback" (p. 134). This approach to coaching clearly defines the role of coach and trainee and makes the goals and expectations clear to each partner in the coaching relationship. What is noteworthy about PBC is that it was based on a thorough review of the coaching literature (see Snyder et al., 2012) and that the literature shows that it is effective for improving outcomes for teachers such as higher fidelity of implementation of practices and curricula, as well as improved outcomes for children (e.g., engagement, early literacy, language, social skills). Using a systematic approach to professional development such as PBC will assist programs is achieving and sustaining the quality of Tier 1 that they are hoping to achieve to improve learning for all children in the classroom.

CONCLUSION

The starting point to providing high-quality educational experiences in early literacy and language to all children is ensuring that a strong foundation is in place—an evidence-based Tier 1 curriculum that is implemented with fidelity. This chapter reviews the critical aspects of implementing Tier 1 and describes the steps a program might take to examine the strength of their core curriculum, its implementation, and how well children are responding to it. The chapter describes the challenges that programs often face in implementing high-quality Tier 1 instruction. It offers tools and resources that programs can use for examining and strengthening their Tier 1 early literacy and language practices and describes an evidence-based coaching model that can be used to support teaching staff in implementing high-quality practices.

When the leadership team at Maplewood School carried out the steps to gather the multiple sources of information about Tier 1 in their program, they learned that they had many strengths on which to build an MTSS approach to their program. Their curriculum was evidence-based, and for the most part, it was being implemented with fidelity. When they took a close look at their curriculum using the rubric contained in the Language and Literacy Preschool Curriculum Consumer Report (NCQTL, 2015), they discovered that it covered the language and vocabulary domains well but failed to address phonological awareness, alphabet knowledge, and print concepts—all of which are important predictors of later reading success. They needed to develop two different sets of strategies: one for strengthening Tier 1 in language/vocabulary, and the other for strengthening early literacy/phonological awareness. In language, for example, when they looked at programwide data from the universal screener, they began to see that the students' overall vocabulary performance was below the targeted level. Moreover, students who started out below the targeted level in knowledge of words and their meanings were not closing the word gap, so the team weighed several options to provide a more robust, vocabulary-building experience in their classrooms. They looked at the curriculum and felt that the evidence-based skill scope and sequence was appropriate; however, they needed to bolster the instructional methodology for teaching the targeted skills. They added the IDEAS strategy to their Tier 1; a mentor teacher served as a coach to provide training and then embedded professional development.

Examining Tier 1 in early literacy, however, revealed a somewhat different picture. Universal screening of children in phonological awareness revealed about 30% of children not meeting benchmarks in this domain across almost all classrooms. This was not surprising given that phonological awareness was not being addressed in the core curriculum. Also, classroom observations using CIRCLE (Atwater et al., 2012) revealed a low level of literacy-focused instruction and children actively engaged in literacy activities. After a few weeks of searching, the leadership team found a focused phonological awareness (PA) curriculum that they could use to supplement their core curriculum. The curriculum was evidence-based and included fun, developmentally appropriate activities that teachers found acceptable and usable because they could be easily integrated into their existing core literacy and language. They felt that they would be able to embed many instructional activities throughout the day and increase children's opportunities to learn PA skills. In summary, the team felt that the time and effort it took to examine all of the different facets of Tier 1 (i.e., the strength of the curriculum and its domains, the fidelity and frequency with which teachers were implementing instructional procedures associated with the curriculum, and the universal screening of all children on key domain areas) were all well worth it. Coming together to reflect on these different sets of data describing the various facets of Tier 1 gave them a clear picture of what was needed to strengthen their program so that all of their children would receive a more effective foundation in the skills needed for later academic success.

RESOURCES

Archer, A., & Hughes, C. (2011). *Explicit instruction: Effective and efficient teaching.* New York, NY: Guilford Press.

Eunice Kennedy Shriver National Institute of Child Health and Human Development, National Institutes of Health, Department of Health and Human Services. (2010). *Developing early literacy: Report of the National Early Literacy Panel (NA).* Washington, DC: U.S. Government Printing Office.

National Association for the Education of Young Children (NAEYC) & National Association of Early Childhood Specialists in State Departments of Education (NAECS-SDE). (2003). *Guidelines for appropriate curriculum content and assessment in programs serving children ages 3 through 8.* Joint position statement. Washington, DC: NAEYC.

National Center on Quality Teaching and Learning (NCQTL). (2015). *Language and literacy preschool curriculum consumer report.* Retrieved from Head Start: An Office of the Administration for Children and Families Early Childhood Learning & Knowledge Center's web site: https://eclkc.ohs.acf.hhs.gov/hslc/tta-system/teaching/docs/curriculum-report-ll.pdf

What Works Clearinghouse Report on Early Childhood (Pre-K) Curriculum. (2016). Retrieved from http://ies.ed.gov/ncee/wwc/FWW/Results?filters=,Pre-K

REFERENCES

Abbott, M., Beecher, C., Petersen, S., Greenwood, C. R., & Atwater, J. (2016). A team-approach to data-driven decision-making literacy instruction in preschool classrooms: Child assessment and intervention through classroom teach self-reflection. *Young Exceptional Children, 37,* 1–13. doi:10.1177/109625061560229

Abbott, M., Greenwood, C. R., Beecher, C., Petersen, S., & Payette, C. (2012). *The literacy 3D top 10 strategies for improving tier 1 instruction: IDEAS*. Kansas City: University of Kansas, Juniper Gardens Children's Project.

Abbott, M., Knoche, L., Petersen, S., & Payette, C. (2012). *The tune-up checklist: A data-driven, decision-making tool to facilitate preschool teacher/coach discussions about making literacy/oral language strategies more intensive by modifying instruction*. Kansas City: University of Kansas.

Archer, A., & Hughes, C. (2011). *Explicit instruction: Effective and efficient teaching*. New York, NY: Guilford Press.

Atwater, J. B., Reynolds, L. H., Schiefelbusch, J., Lee, Y., Montagna, D., & Tapia, Y. (2012). *Classroom CIRCLE: Classroom code for interactive recording of children's learning environments (version 2.0)*. Kansas City: University of Kansas, Juniper Gardens Children's Project.

Bailet, L. L., Repper, K., Murphy, S., Piasta, S., & Zetter-Greeley, C. (2013). Emergent literacy intervention for prekindergarteners at risk for reading failure: Years 2 and 3 of a multiyear study. *Journal of Learning Disabilities, 46*, 133–153. doi:10.1177/0022219411407925

Burchinal, M., Howes, C., Pianta, R., Bryant, D., Early, D., . . . Barbarin, O. (2008). Predicting child outcomes at the end of kindergarten from the quality of pre-kindergarten teacher-child interactions and instruction. *Applied Development Science, 12*, 140–153.

Cabell, S. Q., Justice, L. M., Konold, T. R., & McGinty, A. S. (2011). Profiles of emergent literacy skills among preschool children who at risk for academic difficulties. *Early Childhood Research Quarterly, 26*, 1–14.

Carta, J. J., Greenwood, C. R., Goldstein, H., McConnell, S., Kaminski, R., Bradfield, T., . . . Atwater, J. (2016). Advances in multi-tiered systems of support for prekindergarten children: Lessons learned from 5 years of research and development from the Center for Response to Intervention in Early Childhood. In M. K. Jimerson, A. M. Burns, & A. M. VanDerHeyden (Eds.), *The handbook of Response to Intervention: The science and practice of multi-tiered systems of support* (2nd ed., pp. 587–606). New York, NY: Springer.

Chien, N. C., Howes, C., Burchinal, M., Pianta, R., Ritchie, S., Bryant, D. M., . . . Barbarin, O. A. (2010). Children's classroom engagement and school readiness gains in prekindergarten. *Child Development, 8*, 1534–1549.

Diamond, K. E., Justice, L. M., Siegler, R. S., & Snyder, P. A. (2013). *Synthesis of IES research on early intervention and early childhood education* (NCSER 2013-3001). Retrieved from http://ies.ed.gov/ncser/pubs/20133001/pdf/20133001.pdf

Dickinson, D. K. (2011). Teachers' language practices and academic outcomes of preschool children. *Science*, 333.

Downer, J. T., Rimm-Kaufman, S., & Pianta, R. (2007). How do classroom conditions and children's risk for school problems contribute to children's engagement in learning? *School Psychology Review, 36*, 413–433.

Durlak, J. A., & DuPre, E. P. (2008). Implementation matters: A review of research on the influence of implementation on program outcomes and the factors affecting implementation. *American Journal of Community Psychology, 41*, 327–350.

Eunice Kennedy Shriver National Institute of Child Health and Human Development, NIH, DHHS. (2010). *Developing early literacy: Report of the National Early Literacy Panel (NA)*. Washington, DC: U.S. Government Printing Office.

Finn, J. D., & Zimmer, K. S. (2012). Student engagement: What is it? Why does it matter? In S. L. Christenson, A. L. Reschly, & C. Wylie (Eds.), *Handbook of research on student engagement* (pp. 97–131). New York, NY: Springer. http://dx.doi.org/10.1007/978-1-4614-2018-7_5

Foorman, B. R., Francis, D. J., Fletcher, J. M., Schatschneider, C., & Mehta, P. (1998). The role of instruction in learning to read: Preventing reading disabilities in at-risk children. *Journal of Educational Psychology, 90*, 37–55.

Fredricks, J. A., Blumenfeld, P. C., & Paris, A. H. (2004). School engagement: Potential of the concept, state of the evidence. *Review of Educational Research, 74*(1), 59–109. http://dx.doi.org/10.3102/00346543074001059

Greenwood, C. R., Abbott, M., Beecher, C., Atwater, J., & Petersen, S. (2016). Development, validation, and evaluation of literacy 3D: A package supporting tier 1 preschool literacy instruction implementation and intervention. *Topics in Early Childhood Special Education*, 1–13. doi:10.1177/0271121416652103

Greenwood, C. R., Carta, J. J., Atwater, J., Goldstein, H., Kaminski, R., & McConnell, S. R. (2013). Is a Response to Intervention (RTI) approach to preschool language and early literacy instruction needed? *Topics in Early Childhood Special Education, 33*(1), 48–64.

Guo, Y., Sawyer, B. E., Justice, L., & Kaderavek, J. (2013). Quality of the literacy environment in inclusive early childhood special education classrooms. *Journal of Early Intervention, 34*(1), 40–69.

Justice L. M., Chow, S. M., Capellini, C., Flanigan, K., & Colton, S. (2003). Emergent literacy intervention for vulnerable preschoolers: Relative effects of two approaches. *American Journal of Speech-Language Pathology, 12*, 320–332.

Justice, L. M., Mashburn, A., Hamre, B., & Pianta, R. (2008). Quality of language and literacy instruction in preschool classrooms serving at-risk pupils. *Early Childhood Research Quarterly, 23*(1), 51–68. http://doi.org/10.1016/j.ecresq.2007.09.004

Kaminski, R. A., Abbott, M., Bravo Aguayo, K., Latimer, R., & Good, R. H. (2014). The Preschool Early Literacy Indicators: Validity and benchmark goals. *Topics in Early Childhood Special Education, 34*, 71–82.

Koutsoftas, A. D., Harmon, M. T., & Gray, S. (2009). The effect of Tier 2 intervention for phonemic awareness in a response to intervention model in low-income preschool classrooms. *Language, Speech, and Hearing Services in Schools, 40*, 116–130.

Marulis, L. M., & Neuman, S. B. (2010). The effects of vocabulary intervention on young children's word learning: A meta-analysis. *Review of Educational Research, 80*, 300–335.

Mashburn, A. (2008). Evidence for creating, expanding, designing, and improving high-quality preschool programs. In L. M. Justice & C. Vukelich (Eds.), *Achieving excellence in preschool literacy instruction* (pp. 5–24). New York, NY: Guilford.

Maxwell, K. L., Early, D. M., Bryant, D., Kraus, S., Hume, K., & Crawford, G. (2009). *Georgia study of early care and education: Findings from Georgia's pre-k program*. Chapel Hill, NC: The University of North Carolina at Chapel Hill, FPG Child Development Institute.

McConnell, S. R., & Missall, K. N. (2008). Best practices in monitoring progress for preschool children. In A. Thomas & J. Grimes (Eds.), *Best practices in school psychology* (5th ed., pp. 561–573). Washington, DC: National Association of School Psychologists.

McElhattan, T. (2014). *The influence of preschool teachers' implementation behavior on children's engagement and literacy growth within a phonological awareness intervention* (Unpublished doctoral dissertation). University of Kansas, Lawrence, KS.

McGinty, A. S., Breit-Smith, A., Justice, L. M., Kaderavek, J., & Fan, X. (2012). Does intensity matter? Preschoolers' print knowledge development within a classroom-based intervention. *Early Childhood Research Quarterly, 26*, 255–267.

McGinty, A. S., Justice, L. M., Piasta, S. B., & Kaderavek, J. N. (2011). Does context matter? Explicit print instruction during reading varies in its influence by child and classroom factors. *Early Childhood Research Quarterly, 27*, 77–89.

National Association for the Education of Young Children (NAEYC) & National Association of Early Childhood Specialists in State Departments of Education (NAECS-SDE). (2003). *Guidelines for appropriate curriculum content and assessment in programs serving children ages 3 through 8*. Joint position statement. Washington, DC: NAEYC.

National Center on Quality Teaching and Learning (NCQTL). (2015). *Language and literacy preschool curriculum consumer report*. Retrieved from Head Start: An Office of the Administration for Children and Families Early Childhood Learning & Knowledge Center's web site: https://eclkc.ohs.acf.hhs.gov/hslc/tta-system/teaching/docs/curriculum-report-ll.pdf

Phillips, B. M., Menchetti, J. C., & Lonigan, C. J. (2008). Successful phonological awareness instruction with preschool children: Lessons from the classroom. *Topics in Early Childhood Special Education, 28*, 3–17.

Pianta, R., La Paro, K. M., & Hamre, B. K. (2008). *Classroom Assessment Scoring System (CLASS): Manual Pre-K*. Baltimore, MD: Paul H. Brookes Publishing Co.

Powell, D. R., & Diamond, K. E. (2011). Improving the outcomes of coaching-based professional development interventions. In S. B. Neuman & D. K. Dickinson (Eds.), *Handbook of early literacy research* (Vol. 3, pp. 295–307). New York, NY: Guilford.

Preschool Curriculum Evaluation Research Consortium. (2008). *Effects of preschool curriculum programs on school readiness* (NCER 2008–2009). Washington, DC: U.S. Government Printing Office.

Shanahan, T., & Lonigan, C. J. (2008). *Developing early literacy: A report of the National Early Literacy Panel.* Retrieved from https://lincs.ed.gov/publications/pdf/NELPReport09.pdf

Snyder, P., Hemmeter, M. L., Artman, K., Kinder, K., Pasia, C., & McLaughlin, T. (2012). Characterizing key features of the early childhood professional development literature. *Infants and Young Children, 25,* 188–212.

Snyder, P., Hemmeter, M. L., & Fox, L. (2015). Supporting implementation of evidence-based practices through practice-based coaching. *Topics in Early Childhood Special Education, 35,* 133–143.

van Kleeck, A., Vander Woude, J., & Hammett, L. A. (2006). Fostering literal and inferential language skills in Head Start preschoolers with language impairment using scripted book-sharing discussions. *American Journal of Speech-Language Pathology, 15,* 85–95.

Wasik, B. A., Mattera, S. K., Lloyd, C. M., & Boller, K. (2013). *Intervention dosage in early childhood care and education: It's complicated* (OPRE Research Brief OPRE 2013-15). Washington, DC: Office of Planning, Research and Evaluation, Administration for Children and Families, U.S. Department of Health and Human Services.

What Works Clearinghouse Report on Early Childhood (Pre-K) Curriculum. (2016). Retrieved from http://ies.ed.gov/ncee/wwc/FWW/Results?filters=,Pre-K

Appendix 5A

Tune-Up Checklist

Date goal complete: _____

Teachers: _____ Coach: _____ Date: _____
School: _____ Area of need: PA   PAK   V/OL   COMP

Reflection Questions			
Content of Instruction	Circle One		Notes
Is there a specific skill within the area of need to be targeted?	YES	NO	
Is there an established classroom routine to teach this skill?	YES	NO	
Is there an opportunity to re-teach the skill?	YES	NO	
Is there a pre-skill that the children need to learn?	YES	NO	
Can instruction be more concrete with physical objects incorporated?	YES	NO	
Opportunities to Learn			
Does lesson plan/instruction provide many opportunities to respond?	YES	NO	
Can the skill be emphasized during another part of the day?	YES	NO	
Are transitions being utilized as learning opportunities?	YES	NO	
Is there specific instructional planning for Center Time?	YES	NO	
Are small groups being utilized to teach this skill?	YES	NO	
Grouping for Instruction			
Are children grouped appropriately for instruction?	YES	NO	
Can grouping sizes be changed?	YES	NO	
Explicitness of Instruction			
Is it possible to include more I do it/we do it/you do it?	YES	NO	
Can child response be changed (choral and group responding)?	YES	NO	
Are there opportunities to better monitor accuracy of child responses and then provide immediate, appropriate, positive feedback?	YES	NO	
Language Challenge (LC) Considerations			
Is there strong enough emphasis of LC strategies throughout the day?	YES	NO	
Can children be regrouped to better fit their LC need?	YES	NO	
Are there specific key words/phases that the teacher can learn and use to facilitate understanding?	YES	NO	

Note: LC = Language Challenge; PA = Phonological Awareness; PAK = Print/Alphabet Knowledge; V/OL = Vocabulary, Oral Language; COMP = Comprehension

Goal: _____
_____
_____
_____
_____
_____
_____

Abbott, M., Knoche, L., Beecher, C. C., Petersen, S., & Payette, C. (2012). *The Tune-Up Checklist*. Kansas City, KS: University of Kansas, Juniper Gardens Children's Project. Reprinted with permission. All rights reserved.

6

Designing and Implementing Tier 2 Instructional Support in Early Literacy and Language

Arnold Olszewski, Christa Haring, Xigrid T. Soto, Lindsey Peters-Sanders, and Howard Goldstein

Martin is a 5-year-old boy who has attended preschool since he was 3 years old. He will be eligible to start kindergarten next year. He is a very friendly, well-behaved child. On the surface, Martin seems to be developing quite well, and his parents and teachers have little cause for concern. Although Martin started talking a bit later than his siblings and other children his age, his social-emotional development is age appropriate. He has established friendships with his peers, and he expresses himself appropriately. Martin's preschool teacher utilized curriculum-based language and literacy assessments in the classroom and found his scores to be slightly below his peers. For example, he can name only a few letters of the alphabet, whereas his peers can name 15. He is unable to write letters in his name, although most of his peers can write the first letter of their names, and many of them can write their whole names. He struggles with identifying rhyming words, although most of his peers can produce rhymes on their own. Martin rarely uses new words, whereas many of the children in the classroom use vocabulary from the classroom curriculum during daily activities. His teacher assumes he will catch up once he begins kindergarten.

The research reported here was supported by the Institute of Education Sciences, U.S. Department of Education, through Grant R324A150132 to the University of South Florida. The opinions expressed are those of the authors and do not represent views of the Institute or the U.S. Department of Education.

Howard Goldstein is an author of *Story Friends* and *PAth to Literacy*, which are supplemental preschool curricula described in this chapter. He has a financial interest in these products, as he receives royalties from sales of these products through Paul H. Brookes Publishing. This interest has been reviewed by the University in accordance with its Individual Conflict of Interest policy, for the purpose of maintaining the objectivity and the integrity of research at the University of South Florida.

INTRODUCTION

Martin is an example of a child who is an ideal candidate for Tier 2 language and literacy instruction. Preschool is a sensitive period for language and early literacy skills to develop. In fact, developmental trajectories for preschool children often remain fairly stable through the school years (Foster & Miller, 2007), meaning children who fall behind during this period often continue to struggle in later grades. Language and literacy skills in preschool are strong predictors of later reading ability. Even though Martin is performing only slightly below his peers, without appropriate instruction this gap may continue to grow exponentially. By the time Martin is in second grade, he may be at high risk for a reading disability. It is estimated that 30%–35% of preschool children are candidates for supplemental instruction in language and early literacy skills (Carta et al., 2015). Furthermore, 40%–75% of children with preschool language difficulties later develop reading disabilities, often coupled with additional academic problems (Griffin, Burns, & Snow, 1998). This begs the question, "What can be done to prevent reading disabilities in young children?"

Children struggling to master essential curricular skills are ideal candidates for Tier 2 supplemental instruction. In preschool, Tier 2 is defined as a secondary tier of selected instruction for children who may require more or different instruction to meet kindergarten benchmarks (Greenwood et al., 2015). Ideally, providing efficacious supplemental instruction in preschool will reduce the need for remedial services in kindergarten and the later grades. In early childhood settings, Tier 2 is a means of preventing later disabilities through early intervention and progress monitoring. In this chapter, we provide an overview of the language and literacy skills that should be taught in preschool. We discuss the assessment process for identifying children who might need additional instructional support beyond that provided to all children with the general curriculum and then for monitoring children receiving Tier 2 instruction. Then, we highlight effective Tier 2 interventions for language and literacy, including the professional development supports necessary for classroom implementation. Finally, we discuss considerations for implementing Tier 2 instructional supports in preschool classrooms. The assessment and instructional components of Tier 2 supports are also illustrated in Video 4 of the accompanying video series.

EARLY LITERACY SKILLS

The preschool years are a particularly important time for literacy development. To provide the optimal support for children to become skilled readers, it is important to understand what skills form the necessary precursors. "The Simple View of Reading" defines *reading* as the product of decoding and linguistic comprehension (Hoover & Gough, 1990). To become a skilled reader, you must decode letters into words and comprehend the message of those words. Consequently, reading instruction is divided into two skill categories: code-focused and meaning-focused (Whitehurst & Lonigan, 1998). Code-focused skills are related to decoding and include phonological awareness, print awareness, and phonics. Meaning-focused skills include language-based skills such as vocabulary, syntax, and appropriate use of language across contexts. For children to become proficient readers, they must master both categories of skills.

The National Early Literacy Panel (2008) conducted a review of research on precursors to reading and identified a set of preschool skills that are correlated with later conventional reading. These skills include phonological awareness, phonological memory, rapid automatic naming (of letters, digits, objects, and colors), alphabet knowledge, and writing. In addition, the panel conceptualized other skills that, although not directly correlated, are related to later reading ability: concepts about print, print knowledge, reading readiness, oral language, and visual processing. Weaknesses in one or more of these areas are associated with later reading difficulties in the school years.

There are notable achievements in language and literacy development that occur during preschool. For example, children often begin to learn letter names and sounds, start to associate print with language, exhibit shallow phonological awareness skills (e.g., recognizing rhymes, counting syllables, blending sounds, segmenting words), explore decontextualized language, and begin using compound and complex sentence structures (Pence Turnbull & Justice, 2011). Some organizations have set forth benchmarks for kindergarten readiness. For example, the 2015 Head Start Early Learning Outcomes Framework sets out benchmarks across five domains necessary for later success (Office of Head Start, 2015). Examples of benchmarks in the language and literacy domain include recognizing and using simple words, phrases, and sentences; demonstrating joint attention; asking a variety of questions; understanding at least 300 words; categorizing words; demonstrating the proper way to hold a book and turn pages; naming 18 uppercase and 15 lowercase letters; demonstrating narrative structure in storytelling/retelling; and imitating writing. It is important that children enter kindergarten with a solid foundation in these skills.

School readiness skills are often the focus of preschool curricula. Specific school readiness skills include language and early literacy skills, science and numeracy skills, and social-emotional regulation. Arguably, language skills underlie each of these school readiness domains. For example, social skills rely on language, as instruction on emotional regulation strategies often targets vocabulary related to expressing one's desires and feelings. Likewise, numeracy skills are often vocabulary-related and rely on the teaching of basic concepts. Language may be necessary for instruction on all school readiness skills, but the relations among domains may be reciprocal. Exposure to content-area knowledge provides students a contextual framework and vocabulary that may, in turn, foster development of oral language skills and help students practice and generalize skills learned across settings (Dickinson & Darrow, 2013).

Although language and literacy skills are vital and often easy to integrate into various classroom activities, these skills are not taught consistently in preschools (Greenwood et al., 2013). Observational studies of preschool classrooms have indicated that the overall amount of instructional time spent teaching language and early literacy is somewhat low and quite variable across classrooms. On average, preschoolers spend only 16%–30% of instructional time focused on language- or literacy-related activities (Connor, Morrison, & Slominski, 2006; Greenwood et al., 2013; Pelatti, Piasta, Justice, & O'Connell, 2014). The range of instructional time and quality of instruction on these skills varies across different types of programs (e.g. Head Start, tuition-based pre-K, public pre-K; Greenwood et al., 2013). In addition, the time spent focusing on specific language and early literacy skills varies, with more focus on oral language and meaning-focused skills than alphabet or phonological processing and other code-focused skills (Connor et al., 2006). Even within each classroom, children's experiences are quite different, with some children afforded more learning opportunities than others (Pelatti et al., 2014). There is a need for preschool educators to provide consistent instruction across skills such that all children in the classroom are given adequate exposure and opportunities to practice foundational literacy skills.

Although there are many preschool curricula commercially available, these curricula do not ensure that children will have opportunities to practice and acquire all the necessary early literacy skills. For example, many curricula include vocabulary lists; however, they lack specific guidance for teaching vocabulary (Neuman & Dwyer, 2009). That is, they often fail to provide explicit definitions that teachers can use when introducing new words to children. Furthermore, research has found that adhering to a specific curriculum does not necessarily improve the quality of instruction in a classroom (Justice, Mashburn, Hamre, & Pianta, 2008). For example, teachers may ignore evidence-based instructional strategies in lieu of completing activities as prescribed in a curriculum. Therefore, choice of curriculum should not overshadow the importance of high-quality instructional strategies.

Martin, our example child, demonstrates deficits in alphabet skills and vocabulary. This indicates that Martin may need additional support in both code-focused and meaning-focused domains. Within a multi-tiered systems of support (MTSS) framework, it is necessary to utilize more thorough assessment information to determine the best way to support Martin. The following section will describe language and literacy assessments for children in need of Tier 2 supports.

ASSESSMENT

There are two different types of assessment for children who may need Tier 2 supports: 1) universal screening measures to identify children who are falling behind their peers and might benefit from supplementary instruction, and 2) progress-monitoring measures to ascertain whether children are responding to the supplementary instruction. The following section includes a discussion of each type of assessment, including examples and considerations for their use.

Universal screenings throughout the school year should identify children who may need extra instruction to overcome risk factors that put them in jeopardy for reading disabilities. Children at risk for reading disabilities vary in their language and literacy profiles (Cabell, Justice, Konold, & McGinty, 2011). Some children have low oral language skills, with relative strengths in code-focused skills (e.g., phonological awareness, alphabet knowledge, print awareness). Other children may have typically developing oral language skills but may be struggling with code-focused skills. A third group of children may have difficulties in both oral language and code-focused skills. Assessing only one category of skills may obscure some of the reading difficulties children might encounter in the future. Conducting universal screenings of language and literacy skills at different time points throughout the school year may identify children who, without preventative interventions, may develop reading difficulties. The assessment process is critically important because it is integral to the data-based decision-making process (see Chapter 4; McConnell, Wackerle-Hollman, Roloff, & Rodriguez, 2014). Identifying children for Tier 2 supports in preschool may be tricky because a delay may not necessarily mean that the child has not responded to Tier 1 instruction; it may be that the child has had very limited exposure or instruction to a specific set of literacy skills. For example, some children may show delays in code-focused skills because they have had limited instruction in this area. Assessment will determine whether these children respond quickly to Tier 1 instruction or need additional Tier 2 supports.

Once children are identified as needing Tier 2 instruction and begin receiving supplemental instruction, a second type of assessment, progress monitoring, is employed. For example, if Martin were receiving Tier 2 instruction targeting his alphabet knowledge skills, his teacher could monitor the number of letters and sounds he was learning each week. Close monitoring of his performance would determine the extent to which he is benefiting from Tier 2 instruction. Progress-monitoring data of this type help inform decisions about whether children need more or less support in tiered instruction. For example, if weekly assessments of Martin's alphabet knowledge skills indicated he was mastering the letter names taught as a result of Tier 2 instruction, his level of support might be reduced when progress monitoring showed that his performance was on par with that of his peers. Those data may show that Martin no longer needs Tier 2 supports and that he will make adequate progress via Tier 1 instruction. However, if progress-monitoring data reveal that he continues to struggle with learning the letters, this would indicate that he needs more intensive, individualized Tier 3 instruction. Unlike assessments that are conducted once per semester or year, assessments during Tier 2 instruction occur frequently. In fact, progress monitoring should be occurring during lessons with more formal curriculum-based measurement at least once per month. This type of assessment informs educators when Tier 2 instruction is not working for a specific child and when additional support will be needed to help that child succeed.

Figures 6.1 and 6.2 provide examples of using a progress-monitoring assessment for Martin's alphabet skills. The instructor places cards with all the letters of the alphabet on the table and asks Martin to name each letter and produce its corresponding sound. For young children, this can be made more engaging through creative, game-like modifications (e.g., printing the letters on fish-shaped cards and having children "fish" for letters). Using the Alphabet Monitor in Figure 6.1, the instructor can keep track of Martin's progress. This assessment can be quickly administered once per week to document Martin's acquisition of letter names. Data can then be graphed (Figure 6.2) to aid in decision-making regarding instruction. For example, by Week 9, Martin demonstrates consistent proficiency on the measure. At this point, he may no longer require Tier 2 alphabet instruction. However, it is important to continue screening Martin to ensure that he maintains these skills after finishing Tier 2 instruction.

Examples of Early Literacy and Language Measures for MTSS in Early Childhood

A few early literacy and language measures are available for universal screening and progress monitoring of preschoolers. The Dynamic Measurement Group recently developed the *Preschool Early Literacy Indicator* (PELI; Kaminski, Abbott, Bravo Aguayo, Latimer, & Good, 2014). The *PELI* is a storybook-based assessment of alphabet knowledge, vocabulary and oral language, phonological awareness, and listening comprehension developed for 3- to 5-year-old children. The PELI includes research-based benchmark goals for children. It was developed as a universal

Alphabet Monitor

Child's name: _____ Date _____

<u>Directions</u>: Say, "I'm going to show you some letters. I want you to tell me the name of each letter and the sound it makes. Let's try this one first."

- What letter is this? (Testing prompts may be faded if the child responds independently.)
  - If the child doesn't respond after 3 seconds, ask, "**What letter is this?**" If the child doesn't respond after 3 more seconds, say, "**That's ok. Let's try the sound.**"
  - If the child provides the letter sound instead of the name, circle "1" for the letter sound, and say, "**Yes, that's the sound the letter makes. Now, what's the <u>name</u> of the letter?**" If the child provides the letter sound again, say, "**Remember to tell me the <u>name</u> of the letter.**" If the child provides the letter sound again, circle "0" and show the next letter.
- What sound does this letter make?
  - If the child doesn't respond after 3 seconds, ask, "**What sound does this letter make?**" If the child doesn't respond after 3 more seconds, say, "**That's ok. Let's try the next one.**"
  - If the child provides the letter name instead of the sound, circle "1" for the letter name (if necessary), and say, "**Yes, that's the name of the letter. Now, what <u>sound</u> does it make?**" If the child provides the letter name again, say, "**Remember to tell me the <u>sound</u> the letter makes.**" If the child provides the letter name again, circle "0" and show the next letter.

<u>Scoring</u>: Circle "1" if child responded correctly; circle "0" if child responded incorrectly or did not respond.

Letter	Name	Sound
B	1 0	1 0
C	1 0	1 0
T	1 0	1 0
J	1 0	1 0
H	1 0	1 0
D	1 0	1 0
G	1 0	1 0
K	1 0	1 0
Total 1		

Letter	Name	Sound
W	1 0	1 0
F	1 0	1 0
N	1 0	1 0
L	1 0	1 0
P	1 0	1 0
M	1 0	1 0
S	1 0	1 0
R	1 0	1 0
Total 2		
Grand Total		

Figure 6.1a. Progress monitoring blank form.

Multi-Tiered Systems of Support for Young Children: Driving Change in Early Education
by Judith J. Carta and Robin Miller Young.
Copyright © 2019 by Paul H. Brookes Publishing Co., Inc. All rights reserved.

Alphabet Monitor

Child's name: __Martin__ Date __09/12/2017__

Directions: Say, "I'm going to show you some letters. I want you to tell me the name of each letter and the sound it makes. Let's try this one first."

- What letter is this? (Testing prompts may be faded if the child responds independently.)
    - If the child doesn't respond after 3 seconds, ask, "What letter is this?" If the child doesn't respond after 3 more seconds, say, "That's ok. Let's try the sound."
    - If the child provides the letter sound instead of the name, circle "1" for the letter sound, and say, "Yes, that's the sound the letter makes. Now, what's the name of the letter?" If the child provides the letter sound again, say, "Remember to tell me the name of the letter." If the child provides the letter sound again, circle "0" and show the next letter.
- What sound does this letter make?
    - If the child doesn't respond after 3 seconds, ask, "What sound does this letter make?" If the child doesn't respond after 3 more seconds, say, "That's ok. Let's try the next one."
    - If the child provides the letter name instead of the sound, circle "1" for the letter name (if necessary), and say, "Yes, that's the name of the letter. Now, what sound does it make?" If the child provides the letter name again, say, "Remember to tell me the sound the letter makes." If the child provides the letter name again, circle "0" and show the next letter.

Scoring: Circle "1" if child responded correctly; circle "0" if child responded incorrectly or did not respond.

Letter	Name	Sound
B	① 0	① 0
C	① 0	1 ⓪
T	① 0	1 ⓪
J	1 ⓪	1 ⓪
H	1 ⓪	1 ⓪
D	① 0	1 ⓪
G	1 ⓪	1 ⓪
K	① 0	① 0
Total 1	5	2

Letter	Name	Sound
W	1 ⓪	1 ⓪
F	1 ⓪	1 ⓪
N	① 0	1 ⓪
L	1 ⓪	1 ⓪
P	① 0	1 ⓪
M	① 0	① 0
S	1 ⓪	1 ⓪
R	① 0	1 ⓪
Total 2	4	2
Grand Total	9	4

Figure 6.1b. Progress monitoring example.

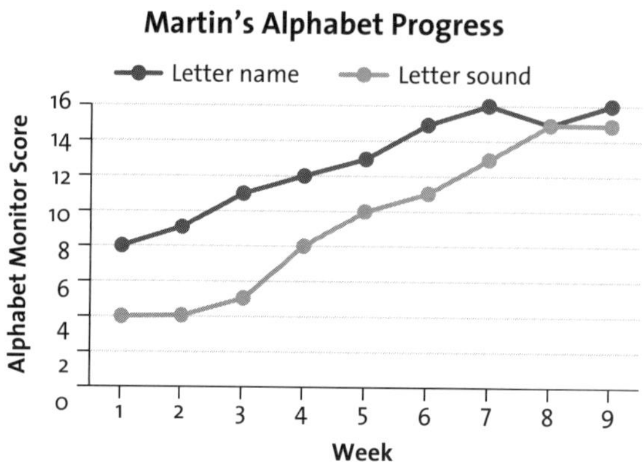

Martin's Alphabet Progress

Figure 6.2. Martin's alphabet progress.

screening tool; thus, it is appropriate for all children in the classroom. Children who do not meet the benchmarks are candidates for Tier 2 instruction.

Another example of a screening and progress-monitoring measure is the *Individualized Growth and Development Indicators of Early Literacy* (IGDIs-EL; McConnell, Bradfield, Wackerle-Hollman, & Rodriguez, 2012). The IGDIs-EL measures language and literacy skills such as vocabulary (picture naming), phonological awareness (alliteration), and alphabet knowledge (sound identification). Scales with established benchmarks are available for universal screening in the fall, winter, and spring sessions to identify children in need of additional supports. Furthermore, IGDIs-EL progress-monitoring measures can be used to monitor children's response to supplemental intervention support. These measures were designed specifically for implementation in an MTSS context. IGDIs-EL is available in English and Spanish (Wackerle-Hollman, Durán, Rodriguez, Palma, & Brunner, 2014).

Progress-monitoring measures should be sensitive to change and should identify both the amount and rate of growth demonstrated by children (Peisner-Feinberg & Buysse, 2013). Children who are not making progress may need more individualized instruction, and children who are making rapid progress may be successful with the general curriculum alone. Members of the educational team, including families, may monitor progress using objective, observational performance data. Clearly, assessments in MTSS models do more than identify skill deficits or simply serve to place students into an appropriate tier of support. Progress-monitoring measures can help identify areas where some children will benefit from more focused, individualized practice. Teachers who use assessments proactively as tools to help guide them while planning lessons and providing opportunities to respond will find that more targeted instruction pays off, especially with struggling students.

TIER 2 INSTRUCTIONAL APPROACHES FOR LANGUAGE AND LITERACY

Tier 2 instruction is designed to supplement rather than replace the general curriculum. Instruction is frequently delivered to small groups of children who are falling behind their peers in early literacy and language skills. Instruction may be modified to focus on the most important skills for the particular domain. The idea is to provide consistent, high-quality instruction with ample opportunities for children to practice targeted skills so they have a good chance to catch up with their peers. This does not necessitate that the lead teacher be responsible for all tiers of instruction, however. Teachers may be so busy delivering the general, classroomwide curriculum that it may be difficult to carve out time to provide supplementary instruction for children needing higher levels of support. One option is to arrange Tier 2 instruction so it can be delivered effectively by other individuals, including paraprofessionals, speech-language pathologists, classroom volunteers, or parents.

Two broad approaches for supplemental instruction within MTSS models have been identified: the *problem-solving approach* and *standard treatment protocols* (Fuchs, Mock, Morgan, & Young, 2003). The problem-solving approach is an individualized method of providing supports to struggling learners. Within a problem-solving approach, a team of educators (often including special educators, speech-language pathologists, or school psychologists) and the child's family work together to specify recommendations to supplement general instruction with specific Tier 2 interventions based on the child's learning profile and the family's priorities (Fuchs et al., 2003). The classroom team works together to identify evidence-based strategies that can be used to promote the child's learning. Some of these practices might include providing more explicit instruction on a focused content area or embedding more carefully planned opportunities throughout the classroom day for practicing a specific set of skills. Although the individualized nature of the problem-solving approach allows educators to target children with unique profiles and offers a great degree of flexibility, it does not guarantee that evidence-based treatments will be utilized. Because the problem-solving approach relies upon the knowledge and experience of the team members, planning, implementation, and effects may vary greatly depending on the strengths of the team.

An evidence-based example of the problem-solving approach in early childhood is EMERGE: Exemplary Model of Early Reading Growth and Excellence (Gettinger & Stoiber, 2007). EMERGE is an early literacy and language program designed to be implemented with preschool children from low-income families. There are four major components of EMERGE: 1) a multi-tiered instructional model that uses research-based practices and a research-supported curriculum, 2) screening and progress monitoring to identify children in need of more intensive instruction, 3) literacy-rich classroom environments, and 4) ongoing professional development and literacy coaching for teachers. The research-supported curriculum focuses instruction on early literacy skills such as phonological awareness, letter knowledge, print awareness, and oral language. In a preliminary efficacy study, children who participated in the EMERGE program performed higher on outcome measures assessing early literacy and language development indicators compared to those children from control classrooms (Gettinger & Stoiber, 2007).

In contrast to the problem-solving approach, standard treatment protocols for Tier 2 instruction offer standardized, evidence-based intervention approaches that target specific academic skills (Fuchs et al., 2003). Protocols are applied broadly, often in small-group settings, to children demonstrating deficits in particular developmental domains. One benefit of the standard treatment protocol is that it utilizes evidence-based instruction, often entailing lessons that are highly specified or scripted. This may facilitate ease of implementation and allow educators to target multiple children with similar deficits. A disadvantage of this approach is that many standard treatment protocols are manualized interventions that do not allow flexibility in implementation. This approach may be efficient because it can be applied to many children in the classroom. However, it may not allow the individualization necessary to target children with varied learning profiles.

The remaining examples of Tier 2 instruction for early literacy are standard treatment protocols. We will present basic characteristics of each intervention along with a summary of research supporting them. See Table 6.1 for a quick review of the interventions. These are not the only Tier 2 interventions available. They were chosen because they have shown evidence in peer-reviewed research reports and fit the characteristics of appropriate Tier 2 instruction. Nevertheless, we encourage educators to utilize resources such as the What Works Clearinghouse (http://ies.ed.gov/ncee/wwc) to find additional evidence-based interventions.

PAth to Literacy (Goldstein, 2016) is a supplementary phonological awareness and alphabet knowledge curriculum designed specifically as a Tier 2 intervention for children with delayed emergent literacy skills. The curriculum contains 12 units of instruction that introduce four specific phonological awareness skills: blending, segmenting, first word-part identification, and first sound identification. Instruction follows a developmental sequence from large to small sound units. Letter names and sounds are introduced at the beginning of each lesson to integrate alphabet instruction. Scripted lessons are delivered to groups of three children. Children are given feedback contingent upon their responses and multiple opportunities to respond. Lessons take 10–15 minutes to complete. Goldstein and colleagues (2017) found that 81% of the children with persisting delays in phonological awareness who received this intervention met the kindergarten early literacy benchmark on

Table 6.1. Examples of Tier 2 interventions for language and literacy skills

Intervention	Skills	Format	Intensity
PAth to Literacy (Goldstein, 2016; Goldstein et al., 2017)	Phonological awareness Alphabet knowledge	Small group	36 lessons 8–12 weeks 10 minutes 3–5× week
Story Friends (Goldstein & Kelley, 2016; Goldstein et al., 2016; Kelley & Goldstein, 2015; Kelley, Goldstein, Spencer, & Sherman, 2015; Spencer et al., 2012)	Vocabulary Comprehension	Small group	26 books 26 weeks 10 minutes 3× week
Read It Again! Pre-K (Justice & McGinty, 2009)	Vocabulary Narrative Phonological awareness Print knowledge	Whole group Small group	60 lessons 30 weeks 20–30 minutes 2× week
Story Champs (Petersen & Spencer, 2016)	Narrative story Grammar Complex language	Whole group Small group Individual	12 stories (each has levels A and B) 15–20 minutes
EMERGE (Gettinger & Stoiber, 2007)	Phonological awareness Letter knowledge Print awareness Oral language	Whole group Small group Individual	Shared book reading (2× day for 25 minutes) (10–15 minutes) Tier 3 tutoring (20 minutes for 2–3×/week)

the DIBELS First Sound Fluency after 12 weeks of intervention. As a comparison, only 34% of children in a control group met the benchmark, indicating that *PAth to Literacy* was efficacious for teaching phonological awareness.

Story Friends™ (Goldstein & Kelley, 2016) is an early literacy intervention for improving oral language skills in preschoolers. The program provides explicit instruction for academic vocabulary (e.g., *enormous, cautious, ruin*), basic concept words (e.g., *up/down, empty/full*), and comprehension skills embedded within prerecorded storybooks. This curriculum was designed specifically as a Tier 2 intervention for children demonstrating delays in oral language and vocabulary development. Children listen to 10-minute audio stories with embedded vocabulary lessons presented via headphones and follow along with printed books. There are two series, *Jungle Friends* and *Forest Friends*, each consisting of 13 books: 1 introduction book, 9 instructional books, and 3 review books. The vocabulary lessons provide multiple contexts for academic vocabulary words, allow for active responding, and provide multiple opportunities for practice and learning. The comprehension activities focus on answering inferential questions about the story and are designed to encourage generalization of comprehension skills. In experimental studies, children learned to define about half the novel words taught, compared to children who did not receive embedded lessons and demonstrated negligible learning (Goldstein et al., 2016; Spencer et al., 2012).

Read It Again Pre-K! (RIA; Justice & McGinty, 2009) is an early language and literacy preschool curriculum that focuses instruction on literacy skills related to vocabulary (naming and describing objects; using words relating to spatial and time concepts, thinking processes, and feelings), narrative generation (identifying and describing the setting, characters, and events of a story; clearly producing a story with beginning, middle, and end), phonological awareness (rhyming, blending, segmenting, and first-sound identification), and print knowledge (differentiating print from pictures and letters from words, conventions of reading, and sight word recognition). Children's storybooks are used and repeated to support the instruction of these targeted skills. The program includes 60 scripted, sequenced lessons designed to address skills from each of the four areas every week. These lessons provide repeated exposure and multiple opportunities for learning. This program can be used classroomwide as a Tier 1 curriculum or in small groups as a Tier 2 intervention. Hilbert and Eis (2014) and Buysse and colleagues (2016) implemented the RIA program as a Tier 2 intervention with small groups of children at risk for reading difficulties. Children who received the intervention had greater gains in the areas of vocabulary, phonological awareness, and print knowledge compared to children who did not receive the intervention.

Story Champs (Petersen & Spencer, 2016) is a narrative-based language intervention that focuses instruction on comprehension through explicit teaching of story grammar and complex language. The intervention is a multi-tiered language curriculum that can be delivered in whole-group, small-group, and individual settings. There are two sets of 12 stories, including a beginner level and an advanced level that contains more story grammar elements. Each of the 12 stories center on a personal theme familiar to children (e.g., getting hurt) and is accompanied by illustrations depicting elements of story grammar (e.g., character, problem, feeling, or action). This intervention can be used in a variety of settings and adapted based on children's individual needs. *Story Champs* has been implemented with preschoolers who are typically developing, who are linguistically diverse, and who have poor language abilities (Petersen & Spencer, 2016). When used as a small-group Tier 2 intervention, children demonstrated improved story comprehension, retelling, and generation of personal narratives (Spencer & Slocum, 2010; Weddle, Spencer, Kajian, & Petersen, 2015). Over the course of the intervention, the frequency in which personal narratives were produced significantly increased, as did the quality of the narrative. In addition, personal stories of children receiving this intervention became more complex and included more elements of story grammar over the weeks of treatment.

Based on this research, it is evident that preschoolers who have low language and literacy skills benefit from early intervention and targeted instruction using these Tier 2 instructional programs. Table 6.1 lists the specific skills addressed in each program. Within each program, teachers are provided a comprehensive scope and sequence that clearly identifies the targeted skills and topics addressed. All of the interventions are either scripted (*PAth to Literacy, Read It Again Pre-K!, Story Champs*) or automated (*Story Friends*), making it easy for teachers or other school-based personnel to implement instruction. Furthermore, all interventions may be delivered to small groups of 3–4 children exhibiting deficits in specific language and literacy skills. Progress-monitoring tools are included for each intervention to assess and adapt instruction as needed. The differences in targeted skills and instructional approaches allow teachers to select the intervention program with which they are most comfortable and that best meets the needs of their students. Tier 2 interventions that promote successful high-fidelity implementation have the following features: 1) are easy enough to be delivered by staff members other than teachers; 2) can be delivered in small groups within a center that is part of a classroom's daily routine; and 3) offer multiple opportunities for children to practice targeted skills (Kelley & Goldstein, 2015).

Although these examples of problem-solving approaches and standard treatment protocols have shown promise, both approaches come with their own strengths and weaknesses. Therefore, a hybrid approach offers a logical compromise. Similar to a problem-solving approach, a hybrid approach utilizes a team of educators and family members to create a plan for supplementing instruction to complement the general curriculum. However, standard treatment protocols are utilized to provide evidence-based treatments for children with specific needs. The team should utilize appropriate progress-monitoring tools to determine each child's response to intervention to inform future decisions. In Martin's case, his teacher, paraeducators, and parents may decide to supplement his code-focused and meaning-focused literacy skills with evidence-based interventions. For example, his vocabulary skills may be bolstered by participating in small-group instruction using *Story Friends*, and his parents may provide at-home instruction on letter names and sounds in an effort to improve Martin's alphabet skills. He will continue to receive whole-class instruction on language and literacy skills.

PROFESSIONAL DEVELOPMENT

Key components of successful Tier 2 curriculum include evidence-based instructional practices and clearly defined benchmarks and learning objectives. When a child such as Martin does not appear to be mastering objectives within an MTSS model, classroom teachers in concert with their instructional team may want to evaluate not only the child's progress but how well they have been implementing the Tier 2 intervention. As instructors move through the scope and sequence of the selected Tier 2 curriculum, especially if it is a curriculum that they have used over a period of years, they may drift off the specific practices of the program specifically outlined by the authors of the program. This potential problem may be avoided by using an implementation checklist associated with the intervention and by moving either through a self-check or having another teacher who uses the same program do a peer-to-peer checklist. In the example case of Martin, his educators should monitor their own adherence to standard treatment protocols as well as his progress toward early literacy benchmarks during intervention.

As depicted in Chapter 3, the emerging field of implementation science has outlined some important considerations for improving the fidelity with which practitioners implement evidence-based practices. The implementation process typically involves multiple levels of collaboration, including the practitioner, direct leadership, organizational support, and environmental contexts (Aarons, Hurlburt, & Horwitz, 2011). In regard to educational interventions, close collaboration among researchers, intervention developers, and classroom educators may improve the acceptability and sustainment of these interventions within the classroom (for an example, see Goldstein & Olszewski, 2015). Furthermore, appropriate training and professional development support are necessary to facilitate implementation of evidence-based practices within classrooms.

Just as students require adaptive levels of support to succeed in the classroom, educators require instruction and support when attempting to put newly learned practices in place and sustain those practices. Implementing an MTSS framework is no different. To implement the components of Tier 2 effectively and efficiently, professional development is needed, requiring support on different levels, including at the administrative level where processes are outlined, and the classroom level where procedures are put in place.

Professional development at the classroom level is fundamental to implementing Tier 2 instruction effectively. Whereas an initial introduction to Tier 2 may be done in an organization-level meeting, research shows that to effectively incorporate any new practice or framework, teachers require modeling and consistent coaching support (Knight, 2008). At the crux of Tier 2 is the practice of adapting instruction and providing appropriate levels of support to meet the needs of all learners. Thus, professional development and coaching support at the classroom level should focus on using assessment information to inform the intervention process and on incorporating evidence-based strategies as necessary. Components of effective professional development for Tier 2 curricula include a brief synthesis of the rationale, a straightforward focus on the logistics of implementation (i.e., the steps educators must take to conduct lessons in the classroom), and in-person as opposed to training modules that allow for practitioner engagement (Kelley & Goldstein, 2015).

Coaches promote fidelity of implementation of evidence-based practices and train teachers to use benchmark assessments and progress-monitoring tools to shape instruction. By reviewing data from assessments and taking time to discuss anecdotal reports, teachers and coaches working side by side can create lesson plans with activities that provide for direct instruction in deficit areas as well as multiple opportunities for practice and response for struggling students. As a second set of eyes both in the classroom and with data, coaches can provide valuable insight and suggestions for alternative ways to approach problems for teachers who may feel they have exhausted their own resources. In addition, coaches can work with educators to adapt evidence-based practices in a way that is feasible for delivery in the classroom. This may include incorporation of Tier 2 standard treatment protocols within a classroom center rotation or modifications to existing classroom activities to promote the number of learning opportunities for children. Martin's teachers would certainly benefit from additional professional development opportunities to ensure Tier 2 interventions are feasibly delivered with high fidelity.

GETTING STARTED WITH TIER 2

This section outlines the steps that inform the adoption of a Tier 2 intervention system that can be feasibly delivered in the classroom. As discussed in Chapter 4, data-based decision making is crucial to successful implementation of MTSS, including Tier 2 supports. This section provides important considerations for each step in the problem-solving process for educators beginning to implement Tier 2 assessment and instruction for language and literacy. These steps include defining the problem, problem analysis, implementing a plan, and evaluating response to intervention. Therefore, an important first step in implementing Tier 2 is to define the problem: Identifying children who are struggling to acquire foundational language and literacy skills during Tier 1 instruction. In this step, questions include

- Is the Tier 1 curriculum providing enough opportunities for children to learn skills targeted in the program?
- For which skills will children likely need supplemental support?
- Which assessments address the specific language and literacy skills of concern?
- Which assessments are feasible for implementation on a regular basis?

Once the problem has been defined and systematically measured, a plan for identifying the Tier 2 intervention or curriculum to address this problem should be carried out. Issues such as how well the curriculum targets the language and literacy skills of concern, how well the curriculum aligns with Tier 1, the organization of the classroom, and the availability and expertise of staff available are among the factors needing consideration. In this step, questions to ask include

- Will Tier 2 fit within the existing structure of the classroom or are changes necessary?
- Who has the knowledge and resources to contribute to assessment and intervention?
- How will instruction of target skills be coordinated across tiers?

In implementing the plan, the team must consider how the specific instruction will affect the school readiness skills of the children in the classroom. For example, if most children in the classroom are mastering alphabet knowledge but struggling with phonological awareness, a team might prioritize goals focused on improving phonological awareness. Tier 1 instruction should cover the full spectrum of early literacy skills so that Tier 2 interventions can focus on those specific skills that children require additional support to master. In this step, questions to ask include

- Which Tier 2 interventions can be put in place to target code-focused literacy skills?
- Which Tier 2 interventions can be put in place to target meaning-focused literacy skills?
- Who will be responsible for screening, intervention, and progress monitoring?
- How can professional development needs, including coaching, be met?

An important consideration for instructional teams is remembering that Tier 2 is a gradual process and the model should be continually refined using data-based decision making. Ongoing authentic assessments during classroom activities and routines will determine how well children are responding to supplementary instruction. Feedback from educators and parents will determine the feasibility of instruction on a daily basis. The team should refine the model and modify instruction as necessary throughout the implementation process to ensure that the treatments will be sustained and children will continue to demonstrate progress on key language and literacy skills. In this step, questions to ask include

- How can we improve the feasibility of Tier 2 intervention and progress monitoring?
- Are there additional skills that should be targeted?
- What professional development is necessary to sustain Tier 2 in the classroom?

CONCLUSION

Children who struggle to acquire key early language and literacy skills may require Tier 2 additional supports to acquire both code-focused and meaning-focused language and literacy skills critical for school readiness. Universal screening of these skills can identify children in need of Tier 2 supports. Regular progress-monitoring assessments can inform decision making regarding movement among tiers (e.g., if a child needs additional Tier 3 support or if a child no longer requires Tier 2 instruction). This chapter provided an overview of available screening and progress-monitoring assessments that can be used within an MTSS system. Effective Tier 2 instruction can be provided by utilizing the aforementioned evidence-based standard treatment protocols within a problem-solving framework that incorporates input from multiple sources (i.e., families, teachers, clinical service providers). Professional development across multiple levels will promote effective implementation of interventions. This chapter concluded with considerations for adopting a Tier 2 MTSS framework for language and literacy in early childhood classrooms.

We have every reason to be optimistic about Martin's future. Using assessments such as the IGDIs-EL and PELI, Martin's teacher identified strengths and weaknesses of Martin's language and literacy profile. Within a system of Tier 2 supports that includes family involvement and standard treatment protocols such as *Story Friends*, Martin receives explicit instruction on vocabulary and alphabet knowledge with frequent opportunities throughout the day to practice these skills. Given this amount of supplemental support,

Martin will likely develop these skills quickly. Throughout the school year, Martin's teacher will monitor his progress and adjust instruction accordingly. Therefore, by the time he enters kindergarten, Martin should have the foundational skills in place for success. Children who have fewer language skills going into school often learn at a slower rate, and as they progress into the higher grades, they often fall further and further behind their peers in reading and other academic areas (Foster & Miller, 2007). Nevertheless, with the appropriate early interventions in place, Martin can match the level of his peers at the start of kindergarten. Thus, Tier 2 supports in early education settings can provide an opportunity for children to begin school ready to succeed.

RESOURCES

Brookes Publishing Co. provides information for purchasing both *Story Friends* (http://products.brookespublishing.com/Story-Friends-Classroom-Kit-P963.aspx) and *PAth to Literacy* (http://products.brookespublishing.com/PAth-to-Literacy-P965.aspx).

Division for Early Childhood (DEC), National Association for the Education of Young Children (NAEYC), & National Head Start Association (NHSA). (2013). *Frameworks for Response to Intervention in early childhood: Description and implications.* Missoula, MT: Author. Retrieved from http://www.dec-sped.org/position-statements

The Crane Center for Early Childhood Research and Policy at The Ohio State University (https://earlychildhood.ehe.osu.edu/research/practice/read-it-again-prek) provides intervention materials and training videos for the *Read It Again-PreK!* curriculum.

The Florida Center for Reading Research web site (http://www.fcrr.org) offers evidence-based language and literacy activities for preschool educators, including resources for providing differentiated instruction to children requiring different tiers of support.

The Language Dynamics Group (http://www.languagedynamicsgroup.com/story champs.html) provides resources and purchasing information for the *Story Champs* curriculum.

Reading Rockets (http://www.readingrockets.org/) offers resources for implementing MTSS, sample lessons, and videos about developing school readiness skills.

REFERENCES

Aarons, G. A., Hurlburt, M., & Horwitz, S. M. (2011). Advancing a conceptual model of evidence-based practice implementation in public service sectors. *Administration & Policy in Mental Health, 38*(1), 4–23. doi:10.1007/s10488-010-0327-7

Buysse, V., Peisner-Feinberg, E., Soukakou, E., Fettig, A., Schaaf, J., & Burchinal, M. (2016). Using Recognition & Response (R&R) to improve children's language and literacy skills: Findings from two studies. *Early Childhood Research Quarterly, 36,* 11–20.

Cabell, S. Q., Justice, L. M., Konold, T. R., & McGinty, A. S. (2011). Profiles of emergent literacy skills among preschool children who are at risk for academic difficulties. *Early Childhood Research Quarterly, 26*(1), 1–14. doi:10.1016/j.ecresq.2010.05.003

Carta, J. J., Greenwood, C. R., Atwater, J., McConnell, S. R., Goldstein, H., & Kaminski, R. A. (2015). Identifying preschool children for higher tiers of language and early literacy instruction within a Response to Intervention framework. *Journal of Early Intervention, 36*, 281–291. doi:10.1177/1053815115579937

Connor, C. M., Morrison, F. J., & Slominski, L. (2006). Preschool instruction and children's emergent literacy growth. *Journal of Educational Psychology, 98*, 665–689. doi:10.1037/0022-0663.98.4.665

Dickinson, D. K., & Darrow, C. L. (2013). Methodological and practical challenges of curriculum-based language interventions. In T. Shanahan & C. Lonigan (Eds.), *Early childhood literacy: The National Early Literacy Panel and beyond* (pp. 195–216). Baltimore, MD: Paul H. Brookes Publishing Co.

Foster, W. A., & Miller, M. (2007). Development of the literacy achievement gap: A longitudinal study of kindergarten through third grade. *Language, Speech, and Hearing Services in Schools, 38*(3), 173–181. doi:10.1044/0161-1461(2007/018)

Fuchs, D. F., Mock, D., Morgan, P. L., & Young, C. L. (2003). Responsiveness-to-Intervention: Definitions, evidence, and implications for the learning disabilities construct. *Learning Disabilities Research & Practice, 18*, 157–171. doi:10.1111/1540-5826.00072

Gettinger, M., & Stoiber, K. (2007). Applying a Response-to-Intervention model for early literacy development in low-income children. *Topics in Early Childhood Special Education, 27*, 198–213. doi:10.1177/0271121407311238

Goldstein, H. (2016). *PAth to Literacy: A phonological awareness intervention for young children*. Baltimore, MD: Paul H. Brookes Publishing Co.

Goldstein, H., & Kelley, E. S. (2016). *Story Friends: An early literacy intervention for improving oral language*. Baltimore, MD: Paul H. Brookes Publishing Co.

Goldstein, H., Kelley, E., Greenwood, C., McCune, L., Carta, J., Atwater, J., . . . Spencer, T. (2016). Embedded instruction improves vocabulary learning during automated storybook reading among high-risk preschoolers. *Journal of Speech, Language, and Hearing Research, 59*, 484–500. doi:10.1044/2015_JSLHR-L-15-0227

Goldstein, H., & Olszewski, A. (2015). Developing a phonological awareness curriculum: Reflections on an implementation science framework. *Journal of Speech, Language, and Hearing Research, 58*(6), S1837–S1850. doi:10.1044/2015_JSLHR-L-14-0351

Goldstein, H., Olszewski, A., Haring, C., Greenwood, C. R., McCune, L., . . . Kelley, E. S. (2017). Efficacy of a Tier 2 curriculum to teach phonemic awareness to preschoolers with delays in early literacy development. *Journal of Speech, Language, and Hearing Research, 60*(1), 89–103. doi:10.1044/2016_JSLHR-L-15-0451

Greenwood, C. R., Carta, J. J., Atwater, J., Goldstein, H., Kaminski, R., & McConnell, S. (2013). Is a Response to Intervention (RTI) approach to preschool language and early literacy instruction needed? *Topics in Early Childhood Special Education, 33*, 48–64. doi:10.1177/0271121412455438

Greenwood, C. R., Carta, J. J., Goldstein, H., Kaminski, R. A., McConnell, S. R., & Atwater, J. (2015). The Center for Response to Intervention in Early Childhood: Developing evidence-based tools for a multi-tier approach to preschool language and early literacy instruction. *Journal of Early Intervention, 36*, 246–262. doi:10.1177/1053815115581209

Griffin, P., Burns, M. S., & Snow, C. E. (Eds.). (1998). *Preventing reading difficulties in young children*. Washington, DC: National Academies Press.

Hilbert, D. D., & Eis, S. D. (2014). Early intervention for emergent literacy development in a collaborative community pre-kindergarten. *Early Childhood Education Journal, 42*, 105–113.

Hoover, W. A., & Gough, P. B. (1990). The simple view of reading. *Reading and Writing: An Interdisciplinary Journal, 2*(2), 127–160. doi:10.1007/BF00401799

Justice, L. M., Mashburn, A. J., Hamre, B. K., & Pianta, R. C. (2008). Quality of language and literacy instruction in preschool classrooms serving at-risk pupils. *Early Childhood Research Quarterly, 23*(1), 51–68. doi:10.1016/j.ecresq.2007.09.004

Justice, L. M., & McGinty, A. S. (2009). Read It Again Pre-K. *A preschool curriculum supplement to promote language and literacy foundations*. Columbus, OH: The Children's Learning Research Collaborative.

Kaminski, R. A., Abbott, M., Bravo Aguayo, K., Latimer, R., & Good, R. H. (2014). The Preschool Early Literacy Indicators: Validity and benchmark goals. *Topics in Early Childhood Special Education, 34*(2), 71–82.

Kelley, E. S., & Goldstein, H. (2015). Building a Tier 2 intervention: A glimpse behind the data. *Journal of Early Intervention, 36,* 292–312. doi:10.1177/1053815115581657

Kelley, E. S., Goldstein, H., Spencer, T. D., & Sherman, A. (2015). Effects of automated Tier 2 storybook intervention on vocabulary and comprehension learning in preschool children with limited oral language skills. *Early Childhood Research Quarterly, 31,* 47–61. doi:10.1016/j.ecresq.2014.12.004

Knight, J. (2008). *Coaching approaches and perspectives.* Thousand Oaks, CA: Corwin Press.

McConnell, S., Bradfield, T., Wackerle-Hollman, A., & Rodriguez, M. (2012). *Individualized Growth and Development Indicators of Early Literacy* (2nd ed.). St Paul, MN: Early Learning Labs.

McConnell, S. R., Wackerle-Hollman, A. K., Roloff, T. A., & Rodriguez, M. (2014). Designing a measurement framework for response to intervention in early childhood programs. *Journal of Early Intervention, 36,* 263–280. doi:10.1177/1053815115578559

National Early Literacy Panel. (2008). *Developing early literacy: Report of the National Early Literacy Panel.* Washington, DC: National Institute for Literacy.

Neuman, S. B., & Dwyer, J. (2009). Missing in action: Vocabulary instruction in Pre-K. *The Reading Teacher, 62,* 384–392. doi:10.1598/RT.62.5.2

Office of Head Start. (2015). *Head Start Early Learning Outcomes Framework: Ages Birth to Five.* Washington, DC: U.S. Department of Health and Human Services.

Peisner-Feinberg, E. S., & Buysse, V. (2013). The role of assessment within response to intervention in early education. In V. Buysse & E. S. Peisner-Feinberg (Eds.), *Handbook of Response to Intervention in early childhood* (pp. 121–142). Baltimore, MD: Paul H. Brookes Publishing Co.

Pelatti, C. Y., Piasta, S. B., Justice, L. M., & O'Connell, A. (2014). Language-and literacy-learning opportunities in early childhood classrooms: Children's typical experiences and within-classroom variability. *Early Childhood Research Quarterly 29*(4), 445–456. doi:10.1016/j.ecresq.2014.05.004

Pence Turnbull, K. L., & Justice, L. M. (2011). *Language development from theory to practice* (2nd ed.). Boston, MA: Pearson.

Petersen, D. B., & Spencer, T. D. (2016). Using narrative intervention to accelerate canonical story grammar and complex language growth in culturally diverse preschoolers. *Topics in Language Disorders, 36*(1), 6–19. doi:10.1097/TLD.0000000000000078

Spencer, E., Goldstein, H., Sherman, A., Noe, S., Tabbah, R., Ziolkowski, R., & Schneider, N. (2012). Effects of an automated vocabulary and comprehension intervention. *Journal of Early Intervention, 43,* 195–221. doi:10.1177/1053815112471990

Spencer, T. D., & Slocum, T. A. (2010). The effect of a narrative intervention on story retelling and personal story generation skills of preschoolers with risk factors and narrative language delays. *Journal of Early Intervention, 32,* 178–199. doi:10.1177/1053815110379124

Wackerle-Hollman, A., Durán, L., Rodriguez, M., Palma, J., & Brunner, S. (2014). *Technical Report #3: Evaluating S-IGDI measures: Iterative decision-making in the development process.* Unpublished manuscript, University of Minnesota IGDI Lab, Minneapolis, MN.

Weddle, S. A., Spencer, T. D., Kajian, M., & Petersen, D. B. (2015). An examination of a multi-tiered system of language support for culturally and linguistically diverse preschoolers: Implications for early and accurate identification. *School Psychology Review, 45*(1), 109–132.

Whitehurst, G. J., & Lonigan, C. J. (1998). Child development and emergent literacy. *Child Development, 69,* 848–872. doi:10.1111/j.1467-8624.1998.tb06247.x

7

Designing and Implementing Tier 2 Instructional Supports to Promote Social-Emotional Outcomes

Mary Louise Hemmeter, Lise Fox, Phillip S. Strain, Jessica K. Hardy, and Jaclyn D. Joseph

Becky teaches in an inclusive preschool classroom. She uses the district-adopted assessment and curriculum and is diligent about completing the required child assessments and ongoing progress-monitoring checks. Becky also uses the district-adopted social-emotional curriculum that has lessons that focus on promoting skills for learning (e.g., paying attention, following rules), skills to use in social interactions with others, conflict resolution skills, expressing emotions and responding to the emotions of others, and using social conventions (e.g., being helpful, providing compliments).

Becky has five children in her classroom who are not making adequate progress on social-emotional skills even though the curriculum is being implemented with fidelity. Of these five children, two (Lei and Brian) have individualized behavior support plans that were recently developed for Becky and her classroom team to implement. The three other children have behavior issues that are not as overwhelming to Becky. She sees these children as likely to develop more severe behavior issues if they don't learn the social-emotional skills that are needed to be successful in a classroom. Ryan has a quick temper and becomes easily frustrated when playing with peers. He wants the children who play with him to follow his plan, and when they don't, he might stomp around, shout at them, or take toys from them. Faisal is the opposite. He is socially withdrawn, wanders around during center activities, watches other children without joining in, and tends to verbally interact only with adults in the classroom. Finally, there is Emily, who is very active, has difficulty focusing on an activity, does not listen during group, and is often off-topic in her conversations. Her behavior has affected her relationships with other children, who express annoyance with her, complain to adults that she is bothering them, and avoid asking her to join in their activities.

These children are in need of supplementary social-emotional supports. Lei and Brian need intensive individualized interventions (Tier 3 intervention) in addition to participating in the social-emotional universal curriculum and Tier 2 social skills instruction. Ryan, Faisal, and Emily need Tier 2 instructional supports that are carefully designed, delivered with fidelity, and matched to their social-emotional skill gaps.

INTRODUCTION

Social-emotional development is widely recognized to be of critical importance to the development and school readiness of young children. In their seminal report, *From Neurons to Neighborhoods: The Science of Early Childhood Development*, Shonkoff and Phillips (2000) identified three domains of development in early childhood that are best summarized as: 1) moving to self-regulation of emotions, behaviors, and attention; 2) learning to communicate, reason, and problem-solve; and 3) resolving conflicts and build friendships with other children. These domains are broad and include many skills, but social-emotional development plays a central role in each of those areas.

Social-emotional development has also been emphasized in federal accountability requirements for states. The Office of Special Education Programs (OSEP) requires that states report data on child and family outcomes in early intervention and early childhood special education. For child outcomes, states must report data on the following three outcomes: 1) positive social-emotional skills (including social relationships), 2) acquiring and using knowledge and skills, and 3) taking appropriate actions to meet needs (Early Childhood Technical Assistance Center, 2017). The first outcome, positive social-emotional skills (including social relationships), includes how a child relates to adults, relates to other children, and follows rules related to groups or interacting with others (note that following rules applies only to children older than 18 months).

While highly influential, *From Neurons to Neighborhoods* was not specifically designed to be a framework for understanding social-emotional skills. Similarly, OSEP's delineation of the three child outcomes does not include an in-depth exploration of positive social-emotional skills. However, frameworks of social-emotional skills do exist. One prominent framework comes from the Collaborative for Academic, Social, and Emotional Learning (CASEL; see Resources at the end of this chapter). Another important framework is the *Head Start Early Learning Outcomes Framework: Ages Birth to Five* (Office of Head Start, 2015), which is intended to guide instruction in Head Start programs. States also have their own early learning and development standards that typically include social-emotional skills.

Although there are differences among these conceptualizations, frameworks, and standards, there is a great deal of overlap. For the purposes of this book, we identify the following social-emotional competency areas: 1) positive self-concept, 2) emotional literacy, 3) social problem solving, and 4) friendship skills. Each of these competency areas includes specific skills. These skill areas are represented in Figure 7.1.

As illustrated in Figure 7.1, positive self-concept includes skills related to the child being aware of his or her own strengths, demonstrating confidence in tasks he or she undertakes, being able to advocate for oneself, and making appropriate choices. Emotional literacy includes recognizing, identifying, and labeling one's own emotions, as well as the emotions of others and the skills related to regulating emotions. The third area of competence, social problem solving, includes the skills of recognizing and identifying problems and identifying solutions to problems. In addition, social problem solving includes the skills of recognizing and acknowledging the feelings and perspectives of others. Finally, the competency area of friendship skills includes interacting positively with others and playing cooperatively with peers.

Although these skills are presented in distinct competency areas, the skills overlap with one another in practice. For example, a child's ability to recognize and acknowledge the emotions and perspectives of others will affect that child's ability

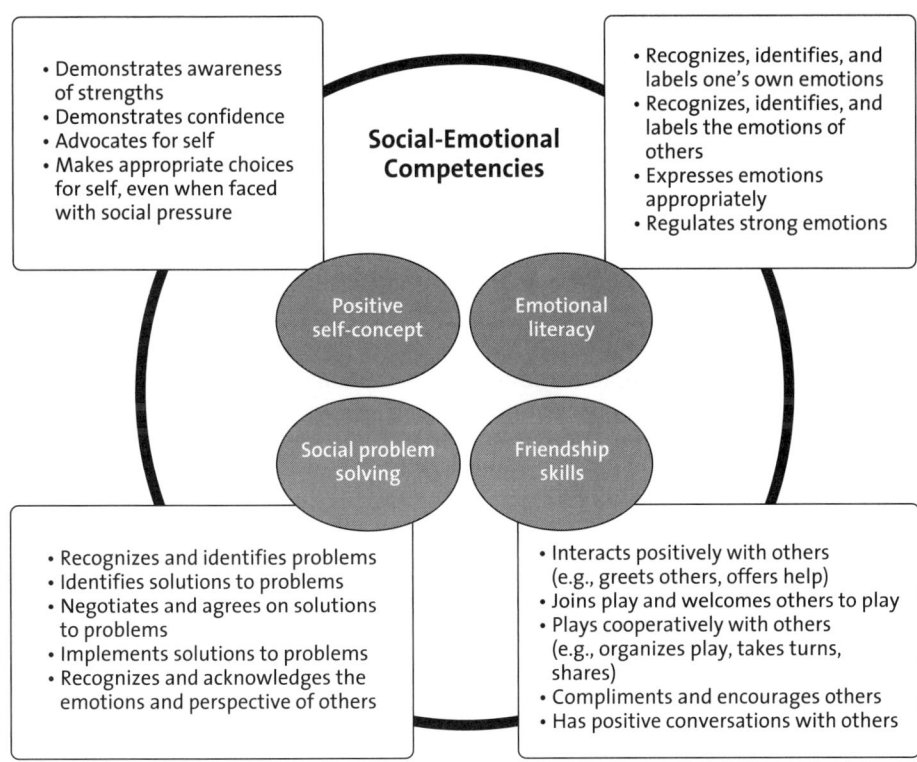

Figure 7.1. Competency areas and skills within the social-emotional domain.

to compliment and encourage others. Similarly, a child with a positive self-concept will be better equipped to solve problems with others.

TIERED MODELS FOR PROMOTING SOCIAL-EMOTIONAL COMPETENCE

Overwhelming evidence indicates that when young children are not successful in mastering social-emotional skills, they are highly likely to continue on a developmental trajectory that includes significant challenging behavior, school failure, and continued challenges into adulthood that ultimately affect social adjustment, mental health, violence and drug crime convictions, and well-being (Brennan, Shaw, Dishion, & Wilson, 2012; Dodge et al., 2014; Jones, Greenberg, & Crowley, 2015). Thus, the provision of a rich universal social-emotional curriculum is essential for young children and should include tiered interventions to ensure that all children receive intervention that results in social-emotional competence. In this chapter, we will describe the design and implementation of Tier 2 instructional supports that are used within multi-tiered systems of support (MTSS) related to social-emotional skills.

A discussion about the design of Tier 2 instructional supports must begin with an examination of the strength of the universal curriculum to deliver a core of instruction that promotes the social-emotional competence of the majority of children in the program. It is increasingly more common for preschool classroom teachers to use commercially available social-emotional curricula such as *Incredible Years Classroom Dinosaur Curriculum* (Webster-Stratton, 2002), *PATHS Preschool* (Domitrovich, Greenberg, Kusche, & Cortes, 2004), and *Second Step* (Committee for Children, 1991) that stand alone and supplement their academic curricula, or multi-domain curricula that include social-emotional skills such as *Connect4Learning* (Sarama, Brenneman, Clements, Duke, & Hemmeter, 2016) and *The Creative Curriculum* (Dodge et al., 2016). In addition to teaching social-emotional skills and knowing how to support children's engagement in planned learning activities, preschool teachers must provide a context that promotes the use of social-emotional skills in all interactions and activities within the classroom community. Thus, successful social-emotional teaching also includes careful consideration of the development of relationships, partnerships with the family, the classroom environment, use of culturally responsive approaches, the design of instructional activities, anticipatory child guidance procedures, and appropriate responses to behavior challenges. Because social-emotional skills are used and supported within every interaction and activity, the universal curriculum should include skill sequences, teaching practices, and careful environmental arrangements.

Many programs have used the Pyramid Model for supporting social-emotional competence in infants and young children (see Figure 7.2) to implement the framework of teaching practices needed for MTSS (Fox, Carta, Dunlap, Strain, & Hemmeter, 2010; Fox, Dunlap, Hemmeter, Joseph, & Strain, 2003; Fox & Hemmeter, 2009; Hemmeter, Fox, & Snyder, 2013). The Pyramid Model is a framework based on

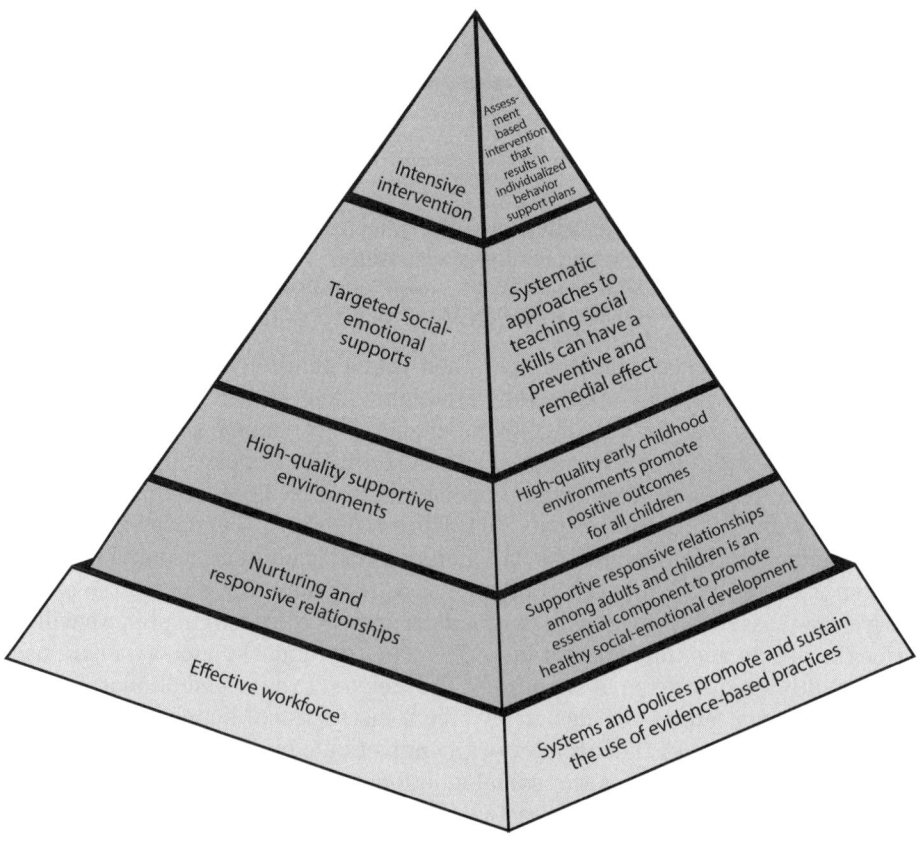

Figure 7.2. Pyramid Model for supporting social-emotional competence in infants and young children. From the Center on the Social and Emotional Foundations for Early Learning at Vanderbilt University.

evidence-based practices that early educators can use for promoting all children's social-emotional competence and to prevent and address challenging behavior. The Pyramid Model practices come from the growing body of research on effective instruction in early education (Burchinal, Vandergrift, Pianta, & Mashburn, 2010), practices and strategies to promote engagement and appropriate behavior (Chien et al., 2010), the teaching of children's social skills and emotional competencies (Domitrovich, Moore, & Greenberg, 2012; Vaughn et al., 2003), and the use of an individualized, assessment-based approach to the development of positive behavior support plans for children with persistent and severe challenging behavior (Blair, Fox, & Lentini, 2010; Conroy, Dunlap, Clarke, & Alter, 2005).

The universal promotion level of the Pyramid Model, or Tier 1, focuses on the importance of establishing nurturing and responsive relationships with children and families, and among the adults in the classroom (Hemmeter, Fox, & Snyder, 2014). The Pyramid Model practices related to nurturing and responsive relationships include engaging in supportive, warm, responsive, and positive interactions with children, and establishing constructive partnerships with families and team members in the collaborative support of the child's social-emotional competence. In addition to relationship-building practices, Tier 1 includes practices related to providing supportive classroom environments that include promoting the communication of children, joining in children's play, providing positive descriptive feedback, promoting child engagement in learning activities, teaching rules and expectations, and supporting families to use these practices. In addition to the interactional and classroom practices that support social-emotional skill development, teachers must also provide explicit instruction in social-emotional skills.

At Tier 2, the Pyramid Model includes the explicit instruction of social skills and emotional competencies for children who have social-emotional delays or problem behaviors that are concerning to their teachers and family members. Those Tier 2 instructional supports include the provision of more frequent and intensive instruction that is delivered with a high degree of fidelity. It is designed to support skill development in targeted areas and prevent children from developing more intensive behavior challenges or social-emotional needs (Fox et al., 2010). Tier 2 interventions may occur in the context of small groups and are focused on children who need more intensive supports than those provided in Tier 1. Tier 3 interventions in the Pyramid Model are designed for children with persistent challenging behavior or who have severe social or emotional skill deficits. For Tier 3, a team-based process is used to conduct assessments and develop an individualized comprehensive behavior support plan in partnership with the family (Dunlap & Fox, 2011). In the Pyramid Model, all tiers build upon the previous tier(s), with Tier 2 and 3 interventions reliant on the lower tier(s) for the provision of practices that are necessary to promote social-emotional outcomes.

When the Pyramid Model is implemented programwide through the support of a program leadership team, it can be used effectively as an MTSS (Fox et al., 2010; Hemmeter et al., 2013), see Chapter 11. The program leadership team develops the procedures and supports, including data-based decision-making, that guide implementation fidelity of the model. For example, the leadership team guides staff in establishing programwide expectations, develops program-level family engagement strategies, establishes the process for universal screening and data collection, provides teachers with the mechanisms to receive problem-solving support related to child progress, provides classroom coaching for intervention fidelity, and establishes the data systems that can be used to ensure that children receive needed interventions that are implemented with fidelity and efficiency.

IDENTIFYING CHILDREN IN NEED OF TIER 2 SUPPORTS

An important feature of an MTSS is ensuring that children receive needed intervention efficiently. This requires the use of tools or procedures to identify children who may need more intensified instructional support as soon as possible. Several common approaches might be used by a classroom teacher or as an established system-level team within the program to help identify children in need of Tier 2 social-emotional interventions. These approaches are described next: 1) behavior rating scales and social-emotional screening tools, 2) teacher observation and reporting, and 3) behavior incident tracking. To obtain the most useful and accurate information, a multi-method assessment, using more than one of these approaches, is recommended.

One approach to identifying children with social-emotional instructional needs is the use of a behavior rating scale or checklist that can be completed by the teacher or parent. For example, a program might use tools such as the Social Skills Improvement System (Gresham & Elliott, 2007) or the Preschool and Kindergarten Behavior Scales (Merrell, 2002), which provide summary scores on child social skills and problem behavior. Standardized behavior rating scales are appealing in that they are easy to use, easy to score, and reliable and valid for screening purposes (Merrell, 2001).

Another option is a social-emotional screening tool. Social-emotional screening tools can be used with all children in the program to identify children who need additional instruction and to provide program information on the adequacy of the universal curriculum in meeting children's needs (Bagnato, Neisworth, & Pretti-Frontczak, 2010; Ikeda, Neessen, & Witt, 2008). Screening tools are developed to be quick, easy to use, and inexpensive for administration. A popular social-emotional screening tool designed especially for young children is the Ages & Stages Questionnaires®: Social-Emotional, Second Edition (ASQ:SE-2; Squires, Bricker, & Twombly, 2015).

A program might also rely on teacher observation and referral for identifying children who are in need of Tier 2 social-emotional instructional supports. Although the knowledge that the teacher has about a child's social-emotional challenges, lack of progress in the curriculum, and interactions with other children are critical to this process, there are concerns about relying on this approach as a sole source of data for Tier 2 identification. These concerns include issues related to teachers' biases about the kinds of behaviors or skill deficits that might be flagged as concerning, teachers' lack of knowledge of normative child development for identifying a child as having social-emotional concerns, and the need to have a more systematic and objective mechanism to ensure all children are screened (Severson, Walker, Hope-Doolittle, Kratochwill, & Gresham, 2007).

Finally, some programs have used a system for collecting behavior incident data across the program and analyzing those data to identify children who have intervention needs (Fox & Hemmeter, 2009; Steed, Pomerleau, & Horner, 2012). In this approach, classroom personnel record incidents that are of significant concern on a form that is quick to complete (see Figure 7.3), and then provide the form to a central person to enter into a data system (using a spreadsheet or a web-based program). The data offer information on when behavior incidents are occurring, the nature of the behavior incident(s), the responses that are used to address the incident(s), and other variables that are useful in revealing patterns to identify

Behavior Incident Report

Program ID: _____

Classroom ID:	Child ID:	Date:	Time:
Behavior Description:			

Problem Behavior (check most intrusive)

❑ Physical aggression	❑ Noncompliance	❑ Repetitive behaviors
❑ Disruption/tantrums	❑ Social withdrawal/isolation	❑ Hurting self
❑ Inconsolable crying	❑ Running away	❑ Trouble falling asleep
❑ Verbal aggression	❑ Breaking/destroying objects or items	❑ Other: _____
❑ Inappropriate language	❑ Unsafe behaviors	

Activity (check one)

❑ Arrival	❑ Outdoor play	❑ Departure
❑ Circle/large-group activity	❑ Special activity	❑ Therapy
❑ Small-group activity	❑ Field trip	❑ Quiet time/nap
❑ Centers/indoor play	❑ Self-care/bathroom	❑ Transportation
❑ Diapering	❑ Transition	❑ Individual activity
❑ Meals	❑ Clean-up	❑ Other: _____

Others Involved (check one)

❑ Teacher	❑ Family member	❑ Transportation driver
❑ Assistant teacher	❑ Support/administrative staff	❑ Kitchen staff
❑ Peers	❑ Substitute	❑ None
❑ Therapist	❑ Classroom volunteer	❑ Other: _____

Possible Motivation (check one)

❑ Obtain desired item	❑ Gain adult attention/comfort	❑ Avoid sensory
❑ Obtain desired activity	❑ Avoid adults	❑ Don't know
❑ Gain peer attention	❑ Avoid task	❑ Other: _____
❑ Avoid peers	❑ Obtain sensory	

Response (check one or the most intrusive)

❑ Verbal reminder	❑ Provide physical comfort	❑ Teacher contact family
❑ Redirect to different activity/toy	❑ Curriculum modification	❑ Time out
❑ Move within group	❑ Re-teach/Practice expected behavior	❑ Physical guidance
❑ Remove from activity	❑ Loss of activity	❑ Physical hold/Restrain
❑ Remove from area	❑ Time with a teacher	❑ Other: _____
❑ Remove item	❑ Time in a different classroom or adult outside of classroom	

Administrative Follow-Up (check one or most intrusive)

❑ Not applicable	❑ Targeted group intervention	❑ Transfer to another program
❑ Talk with child	❑ Temporary removal from classroom	❑ Reduce hours in program
❑ Contact family	❑ Sent home for remainder of day	❑ Dismissal from program
❑ Family meeting	❑ Sent home for 1 or more days	❑ Other: _____
❑ Arrange behavioral consultation/team	❑ Conditional enrollment	

Comments:

If this is the first BIR for the child, please select the following demographic Information:	___ Male ___ Female	___ IEP in place ___ No IEP ___ Dual language	Select ONE: ___ American Indian or Alaskan Native ___ Asian ___ Black or African American ___ Hispanic/Latino ___ Native Hawaiian or Other Pacific Islander ___ Two or more races ___ White

Figure 7.3. Example of a behavior incident report. (*Key*: BIR, Behavior Intervention Report; IEP, individualized education program.) National Center for Pyramid Model Innovations (2018). Behavior Incident Report Form. Tampa, Florida: Author. Reprinted with permission.

students who might need interventions and the types of interventions that might match an individual student's (or students') needs.

Once children are identified as needing additional instructional supports to meet social-emotional benchmarks or milestones, the target skill for the Tier 2 intervention must be identified. For some children, the identification of the Tier 2 intervention skill might occur through an examination of the child's performance on a curriculum-based assessment such as the Assessment, Evaluation, and Planning System (AEPS®; Bricker et al., 2002) or Teaching Strategies Gold (Heroman, Burts, Berke, & Bickart, 2010).

The identification of a Tier 2 social-emotional instructional target sometimes comes from teachers' observations of children's behavior and interactions within the classroom with peers and adults and the identification of skills that are needed to be successful within the classroom environment and in interactions with others. Although assessment tools can be highly valuable in the identification of the child's performance on curriculum benchmarks and potential intervention objectives, many children will need intervention related to a social-emotional skill that is individually specified and might not be specifically listed on a general assessment tool.

OVERVIEW OF TIER 2 INSTRUCTIONAL SUPPORTS

In this section, we discuss characteristics of effective instruction for supporting children's social-emotional development, as well as how these interventions might vary based on the needs of individual or small groups of children.

Characteristics of Effective Instruction for Teaching Social-Emotional Skills

Dozens of studies over the last 25 years have examined the impact of various teaching procedures on young children's social-emotional competence (e.g., Domitrovich, Cortes, & Greenberg, 2007; Hemmeter, Snyder, Fox, & Algina, 2016; Strain & Bovey, 2011; Webster-Stratton, Reid, & Stoolmiller, 2008). These studies, involving children with and without special needs, include brief interventions, as well as intensive, long-term interventions. From this broad array of research, a few pivotal characteristics of interventions are associated most reliably with rapid and durable behavior change. Each characteristic is briefly described next.

Focus on Skills That Lead to the Most Important Outcomes The array of potential skills to teach to children in the social-emotional domain is extensive. Many intervention developers have attempted to hone in on children's skills that are predictors of children's future development, including friendship skills, emotional literacy and regulation, problem solving, and social interaction skills (Domitrovich et al., 2007; Hemmeter et al., 2016; Strain & Bovey, 2014; Webster-Stratton et al., 2008). What is important is to select skills to teach that offer children the best chance for success now and in the future. In some cases, this decision will be made at the individual child level based on the child's delays and what skills will be most likely to assist the child in gaining access to important social interaction opportunities.

Directly Teach to Enhance Skill Acquisition Joseph, Rausch, and Strain (2016) have noted that a substantial number of early educators propose that children will acquire needed social-emotional skills simply by being given the opportunities to interact with each other. And, while doubtless there are children who will acquire skills under such conditions, this is clearly not the case for a large segment of the population (Wolery, Strain, & Bailey, 1992). Like most other skills (e.g., using a utensil, riding a scooter, counting), many children need explanation, demonstration, and practice to learn and become fluent in their use of social-emotional skills. Direct teaching of these skills should occur for all children in a classroom, and practitioners also need to provide more individualized instruction for children who might need even more support to independently use particular social-emotional skills. Direct teaching has been used in a wide variety of specific approaches, including the use of puppets in circle-time lessons to model specific skills (Webster-Stratton & Reid, 2004), role-play and rehearsal (Center on the Social and Emotional Foundations for Early Learning, 2013), and peer-mediated intervention (Kohler & Strain, 1999), to name a few. An effective teacher will employ a variety of these approaches to ensure that all children learn and use particular skills.

Use Motivational Incentives to Support New Skills   Similar to the diversity in instructional practices, successful intervention approaches have utilized a wide variety of carefully arranged consequences to encourage children to use emerging social-emotional skills. More specifically, consequences in the form of varied reinforcement strategies result in positive outcomes for improving children's use of social-emotional skills. These reinforcement strategies may include 1) special recognition for extraordinary skill use (e.g., wearing the "super friend" cape or receiving a "super friend" certificate [see Figure 7.4]), or 2) giving children behavior-specific praise (e.g., "You worked so hard to solve that problem!"). Teachers may

Figure 7.4.   Example of a super friend certificate.

employ a variety of group and individualized motivational incentives specific to children's use of social-emotional skills.

INDIVIDUALIZING INSTRUCTION WITHIN TIER 2

In this section, we offer five types of accommodations and/or modifications to the typical delivery of instruction that can be used singly or, more likely, in some combination to facilitate learning. These modifications/accommodations could be used to design and deliver Tier 2 instructional supports.

Conduct a Task Analysis of Specific Skills

A common peer social skill incorporated in every approach we know of is taking turns. At one level, this may appear to be a simple, straightforward behavior. However, a careful analysis suggests otherwise. To take turns, children must first be in proximity to peers, have the receptive language skills to process the request, and have the ability to request, either verbally or with the use of pictures (e.g., "Can I have the truck?"). Turn taking most often involves someone asking and then someone responding to the request. Turn taking often has an important verbal language component, such as when the child who is giving up an item accompanies the item with a statement such as, "You can have it for a little bit" or "Now can I have the car?"

When and if children begin to struggle with acquiring a skill, the first instructional modification is to consider all prerequisite cognitive and language skills. Then, to teach the specific skill, it is beneficial for practitioners to also consider and teach all of the actual behaviors that are associated with the skill itself. To teach turn taking to children, the following has to occur: 1) a peer has to obtain the attention of the child with the truck (e.g., peer taps the shoulder of the child with the truck, looks at him, says his name), 2) the peer says, "Can I have a turn with the truck?", and 3) the child hands the truck to his peer while saying, "Here you go." Furthermore, the child has to learn what to do if the peer does not want to give up the toy. The development of a task analysis like the one above when teaching skills is important so all adults and children in the classroom understand what to teach and what to do when using a particular social-emotional skill.

Increase Opportunities to Practice

For children in risk categories or with special needs, skill acquisition is dependent on large numbers of meaningful practice opportunities. Consider the goal of teaching a child to greet peers upon arrival. The obvious, most functional time to teach greeting would be at the morning arrival time. However, should those opportunities prove insufficient, it would be possible to greatly expand practice opportunities. For example, the child in question could come to opening circle and storytime first and then greet each peer as he or she arrives. Modifications could also be made to center time whereby the target child could come to dramatic play area first, then greet peers as they enter the area. To optimize the effectiveness and efficiency of social skill interventions, maximizing the number and quality of practice opportunities throughout the day is essential. Increasing opportunities for practice takes careful planning by adults with a focus on embedding opportunities across multiple classroom routines and activities. This is often done through the

Activity/ Routine	Faisal	Ryan	Emily
Arrival		Greet peers as they come into the classroom	
Breakfast	Hand out plates and napkins to each child and greet each child		
Circle		Teacher's helper job at circle	Prompt Emily to ask a friend to talk during "think-pair-share"
Centers	Practice problem-solving skills Visual schedule and small-group instruction to help Faisal play in centers	Practice problem-solving skills	Embed instruction to help Emily ask a friend to play and to stay engaged with play for longer periods of time

Figure 7.5. Activity matrix.

use of an activity matrix, which has the routines and activities in the classroom in the left column and the children's names across the top. Then, in each cell of the matrix, the teacher writes how to embed instruction on needed skills for the child in each routine or activity (see Figure 7.5 for an example).

Provide Additional Adult and Peer Support

At times it may be necessary for adults and or peers to assist some children by providing visual supports, rehearsal opportunities, and verbal and physical prompts. For example, a key component of the Learning Experiences and Alternative Program (LEAP) model's peer-mediated social skills approach (Strain & Bovey, 2016) involves the strategic placement of visual cues around the classroom to provide a continuous reminder of the skill(s) that are to be used in certain physical areas. Related to the task analysis option mentioned earlier, adults can also provide children with sequenced visual supports for skills that have multiple components. For example, a visual for supporting the skill of initiating an interaction with a peer might include photos of the child approaching a friend, tapping the friend on the shoulder, looking at the friend, and saying the friend's name.

Rehearsal opportunities can also facilitate learning. For example, in a circle time that immediately precedes center time where the goal is to "invite peers to play," the teacher might role-play with several children, reminding them that they should do this during center time. Rehearsal opportunities provide the opportunity for children to practice a skill with adults, such as inviting others to play, with certainty that the behavior will be responded to in a positive fashion (i.e., the other children will play with their peer who invited them to play). Rehearsal opportunities might be particularly important for complex skills such as problem solving. Supporting a child through the problem-solving steps prior to center time would provide the child with practice opportunities immediately prior to when the child would need to use the skill.

Prompting children to engage in a skill can take many forms and be delivered by adults and peers. For some children, prompting can be as simple as verbally reminding them to use particular skills. Such verbal reminders can come from both adults and children. When peers become proficient at using particular social-emotional skills, they often support other children in the classroom by reminding them that they can use such skills to play, calm down, or solve problems. Other children, however, may require more intense support to engage in particular skills. More intrusive prompts (e.g., hand-over-hand prompting, gently touching a child's elbow to prompt her to tap her friend on the shoulder) can be used and systematically reduced through the use of a prompting hierarchy as the child becomes more successful at using the skill. Peers can be taught how to buddy-up to assist children who might need additional support when passing out napkins at snack time.

Focus on Generalization

When providing instruction on social-emotional skills, it is important to promote children's generalization of skills from the beginning. That is, children should be provided with practice opportunities to use skills with a variety of people, in a number of different places, and across several daily routines. As we have previously discussed, the number and frequency of planned social-emotional skill practice opportunities should be individualized for each child and so should the context of such practice opportunities, including specifying adults and peers, possible places, and selected routines. It is likely that some children in need of Tier 2 supports will need instruction focused on supporting their use of skills that they might have learned as part of the Tier 1 curriculum but that they are not using in more generalized contexts.

At the same time that practice opportunities are embedded into classroom routines and social interactions, all children should have naturally occurring opportunities to practice social-emotional skills. When practitioners focus on teaching and reinforcing the use of a smaller number of critical skills that lead to important outcomes, all of the children in the class will be using the skills (at various levels of competence, of course) with one another. This classroomwide use of particular skills increases the number of potential practice opportunities for all children and particularly for those who need them.

To maximize generalization, using social-emotional skills in a variety of ways becomes important. When first teaching a skill, developing a task analysis and teaching one or a few discrete behaviors at a time can be important for children to know what is expected of them when using the skill. As children become more proficient using a particular skill, they can, and likely should, learn other ways to use the skill or other skills to achieve the same outcome. For example, to teach children to use a problem-solving skill when faced with social situations that cause frustration, a teacher might teach how to request a toy by saying/signing/using a picture that means, "Do you want to trade?" instead of grabbing it from a peer. The teacher could also teach children different ways of asking for desired items by using other statements or other social behaviors that can be used in varied contexts. Children could also be taught that they can use other problem-solving skills such as offering an item to trade or suggesting that they play with the toy and their peer at the same time by taking turns. These scenarios consider the extension of their problem-solving skill repertoires, which will likely promote generalization by increasing their ability to engage with a variety of peers (e.g., peers who share easily, peers who are more likely to trade than share) in varied settings.

Use Intensive Progress Monitoring

As we discussed previously, progress monitoring is critical for confirming that children are learning the social-emotional skills that are being taught. Earlier in this chapter, we discussed a variety of progress-monitoring strategies for teachers to use depending on the children's abilities and individualized needs regarding their social-emotional competence. However, the delivery of a Tier 2 instruction will require that individualized progress monitoring occur frequently (e.g., daily, weekly) to ensure that the child is responding to the intervention. Because children's goals are more individualized at this point, it will be important to use progress-monitoring tools and approaches that are based on the individual skills children are working on at Tier 2.

To develop a progress-monitoring tool, practitioners must identify the skills or behaviors that will be evaluated and identify how meaningful data might be collected to indicate a child's progress toward the targeted goal. Data collection methods can be simple such as the use of frequency counts of the number of times a child uses a target skill (e.g., number of times a child initiates joining the play of other children during center-time activities) or might involve an examination of the rate of responding to opportunities that is expressed as a percentage of opportunities (e.g., the percentage of opportunities that a child shares an item when asked by another child). Other measures might be used such as duration recording (e.g., duration that a child engages in cooperative play with others) or time sampling (e.g., teacher looks to see if child is playing cooperatively at predetermined time intervals). In addition to these methods, teachers should consider the use of a practitioner-developed behavior rating scale to monitor progress. A behavior rating scale can provide an accurate indication of child progress while requiring less effort toward data collection (Christ, Riley-Tillman, & Chafouleas, 2009; Dunlap, Wilson, Strain, & Lee, 2013). A behavior rating scale (see Figure 7.6 for an example) is constructed by designing an individualized rating scale that captures the increments of the relevant dimension of the skill to be rated. The frequency of progress monitoring will depend on the children's needs; however, tracking children's use of

---

Directions: Write the child's name and define the behavior of interest. Write the date. For each routine or activity of interest, circle the number on the rating scale that corresponds with the child's demonstration of that behavior.

Child: _____

Behavior definition: _____

Date: _____ Routine/activity: _____

Rating	1	2	3	4
Definition	Does not demonstrate behavior	Occasionally demonstrates behavior	Often demonstrates behavior	Demonstrates behavior at level similar to peers

Multi-Tiered Systems of Support for Young Children: Driving Change in Early Education
by Judith J. Carta and Robin Miller Young. Copyright © 2019 by Paul H. Brookes Publishing Co., Inc. All rights reserved.

Figure 7.6. Progress-monitoring data collection sheet: Rating scale.

> *Directions: Write the child's name and define the behavior of interest. Write the date. For each routine or activity of interest, make a tally mark for each instance of the behavior of interest.*
>
> Child: _____
> Behavior definition: _____
>
> Date: _____ Routine/activity: _____
>
> Tally each routine or activity of interest in the space below.
>
> Sum: _____
>
> *Multi-Tiered Systems of Support for Young Children: Driving Change in Early Education*
> by Judith J. Carta and Robin Miller Young. Copyright © 2019 by Paul H. Brookes Publishing Co., Inc. All rights reserved.

Figure 7.7. Progress-monitoring data collection sheet: Frequency count.

particular skills on at least a daily basis is recommended. Daily progress-monitoring data can be transferred to a visual representation of data (e.g., line graph) that can and should be used for making data-based decisions.

See Figure 7.7 for an example of a progress-monitoring tool used to measure the frequency of a behavior. This tool can be used to collect data on appropriate, as well as challenging, behavior. See Figure 7.8 for a graph of a child's challenging behavior and initiations on the playground, both prior to and during intervention.

In this section, we have discussed critical instructional practices for teaching social-emotional skills and have provided examples of how these instructional approaches might be used to support children who are in need of Tier 2 instructional supports. It is important to note that the majority of these practices can be implemented in the context of ongoing classroom activities and routines and do not require teachers to spend a significant amount of time outside those activities and routines to support children's instructional needs. Many of the practices that require more individualized time with the child can be implemented in the context

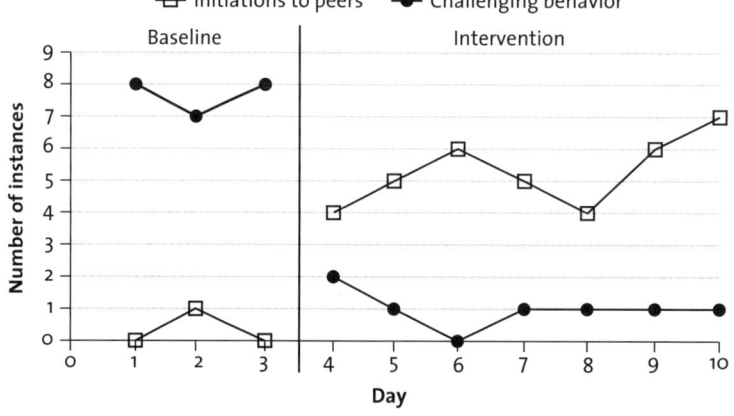

Figure 7.8. Graph example.

of a small group. Although Tier 2 supports require more frequent, more individualized, or more intensive levels of instruction, the majority of that instruction can and should occur in the context of ongoing classroom activities and routines.

STEPS FOR DEVELOPING TIER 2 INSTRUCTIONAL SUPPORTS

Considering the evidence base about effective instruction related to young children's social-emotional development, the following steps are recommended for developing Tier 2 instructional supports, which are illustrated using the children from Becky's classroom.

Becky has five children who have been identified as needing more intensive supports around social-emotional skills. Two of the children are Faisal and Ryan. Faisal is socially withdrawn and rarely interacts with other children, and Ryan is easily frustrated and aggressive toward other children. Based on her progress-monitoring data, Becky decides that both children need more supports around social problem solving. When faced with a social problem, Faisal generally walks away, and Ryan typically is aggressive toward other children in order to get what he wants. Becky uses the following steps to design instructional supports:

1. Identify the target skill: Becky realizes that social problem solving requires a broad set of skills. She decides to start by teaching Faisal and Ryan three solutions to common problems: trade, wait until the child is finished with the toy, and get a teacher. She selects these three solutions because they can be used to solve many different social problems.
2. Select instructional approaches: Becky decides she will use 1) prompting and feedback during small-group instruction to teach the solutions, 2) role-play during small group to practice the solutions, and 3) prompting and feedback during center time to promote the use of the solutions in the context in which they will be needed. To accomplish this, she will make visuals to represent each solution, teach the children what the visuals mean, and use the visuals during center time to decrease the extent to which she interrupts the children's interactions with each other. She generates a number of vignettes that she can use during small-group instruction to practice the solutions. Furthermore, she uses an activity matrix to plan opportunities during the day for Faisal and Ryan to practice the skills even when they don't have a significant social problem. Finally, she has been talking to both children's parents, and they are excited to help out. She works with the parents to identify ways that the children can work on these skills at home or in the community, and the parents and Becky agree to communicate each week about how the children are doing.
3. Monitoring implementation and outcomes: Becky wants to closely monitor how Faisal and Ryan are doing related to problem solving. She wants the intervention to work but she also wants to ensure that if it isn't working, she knows so she can make modifications quickly. She determines how many instructional trials she will deliver during small group and makes a data sheet with space for scoring four trials for each solution. For each trial, she will indicate if the child demonstrated the solution independently or if the child needed a prompt to complete the trial. She will also ensure that each child has opportunities to practice the solutions at least three times

during centers. Furthermore, she will include a space to note how many trials were conducted so she can ensure that the children receive the amount of instruction planned. In addition, she develops a behavior rating scale and asks other classroom staff and family to complete the behavior rating once a week.

4. Making instructional decisions: The classroom team has a meeting each Friday. Becky plans to review the data during those meetings to determine if they are implementing the instructional supports as planned, if the children are learning the skills, and whether changes are needed in the instructional plan.

SUPPORTING TEACHERS DURING TIER 2 INSTRUCTION

The development and implementation of Tier 2 instructional supports related to young children's social-emotional development and challenging behavior is a complex process. As discussed previously, it involves the use of universal screening to determine which children might be in need of Tier 2 supports, assessment to identify individual needs, and the development of instructional supports and progress monitoring for determining if the instructional supports are effective and, if not, how they might need to be refined to increase their effectiveness.

Researchers have looked at professional development related to implementing positive behavior supports and social-emotional interventions (e.g., Barton, Pribble, & Chen, 2014; Conroy et al., 2015; Domitrovich et al., 2009; Hemmeter et al., 2016; Stormont, Smith, & Lewis, 2007). In these studies, researchers have consistently used a combination of high-quality training and systematic coaching with performance-based feedback (e.g., practice-based coaching [PBC]; Snyder, Hemmeter, & Fox, 2015). Teachers have learned to use individual strategies (e.g., descriptive praise, expansions, precorrections), multi-component interventions (e.g., Pyramid Model, embedded instruction practices), and social-emotional curricula (e.g., *PATHS Preschool*). Supporting teachers to use multi-component interventions has required a significant dosage of coaching. For example, Hemmeter and colleagues (2016) provided 16 weeks of coaching following 3 days of high-quality workshops. Conroy and colleagues (2015) used 14 weeks of individualized coaching to support teachers to use BEST in CLASS, which is a Tier 2 intervention.

High-quality training and PBC are effective for supporting teachers to implement Tier 1 and Tier 2 instructional practices. However, there are some practical issues related to these findings. First, there is limited evidence of effective strategies for supporting teachers to design individualized interventions and to use data-based decision making related to instructional decisions. Second, although the professional development interventions are effective, they are also resource-intensive. It is unlikely that most programs will be able to deliver 16 coaching sessions to each teacher on Tier 1 practices followed by more coaching related to Tier 2 and 3 practices.

Comprehensive programwide supports that include ongoing coaching are necessary for supporting teachers to implement tiered models (Fixsen, Naoom, Blasé, Friedman, & Wallace, 2005; Fox & Hemmeter, 2009). These programwide supports include but are not limited to 1) ongoing coaching (e.g., PBC; Snyder et al., 2015) focused not only on implementation of universal practices but also around designing, implementing, and evaluating Tier 2 instructional supports; 2) programwide implementation of universal screening; 3) personnel who can support teachers around the development of Tier 3 interventions; and 4) ongoing support around using data to make instructional decisions.

INCLUDING FAMILIES IN DEVELOPMENT AND IMPLEMENTATION

Families should be included in all aspects of a tiered model. At the base of a tiered model, families should be engaged around efforts to support children's social-emotional development and prevent challenging behavior. This would include a variety of strategies focused on 1) building relationships with families as partners in their children's education; 2) sharing information with families about creating consistent and predictable routines, implementing positive guidance strategies, and being responsive to their children's communication; and 3) providing families with information on how to promote social-emotional development at home and in the community.

By supporting and engaging families at Tier 1, early childhood programs provide a context for engaging families in developing and implementing Tier 2 supports. It creates a context where the family trusts the professionals and feels like an important part of their child's educational team. Second, professionals are more likely to understand the child's needs across environments when they have worked with the family previously. This information can then be useful when developing Tier 2 interventions. Third, when educators share information with families about the importance of Tier 1 strategies at home and in the community, families may be more prepared to implement Tier 2 strategies.

CONCLUSION

Recent attention on young children's challenging behavior and social-emotional needs has resulted in a focus on how to support young children in early childhood settings. While tiered models have been described, there has been relatively little discussion on how to identify children who are not responding to the universal curriculum; how to design instructional supports to address their social, emotional, and behavioral needs; and how to support teachers to implement the practices needed to implement tiered models. However, there has been a great deal of research on effective instruction and effective supports for teachers. In this chapter, we have attempted to use this research to articulate how to design and monitor Tier 2 instructional supports. This work is limited to some extent by lack of efficient universal screening and progress-monitoring tools. Nonetheless, there are tools and strategies necessary for designing, delivering, and monitoring Tier 2 instructional supports.

The diversity of social-emotional instructional needs within Becky's classroom is not uncommon. Because Becky taught in a school that provided an implementation infrastructure of MTSS, she had assistance in identifying children who needed more support and designing their interventions. The development of her plan for providing Tier 2 supports to Ryan and Emily occurred during a meeting with her classroom coach and the classroom team. She shared the children's progress-monitoring data with her coach and discussed how their behavior was interfering in their interactions with other children. Becky and her coach developed a plan for each child and designed a progress-monitoring tool that would capture a daily rating of the child's use of the target skill. Becky set a date to begin implementing the Tier 2 interventions, and her coach identified a day that she could come by to observe implementation with Ryan and Emily and provide coaching to Becky and her teaching assistants.

Becky and her coach were more puzzled by Faisal's challenges and how to support him with engagement in activities and initiating interactions with peers and adults. Becky's coach suggested that they bring the data related to Faisal's social challenges to the next monthly meeting of the grade-level intervention support group (ISG). Becky and her coach are members of the preschool-kindergarten intervention support group that meets each month to assist teachers with the interpretation of progress-monitoring data and the design of interventions. Becky and her coach presented the concerns about Faisal at the next ISG meeting and were able to receive some valuable suggestions from a kindergarten teacher who successfully intervened with a similar child the previous year. Following the ISG meeting, Becky and her coach designed a Tier 2 intervention plan for Faisal and a progress-monitoring behavior rating scale.

The Tier 2 interventions Becky planned for Faisal, Ryan, Emily, Lei, and Brian included the following components:

- Instruction in how to identify problems, engage in the problem-solving process, and try solutions to problems
- Instruction in how to interact with peers appropriately in a variety of activities (e.g., different centers, playground, meal times)
- Instruction in how to use materials in the classroom to play with peers and independently

Becky used an activity matrix similar to the one provided in Figure 7.5 to ensure that she and the classroom team embedded instruction throughout the day. Her coach helped collect data on Becky and her classroom team's implementation of instruction. The classroom team also collected data regularly on children's challenging behavior and appropriate behavior, using tools such as those provided in Figures 7.6 and 7.7. Becky was unsure of how to graph the data, so her coach helped her to graph the data and understand what it meant. Over time, they began to see changes in the children's prosocial behaviors.

RESOURCES

Specific tools related to assessment of social-emotional skills that are cited in the chapter are indicated with an *asterisk in the reference list.

Center for Early Childhood Mental Health Consultation. http://www.ecmhc.org/index.html. The Center provides "Choose and Use Guides" to social-emotional screening tools and social-emotional curricula that programs and practitioners might find valuable as they consider the components needed for the MTSS.

Collaborative for Academic, Social, and Emotional Learning (CASEL) Guide. http://www.casel.org/guide. This guide includes an evaluation of social-emotional programs and their effectiveness.

Division for Early Childhood (DEC), National Association for the Education of Young Children (NAEYC), & National Head Start Association (NHSA). (2013). *Frameworks for Response to Intervention in early childhood: Description and implications.* Missoula, MT: Author. Retrieved from http://www.dec-sped.org/position-statements

Illinois Early Learning Project. http://illinoisearlylearning.org/faqs/socialcomp.htm. This site answers many frequently asked questions about social-emotional skills and has links to a variety of resources.

Promoting Children's Social and Emotional Development Through Preschool Education: NIEER Preschool Policy Brief. http://nieer.org/policy-issue/policy-report-promoting-childrens-social-and-emotional-development-through-preschool-education. This brief provides an overview of social-emotional development and teaching. It also includes recommendations for practice.

Technical Assistance Center on Social Emotional Intervention for Young Children. http://www.challengingbehavior.org. On this web site are many materials that can be used to establish partnerships with families to teach targeted social-emotional skills. In addition, a roadmap document is available with guidance on selecting a social-emotional screening tool.

The Center on the Social and Emotional Foundations for Early Learning (CSEFEL). http://csefel.vanderbilt.edu. CSEFEL has compiled a variety of activities, materials, and tools to help children learn social-emotional skills. Examples of strategies and materials you will find here are handouts that feature emotion faces, the "turtle technique," and feeling charts as well as solution kits to help children come up with solutions around problems such as learning how to share, trade, and ask nicely.

REFERENCES

*Bagnato, S. J., Neisworth, J. T., & Pretti-Frontczak, K. (2010). *LINKing authentic assessment and early childhood intervention: Best measures for best practices*. Baltimore, MD: Paul H. Brookes Publishing Co.

Barton, E. E., Pribble, L., & Chen, C. (2014). The use of e-mail to deliver performance-based feedback to early childhood practitioners. *Journal of Early Intervention, 35*, 270–297.

Blair, K. S. C., Fox, L., & Lentini, R. (2010). Use of positive behavior support to address the challenging behavior of young children within a community early childhood program. *Topics in Early Childhood Special Education, 30*, 68–79.

Brennan, L. M., Shaw, D. S., Dishion, T. J., & Wilson, M. (2012). Longitudinal predictors of school-age academic achievement: Unique contributions of toddler-age aggression, oppositionality, inattention, and hyperactivity. *Journal of Abnormal Child Psychology, 40*, 1289–1300.

*Bricker, D., Capt, B., Pretti-Frontczak, K., Johnson, J., Slentz, K., Straka, E., & Waddell, M. (2002). *Assessment, Evaluation, and Programming System (AEPS®) for Infants and Children* (2nd ed., Vol. 2). Baltimore, MD: Paul H. Brookes Publishing Co.

Burchinal, M., Vandergrift, N., Pianta, R., & Mashburn, A. (2010). Threshold analysis of association between child care quality and child outcomes for low income children in pre-kindergarten programs. *Early Childhood Research Quarterly, 25*, 166–176.

Chien, N. C., Howes, C., Burchinal, M., Pianta, R. C., Ritchie, S., Bryant, D. M., . . . Barbarin, O. A. (2010). Children's classroom engagement and school readiness gains in pre-kindergarten. *Child Development, 81*, 1534–1549.

Christ, T. J., Riley-Tillman, T. C., & Chafouleas, S. M. (2009). Foundation for the development and use of direct behavior rating (DBR) to assess and evaluate student behavior. *Assessment for Effective Intervention, 34*, 201–213.

Collaborative for Academic, Social, and Emotional Learning. (n.d.). *Social and Emotional Learning Core Competencies*. Retrieved from http://www.casel.org/social-and-emotional-learning/core-competencies

Committee for Children. (1991). *Second Steps: Early Learning*. Retrieved from http://www.secondstep.org/early-learning-curriculum.

Conroy, M. A., Dunlap, G., Clarke, S., & Alter, P. J. (2005). A descriptive analysis of behavioral intervention research with young children with challenging behavior. *Topics in Early Childhood Special Education, 25*, 157–166.

Conroy, M. A., Sutherland, K. S., Algina, J. J., Wilson, R. E., Martinez, J. R., & Whalon, K. J. (2015). Measuring teacher implementation of the BEST in CLASS intervention program and corollary child outcomes. *Journal of Emotional and Behavioral Disorders, 23*, 144–155.

Dodge, K. A., Bierman, K. L., Coie, J. D., Greenberg, M. T., Lochman, J. E., McMahon, R. J., & Pinderhughes, E. E. (2014). Impact of early intervention on psychopathology, crime, and well-being at age 25. *American Journal of Psychiatry, 172*(1), 59–70.

Dodge, D. T., Heroman, C., Berke, K., Colker, L., Bickart, T., . . . Tabors, P. O. (2016). *The Creative Curriculum for Preschool* (6th ed.). Bethesda, MD: Teaching Strategies.

Domitrovich, C. E., Cortes, R. C., & Greenberg, M. T. (2007). Improving young children's social and emotional competence: A randomized trial of the preschool "PATHS" curriculum. *The Journal of Primary Prevention, 28*, 67–91. doi:10.1007/s10935-007-0081-0

Domitrovich, C. E., Gest, S. D., Gill, S., Bierman, K. L., Welsh, J. A., & Jones, D. (2009). Fostering high-quality teaching with an enriched curriculum and professional development support: The Head Start REDI program. *American Educational Research Journal, 46*, 567–597.

Domitrovich, C., Greenberg, M., Kusche, C., & Cortes, R. (2004). *PATHS preschool program*. South Deerfield, MA: Channing Bete.

Domitrovich, C. E., Moore, J. E., & Greenberg, M. T. (2012). Maximizing the effectiveness of social-emotional interventions for young children through high-quality implementation of evidence-based interventions. In B. Kelly & D. F. Perkins (Eds), *Handbook of implementation science for psychology in education* (pp. 207–229). New York, NY: Cambridge.

Dunlap, G., & Fox, L. (2011). Function-based interventions for children with challenging behavior. *Journal of Early Intervention, 33*, 333–343.

Dunlap, G., Wilson, K., Strain, P., & Lee, J. K. (2013). *Prevent, teach, reinforce for young children*. Baltimore, MD: Paul H. Brookes Publishing Co.

Early Childhood Technical Information Center (2017) *Using COS for Federal Reporting* (2017, November, 20). Retrieved from http://ectacenter.org/#2

Fixsen, D. L., Naoom, S. F., Blasé, K. A., Friedman, R. M., & Wallace, F. (2005). *Implementation research: A synthesis of the literature*. Tampa: University of South Florida, Louis de la Parte Florida Mental Health Institute, The National Implementation Research Network.

Fox, L., Carta, J., Dunlap, G., Strain, P., & Hemmeter, M. L. (2010). Response to Intervention and the Pyramid Model. *Infants and Young Children, 23*, 3–14.

Fox, L., Dunlap, G., Hemmeter, M. L., Joseph, G. E., & Strain, P. S. (2003). The Teaching Pyramid: A model for supporting social competence and preventing challenging behavior in young children. *Young Children, 58*, 48–52.

Fox, L., & Hemmeter, M. L. (2009). A program-wide model for supporting social emotional development and addressing challenging behavior in early childhood settings. In W. Sailor, G. Dunlap, G. Sugai, & R. Horner (Eds.), *Handbook of positive behavior support* (pp. 177–202). New York, NY: Springer.

Gresham, F. M., & Elliott, S. N. (2008). *Social Skills Improvement System Rating Scales manual*. Minneapolis, MN: NCS Pearson.

Hemmeter, M.L., Fox, L., & Snyder, P. (2013). A tiered model for promoting social-emotional competence and addressing challenging behavior. In V. Buysse & E. Peisner-Feinberg (Eds.), *Handbook of Response to Intervention in early childhood* (pp. 85–101). Baltimore, MD: Paul H. Brookes Publishing Co.

Hemmeter, M. L., Fox, L., & Snyder, P. (2014). *Teaching Pyramid Observation Tool—Research edition* [manual]. Baltimore, MD: Paul H. Brookes Publishing Co.

Hemmeter, M. L., Snyder, P. A., Fox, L., & Algina, J. (2016). Evaluating the implementation of the Pyramid Model for promoting social-emotional competence in early childhood classrooms. *Topics in Early Childhood Special Education*. Advance online publication. doi:10.1177/0271121416653386

Heroman, C., Burts, D. C., Berke, K., & Bickart, T. S. (2010). *Teaching Strategies GOLD: Objectives for development and learning: Birth through kindergarten*. Bethesda, MD: Teaching Strategies.

Ikeda, M. J., Neessen, E., & Witt, J. C. (2008). Best practices in universal screening. *Best Practices in School Psychology, 5*, 103–114.

Jones, D. E., Greenberg, M., & Crowley, M. (2015). Early social-emotional functioning and public health: The relationship between kindergarten social competence and future wellness. *American Journal of Public Health, 105*, 2283–2290.

Joseph, J. D., Rausch, A., & Strain, P. S. (2016). Social competence and young children with special needs: Debunking "mythconceptions." *Young Exceptional Children*. (Advance online publication). doi:10.1177/1096250615621359

Kohler, F. W., & Strain, P. S. (1999). Maximizing peer-mediated resources in integrated preschool classrooms. *Topics in Early Childhood Special Education, 19,* 92–102. doi:10.1177/027112149901900203.

Merrell, K. W. (2001). Assessment of children's social skills: Recent developments, best practices, and new directions. *Exceptionality, 9*(1–2), 3–18.

Merrell, K. W. (2002). *Preschool and Kindergarten Behavior Scales: Test manual.* Brandon, VT: Clinical Psychology Publishing Co.

Office of Head Start. (2015). *Head Start Early Learning Outcomes Framework: Ages Birth to Five.* Retrieved from http://eclkc.ohs.acf.hhs.gov/hslc/hs/sr/approach/pdf/ohs-framework.pdf

Sarama, J., Brenneman, K., Clements, D. H., Duke, N. K., & Hemmeter, M. L. (2016). *Connect4Learning: The pre-k curriculum.* Lewisville, NC: Connect4Learning.

Severson, H. H., Walker, H. M., Hope-Doolittle, J., Kratochwill, T. R., & Gresham, F. M. (2007). Proactive, early screening to detect behaviorally at-risk students: Issues, approaches, emerging innovations, and professional practices. *Journal of School Psychology, 45,* 193–223.

Shonkoff, J. P., & Phillips, D. A. (Eds.). (2000). *From neurons to neighborhoods: The science of early childhood development.* Washington, DC: National Academies Press.

Snyder, P. A., Hemmeter, M. L., & Fox, L. (2015). Supporting implementation of evidence-based practices through practice-based coaching. *Topics in Early Childhood Special Education, 35,* 133–143.

Squires, J., Bricker, D., & Twombly, E. (2015) *Ages & Stages Questionnaires®: Social-Emotional, Second Edition (ASQ:SE-2).* Baltimore, MD: Paul H. Brookes Publishing Co.

Steed, E. A., Pomerleau, T. M., & Horner, R. (2012). *Preschool-wide Evaluation Tool (Pre-SET™) manual, research edition.* Baltimore, MD: Paul H. Brookes Publishing Co.

Stormont, M. A., Smith, S. C., & Lewis, T. J. (2007). Teacher implementation of precorrection and praise statements in Head Start classrooms as a component of a program-wide system of positive behavior support. *Journal of Behavioral Education, 16,* 280–290.

Strain, P. S., & Bovey, E. H. (2011). Randomized, controlled trial of the LEAP model of early intervention for young children with autism spectrum disorders. *Topics in Early Childhood Special Education, 31,* 133–154. doi:10.1177/0271121411408740

Strain, P. S., & Bovey, E. H. (2014). Promoting peer relations for young children with autism spectrum disorder: The LEAP preschool experience. In S. Madrid, D. E. Fernie, & R. Kantor (Eds.), *Reframing the emotional worlds of the early childhood classroom* (pp. 177–190). New York, NY: Routledge.

Strain, P. S., & Bovey, E. H. (2016). The power of peers to influence social outcomes for children with special needs. In K.R. Harris & L. Meltzer (Eds.), *The power of peers: Enhancing learning, development and social skills* (pp. 288–316) New York, NY: Guilford Press.

Vaughn, S., Kim, A., Sloan, C. V. M., Hughes, M. T., Elbaum, B., & Sridhar, D. (2003). Social skills interventions for young children with disabilities: A synthesis of group design studies. *Remedial and Special Education, 24,* 2–15.

Webster-Stratton, C. (2002). *Effective classroom management skills training and Dina dinosaur's social skills and problem-solving curriculum training for the classroom: Leader's guide.* Seattle, WA: Incredible Years.

Webster-Stratton, C., & Reid, M. J. (2004). Strengthening social and emotional competence in young children—The foundation for early school readiness and success: Incredible Years Classroom Social Skills and Problem-Solving Curriculum. *Infants and Young Children, 17,* 96–113. doi:10.1097/00001163-200404000-00002

Webster-Stratton, C., Reid, M. J., & Stoolmiller, M. (2008). Preventing conduct problems and improving school readiness: Evaluation of the Incredible Years Child Training Programs in high-risk schools. *The Journal of Child Psychology and Psychiatry, 49,* 471–488. doi:10.1111/j.1469-7610.2007.01861.x

Wolery, M., Strain, P. S., & Bailey, D. B. (1992). Reaching the potentials of children with special needs. In S. Bredekamp & T. Rosegrant (Eds.), *Reaching potentials: Appropriate curriculum and assessment for young children* (pp. 92–111). Washington, DC: National Association for the Education of Young Children.

8

Creating and Providing Tier 3 Instructional Support

Ruth A. Kaminski, Kelly A. Powell-Smith, and Katherine Bravo Aguayo

Marta is the teacher of a public preschool classroom of 15 students. A summer professional development workshop has motivated her to focus on building phonological awareness (PA) skills with her students in the hopes of putting them on the path to becoming successful readers in elementary school.

Many of the children in her classroom started the school year with low PA skills, although after 2 months of instruction, most are beginning to make progress developing initial skills such as rhyming, syllable segmentation, and saying the first sounds in words. She is concerned about two children. Ella has an identified speech delay and is on an individualized education program (IEP). Marta frequently asks her questions during classroom PA activities, and she either does not respond or does not respond correctly. James does not have an identified disability but similarly struggles to grasp basic PA concepts. He demonstrates challenging behaviors and is rarely able to sit still and pay attention during instruction.

In addition, Marta is concerned about Mateo, who is a dual language learner (DLL) with very limited English. His limited English language skills impact his peer interactions and his participation in classroom activities. Marta has identified only 10 English words that Mateo has used in the classroom. She knows that Mateo needs to develop his English vocabulary before he can benefit from core classroom instruction in PA and other important skills.

Marta incorporates small-group instruction in her classroom, providing instruction that is comparable to Tier 2 support, but she is less sure about when, if, and how to modify what she is doing to meet the needs of the three lowest performing children in her classroom. Multi-tiered systems of support (MTSS) has been implemented in the elementary grades at her school for about 3 years, and Marta wonders if this model could be useful in meeting the needs of all of the children in her classroom.

INTRODUCTION

As you can see in the opening scenario, Marta has several students in her class who may need extra assistance to make adequate progress in the development of critical literacy and language skills if they are to be on track for success when they enter kindergarten. In particular, Marta needs some assistance in implementing what would be considered Tier 3 interventions within an MTSS model of service delivery and decision making. Tier 3 instruction offers more individualized, targeted, and intensive instructional support either one to one or in small groups when Tier 2 instruction does not lead to improved child outcomes.

As a service delivery/decision-making model, MTSS is complex and has many moving parts, making implementation challenging. Among the components of an MTSS model, Tier 3 intervention is one of the most challenging to implement, in part because of lack of research regarding the specific features of intervention that will work with the group of young students whose response to typically effective instruction is low (e.g., Harn, Linan-Thompson, & Roberts, 2008; Hill, King, Lemons, & Partanen, 2012). Research with early elementary-age students who have not responded to Tier 1 and/or Tier 2 interventions indicates that these students frequently demonstrate needs in multiple areas (e.g., oral language, phonological processing, attention, behavior) (Al Otaiba & Fuchs, 2002; Denton et al., 2013). Furthermore, a proportion of students continue to struggle to make adequate progress even when provided with more intensive evidence-based intervention that is generally effective for most students (Denton, Fletcher, Anthony, & Francis, 2006; Wanzek & Vaughn, 2008). Our own experience and research confirms these findings at the preschool level (Kaminski & Powell-Smith, 2016; Kaminski, Powell-Smith, Hommel, McMahon, & Bravo Aguayo, 2015). The primary purpose of this chapter is to review the research on Tier 3 intervention within an MTSS model and provide an overview of considerations for the implementation of Tier 3 intervention in early childhood settings. An additional purpose is to provide helpful implementation resources for professionals. One of those resources is Video 5 in which a young child benefits from receipt of intensive instruction matched to his needs through application of the problem-solving process.

See Video 5 for a demonstration of intensive instruction matched to a student's individual needs through the application of the problem-solving process.

WHAT DO WE KNOW ABOUT TIER 3 INTERVENTION?

Whether Tier 3 interventions are needed at the preschool level is an important question to address at the outset. An argument could be made that children entering preschool have not yet had the opportunity to benefit from formal schooling and that providing intensive intervention in preschool is intrusive and unnecessary. We disagree with this perspective and would argue for the benefit of providing Tier 3 support as early as it is viable to do so in the preschool years. When children start their prekindergarten year in a typical early childhood program with lower than average early literacy and language performance levels, they rarely close initial skill gaps without some type of intensified instruction (Greenwood et al., 2012). Moreover, decades of research indicate that the skills with which children enter kindergarten make a significant difference to later academic success (e.g., National Early Literacy Panel, 2008). Furthermore, a substantial body of converging evidence supports the finding that there are larger effects for interventions provided in the early stages of reading acquisition, especially in kindergarten and first grade, than for interventions provided in grade 3 and higher (e.g., Cavanaugh, Kim, Wanzek, & Vaughn, 2004; Wanzek & Vaughn, 2007). Thus, it is critical that programs serving young children provide strong support for the development of critical skills necessary for later school success, especially for those preschool students with the lowest skills.

Tier 3 is one component of an overarching service delivery/decision-making model (i.e., MTSS) and can apply to any instructional or curricular area—academic or developmental as well as social-behavioral. While initially and most extensively applied to the area of reading instruction, MTSS is increasingly being implemented in other academic areas such as math (e.g., Bryant et al., 2016). The use of Positive Behavioral Interventions and Support (PBIS) to address social-behavioral concerns also has been integrated with an MTSS model both at school age (Lewis, Mitchell, Bruntmeyer, & Sugai, 2016) and preschool (Fox, Carta, Strain, Dunlap, & Hemmeter, 2010).

Tier 3 is described as consisting of supplemental instruction or support that is more intensive than lower levels of instructional support. Exactly how the intensity is increased—that is, what instructional variables are modified and how—is described in various ways in the literature. In the area of social-behavioral support, Tier 3 is addressed through conducting a functional behavioral assessment and developing and implementing an individual behavioral plan. The effectiveness of these procedures is widely documented in the literature (e.g., Dunlap & Fox, 2011; Horner et al., 2014), so it will not be a focus of this chapter. For a discussion of the application of support for social-behavioral concerns within an MTSS framework, please see Chapter 7. This chapter focuses on the implementation of Tier 3 in early childhood in the area of preacademic and developmental skills.

Tier 3 Implementation

Tier 3 in preschool typically is described as being more intensive and individualized with the addition of more frequent progress monitoring, structured problem solving, and more intensive empirical interventions (Barnett, VanDerHeyden, & Witt, 2007). Unfortunately, few descriptions of actual implementations of Tier 3 interventions within an MTSS model exist in the literature—and none that have been carried out in early education settings. A review of Tier 3 implementations at school age found some generalities about the implementation of Tier 3 and how it differed from Tier 2. Specifically, compared to Tier 2 interventions, Tier 3 interventions 1) used smaller group sizes (i.e., 2–4 students as opposed to 3–15); 2) allocated more time for intervention (i.e., more days per week and for more minutes per day); 3) conducted more frequent progress monitoring; and 4) more frequently used special educators to implement the Tier 3 intervention (Jenkins, Schiller, Blackorby, Thayer, & Tilly, 2013). These features of Tier 3 are supported by the research on intensive interventions in which higher effects are generally found for studies providing intervention with increased instructional time in the smallest group sizes and incorporating elements of effective instruction such as increased opportunities to respond and the provision of individual feedback (Connor, Alberto, Compton, & O'Connor, 2014).

Effectiveness of Tier 3

Although there is a great deal of research on the effectiveness of interventions for specific skills (e.g., language, literacy, math) in preschool (e.g., National Early Literacy Panel, 2008), most of the research is focused on interventions for students who are at risk and thus is more applicable to Tiers 1 and 2 than to Tier 3 (Noe, Spencer, Kruse, & Goldstein, 2014). Students needing Tier 3 intervention are no longer at risk—by definition they are already identified as needing additional support. The other body of literature on effectiveness of interventions comes out of the work with children with disabilities (Carta & Driscoll, 2013). Although some of the procedures used in these studies may be applicable to Tier 3, few studies, either at school age or in preschool, have examined response to Tier 3 interventions within the context of a full MTSS implementation. Furthermore, in most studies of intensive interventions, information about Tier 1 is not provided, restricting the assertions that can be made about the effectiveness of Tier 3. If children did not receive high-quality instruction in Tier 1 (and/or Tier 2), they are more likely to respond when provided intervention than those children who failed to make progress when provided with generally effective instruction (Gersten & Dimino, 2006).

Despite the limitations of the research in this area, there is evidence that increasing the intensity of intervention in early elementary grades can have significant effects on reading achievement (Harn et al., 2008; O'Connor, Harty, & Fulmer, 2005) and/or prevent reading difficulties for some students (O'Connor, Bocian, Sanchez, & Beach, 2014). Recent studies of Tier 3 interventions for preschool in the area of language and early literacy provide some support for the effectiveness of Tier 3 instruction for the lowest performing preschool children in these areas (Connor et al., 2014; Kaminski & Powell-Smith, 2016; Noe et al., 2014). The question, then, is not whether we should provide Tier 3 support in preschool, but rather, what is the most effective and efficient way to do so?

IMPLEMENTATION OF TIER 3 IN EARLY CHILDHOOD

In this section, we will discuss considerations for implementation of Tier 3 in early childhood settings including 1) which children need this level of support in preschool, 2) how to identify children for Tier 3 intervention, 3) features of effective Tier 3 instruction, 4) how to manage and implement interventions, and 5) how to monitor progress. We will also discuss the relationship between Tier 3 intervention and early childhood special education.

Children Who Need Tier 3 Support

Preschool children who are recipients of Tier 3 interventions are those who are significantly behind their peers in acquiring the skills needed to be successful in school. The significant learning needs of these children may stem from a number of factors. For example, severely limited or delayed early literacy skills may be due to limited experiences with language or with print materials (e.g., books) or due to speaking a first language other than English. In addition, disabilities (e.g., autism, cognitive delay), delays, or impairment in development of speech and language skills can contribute to the need for Tier 3 interventions. Another group of children who are more likely to need Tier 3 interventions are children with challenging behaviors. Disruptive behaviors as well as difficulties attending to tasks, even for short periods of time, can result in significant learning gaps. In their review of the literature, Al Otaiba and Fuchs (2002) found that one of the learner characteristics that corresponded to a lack of response to intervention were problem behaviors. The authors found that children with problem behaviors were unresponsive to early literacy interventions even when those interventions were provided in a one-to-one format.

It is important to point out here that Tier 3 is not synonymous with early childhood special education. Children receiving Tier 3 support in a particular skill area (e.g., early literacy, language, social-emotional/behavioral) may or may not have identified disabilities in that domain. Furthermore, children with identified disabilities may be appropriately served in Tier 1 and/or Tier 2 depending upon their individual learning needs. Please see Chapter 10 for information on meeting the needs of young children with identified disabilities in an MTSS framework.

Identification

While providing intensive support in preschool may prevent future academic and social-behavioral difficulties, it is challenging to identify children who need Tier 3 support at this age. Young children by nature are inconsistent in performance and often have difficulty maintaining attention to specific tasks or activities. It is also the case that children enter preschool with varying levels of skills and need to have opportunities to respond to appropriate instructional experiences that foster the preschool skills that are critical for later school success (e.g., social, language, and emergent literacy skills) before it is possible to identify which children are at risk for later learning difficulties. It is possible that efforts to identify children in preschool may identify children as needing support who may acquire critical skills and ultimately be successful without intervention. To address this issue, Catts and colleagues suggest that differential progress in the first few months of the school year can be useful to assess the risk for later academic and/or social-behavioral difficulties (Catts, Nielsen, Bridges, Liu, & Bontempo, 2015). In a study of identification of risk for reading disabilities in kindergarten, they found that a child's performance at the beginning of the year, coupled with progress during the first half of the year, provided a good indicator of risk.

A key element of screening for identification of children who need support is the use of reliable and valid measures that are appropriate for screening and progress monitoring of preschool children. In recent years, measures have been developed for this purpose that have evidence of validity and utility for making these decisions (e.g., Kaminski, Abbott, Bravo Aguayo, Latimer, & Good, 2014; McConnell, Wackerle-Hollman, Roloff, & Rodriguez, 2015). Essential to the use of such measures is a measurement framework that supports data-based decision making, including the identification of young children who are candidates for intensive support (see Chapter 4; McConnell et al., 2015).

We propose the following framework for the identification of preschool children for Tier 3. This framework is based on the notion of periodic screening of all children to identify those who are not making expected progress. It is a framework that we have used effectively with early school-age students (Kaminski, Cummings, Powell-Smith, & Good, 2008) and is consistent with recommendations for universal screening within an MTSS model for early childhood (e.g., Division of Early Childhood [DEC] of the Council for Exceptional Children, National Association for the

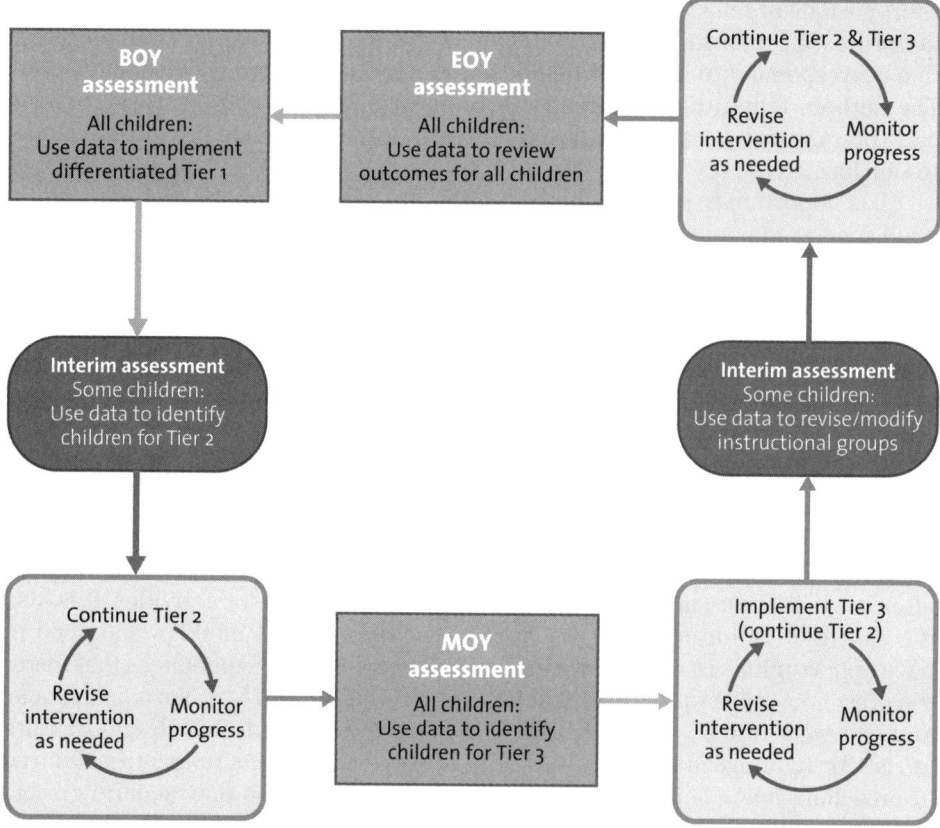

Figure 8.1. Early childhood multi-tiered systems of support (MTSS) assessment framework. (*Key:* BOY, beginning of year; MOY, middle of year; EOY, end of year.)
Source: Good, R. H. III & Kaminski R. A. (2011).

Education of Young Children [NAEYC], & National Head Start Association [NHSA], 2013; McConnell, & Greenwood, 2013; Spencer, Spencer, Goldstein, & Schneider, 2013). This framework is illustrated in Figure 8.1. Within this framework a screening measure is administered to all children three times over the course of the year—at the beginning (beginning of year = BOY), middle (middle of year = MOY), and end (end of year = EOY). At the beginning of the year, the initial screening can serve as a guide for differentiating instruction for all children in Tier 1. Midway through the year, approximately 6 weeks to 2 months into the first semester, we recommend an interim assessment or progress-monitoring probe for children who demonstrated low skills initially, along with any other children about whom there are concerns. These data will provide information on which children are and are not making progress when provided with core, Tier 1 instruction. This information, along with other sources of data collected over the course of the first few weeks and months of school (e.g., anecdotal records, classroom observations), can then be used to further differentiate core instruction. Some students may begin to receive small-group Tier 2 instruction at this time with the incorporation of more frequent progress monitoring, for example, every 2 weeks.

The mid-year screen of all children will provide information regarding which children are making progress in Tiers 1 and 2. We would recommend beginning Tier 3 intervention at this time for those children who have not made adequate progress in Tier 1 and/or Tier 2 in the first half of the school year. Starting Tier 3 in January allows for almost 5 months or 20 weeks to accelerate development and should not be postponed until the final 2 months of the school year. Research on providing Tier 3 interventions in preschool indicates that 8 weeks of intervention is enough time to accelerate growth for some children but is not enough time for all children (Kaminski & Powell-Smith, 2016). Allowing greater duration for intervention is also consistent with the majority of effective Tier 3 interventions for early school-age students, which provide daily intervention for 20–30 weeks (e.g., Denton et al., 2006; Wanzek & Vaughn, 2007).

Low-stakes decisions within a well-designed and executed classroom system of support, in which the classroom instruction is differentiated, are formative decisions focused on supporting student learning as opposed to decisions related to funding or teacher evaluation, for example. Students are placed into dynamic and flexible groups for instruction in Tier 1. Throughout the year, increasing tiers of support are provided as needed, with children receiving support matched to their current needs. If children make sufficient progress, they move to less intensive levels of support. Those students who need the more intensive support continue to receive support. For further information on data-based decision making, see Chapter 4.

It is important to point out that not all children will need to go through Tier 2 to get to Tier 3. This has been found to be true in early elementary grades (Compton et al., 2012; Greulich et al., 2014), and we support this recommendation in preschool. The purpose of MTSS in preschool is to prevent later reading and academic problems. Some young children will demonstrate substantial delays and lack of progress despite a generally effective Tier 1 such that the provision of an intervention more intensive than can be provided in Tier 2 may be warranted. Of course, as noted by Compton and colleagues (2012), in order to fast-track children into Tier 3, intervention must be with appropriate intensity and individualization to meet their needs.

FEATURES OF TIER 3 INTERVENTION

As previously noted, the students who need Tier 3 intervention often have deficits relative to their peers in attention to tasks, social-behavioral skills, oral language skills, and/or phonological processing (Al Otaiba & Fuchs, 2002). In addition, these children are making less than adequate progress in many of these areas than their peers and thus are not likely to catch up to their peers by the end of the school year. Instruction that is more intensive than Tier 2 support is needed to accelerate progress and close the achievement gap.

Over the past two decades, educational researchers have identified evidence-based instructional practices that are associated with student achievement across a wide range of skill areas for all students, and especially for those with significant learning needs and/or disabilities. For students with significant learning needs to benefit most from Tier 3 instruction, it must 1) be more systematic, 2) be more explicit, 3) focus on prioritized content, 4) include more opportunities to respond, and, to the greatest extent possible, 5) be more individualized than Tier 2 instruction (Connor et al., 2014; Simmons, 2015).

Kaminski and colleagues (2014) described a Tier 3 intervention in the area of early literacy that incorporates the features described previously. The lesson starts with a brief review of five letters of the alphabet, then moves on to a 2-minute introduction, demonstration, and instruction of the target skill for the day, which is focused on teaching children to identify the two parts of a two-syllable compound word. The majority of the intervention time is then spent on guided practice using engaging instructional materials such as picture cards, game boards, and puppets. After guided practice, the interventionist conducts a brief "checkout" in which the student is asked to independently respond to a predetermined number of items related to the target skill. Performance on the checkout determines whether the child will move on to a new skill or continue instruction on the same skill during the following session. Finally, a few minutes are spent at the end of the intervention to contextualize the skill by incorporating the skill in the reading of a poem/finger play, short story, or song. In such a session, within 10–15 minutes, the child has more than 100 opportunities to practice important early literacy skills with teacher guidance. A description of each of the intervention features and examples from the Reading Ready Early Literacy Intervention (RRELI) lesson are provided next.

Systematic Instruction

Instruction that is systematic specifies a carefully designed scope and sequence of skills. Skills are sequenced logically so as to avoid confusing the learner. Prerequisite skills are taught first; easier skills are taught before harder ones; and complex skills are broken down in smaller chunks of information to be learned. An optimal sequence is one that introduces skills in a manner that reduces the likelihood of confusing the student (Vaughn, Wanzek, Murray, & Roberts, 2012). For example, the RRELI follows a systematic sequence of skills that begin with easier skills, such as identifying the parts of a compound word and identifying syllables in words before identifying first sounds in words. The specific sounds were selected because they are relatively easy to say, are represented by the same letter in English and Spanish, and occur frequently at the beginning of common words.

Explicit Instruction

Explicit instruction is a direct approach to teaching that provides clear and concise language for step-by-step, teacher-guided instruction. Explicit instructions involve clear explanations and demonstrations (i.e., modeling) of the skill followed by guided practice with corrective feedback before the student performs the skill independently. Termed "I do, we do, you do," this approach reduces ambiguity for the learner and provides support (i.e., scaffolding) to perform the skill independently (Archer & Hughes, 2011). The RRELI uses the "I do, we do, you do" model in its lessons. For example, if a child is learning to clap the parts of a compound word, after a brief introduction, the teacher models the skill for the pictured words "backpack" and "cupcake" ("I do"). The teacher then says, "Let's do it together," and the child claps and says the parts of the words with the teacher ("We do"). Next, the child does the skill in guided practice during a game ("You do" with encouragement and guidance). Finally, the child performs the skill independently in the checkout.

Focus on Prioritized Content

Whereas Tier 2 intervention is often aligned with the core curriculum to provide greater opportunities to learn and practice what is taught in the core (Hill et al., 2012), Tier 3 interventions must not only remediate but also accelerate learning. Thus, it is recommended that Tier 3 intervention prioritize the essential skills—that is, focus on teaching the most critical skills—in an optimum sequence and at an optimum rate (Simmons, 2015). Students experience greater difficulty in learning the most important skills when there are too many skill objectives, likely because less time may be spent on mastery of any one skill. Focusing on critical skills is an approach that has been used in several Response to Intervention (RtI) studies, both with preschool students and older students (e.g., Foorman, Fletcher, Francis, Schatschneider, & Mehta, 1998; Gillon, 2000).

Following this reasoning, the RRELI does not teach all skills in the broad array of PA skills, such as rhyming and identifying words and onset rimes, but focuses primarily on effectively and efficiently teaching children to identify first sounds in words. In general, phonemic awareness at the phoneme level is more strongly related to later reading success than are syllable and rhyme awareness (e.g., Hulme, Bowyer-Crane, Carroll, Duff, & Snowling, 2012), and if we want to accelerate the development of preschool children in need of Tier 3 interventions, it is important to focus on the most critical skills.

Increased Opportunities to Respond

One of the most critical components of highly effective Tier 3 intervention is providing a high number of response opportunities during individualized instruction. Children with the most intensive instructional needs require numerous opportunities to practice and receive immediate feedback on the skills they are learning. This means that most of the intervention time should be spent practicing the skills taught. Having young children respond frequently not only helps them to focus on the lesson content but also keeps them actively engaged in the instructional activities. Furthermore, frequent child responses provide the teacher opportunities to check the child's understanding and provide guidance and feedback as needed (Archer & Hughes, 2011).

One of the ways to increase opportunities to respond is by providing instruction in smaller groups. The RRELI is designed to be done one to one or with a group of two children who need Tier 3 support. During the game format, the children have numerous opportunities to practice the skills and receive guidance and feedback from the teacher.

Individualized Instruction

In a synthesis of Institute of Educational Sciences (IES) studies on improving reading outcomes, Connor and colleagues concluded that one-size-fits-all approaches to intervention for students with or at risk for disabilities are not likely to be successful and recommended that instruction be individualized to children's strengths and weaknesses and modified on an ongoing basis as children progress and their needs change (Connor et al., 2014). Learning may be individualized for Tier 3 in several ways, including differentiating content and/or delivery of instruction. Some options illustrated in a study by Denton et al. (2013) included changing the activities used to engage each component and altering the amount of time spent on different intervention components. Included among the options for individualization is the allowance for increasing lesson duration, altering the pace of a lesson, making greater use of lesson activities that have prompting or scaffolding, and repeating lessons as needed to achieve results.

In summary, Tier 3 interventions need to be developed and packaged in such a way as to allow educators the flexibility to individualize the lessons to meet unique learner needs. Along with this flexibility, however, interventions must be sufficiently structured so implementers understand and can carry out key ingredients of the intervention with a high degree of fidelity. A sample Fidelity Checklist for the RRELI intervention is provided in Figure 8.2.

TIER 3 INTERVENTION IMPLEMENTATION

In a study investigating the proportions of children for higher tiers of instruction within an MTSS framework, Carta and colleagues found that 9%–14% of children were identified as needing Tier 3 support based on the Get Ready to Read screening tool (Carta et al., 2015). This proportion would translate to approximately two to three children out of a class of 20 and possibly more in sites serving large numbers of children who are DLLs or who have identified developmental delays. It is possible that when multiple students in a class require Tier 3 support, these students could receive intervention together as a small group. It is just as likely, however, that they would have different learning needs and would benefit most from individualized, one-to-one intervention. Given that the most effective intensive interventions for the lowest performing students are given daily, how is the preschool teacher to organize the classroom and arrange the schedule to conduct such individualized interventions? Is it even feasible to provide individualized interventions in a half-day preschool program?

A final feature of Tier 3 intervention in preschool settings, then, is that it must be feasible to implement. Two primary issues can affect feasibility: 1) teacher training and 2) the manner in which instruction is organized in typical preschool classrooms. It would be ideal for preschool teachers to be sufficiently skilled and have the time available to adapt curricula using best practices so that instruction can meet the needs of students in Tier 3. The reality is that most preschool teachers have limited time and limited training to equip them for such a task. In lieu of extensive training for preschool teachers, Tier 3 interventions need to be prepared in such a manner that a typical preschool teacher could implement the intervention successfully.

With respect to the second issue, variables to consider include the class size and teacher–child ratio (VanDerHeyden & Snyder, 2006). Most preschool classrooms are organized with a single teacher or a single teacher plus paraprofessional. As such, any intervention that requires the use of small groups or individual instruction will mean that the other children in the classroom must be engaged in activities that do not require the teacher (e.g., free choice, center time). An additional concern is the space available. Typically, preschools have limited space and support staff, so interventions must take place within the classroom and be conducted by classroom personnel.

Thus, the implementation of Tier 3 intervention in preschool not only requires well-designed interventions but careful planning and strategic classroom

Reading Ready Intervention Fidelity Checklist: Early Literacy

Observer: _____ Date: _____ Time: _____ to _____
Interventionist: _____ Lesson: _____ Student ID: _____

Fidelity of Intervention	Y	P	N	Notes
1. The teacher leads the children in practicing the alphabet, using the appropriate level of support (i.e., children name the letters after the teacher, with the teacher, or independently).				
2. The teacher introduces the lesson.				
3. The teacher reviews the past skill.				
4. The teacher uses "I do, we do, you do" approach to teach the new skill.				
5. The teacher uses explicit and consistent instructional language.				
6. The teacher provides 6–12 opportunities per minute for each child to respond during the activity.				
7. The teacher uses designated procedures for encouragement and guidance throughout the lesson.				
8. The teacher ends the activity by having the children practice the skill in the context of a printed poem, story, or finger play.				

Activity Management (Check all that apply)

❑ Materials for the lesson are ready and organized.
❑ The teacher paces the lesson to maintain attention.
❑ The teacher proactively provides positive attention to children for attention and appropriate behavior.
❑ Ratio of positive teacher attention for appropriate behavior to attention for misbehavior is at least 5:1.

Child Behavior

Accuracy of responses (Check one)
❑ ≥ 80% appropriate/accurate responses
❑ 40%–80% appropriate/accurate responses
❑ ≤ 40% appropriate/accurate responses

Level of engagement (Check one)
❑ Had difficulty attending/keeping engaged
❑ Generally attentive and engaged, occasionally had difficulty
❑ Was highly engaged with activities

Language abilities (Check one)
❑ Nonverbal or 1- to 2-word responses
❑ Communicated with brief utterances, phrases, short sentences
❑ Typical language for a preschooler (e.g., simple sentences, can carry on a short conversation about what he/she did last night)

Key: Y = Yes, P = Partial, N = No

Additional Notes/Comments (Use reverse side as needed):

Figure 8.2. Reading Ready Intervention Fidelity Checklist: Early Literacy. (From Kaminski, R., Reading Ready Early Literacy Intervention [RRELI]. Adapted and reprinted with permission.)

In *Multi-Tiered Systems of Support for Young Children: Driving Change in Early Education*
by Judith J. Carta and Robin Miller Young. (2019; Paul H. Brookes Publishing Co., Inc.)

management. In the preacademic and developmental skill areas (e.g., early literacy, language, math), the most effective interventions are likely to be an integrated approach utilizing both highly focused small-group/one-to-one instruction and intentional embedded approaches. Such an integrated approach maximizes effectiveness and efficiency of teaching and learning by providing opportunities for the child to receive the individualized instruction needed to acquire new skills combined with opportunities to practice, apply, and generalize the skills in multiple contexts across the preschool day.

As described by Wasik (2008), small-group instruction is "one of the most underused and ineffectively implemented strategies in early childhood classrooms" (p. 515). To be used effectively to implement Tier 3 interventions, the following guidelines are provided:

1. The classroom needs to be organized to accommodate small-group instruction daily; however, it is possible that not all children will participate in small-group instruction daily. We strongly recommend that children receiving Tier 3 support receive small-group instruction daily; however, in a half-day program, for example, children receiving Tier 2 support may participate in small-group instruction two or three times per week.

2. Assignment of children to small groups needs to be done intentionally based on child needs. All groups do not have to be of equal size.

3. A plan for managing the groups is necessary. This plan should include who is going to do the Tier 3 instruction, where the instruction will occur, what the other children will be doing, and how all of the children in the classroom will rotate or move through groups.

4. The classroom schedule and small-group time will change throughout the year. For example, it is possible that groups may be 5–10 minutes in length early in the school year or at the beginning of the provision of Tier 3. This time can be extended as children receiving Tier 3 support develop the skills to focus and participate in teacher-led instructional activities and in tandem with all of the children in the classroom, increasing their abilities to engage in independent learning activities in centers.

There are several models to implementing small groups. Most use learning centers and rely on having at least one other adult in the classroom. Two of the most common models for providing one-to-one or small-group intervention will be described. In the first, the children in the classroom are engaged in center activities. The teaching assistant monitors the center activities while the teacher works with individuals or small groups for 5–15 minutes each. In a second model, all children are assigned to one of four groups, and during designated small-group time the groups rotate every 10–20 minutes. At any given time, the teacher and assistant are working directly with one group and monitoring the independent work of children in an adjoining center. In both approaches, the grouping is flexible and dynamic, changing as children's needs change and can be further differentiated by assigning partners or grouping within a group (Wasik, 2008).

To maximize the effectiveness of the small-group instruction, it will be important to strategically integrate learning objectives into daily activities. Procedures and strategies that have evidence of effectiveness for embedding instruction

Table 8.1. Example of embedded intervention

Small-group instruction		Choice time	Snack	Outside	Story time
RRELI Lesson 2	Block area: It looks like you are building a big highway. We can clap and say the parts of the word "highway." "High" (clap) — "way" (clap). Housekeeping area: You poured some tea in the teacup. Clap and say the parts of the word "teacup" with me. "Tea" (clap) — "cup" (clap).	We have grapefruit today. We can clap and say the parts of the word "grapefruit." "Grape" (clap) — "fruit" (clap). Don't forget to get a placemat. "Place" (clap) — "mat" (clap).	We are getting ready to go outside. Clap and say the parts of the word "outside" with me. Ready? "Out" (clap) — "side" (clap).	This is a story about Gilbert Goldfish. Let's all clap and say the parts of the word "goldfish." "Gold" (clap) — "fish" (clap).

Key: RRELI, Reading Ready Early Literacy Intervention.

Skill: The child will clap and say the parts of compound words.

in activities throughout the day include, for example, individualized scaffolding (*Recognition & Response*, Buysse et al., 2013), explicit child-focused instructional strategies (*Building Blocks*, Sandall & Schwartz, 2013), and activity-based intervention (*Activity-Based Approach to Early Intervention*, Johnson, Rahn, & Bricker, 2015). Table 8.1 illustrates how the lesson from RRELI on clapping and saying parts of compound words could be embedded and supported in activities occurring throughout the day.

Additional personnel who may assist with small-group instruction or intervention should be considered as a way to increase feasibility. Personnel resources that may be available to implement Tier 3 interventions in preschools include speech-language pathologists, school psychologists, and early childhood special education teachers. Notably, when curricular materials are scripted and have high utility, it is possible to enlist the help of teaching assistants, paraprofessionals, or trained volunteers to implement interventions.

PROGRESS MONITORING

As stated previously, a key component of an MTSS service delivery approach is the use of ongoing progress monitoring. The rationale for progress monitoring is to make timely decisions about the effectiveness of the intervention. As such, progress monitoring should be integrated into the Tier 3 intervention process, and the data collected for this purpose must be aligned with the desired outcomes of instruction. When insufficient progress is made, a decision is made to alter the intervention in some way to try to increase its efficacy. In a similar manner, children can be moved into less intensive tiers of support when the data suggest that it would be appropriate.

In a preschool MTSS model, assessment needs to be both sensitive to small changes in children's skill and relate to the more distal outcome of school readiness.

As such, both proximal and distal measures may be necessary for progress-monitoring purposes in this context. Proximal measures are those that assess the specific skills taught in the intervention, while distal measures are those that assess skills related to the intervention but are designed to index generalization of skills targeted in the intervention (Noe et al., 2014). Like the Tier 3 intervention itself, the assessment procedures used to evaluate intervention effectiveness need to be efficient, feasible for use, and easily implemented within the preschool setting (i.e., efficient and not time consuming and simple enough to be used with high fidelity by a range of preschool practitioners). Beyond this, it is worth considering assessment approaches that may feel more familiar to preschool children (e.g., storybook format) (Kaminski et al., 2014; Noe et al., 2014).

CONCLUSION

In summary, MTSS methods in preschool settings are designed to provide differentiated levels of support to meet the needs of *all* students. When implementing MTSS, it is important to consider that such systems have many integral parts that must work together. The process begins with high-quality screening and evidence-based core (Tier 1) instruction. As the year progresses, data from an interim assessment should inform the need for Tier 2 and Tier 3 intervention. The implementation of Tier 3 intervention involves the use of individualized, explicit, systematic instruction that is more frequent and intense, and provides more opportunities to respond and be given feedback. A hallmark of Tier 3 is the use of ongoing assessment to inform any adjustments to the intervention. The nature of preschool settings may require greater efficiency and creativity with respect to the use of resources (i.e., space, personnel) to implement Tier 3. As such, Tier 3 interventions in this context will need to be well designed and structured yet provide flexibility. With these ideas in mind, preschools should meet with greater success in improving outcomes for all young children. Preschool provides a critical window of opportunity to accelerate learning for young children with the most significant learning needs. By intensifying earlier rather than waiting until these children get to elementary school, educators may significantly decrease the numbers of children who struggle academically later in school.

With the assistance of the school psychologist in her school, Marta carried out Tier 3 interventions within her classroom. In November, Marta conducted an interim assessment of Ella, James, and Mateo using the high-quality literacy screening that she had utilized at the beginning of the year. The assessment data confirmed very low progress on the acquisition of PA skills for Ella and James and low language and literacy skills for Mateo. All three students began to receive small-group, Tier 2 instruction in groups of five students during choice time.

In January, the mid-year screening showed that Ella, James, and Mateo's skills remained low and that they were not catching up to their peers through the combination of Tier 1 and Tier 2 instruction. Marta determined Tier 3 intervention was needed for her three struggling students. She arranged her hour-long center time into four groups with

15 minutes at each classroom station. Marta spent several days practicing the timing and transitions between centers with her students before beginning intervention. Once her students were familiar with the procedures and she believed behavior could be managed by her classroom assistant, she was ready to start intervention sessions in a quiet corner of the classroom where she could observe the class, but the student receiving intervention was relatively free from distractions. Marta took special care to pull students for intervention during less-preferred center time activities.

Marta started with a small-group PA intervention with both Ella and James. Even with a 2:1 ratio, she struggled to promote positive behavior with James and was spending too much instructional time managing behavior. She then decided to provide individual instruction in 10- to 15-minute increments each day with each child.

Ella thrived in the one-to-one setting and quickly picked up dividing words into syllables and later identified the first sounds in words. Using regular progress-monitoring data, Marta found that Ella's skills were comparable to her peers receiving core instruction after just 8 weeks. Marta made the decision to transition Ella to core-only instruction but continued to monitor her progress monthly to ensure the skills were being maintained. During the transition, Marta faded the intervention support over a 3-week period. First, Marta reduced the number of days per week she met with Ella to every other day. Then, she began reducing the amount of time to 5–8 minutes every other day and eventually moved to 2 days per week for 5–8 minutes before discontinuing the Tier 3 intervention. By the end of the year, Ella achieved important PA goals that indicated she was on track for reading success in kindergarten.

Marta began one-to-one instruction with James by enforcing positive behavior and practicing intervention rules for several days prior to starting PA instruction. James responded well to incentives such as stickers and stamp cards, and both strategies were used liberally throughout the intervention sessions. James was much slower to respond to intervention than Ella. After 3 weeks attempting to teach James to segment two-syllable words into parts without success, Marta transitioned to teaching first sounds. After 3 weeks of instruction and practice, James correctly said the first sounds in a variety of words starting with /m/ and /f/. Marta spent the rest of the school year providing individual instruction to James, and by the end of the year he was successful in providing the first sound in words starting with most letters, with some support. While end-of-year test data do not show that James has met important benchmarks related to PA, he has improved significantly from the beginning of the year.

Each day Marta also spent 15 minutes teaching English vocabulary to Mateo, starting with simple nouns found in the classroom setting (e.g., *pencil, paper, doll*). Progress was slow, but by the end of the school year Mateo was using 1,000+ English words and interacting more with his peers. He even established friendships with two of his classmates. Marta observed that his peer interactions helped to further advance his English. Toward the end of the school year, Marta began to instruct Mateo in PA skills. She was surprised that he quickly picked up the skills, and after minimal instruction he correctly segmented words into parts and produced first sounds in words. Marta continued to provide language intervention throughout the school year but decided Tier 1 PA instruction would be enough for Mateo to meet future English reading goals.

Marta ended the school year confident that she provided the best support possible to her struggling students and helped put them on a path to future school success.

RESOURCES

Archer, A. L., & Hughes, C. A. (2011). *Explicit instruction: Effective and efficient teaching.* New York, NY: Guilford Press.

Division for Early Childhood (DEC), National Association for the Education of Young Children (NAEYC), & National Head Start Association (NHSA). (2013). *Frameworks for Response to Intervention in early childhood: Description and implications.* Missoula, MT: Author. Retrieved from http://www.dec-sped.org/position-statements

Gersten, R., Compton, D., Connor, C. M., Dimino, J., Santoro, L., Linan-Thompson, S., & Tilly, W. D. (2008). *Assisting students struggling with reading: Response to Intervention and multi-tier intervention for reading in the primary grades* (NCEE 2009-4045). Washington, DC: National Center for Education Evaluation and Regional Assistance, Institute of Education Sciences, U.S. Department of Education. Retrieved from https://ies.ed.gov/ncee/wwc/Docs/PracticeGuide/rti_reading_pg_021809.pdf

Gibson, V. (2014). *Classroom management for differentiating instruction and collaborative practice.* Austin, TX: Gibson Hasbrouck & Associates.

Schickedanz, J. A. (2008). *Increasing the power of instruction: Integration of language, literacy, and math across the preschool day.* Washington, DC: National Association for the Education of Young Children.

REFERENCES

Al Otaiba, S., & Fuchs, D. (2002). Characteristics of children who are unresponsive to early literacy intervention. *Remedial and Special Education, 23*(5), 300–316.

Archer, A. L., & Hughes, C. A. (2011). *Explicit instruction: Effective and efficient teaching.* New York, NY: Guilford Press.

Barnett, D. W., VanDerHeyden, A. M., & Witt, J. C. (2007). Achieving science-based practice through Response to Intervention: What it might look like in preschools. *Journal of Educational and Psychological Consultation, 17,* 31–54.

Bryant, B. R., Bryant, D. P., Porterfield, J., Dennis, M. S., Falcomata, T., Valentine, C., . . . Bell, K. (2016). The effects of a Tier 3 intervention on the mathematics performance of second grade students with severe mathematics difficulties. *Journal of Learning Disabilities, 49*(2), 176–188.

Buysse, V., Peisner-Feinberg, E. S., Soukakou, E., LaForett, D. R., Fettig, A., & Schaaf, J. M. (2013). Recognition & response: A model of Response to Intervention to promote academic learning in early education. In V. Buysse & E. S. Peisner-Feinberg (Eds.), *Handbook of Response to Intervention in early childhood.* Baltimore, MD: Paul H. Brookes Publishing Co.

Carta, J. J., & Driscoll, C. (2013). Early literacy intervention for young children with special needs. In T. Shanahan & C. J. Lonigan (Eds.), *Early childhood literacy: The National Literacy Panel and beyond* (pp. 233–253). Baltimore, MD: Paul H. Brookes Publishing Co.

Carta, J. J., Greenwood, C. R., Atwater, J., McConnell, S. R., Goldstein, H., & Kaminski, R. (2015). Identifying preschool children for higher tiers of language and early literacy instruction within a Response to Intervention framework. *Journal of Early Intervention, 36*(4), 281–291.

Catts, H. W., Nielsen, D. C., Bridges, M. S., Liu, Y. S., & Bontempo, D. E. (2015). Early identification of reading disabilities within an RTI framework. *Journal of Learning Disabilities, 48*(3), 281–297.

Cavanaugh, C. L., Kim, A., Wanzek, J., & Vaughn, S. (2004). Kindergarten reading intervention for at-risk students: Twenty years of research. *Learning Disabilities: A Contemporary Journal, 2*(1), 9–21.

Compton, D. L., Gilbert, J. K., Jenkins, J. R., Fuchs, D., Fuchs, L. S., Cho, E., . . . Bouton, B. (2012). Accelerating chronically unresponsive children to Tier 3 instruction: What level of data is necessary to ensure selection accuracy? *Journal of Learning Disabilities, 45*(3), 204–216.

Connor, C. M., Alberto, P. A., Compton, D. L., & O'Connor, R. E. (2014). *Improving reading outcomes for students with or at risk for reading disabilities: A synthesis of the contributions from the Institute of Education Sciences Research Centers (NCSER 2014–3000)*. Washington, DC: National Center for Special Education Research, Institute of Education Sciences, U.S. Department of Education.

Denton, C. A., Fletcher, J. M., Anthony, J. L., & Francis, D. J. (2006). An evaluation of intensive intervention for students with persistent reading difficulties. *Journal of Learning Disabilities, 39*(5), 447–466.

Denton, C. A., Tolar, T. D., Fletcher, J. M., Barth, A. E., Vaughn, S., & Francis, D. J. (2013). Effects of Tier 3 intervention for students with persistent reading difficulties and characteristics of inadequate responders. *Journal of Educational Psychology, 105*, 633–648.

Division for Early Childhood (DEC), National Association for the Education of Young Children (NAEYC), & National Head Start Association (NHSA). (2013). *Frameworks for Response to Intervention in early childhood: Description and implications*. Missoula, MT: Author. Retrieved from http://www.dec-sped.org/position-statements

Dunlap, G., & Fox, L. (2011). Function-based interventions for children with challenging behavior. *Journal of Early Intervention, 33*, 333–343.

Foorman, B. R., Fletcher, J. M., Francis, D. J., Schatschneider, C., & Mehta, P. (1998). The role of instruction in learning to read: Preventing reading failure in at-risk children. *Journal of Educational Psychology, 90*, 37–55.

Fox, L., Carta, J., Strain, P. S., Dunlap, G., & Hemmeter, M. L. (2010). Response to Intervention and the Pyramid Model. *Infants & Young Children, 23*(1), 3–13.

Gersten, R., & Dimino, J. A. (2006). RTI (Response to Intervention): Rethinking special education for students with reading difficulties (yet again). *Reading Research Quarterly, 41*(1), 99–108.

Gillon, G. (2000). The efficacy of phonological awareness intervention for children with spoken language impairment. *Language, Speech, and Hearing Services in Schools, 31*, 126–141.

Greenwood, C. R., Carta, J. J., Atwater, J., Goldstein, H., Kaminski, R., & McConnell, S. (2012). Is a Response to Intervention (RTI) approach to preschool language and early literacy instruction needed? *Topics in Early Childhood Special Education, 33*(1), 48–64.

Greulich, L., Al Otaiba, S., Schatschneider, C., Wanzek, J., Ortiz, M., & Wagner, R. K. (2014). Understanding inadequate response to first-grade multi-tier intervention: Nomothetic and ideographic perspectives. *Learning Disabilities Quarterly, 37*, 204–217.

Harn, B. A., Linan-Thompson, S., & Roberts, G. (2008). Intensifying instruction: Does additional instructional time make a difference for the most at-risk first graders? *Journal of Learning Disabilities, 41*(2), 115–125.

Hill, D. R., King, S. A., Lemons, C. J., & Partanen, J. N. (2012). Fidelity of implementation and instructional alignment in Response to Intervention research. *Learning Disabilities Research & Practice, 27*(3), 116–124.

Horner, R. H., Kincaid, D., Sugai, G., Lewis, R., Eber, L., Barrett, S., . . . Johnson, N. (2014). Scaling up school-wide positive behavioral interventions and supports: Experiences of seven states with documented success. *Journal of Positive Behavior Interventions, 16*, 197–208.

Hulme, C., Bowyer-Crane, C., Carroll, J. M., Duff, F. J., & Snowling, M. J. (2012). The causal role of phoneme awareness and letter–sound knowledge in learning to read: Combining intervention studies with mediation analyses. *Psychological Science, 23*(6), 572–577.

Jenkins, J. R., Schiller, E., Blackorby, J., Thayer, S. K., & Tilly, W. D. (2013). Responsiveness to intervention in reading: Architecture and practices. *Learning Disability Quarterly, 36*(1), 36–46.

Johnson, J., Rahn, N., & Bricker, D. (2015). *Activity-based approach to early intervention* (4th ed.). Baltimore, MD: Paul H. Brookes Publishing Co.

Kaminski, R. A., Abbott, M., Bravo Aguayo, K., Latimer, R., & Good, R. H. (2014). The Preschool Early Literacy Indicators: Validity and benchmark goals. *Topics in Early Childhood Special Education, 34*(2), 71–82.

Kaminski, R. A., Cummings, K. D., Powell-Smith, K. A., & Good, R. H., (2008). Best practices in using Dynamic Indicators of Basic Early Literacy Skills (DIBELS) in an outcomes-driven model. In A. Thomas & J. Grimes (Eds.), *Best practices in school psychology.* (5th Ed.) (pp. 1181–1204). Bethesda, MD: National Association of School Psychologists.

Kaminski, R. A., & Powell-Smith, K. A. (2016). Early literacy intervention for preschoolers who need Tier 3 support. *Topics in Early Childhood Special Education.* Advance online publication. doi:10.1177/0271121416642454

Kaminski, R. A., Powell-Smith, K. A., Hommel, A., McMahon, R., & Bravo Aguayo, K. (2015). Development of Tier 3 curricula to teach early language and literacy skills. *Journal of Early Intervention, 36*, 313–332.

Lewis, T. J., Mitchell, B. S., Bruntmeyer, D. T., & Sugai, G. (2016). School-wide positive behavior support and Response to Intervention: System similarities, distinctions, and research to date at the universal level of support. In S. R. Jimeson et al. (Eds.), *Handbook of Response to Intervention* (pp. 703–717). New York, NY: Springer.

McConnell, S., & Greenwood, C. R. (2013). General outcome measures in early childhood and individual growth and development indicators. In V. Buysse & E. S. Peisner-Feinberg (Eds.), *Handbook of Response to Intervention in early childhood.* (pp. 143–154). Baltimore, MD: Paul H. Brookes Publishing Co.

McConnell, S. R., Wackerle-Hollman, A. K., Roloff. T. A., & Rodriguez, M. C. (2015). Designing a measurement framework for Response to Intervention in early childhood programs. *Journal of Early Intervention, 36*(4), 263–280. doi:10.1177/1053815115578559

National Early Literacy Panel. (2008). *Developing early literacy: Report of the National Early Literacy Panel.* Washington, DC: National Institute for Literacy.

Noe, S., Spencer, T. D., Kruse, L., & Goldstein, H. (2014). Effects of a Tier 3 phonological awareness intervention on preschoolers' emergent literacy. *Topics in Early Childhood Special Education, 34*, 27–39.

O'Connor, R. E., Bocian, K. M., Sanchez, V., & Beach, K. D. (2014). Access to a responsiveness to intervention model: Does beginning intervention in kindergarten matter? *Journal of Learning Disabilities, 47*, 307–328.

O'Connor, R. E., Harty, K. R., & Fulmer, D. (2005). Tiers of intervention in kindergarten through third grade. *Journal of Learning Disabilities, 38*, 532–538.

Sandall, S. R., & Schwartz, I. S. (2013). Building blocks: A framework for meeting the needs of all young children. In V. Buysse & E. S. Peisner-Feinberg (Eds.), *Handbook of Response to Intervention in early childhood* (pp. 103–117). Baltimore, MD: Paul H. Brookes Publishing Co.

Simmons, D. (2015). Instructional engineering principles to frame the future of reading intervention research and practice. *Remedial and Special Education, 36*(1), 45–51.

Spencer, E. J., Spencer, T. D., Goldstein, H., & Schneider, N. (2013). Identifying early literacy learning needs: Implications for child outcome standards and assessment systems. In T. Shanahan & C. J. Lonigan (Eds.), *Early childhood literacy: The National Early Literacy Panel and beyond* (pp. 45–70). Baltimore, MD: Paul H. Brookes Publishing Co.

VanDerHeyden, A. M., & Snyder, P. (2006). Integrating frameworks from early childhood intervention and school psychology to accelerate growth for all young children. *School Psychology Review, 35*, 519–534.

Vaughn, S., Wanzek, J., Murray, C. S., & Roberts, G. (2012). *Intensive interventions for students struggling in reading and mathematics: A practice guide.* Portsmouth, NH: RMC Research Corporation, Center on Instruction.

Wanzek, J., & Vaughn, S. (2007). Research-based implications from extensive early reading interventions. *School Psychology Review, 36*, 541–561.

Wanzek, J., & Vaughn, S. (2008). Response to varying amounts of time in reading intervention for students with low response to intervention. *Journal of Learning Disabilities, 41*(2), 126–142.

Wasik, B. (2008). When fewer is more: Small groups in early childhood classrooms. *Early Childhood Education Journal, 35*, 515–521.

9

Meeting the Needs of Young Dual Language Learners in Multi-Tiered Systems of Support

Lillian K. Durán and Alisha Wackerle-Hollman

Jasmine lives with her mother and father in Oakland, California. Spanish and English are spoken in her home and neighborhood. Her family immigrated from Guatemala 6 years ago when her older brother was 3, but she was born in the United States. She attends a state-funded preschool program operated by the local school district where English is the primary language of instruction. The lead teacher speaks English, whereas the assistant teacher speaks both Spanish and English. Spanish is used in the classroom about 30% of the time, mostly for social conversations at snack, during transitions, and sometimes to clarify the English used by the lead teacher. About 65% of her classmates also speak at least some Spanish at home. Three other children speak Chinese, and one speaks Vietnamese. Jasmine is learning both English and Spanish at the same time. She is a simultaneous bilingual; however, over the course of the school year she is exposed to more English at school and from other children in the class. Her older brother, who is enrolled in the second grade, also speaks English with Jasmine at home.

Myaing lives in rural Utah and attends a Head Start program. He is an only child, and his mother and father are recent refugees from Burma. The family speaks only Burmese at home. Both the lead teacher and assistant teacher only speak English in Myaing's classroom, and he is the only child in the class who speaks Burmese. After 3 months in the preschool program, Myaing is starting to use single words in English but continues to be mostly silent during the school day, using gestures to communicate when he can.

The stories of these two children illustrate the challenges for teaching staff who are trying to find the best ways to meet the needs of dual language learners (DLLs). This chapter highlights how teachers of young DLLs can use a multi-tiered systems of support (MTSS) framework for assessing children's current skill levels, determining appropriate interventions, monitoring children's progress in response to those interventions and including families in their intervention efforts.

INTRODUCTION

DLLs in the United States are a highly diverse population representing a multitude of languages and cultures (U.S. Department of Health and Human Services [USDHHS], 2013). Children who speak a language other than or in addition to English at home are often referred to as *dual language learners*. This term is used to describe children who will need to maintain their home language or languages to communicate with their families and will also learn English as they begin participating in early education programs or attend kindergarten. Preschool programs often lack bilingual personnel and the financial resources necessary to adequately address the needs of the burgeoning population of DLLs that they serve (Park & McHugh, 2014; USDHHS, 2013). This chapter will build on the applications of MTSS in early childhood education (ECE) that already have been provided in previous chapters by describing the unique and specific considerations necessary for DLLs.

Effective MTSS models can no longer operate under the assumption of a monolingual English-speaking norm: DLLs in preschool settings are not an exception, but rather represent one of the fastest growing populations in the United States (Figueras-Daniel & Barnett, 2013; Fortuny, Hernandez, & Chaudry, 2010). The new mainstream includes a diverse range of languages and cultures and children born in and outside of the United States to parents who are both native and immigrants (Fortuny et al., 2010; Park & McHugh, 2014). More than one quarter of American children younger than 8 years old have at least one immigrant parent (Williams, 2014), and this number rose from 2.9 million in 1990 to 5.8 million in 2011 (Park & McHugh, 2014). Latino children alone represent about 25% of the total population of children younger than 5 years old, and of these 43% have Mexican-born parents and about 70% of all DLLs speak Spanish at home (Figueras-Daniel & Barnett, 2013; Yoshikawa, & Kholoptseva, 2013). However, over 130 different languages are spoken by children enrolled in Head Start programs (USDHHS, 2013). This fact is essential to keep in mind when considering adaptions to MTSS in various communities because the needs of the specific populations served can vary significantly by language.

In addition to the challenges DLLs often face entering U.S. schools with limited English proficiency, they are also more likely to grow up in poverty and with parents who have low educational levels (García & Jensen, 2009). Being bilingual is a long-term asset for these children because of increasing demand for bilingual professionals in the workforce in many sectors of employment, including education, social services, international business, and so forth (Johnston, 2017). In addition, recent studies suggest that bilingual students are more likely to have higher levels of executive functioning and other cognitive capacities (Carlson & Meltzoff, 2008). Unfortunately, teachers often lack adequate training to effectively work with children learning English as a second language, and the curriculum in place often includes minimal supports for language, learning (Connors-Tadros, Barnett, & Nores, 2014; Zepeda, Castro, & Cronin, 2011). Young children of immigrants represent 30% of the total number of children living in poverty in the United States, and 34% of Latino children under the age of 5 live in poverty (Figueras-Daniel & Barnett, 2013; Fortuny et al., 2010). Therefore, the focus on early identification, systematic and targeted instruction, and ongoing progress monitoring are critical components to promoting equity in outcomes for DLLs.

OVERVIEW OF MTSS WITH DUAL LANGUAGE LEARNERS

The essential components of an MTSS model include robust assessment procedures for the early identification of children who may be in need of more instructional support, targeted instruction that is designed to directly address identified learning needs to efficiently and effectively accelerate development in key areas, and ongoing progress monitoring to make informed and data-based instructional decisions. There are currently no evidence-based approaches to implementing MTSS with DLLs. Although specific practice recommendations have been published for school-age populations who are DLLs (Linan-Thompson, & Ortiz, 2009; Sanford & Brown, 2011), models of MTSS in early childhood settings focused on DLLs have not yet been fully developed. The development of the Recognition and Response (R&R-DLL) model focused on the language and early literacy development of Spanish-speaking DLLs has been described, but no child outcome data have been reported. R&R-DLL was developed for classrooms in which English was the predominant language used for instruction, with Spanish-speaking staff available for specific bilingual instructional strategies (LaForett, Peisner-Feinberg, & Buysse, 2013). There are no other studies to date that directly describe the implementation of MTSS with DLLs in early childhood education or describe child-level outcomes as a result of such implementation. This represents a significant gap in the knowledge base, and there is an urgent need for further empirical investigation in this area. Given this limited knowledge base, the content of this chapter is derived from research that focuses more broadly on recommended assessment procedures (Hoff & Core, 2015; Peña & Halle, 2011) and the emerging trends in evidence-based language and early literacy interventions with DLLs (Castro, Páez, Dickinson, & Frede, 2010; Durán, Hartzheim, Lund, Simonsmeier, & Kohlmeier, 2016; USDHHS, 2013).

MTSS are conceptualized as including three tiers of instructional support. Most children should demonstrate growth from participation in Tier 1 instruction and should be well served by the core curriculum and the learning activities provided. Tier 2 is often described as the delivery of more structured and targeted instruction to a smaller group of children who have been identified as needing a higher level of instructional support. Those children identified as needing Tier 3 level of instruction demonstrate more significant learning needs and instruction may need to be individualized. Chapter 1, "Introduction to Multi-Tiered Systems of Support in Early Education," provides an overview of tiered instruction and more details about each tier.

Core components of any MTSS include appropriate assessment for the identification of children in need of more instructional support and evidence-based approaches to meet their educational needs. In this section, we turn our attention first to describing appropriate approaches for assessing DLLs and then to intervention.

Dual Language Assessment

The first step in implementing MTSS is typically universal screening. There are a number of hurdles regarding the state of universal screening with DLLs related to the quality and accuracy of these assessments (Barrera & Liu, 2010). Challenges include a lack of professional knowledge of appropriate screening procedures for DLLs (Banerjee & Luckner, 2013; Peña & Halle, 2011); a scarcity of publicly available, technically adequate screening measures for use with this population (Barrueco, López, Ong, & Lozano, 2012); a shortage of practitioners who speak languages other than English to administer the assessments (Zehler et al., 2003); and the need for training on the use of interpreters to administer assessments (Cheatham, 2011).

Selecting Screening and Progress-Monitoring Measures Given that many DLL universal screening tools were not designed to focus on specific cultural or linguistic features of bilingual development, it can be challenging to locate tools to use in an MTSS model (Castro et al., 2010; Hammer, Scarpino, & Davison, 2011; Peña & Halle, 2011). Two types of tools must be considered: 1) universal screening measures to determine DLL students who are appropriate candidates for higher tiers of intervention, and 2) progress-monitoring measures to evaluate growth over time in response to the intervention. Screening and progress-monitoring measures designed for use with DLLs are sparse in the field. Some measures that were designed in English have been recommended for use with DLLs through the use of an interpreter; however, studies show that simply interpreting English measures compromises claims of validity (Peña, 2007). In addition, measures must attend to the nuances of various languages, including the cultural and social context that informs language use, syntactical and semantic features specific to the targeted languages, and dialectical variations and differences in developmental trajectories so that inferences about performance can be made in the context of how a specific language develops rather than through the lens of English-language development. While some domains offer nearly parallel trajectories to their English counterparts (e.g., mathematics and early numeracy), others are substantially different (e.g., language and literacy development). Therefore, it is important to review potential screening and progress-monitoring measures carefully to evaluate their utility for use with DLL students.

Here, three questions are presented that can help guide decision making as practitioners select measures for use with DLL populations:

- Does the measure have a parallel form in the child's native language (generally Spanish) that allows for dual language (parallel) assessment or conceptual scoring? ("Conceptual scoring considers the total number of concepts for which a child has a word in at least one language"; Gross, Buac, & Kaushanskaya, 2014, p. 574)

- Has the measure been designed with the native language as the focus of the development of the measure or is it a translation of an English measure?

- Have the measures been empirically validated using a DLL sample?

When measures are designed to capture English performance and do not attend to the unique linguistic and cultural features of other languages, they often overlook important factors that may affect child performance and the accuracy of the ability estimates obtained from the measure. These considerations include the unique syntactical features of the language that inform what to measure, the frequency of use and the familiarity of the vocabulary on the measure for young children, and dialectical differences within the languages that must also be accounted for in the scoring of items.

There are many different dialects of various languages spoken across the United States (e.g., White versus Green Hmong, Mexican versus Puerto Rican Spanish). Without attending to these dialects it is difficult to know if the native language was appropriately sampled within the measure. Here, we use Spanish as an example; consider the word for *orange* in Spanish. Frequently Spanish speakers from Mexico will call an orange a "naranja" or "mandarina"; however, when the same image is shown to many children from Puerto Rico they label it a "china." Without consideration for dialectical variation, the later response may be considered incorrect, when in fact it is an appropriate label for a child from that cultural background.

Finally, it is important to consider to what degree the measures were empirically validated with DLLs by asking "Does the measure provide evidence of validity for use with the DLL population in which I am interested?" When measures are appropriately designed and consider the developmental trajectories of other native languages, they are likely to also include normative samples in their empirical reports. However, when measures are simply translated forms of English tools, evidence for their validity with specific DLL populations is often weak. As a result, it is important to review technical manuals to evaluate the degree to which the tools were based on established norms with students who are DLLs, included items constructed based on unique factors of the target language, and avoided direct translation of items or scales initially developed in English. For example, a review of measures indicated the Istation ISIP Early Reading (Mathes, 2015) in Spanish and the Spanish Individual Growth and Development Indicators (S-IGDIs; Wackerle-Hollman, Durán, & Rodriguez, 2015) are two measures that were developed using Spanish language, and literacy development as the construct of interest (rather than translating English). They were normed or calibrated with children who are DLLs, and their test authors reported engaging in item development processes that reflected the unique semantic and syntactical features of Spanish. For additional information on measure reviews, Table 9.1 provides a summary of screening and progress-monitoring measures available for use with preschoolers who are DLLs and documents the available information based on the three questions noted here to allow for comparison and selection of measures that may prove useful in an MTSS framework.

Once a screening and progress-monitoring tool is selected, additional factors must be considered to ensure adherence to the administration protocol of the assessment and to elicit a child's best performance. Research has demonstrated that DLLs know when to use each of their languages with different communicative partners, a skill called *interlocutor sensitivity*. Specifically, educators administering progress-monitoring and screening tools must address interlocutor sensitivity and the role of interpreters in administering assessments. Evidence suggests that interlocutor sensitivity develops as early as 18 months (Pettito et al., 2001). Given that even very young bilinguals are sensitive to the native language of the person with whom they are communicating, it is recommended that assessors should have native or near-native fluency. For example, if the child assumes that the assessor speaks English, then he or she may conclude that it is appropriate to speak English with that assessor even when an assessment is being conducted in another language. Although potentially difficult to accomplish in all early childhood programs, every effort should be taken to hire assessors with the appropriate language skills to elicit children's optimal performance. Furthermore, it is important to test each

Table 9.1. Screening measures for use with early childhood dual language learner students

Measure	Areas	Languages	Does the measure provide information about how to interpret performance of the child in English and the other language through dual language assessment or conceptual scoring?	Is there attention to the construct and trajectory of each language in measure design, including attention to cultural, dialectical, and social contexts?	Does the technical manual provide information specific to dual language learners (DLLs) (e.g., norms, item design, procedures)?
ASQ-3®: Ages & Stages Questionnaires® (3rd ed.) (Squires et al., 2009)	SE, PD, LL, CD	Spanish, Hmong, Somali, French, Korean, Vietnamese, German, Norwegian	No	No. All versions are direct translations of the English version.	Yes, norms only for Spanish, French, Korean, Vietnamese, German, Chinese, and Norwegian
Battelle Developmental Inventory-2, Spanish Screening (Newborg, 2005)	SE, AS, PD, LL, CD	Spanish	Yes, conceptual scoring	No. The Spanish Battelle and the supporting reports and documentation are direct translations of the English Battelle.	None provided
Brigance Early Childhood Screens III–Spanish (Glascoe, 2012)	SE, LL, PD, CD, AS	Spanish	No	No. The Spanish Brigance and the supporting reports and documentation are direct translations of the English Brigance.	None provided
Children's Progress Academic Assessment–Spanish (CPAA; Camacho, 2012)	LL	Spanish	No	No. The CPAA items appear to be direct translations of the English CPAA items.	None provided
Developmental Indicators for the Assessment of Learning-Spanish (DIAL-4; Mardell & Goldenberg, 2011)	SE, LL, PD, CD, AS	Spanish	Yes, conceptual scoring	No. The Spanish DIAL-4 and the supporting reports and documentation are direct translations of the DIAL-4 in English.	Yes, norms only

Table 9.1. (continued)

Measure	Areas	Languages	Does the measure provide information about how to interpret performance of the child in English and the other language through dual language assessment or conceptual scoring?	Is there attention to the construct and trajectory of each language in measure design, including attention to cultural, dialectical, and social contexts?	Does the technical manual provide information specific to dual language learners (DLLs) (e.g., norms, item design, procedures)?
Early Literacy Skills Assessment (ELSA; DeBruin-Parecki, 2005)	LL	Spanish	No	No. The ELSA forms in Spanish are different from those in English. However, there is no information on if they were developed in Spanish or if they were alternate English forms translated to Spanish.	None provided
Get Ready To Read!-Spanish (GRTR; Lonigan, 2003)	LL	Spanish	Yes, dual language assessment comparison	No. The Spanish GRTR and the supporting reports and documentation are direct translations of the English GRTR.	Yes, norms and item design
Spanish Individual Growth and Development Indicators (Wackerle-Hollman, Durán, & Rodriguez, 2015)	LL	Spanish	Yes, dual language assessment comparison	Yes. S-IGDI items and reports were developed independent of the English IGDI items to support Spanish development.	Yes, norms, item design, and procedures
Inventario para la Deteccion-Temprana (IDT-R; Meisels, Marsden, Wiske, & Henderson, 2008)	LL, CD, PD, AS	Spanish	Yes, dual language assessment comparison	No. The Spanish IDT and the supporting reports and documentation are direct translations of the English Early Screening Inventory measure.	Yes, norms, item design, and procedures
Istation ISIP Early Reading-Spanish (Mathes, 2015)	LL, CD	Spanish	Yes, dual language assessment comparison	Yes. ISIP items and reports were developed independent of English items to support Spanish development.	Yes, norms, item design, and procedures
mCLASS Circle (C-PALS; Landry et al., 2004)	LL	Spanish	Yes, dual language assessment comparison	No. No information is provided regarding item or measure design, nor for any supporting documents.	None provided

Key: AS, adaptive skills; CD, cognitive development; LL, early language, literacy, and communication; PD, physical development; SE, social-emotional.

language separately with different examiners and on different days if possible if tests are not conceptually scored.

Engaging Interpreters to Support Assessment   One of the most common approaches to administering assessments in languages other than English is to use an interpreter. However, effective practices for interpreters are often overlooked in these interactions, which can lead to four common challenges of interpretation: addition errors, substitution errors, omission errors, and challenges in maintaining standards of practice (Cheatham, 2011). When interpreters engage in addition errors during assessment administration, they add their opinion, background knowledge, or assumptions about the child's response and may distort the child's performance. For example, during an assessment an interpreter might ask a child a question and report the child's response to the assessor but also add his or her opinion about the response such as, "She's not doing very well; I think we should discontinue," or the assessor may also add to the child's response. For example, the child may respond with two words, but the interpreter may add to the child's utterance to make it more complete. Addition errors can inappropriately influence the assessor to make decisions about the child's performance that may be inaccurate.

In errors of substitution, the interpreter changes the student's response when describing what the child said in English because there may be no equivalent in English. The interpreter may also misunderstand the testing context and may alter the performance of the child. For example, a child might approximate a response on a test of vocabulary that would otherwise be considered incorrect, but the interpreter might make the assumption that the child "knows" the word and therefore deserves the credit for the item and in turn reports that the child said the appropriate vocabulary word. This type of error compromises protocols for test standardization and results in invalid scores on assessments.

Errors of omission occur when interpreters leave out key information because they are unable to track the child's response, do not understand, or no translational equivalent is available. For example, if the child produces a word that the interpreter does not know, he or she may simply omit the word rather than reporting to the assessor that he or she was unable to translate the response provided (Cheatham, 2011).

Finally, some interpreters who work in early childhood settings receive limited professional development and as a result experience challenges in maintaining standards of practice. For example, various studies have reported a need for improved quality both in professional interaction and in the accuracy of the translation (Cheatham, 2011; Klinger & Harry, 2006). Young children are particularly vulnerable to the errors of interpretation because they are generally unable to advocate for themselves because of their young age and developmental level. As a result, it is important to carefully monitor and support interpreters when they are involved in assessment. Continuous professional development and training to protect against common errors and challenges can improve the validity of scores obtained through interpreter interactions. Interpreters are invaluable members of early childhood teams and should be treated professionally and be expected to maintain high standards of practice.

Dual Language Measurement Approaches   As we move toward MTSS models that attend to the unique needs of DLLs, we must adjust our current assessment practices to align with recommended practices (Hoff & Core, 2015; Peña &

Halle, 2011). There is an emerging consensus that measuring bilingual children in both of their languages improves diagnostic accuracy (Hammer, Lawrence, & Miccio, 2007; Peña, Bedore, & Kester, 2015). Experts on MTSS models and DLLs also agree that measuring children in their home language and English is the best approach (Fien et al., 2011; Linan-Thompson & Ortiz, 2009; Sanford & Brown, 2011). Although this may appear to be a logical approach to capture overall language ability, most programs administer screening and progress-monitoring assessments in English only, even when children have limited English proficiency (Sanford & Brown, 2011). Restricting assessment to English could lead to over-identification of children for higher-level tier candidacy and potentially lead to an increase in referrals for special education evaluations (Guiberson, 2010).

A fundamental shift is necessary in program administrators' and teachers' awareness of the importance of measuring children in their home language. This program-level support is necessary to increase resources and includes purchasing technically adequate assessments in the children's home languages, hiring bilingual personnel to administer these assessments, and offering the training necessary for appropriate test administration and interpretation of results. A dual-language measurement approach is feasible at this point with Spanish-speaking DLLs, and there are universal screening measures that have parallel measures available in English and Spanish, including the *Istation ISIP Early Reading-Spanish* (Mathes, 2015), the mCLASS Circle (C-PALS; Landry, Assel, Gunewig, & Swank, 2004), the Phonological Awareness Literacy Screening-Español, (PALS; Ford & Invernizzi, 2014), and the S-IGDIs (Wackerle-Hollman et al., 2015) (see Table 9.1 for a selection of DLL measures).

For children who speak languages other than Spanish, informal approaches to capturing performance in both languages may be necessary. Parent and teacher reporting, language samples, observations, and clinical decision making may be needed to adequately attend to these children's abilities in their home language as well as English (Anaya, Peña, & Bedore, 2016). No matter what approach to measuring the child's native language is taken by the program, the limitations of using English-only assessments must be recognized. In summary, given that screening and progress-monitoring assessment represents one of the principal tenets of MTSS, educators must employ strategies that systematically evaluate the performance of DLLs in both their home language and the language(s) primarily used in the instructional environment to ensure a complete profile of student performance.

Tiered Levels of Instruction

An important first step in designing effective instructional environments for DLLs is to consider their performance in each language, recognizing that their performance in each language will be influenced by their home language exposure.

Researchers have found that the amount and quality of exposure young children have to the various languages used across their natural environments affects their ability level in all of their languages (Bohman, Bedore, Peña, Mendez-Perez, & Gillam, 2010). One way to gather this information is to have families complete a home-language survey. Programs should have a home-language survey in all of the languages of the families served in their program to ensure that they have the opportunity to provide this critical information about their child. If the language is not traditionally a written language (e.g., Hmong, Mam, and many other indigenous languages), then interviewing the family in their native language should be arranged.

Many home-language surveys are available for public use. For example, the Bilingual Input/Output Survey (BIOS; Peña, Gutiérrez-Clellen, Iglesias, Goldstein, & Bedore, 2014), provides a detailed analysis of hourly exposure levels and has been used in research and tested in various studies (e.g., Lugo-Neris, Peña, Bedore, & Gillam, 2015). Similarly, the Preschool Language Scales-5 Home Communication Questionnaire (Zimmerman, Steiner, & Pond, 2012) provides a broad indicator of the languages used in various environments (e.g., community, home, school). Finally, the Language Exposure Evaluation Report (LEER), developed by Durán & Wackerle-Hollman (2016), is designed to maximize information on level of exposure through the three approaches previously described: questions regarding family's immigration time lines and home country, summary reporting on language input/output, and questions regarding age of introduction (see Appendix 9A).

Tier 1 In this section the question of what should be considered a high-quality Tier 1 environment for DLLs will be addressed. Recommended Tier 1 practices can be found in leading research and practice reports, including a publication on principles and practices designed to promote language, literacy, and learning with DLLs (Governor's State Advisory Council on Early Learning and Care, 2013); a research synthesis on language and literacy practices with DLLs (Castro et al., 2010); and a recent report to Congress on DLLs in Head Start (USDHHS, 2013). In addition to these publications, a recent research synthesis describing home-language and dual-language interventions that have been found to improve the language development of DLLs provides guidance (Durán Hartzheim, et al., 2016). The review identified five primary evidence-based practices for at-risk populations, including the following: 1) instruction delivered in children's home language, 2) using adaptive strategies when delivering English-language instruction, 3) using supplemental small-group literacy interventions delivered in English and the children's home language, 4) embedding language-bridging techniques into instruction that intentionally use the child's home language to support English vocabulary acquisition, and 5) incorporating storybook reading interventions delivered by families in their home language. These practices, described next, are those we recommend for providing Tier 1 instruction to DLLs to accelerate development and provide the foundation necessary for improved long-term academic success (Hoff, 2013).

Home-Language Instruction An important consideration is the language of instruction in classrooms (Cárdenas-Hagan, Carlson, & Pollard-Durodola, 2007). Several studies conducted in the United States have found that children in English-only early education settings demonstrated decreased rates of growth in their home language (e.g., Barnett, Yarosz, Thomas, Jung, & Blanco, 2007; Durán, Roseth, Hoffman, & Robertshaw, 2013; Farver, Lonigan, & Eppe, 2009). When English-only programs have been compared to two-way immersion programs, advantages of instruction in both languages have been found for children who are native Spanish speakers on Spanish and English receptive vocabulary and early literacy achievement measures such as Spanish rhyming and English phoneme deletion skills (Barnett et al., 2007). Other advantages of instruction in both languages have been found on Spanish measures of receptive and expressive language and early literacy in preschool that continue into kindergarten (Durán et al., 2013).

Adapting English-Language Instruction After programs carefully consider what level of native language support may be possible given their current resources, it could be that native-language support is simply not feasible. In this case every effort should be taken to adapt English instruction to the child's level of English proficiency. Teachers should provide comprehensible input throughout the day and check often for a child's comprehension.

Total physical response (TPR) is also often recommended as a strategy to teach children with limited English proficiency (Breckinridge Church, Ayman-Nolley, & Mahootian, 2014). TPR involves acting out words or scenes in order to support understanding, and it is based on the coordination of language and physical movement. In TPR, teachers provide instruction in the target language, and children respond with whole-body actions. Examples in an early childhood classroom might include acting out a story like a play instead of reading it, or acting out vocabulary words in order to facilitate learning new words.

Using visual and graphic cues and real objects is also another recommended strategy (Beck, McKeown, & Kucan, 2013; Collins, 2010). Visual cues and real items should be used during lessons to reinforce vocabulary and teach new concepts. For example, when reading *Brown Bear, Brown Bear* (Martin & Carle, 1992) a teacher can bring in various stuffed or plastic animals from the book for the children to handle and include them in a center activity in the classroom. This direct experience with items and being shown images of target vocabulary has been shown to improve vocabulary learning (Collins, 2010).

Supplemental Small-Group Language and Literacy Instruction We propose that small-group instruction should be included in Tier 1 instruction for DLLs given the low levels of language and literacy development widely documented across the population in the United States (Hoff, 2013; Paéz, Tabors, & Lopez, 2007). Farver and colleagues (2009) investigated a model in which children were provided with small-group instruction by bilingual graduate assistants with lessons from the *Literacy Express Curriculum* that included dialogic reading, direct instruction of phonological awareness, alphabet knowledge, and print awareness. Results indicated that children in the English-only and transitional Spanish group showed significantly higher skills than the control group, but only the group that received Spanish instruction demonstrated significant improvement in their Spanish language and literacy skills. This study provides an example of what the focus of small-group instruction can be both in English and Spanish and evidence that this level of support can improve language and early literacy performance in both languages.

Language-Bridging Techniques Language-bridging strategies have also been found to enhance English-language development. These bridging strategies include 1) providing definitions for target vocabulary in the child's native language (Lugo-Neris, Jackson, & Goldstein, 2010) (e.g., "a frog es un animal que puede brincar muy alta"); 2) previewing key vocabulary in the child's native language before a lesson in English (e.g., the bilingual teacher reviews the words *frog* [rana], *bear* [oso], *horse* [caballo], and *look* [mirar] in Spanish before reading *Brown Bear, Brown Bear* in English); and 3) intentionally teaching cognates, which are words in two languages that are from the same root and therefore sound very similar and share the same meaning (e.g., the teacher adds additional animals to the lessons such as *elefante/elephant* or *girafa/giraffe*). Spanish-speaking children have been found to learn more cognates in English than noncognates (Dressler & Kamil, 2006; Kelley & Kohnert, 2012; Perez, Peña, & Bedore, 2010). For a list of cognates see http://www.colorincolorado.org/pdfs/articles/cognates.pdf

Interventions Delivered by Families   Families should be encouraged to read books in their home language to their child, conduct picture walk-throughs of books even if they are written in English, or simply tell the story in their home language. Roberts (2008) compared home storybook reading in the child's primary language to home storybook reading only in English and measured gains in English vocabulary. Storybook reading in the home language was found to improve English vocabulary acquisition over reading the same books in only English at home. Other researchers have also found that children who participated in shared reading interventions with their families in their home language gained significantly more English vocabulary in addition to vocabulary in their home language than children in control groups (Huennekens & Xu, 2010; Roberts, 2008; Tysbina & Eriks-Brophy, 2010).

Tier 2   Very little is currently known about what specifically might accelerate development at the Tier 2 levels of instructional support with young DLLs. In addition, it is also difficult for practitioners to decide when to emphasize enhancing Tier 1 strategies and when to move to providing Tier 2 instructional approaches. To make this determination, programs should assess children regularly and monitor their growth both individually and as a group. When evaluating a group of children as a class, results can be used as a proxy for evaluating Tier 1 instruction. When the majority of students in a classroom are not meeting screening benchmarks, it may be most effective to improve or modify the Tier 1 curriculum or intervention. At the same time, if individual children are not making adequate progress in their language and literacy development, then intensifying intervention and providing targeted small-group instruction may prove most useful. However, very little specific information is available to help researchers and practitioners fine-tune dosage, intensity, and specific intervention targets. In general, however, it can be assumed that most of the same principles described in Chapter 6 on Tier 2 interventions apply with DLLs. What we know about effective instruction generally holds true for DLLs as well (Goldenberg, 2008). Explicit and systematic small-group Tier 2 language- and early literacy-focused interventions are likely to produce the strongest outcomes. However, when working with DLLs, it is also important to consider levels of language proficiency in children's home language and English and how to address instructional needs in both languages (Goldenberg, 2008). It is therefore important to use curricula that both have some evidence of effectiveness with DLLs and that are available in languages other than English.

There are three Tier 2 interventions described in Chapter 6 that also have Spanish versions. *Read It Again-PreK!* (RIA; Justice & McGinty, 2009) was adapted by Durán, Gorman, Kohlmeier, & Callard (2016) for DLLs and is available from the *Read It Again* web site (https://earlychildhood.ehe.osu.edu/research/practice/read-it-again-prek). *Read It Again Dual Language (RIA-DL)* includes 30 lessons built around children's books that are available in both languages. English lessons include adaptations for children with lower levels of English proficiency, and Spanish lessons are designed to challenge children with novel and more complex vocabulary in Spanish. The curriculum also covers phonological awareness, conventions of print, and narrative development. The curriculum has recently been completed, and evidence is emerging regarding its effectiveness with DLLs (Kohlmeier & Durán, 2015).

The English version of *Story Champs* (Petersen & Spencer, 2016) is described in Chapter 6 and is a narrative-based language intervention that holds promise for improving the narrative language development of DLLs. *Puentos de Cuentos* (bridge of stories) was specifically designed in Spanish for dual language implementation (Spencer, Peterson, Arvizu, Restrepo, & Thompson, in preparation) and has 12 Spanish lessons with 12 parallel English lessons. Every lesson centers on a brief, personally themed story in which the targeted vocabulary words and concept are embedded. Lessons consist of three storytelling activities, four vocabulary activities, and two optional activities for teaching nouns and concepts. *Story Champs/Puentos de Cuentos* holds promise as an effective narrative intervention for DLLs in English and Spanish, but more research is needed with larger sample sizes and experimental control to test its efficacy (Spencer et al., in preparation).

Developing Talkers/Hablemos Junto focuses on supporting both expressive and receptive language development (Zucker, Cabell, Solari, & Landry, 2010) and is designed as a Tier 2 intervention to be delivered in small groups. It is a curricular supplement that has a parallel Spanish and English version and focuses on listening comprehension and vocabulary skills in the context of book reading. The lessons, materials, and training are all available at no cost online. There is emerging evidence of the efficacy of the English version, but no studies have been published that report on the efficacy of the Spanish version (Zucker, Solari, Landry, & Swank, 2013).

The three interventions described previously primarily support oral language development, but for those children who specifically need support with phonological awareness, the *Get Ready to Read* web site has skill-building activities focused on phonological awareness that teachers can download and use to guide small-group instruction. The activities are available in English, Spanish, Chinese, Korean, and Arabic and focus on segmenting, blending, rhyming, alliteration, and letter names and sounds. The strategies provided are research based and were developed by the National Center for Learning Disabilities.

Tier 3 In early childhood, Tier 3 intervention has been used in ways that align with and depart from current K–12 MTSS models. In some early childhood models, children must first fail to respond to Tier 2 intervention before moving on to Tier 3 intervention. In other models children may be accelerated to receive Tier 3 intervention immediately after screening suggests they are unsuccessful in the Tier 1 curricula and/or intervention. This is done to maximize efficiency and, potentially, efficacy of intervention delivery during the pre-K year.

Early language and literacy Tier 3 candidacy for DLLs may be indicated by at least three variables, including the following: 1) significant but isolated speech and language delays; 2) more general developmental delays leading to a mismatch between instructional content in Tier 1 or Tier 2 and the child's instructional and developmental level; and 3) significant lack of progress in constrained language and early literacy skills, such as phonological and phonemic awareness and alphabet knowledge.

In early childhood, speech and language delays for DLLs can be difficult to parse out when the language of instruction varies from the home language. That is, it can be difficult to differentiate a delay in language development from a lack of exposure to English, particularly when testing is conducted in English. Teachers may also be inaccurate in their estimation of children's home-language ability if they do not speak the language and have no assessments in the child's language to be able to measure their ability levels accurately.

Children may be candidates for Tier 3 intervention when they demonstrate adequate skill in other domains of early development but show significant lack of skill in language development, even when exposure to their home language and English is high, and instructional content is delivered in both languages. In contrast, Tier 3 candidacy may also be appropriate for children who experience developmental delays across domains and are at a developmental level that is discrepant from the level of the classroom instruction. In this way, the child's performance remains low because the content delivered in the Tier 1 curricula is too difficult across domains and the child is unable to learn in ways that maximize and accelerate his or her performance. Finally, the third way children can be Tier 3 candidates aligns with transitions from Tier 2 intervention to Tier 3 intervention, when children do not make adequate progress. When a child experiences little or no growth, the achievement gap between his or her current performance and the benchmark expectation grows, and more intensive intervention efforts are needed to accelerate growth.

One intervention program that may affect preschool performance at Tier 3 is *Vocabulary Oral Language and Academic Readiness (VOLAR)* (Gutiérrez-Clellan, Simon-Cerejido, & Restrepo, 2014). VOLAR focuses on teaching vocabulary and oral language through shared book reading using common trade books with Spanish and English support. The curriculum was specifically designed for children experiencing language delays. Results indicate that participating in the VOLAR curriculum supports meaningful gains in vocabulary and oral language in English and Spanish for children who have identified speech and language disabilities (Simon-Cereijido, 2015).

To encourage success in these types of Tier 3 interventions, children with disabilities may benefit from strategic techniques to accelerate their performance. For example, families of children with disabilities who receive Tier 3 intervention in their home language may believe that maintaining their home language may be contributing to their developmental delay or specific disability. While evidence suggests this is not the case, making parents aware that home-language maintenance is an asset rather than a constraint in their child's development is an important focus in delivering Tier 3 interventions (Yu, 2013). It is important for families to be informed about the benefits to their children when they maintain their home language. Children need to maintain their connection with their family and will benefit from their continued ability to engage in language interactions in their home (Anderson, 2012; Paradis, Genesee, & Crago, 2011; Yu, 2013).

CONCLUSION

Implementing MTSS with DLLs requires a systematic and intentional focus on understanding children's abilities in the languages they are exposed to and speak. Informed efforts should be taken to improve the accuracy of assessments in place in MTSS and the effectiveness of interventions that are selected at all three tiers with this population. It is critical that programs hire bilingual staff to deliver assessments and instruction in the child's home language and that all staff have appropriate training to implement testing and intervention procedures with fidelity. Implementing high-quality Tier 1 environments that recognize the needs of children with emerging English language proficiency is an important first step in serving DLLs. There are a limited number of Tier 2 and 3 interventions available, and this is an area that demands further exploration and research. Given the demographic shifts in the United States, planning for DLLs in MTSS in early childhood settings should be integral to all program development efforts. The population of young culturally and linguistically diverse children in the United States is rapidly increasing—intensifying the need for systematic investment in their educational success.

Let's consider the two children in the opening vignette and the types of support that might be most appropriate for them. First, consider Jasmine in Oakland. MTSS designed for this setting needs to include Spanish language screening and progress monitoring by selecting one of the measures provided in this chapter. The school will also need to have other procedures in place for evaluating the children who speak other languages in the setting such as parent interviews or interpreters who can be hired to gather language samples in the child's home language. Based on Jasmine's screening performance, she may be an ideal candidate for Tier 2 intervention. The bilingual assistant in the classroom should also be supported in leading small-group literacy instruction in Spanish using a supplemental curriculum such as *Read It Again-DLL*, *Puentos de Cuentos*, or *Hablemos Juntos*. Bilingual assistants should receive professional development to provide high-quality instruction and to maximize their ability to scaffold language development. Jasmine's family should also be encouraged to continue using Spanish at home to help her maintain development in her home language. Materials can be sent home in Spanish, and family literacy nights can be conducted all in Spanish to help families understand how to incorporate more language into daily routines and how to use the materials that are sent home. Teachers can send home pictures of key vocabulary that the family can review and incorporate into daily conversations. Throughout the process, Jasmine's teacher must continue to monitor her progress using progress-monitoring tools to evaluate to what degree the intervention is successful and make instructional adjustments as necessary.

Myaing and his family are both cultural and linguistic minorities in a rural area, and special attention will be needed to make sure his educational needs are met. There are no assessments available in Burmese. To understand Myaing's development, the educational team should work with his family to provide information about his ability to communicate at home and their perception of how he compares to other children his same age in his culture. Teachers can develop a questionnaire to gather developmental information from the family and have an interpreter interview the family. It is likely his receptive language skills will emerge before his expressive skills in English. Teachers can use informal observations to document the receptive commands he responds to and measure how his receptive abilities grow over time in the classroom. This way, Myaing's emerging English skills can be measured while he is in the process of developing his expressive language abilities. These data should be used to determine his tier-level candidacy. Myaing will likely benefit from Tier 2 or Tier 3 English instruction. Given there are no staff who speak Burmese, instruction in his home language cannot be offered, but the English instruction he receives should be adapted to increase the comprehensible input he receives during the day. For example, classroom instruction should be adapted to include the use of visual symbols, intentionally teaching key vocabulary, using total physical response to act out stories, and carefully selecting books with few words and concrete images. His parents should also be provided information about the importance of maintaining his home language and the benefits of bilingualism. Throughout the process, Myaing's progress must be measured to evaluate if instruction is successful or if modifications are required using the types of measures and approaches noted for screening, but with increased frequency to evaluate change over time.

These two examples make clear that children who are DLLs may have very different language learning experiences in their home language and in English. A simple one-size-fits-all approach will not meet the needs of the broad range of DLLs served nationwide in ECE programs. Preschool programs need to be creative and open to innovation to implement evidence-based practices that are likely to produce the best outcomes. Families should also be meaningfully included in the assessment process and in supporting the child's home language. DLLs can no longer be an afterthought when implementing MTSS but need to be an integral part of the initial planning stages to effectively implement MTSS in early childhood programs.

RESOURCES

Developing Talkers/Hablemos Juntos. https://www.childrenslearninginstitute.org/resources/developing-talkershablemos-juntos-curricula-and-training

Division for Early Childhood (DEC), National Association for the Education of Young Children (NAEYC), & National Head Start Association (NHSA). (2013). *Frameworks for Response to Intervention in early childhood: Description and implications.* Missoula, MT: Author. Retrieved from http://www.dec-sped.org/position-statements

Durán, L. K., Hartzheim, D., Lund, E. M., Simonsmeier, V., & Kohlmeier, T. L. (2016). Bilingual and home language interventions with young dual language learners: A research synthesis. *Language, Speech, and Hearing Services in the Schools, 47,* 347–371.

Get Ready to Read. http://www.getreadytoread.org/skill-building-activities

Head Start Center on Cultural and Linguistic Responsiveness. https://eclkc.ohs.acf.hhs.gov/hslc/tta-system/cultural-linguistic

Lynch, E. W., & Hanson, M. J. (2011). *Developing cross-cultural competence: A guide for working with children and their families* (4th ed.). Baltimore, MD: Paul H. Brookes Publishing Co.

Paradis, J., Genesee, F., & Crago, M. B. (2010). *Dual language development and disorders: A handbook on bilingualism and second language learning.* Baltimore, MD: Paul H. Brookes Publishing Co.

Read It Again-PreK. https://earlychildhood.ehe.osu.edu/research/practice/read-it-again-prek

Tabors, P. O. (2008). *One child, two languages: A guide for preschool educators of children learning English as a second language* (2nd ed.). Baltimore, MD: Paul H. Brookes Publishing Co.

REFERENCES

Anderson, R. T. (2012). First language loss in Spanish-speaking children: Patterns of loss and implications for clinical practice. In B. A. Goldstein (Ed.), *Bilingual language development and disorders in Spanish–English speakers* (pp. 187–211). Baltimore, MD: Paul H. Brookes Publishing Co.

Anaya, J. B., Peña, E. D., & Bedore, L. M. (2016). Where Spanish and English come together: A two-dimensional bilingual approach to clinical decision making. *Perspectives of the ASHA Special Interest Groups, 1*(14), 3–16.

Banerjee, R., & Luckner, J. L. (2013). Assessment practices and training needs of early childhood professionals. *Journal of Early Childhood Teacher Education, 34*, 231–248.

Barnett, W. S., Yarosz, D. J., Thomas, J., Jung, K., & Blanco, D. (2007). Two-way and monolingual English immersion in preschool education: An experimental comparison. *Early Childhood Research Quarterly, 22*, 277–293.

Barrera, M., & Liu, K. K. (2010) Challenges of general outcomes measurement in the RTI progress monitoring of linguistically diverse exceptional learners. *Theory Into Practice 49*(4), pp. 273–280.

Barrueco, S., Lopez, M., Ong, C., & Lozano, P. (2012). *Assessing Spanish-English bilingual preschoolers: A guide to best approaches and measures*. Baltimore, MD: Paul H. Brookes Publishing Co.

Beck, I. L., McKeown, M. G., & Kucan, L. (2013). *Bringing words to life: Robust vocabulary instruction* (2nd ed.). New York, NY: Guilford Press.

Bohman, T. M., Bedore, L. M., Peña, E. D., Mendez-Perez, A., & Gillam, R. B. (2010). What you hear and what you say: Language performance in Spanish-English bilinguals. *International Journal of Bilingual Education and Bilingualism, 13*(3), 325–344.

Breckinridge Church, R., Ayman-Nolley, S., & Mahootian, S. (2014). The role of gesture in bilingual education: Does gesture enhance learning? *International Journal of Bilingual Education and Bilingualism, 7*(4), 303–319.

Camacho, C. (2010). *CPAA Technical Report*. New York, NY: Children's Progress. Retrieved from http://www.childrensprogress.com/wpcontent/uploads/2011/11/cpaa-adaptive-assessment-technical-report.pdf

Cárdenas-Hagan, E., Carlson, C. D., & Pollard-Durodola, S. D. (2007). The cross-linguistic transfer of early literacy skills: The role of initial L1 and L2 skills and language of instruction. *Language, Speech, and Hearing in the Schools, 38*(3), 249–259.

Carlson, S. M., & Meltzoff, A. N. (2008). Bilingual experience and executive functioning in young children. *Developmental Science, 11*(2), 282–298.

Castro, D., Páez, M. M., Dickinson, D. K., & Frede, E. (2010). Promoting language and literacy in young dual language learners: Research, practice, and policy. *Child Development Perspectives, 5* (1), 15–21.

Cheatham, G. A. (2011). Language interpretation, parent participation, and young children with disabilities. *Topics in Early Childhood Special Education, 31*, 78–88.

Collins, M. C. (2010). ELL preschoolers' English vocabulary acquisition from storybook reading. *Early Childhood Research Quarterly, 25*(1), 84–97.

Connors-Tadros, L., Barnett, W. S., & Nores, M. (2014). *Young immigrants and dual language learners: Participation in pre-K & gaps at kindergarten entry*. Retrieved from http://ceelo.org/wpcontent/uploads/2014/11/ceelo_nieer_webinar_equity_immigrant_dll_pre_k_slides_final.pdf http://ceelo.org/wpcontent/uploads/2014/11/ceelo_nieer_webinar_equity_immigra%09nt_dll_pre_k_slides_final.pdf.

DeBruin-Parecki, A. (2005). *Early Literacy Skills Assessment*. Ypsilanti, MI: HighScope Press.

Dressler, C., & Kamil, M. L. (2006). First-and second-language literacy. In D. August & T. Shanahan (Eds.), *Developing literacy in second-language learners: Report of the national panel on language minority children and youth*. Mahwah, NJ: Lawrence Erlbaum.

Durán, L. K., Gorman, B. K., Kohlmeier, T., & Callard, C. (2016). The feasibility and usability of the Read It Again Dual Language and Literacy Curriculum. *Early Childhood Education Journal, 44*, 453–461.

Durán, L. K., Hartzheim, D., Lund, E. M., Simonsmeier, V., & Kohlmeier, T. L. (2016). Bilingual and home language interventions with young dual language learners: A research synthesis. *Language, Speech, and Hearing Services in the Schools*. Published online ahead of print. doi:10.1044/2016_LSHSS-15-0030

Durán, L. & Wackerle-Hollman, A. (2016). Language and literacy environment evaluation report. Unpublished Survey. Minneapolis, MN: University of Minnesota.

Durán, L. K., Roseth, C., Hoffman, P., & Robertshaw, M. B. (2013). An experimental study comparing predominantly English and transitional bilingual education on Spanish-speaking preschoolers' early literacy development: Year three results. *The Bilingual Research Journal, 36*(1), 6–34

Farver, J. M., Lonigan, C., & Eppe, S. (2009). Effective early literacy skill development for young Spanish-speaking English language learners: An experimental study of two methods. *Child Development, 80*, 703–719.

Fien, H., Smith, J. L. M., Baker, S. K., Chaparro, E., Luft Baker, D., & Preciado, J. A. (2011). Including English learners in a multitiered approach to early reading instruction and intervention. *Assessment for Effective Intervention, 36*(3), 143–157.

Figueras-Daniel, A., & Barnett, W. S. (2013). *Preparing young Hispanic dual language learners for a knowledge economy.* New Brunswick, NJ: National Institute for Early Education Research.

Ford, K., & Invernizzi, M. (2014). *Phonological Awareness Literacy Screening in Spanish for Preschool (PALS español Pre-K).* Charlottesville: University of Virginia.

Fortuny, K., Hernandez, D. J., & Chaudry, A. (2010). *Young children of immigrants: The leading edge of America's future.* Retrieved from https://www.urban.org/sites/default/files/publication/29106/412203-Young-Children-of-Immigrants-The-Leading-Edge-of-America-s-Future.pdf

García, E., & Jensen, B. (2009). *Early educational opportunities for children of Hispanic origins* (Social Policy Rep. No. 23-2). Ann Arbor, MI: Society for Research in Child Development.

Glascoe, F. P. (2010). *Brigance Early Childhood Screens III.* North Billerica, MA: Curriculum Associates.

Goldenberg, C. (2008). Improving achievement for English language learners. In S. B. Neuman (Ed.), *Educating the other America* (pp. 139–162). Baltimore, MD: Paul H. Brookes Publishing Co.

Governor's State Advisory Council on Early Learning and Care. (2013). *California's best practices for young dual language learners: Research overview papers.* Sacramento: California Department of Education.

Gross, M., Buac, M., & Kaushanskaya, M. (2014). Conceptual scoring of receptive and expressive vocabulary measures in simultaneous and sequential bilingual children. *American Journal of Speech-Language Pathology/American Speech-Language-Hearing Association, 23*(4), 574–586. http://doi.org/10.1044/2014_AJSLP-13-0026

Guiberson, M. (2010). Patterns and implications. *Preventing School Failure, 53*, 167–176, doi:10.3200/PSFL.53.3.167-176

Gutiérrez-Clellan, V., Simon-Cerejido, G., & Restrepo, M. A. (2013). *Improving the vocabulary and oral language of bilingual Latino preschoolers: An intervention for speech-language pathologists.* San Diego, CA: Plural.

Hammer, C., Lawrence, F. R., & Miccio, A. W. (2007). Bilingual children's language abilities and early reading outcomes in Head Start and kindergarten. *Language, Speech, and Hearing Services in Schools, 38*, 237–248.

Hammer, C., Scarpino, S., & Davison, M. (2011). Beginning with language: Spanish–English bilingual preschoolers' early literacy development. In S. B. Neuman & D. K. Dickinson (Eds.), *Handbook of early literacy research: Volume 3* (pp. 118–135). New York: The Guilford Press.

Hoff, E. (2013). Interpreting the early language trajectories of children from low-SES and language minority homes: Implications for closing achievement gaps. *Developmental Psychology, 49*(1), 4–14.

Hoff, E., & Core, C. (2015). What clinicians need to know about bilingual development. *Seminars in Speech and Language, 36*(2), 89–99.

Huennekens, M. E., & Xu, Y. (2010). Effects of a cross-linguistic storybook intervention on the second language development of two preschool English language learners. *Early Childhood Education Journal, 38*(1), 19–26. doi:10.1007/s10643-010-0385-1

Johnston, K. (2017, March 13). Which job seekers are in hot demand? Bilingual workers. *The Boston Globe.* Retrieved from https://www.bostonglobe.com/business/2017/03/12/wanted-bilingual-workers/t8C9txqPmwCtIGDHX1jSTI/story.html

Justice, L., & McGinty, A. (2008). *Read It Again-PreK!* Retrieved from http://www.myreaditagain.com

Kelley, A., & Kohnert, K. (2012). Is there a cognate advantage for typically developing Spanish-speaking English-language learners? *Language, Speech, and Hearing Services in Schools, 43,* 191–204.

Klingner, J., & Harry, B. (2006). The special education referral and decision-making process for English language learners: Child Study Team meetings and placement conferences. *Teachers College Record, 108*(11), 2247–2281.

Kohlmeier, T., & Durán, L. K. (2015, July). *Findings from a quasi-experimental study investigating the effects of the Read It Again-Dual Language Preschool curriculum.* Kona, HI: Society for the Scientific Study of Reading.

LaForett, D. R., Peisner-Feinberg, E. S., & Buysse, V. (2013). Recognition and response for dual language learners. In V. Buysse & E. S. Peisner-Feinberg (Eds.), *Handbook of Response to Intervention on early childhood.* (pp. 355–369). Baltimore, MD: Paul H. Brookes Publishing Co.

Landry, S., Assel, M., Gunewig, S., & Swank, P. (2004). *mCLASS Circle Phonological Awareness Language and Literacy Screener (C-PALS).* Houston, TX: Ridgeways.

Linan-Thompson, S., & Ortiz, A. (2009). Response to Intervention and English-language learners: Instructional and assessment considerations. *Seminars in Speech and Language, 30*(2), 105–120.

Lonigan, C. J. (2003). Technical report on the development of the NCLD Spanish-Language *Get Ready to Read! Screening Tool.* Retrieved from http://www.getreadytoread.org.

Lugo-Neris, M. J., Jackson, C. W., & Goldstein, H. (2010). Facilitating vocabulary acquisition of young English language learners. *Language, Speech, and Hearing Services in Schools, 41*(3), 314.

Lugo-Neris, M. J., Peña, E. D., Bedore, L. M., & Gillam, R. B. (2015). Utility of a language screening measure for predicting risk for language impairment in bilinguals. *American Journal of Speech-Language Pathology, 24*(3), 426–437.

Mardell, C., & Goldenberg, D. S. (2011). *Developmental Indicators for the Assessment of Learning Manual-Spanish* (4th ed.). Bloomington, MN: Pearson.

Martin, B., & Carle, E. (1992). *Brown bear, brown bear, what do you see?* New York, NY: Holt.

Newborg, J. (2005). *Battelle Developmental Inventory* (2nd ed.). Itasca, IL: Riverside Publishing.

Mathes, P. (2015). *Istations' Indicators of Progress (ISIP) Early Reading-Spanish.* Dallas, TX: Istation

Meisels, S. J., Marsden, D. B., Wiske, M. S., & Henderson, L. W. (2008). *Early Screening Inventory–Revised,* (2nd ed.). San Antonio, TX: Pearson.

Páez, M. M., Tabors, P. O., & López, L. M. (2007). Dual language and literacy development of Spanish-speaking preschool children. *Journal of Applied Developmental Psychology, 28,* 85–102.

Paradis, J., Genesee, F., & Crago, M. (2011). *Dual language development and disorders: A handbook on bilingualism and second language learning.* Baltimore, MD: Paul H. Brookes Publishing Co.

Park, M., & McHugh, M. (2014). *Immigrant parents and early childhood programs: Addressing barriers of literacy, culture, and systems knowledge.* Washington, DC: Migration Policy Institute.

Peña, E. D. (2007). Lost in translation: Methodological considerations in cross-cultural research.*Child Development, 78,* 1255–1264.

Peña, E. D., Bedore, L. M., & Kester, E. S. (2016). Assessment of language impairment in bilingual children using semantic tasks: Two languages classify better than one. International Journal of Language & Communication Disorders, (51)192–202. doi:10.1111/1460-6984.12199

Peña, E. D., Gutierrez-Clellen, V., Iglesias, A., Goldstein, B., & Bedore, L. M. (2014). *BESA: Bilingual English–Spanish Assessment manual.* San Rafael, CA: AR-Clinical Publications.

Peña, E. D., & Halle, T. G. (2011). Assessing preschool dual language learners: Traveling a multiforked road. *Child Development Perspectives, 5*(1), 28–32. doi:10.1111/j.1750-8606.2010.00143.x

Perez, A. M., Peña, E., & Bedore, L. M. (2010). Cognates facilitate word recognition in young Spanish–English bilinguals' test performance. *Early Childhood Services Journal, 4*, 55–67.

Petersen, D. B., & Spencer, T. D. (2016). Using narrative intervention to accelerate canonical story grammar and complex language growth in culturally diverse preschoolers. *Topics in Language Disorders, 36*(1), 6–19.

Petitto, L. A., Katerelos, M., Levy, B., Gauna, K., Tétrault, K., & Ferraro, V. (2001). Bilingual signed and spoken language acquisition from birth: Implications for mechanisms underlying bilingual language acquisition. *Journal of Child Language, 28* (2), 1–44.

Roberts, T. (2008). Storybook reading in primary or second language with preschool children: Evidence of equal effectiveness for second-language vocabulary acquisition. *Reading Research Quarterly, 43*(2), 103–130. doi:10.1598/RRQ.43.2.1

Sanford, A. K., & Brown, J. E. (2011). *RTI for English language learners: Appropriately using screening and progress monitoring tools to improve instructional outcomes.* Portland, OR: National Center on Response to Intervention.

Simon-Cereijido, G. (2015). Preschool language interventions for Latino dual language learners with language disorders: What, in what language, and how. *Seminars in Speech and Language, 36*(2), 154–164.

Spencer, T., Perterson, D., Arvizu, M., Restrepo, M., & Thompson, M. (in preparation). *The effect of Spanish and English narrative intervention on the language skills of young dual language learners.*

Squires, J., Bricker, D. & Potter, L. (2009). *ASQ-3®: User's Guide, Ages & Stages Questionnaires®* (3rd ed.). Baltimore, MD: Paul H. Brookes Publishing Co.

Tsybina, I., & Eriks-Brophy, A. (2010). Bilingual dialogic book-reading intervention for preschoolers with slow expressive vocabulary development. *Journal of Communication Disorders, 43,* 538–556. doi:10.1016/j.jcomdis.2010.05.006

U.S. Department of Health and Human Services (UDHHS), Administration for Children and Families, Office of Head Start. (2013). *Report to Congress on dual language learners in Head Start and Early Head Start programs.* Retrieved from http://www.acf.hhs.gov/sites/default/files/opre/report_to_congress.pdf

Wackerle-Hollman, A., Durán, L., & Rodriguez, M. (2015). *Spanish Individual Growth and Development Indicators (S-IGDI).* St Paul, MN: Early Learning Labs.

Williams, C. (2014). *Building on immigrants' strengths to improve their children's early education.* Washington, DC: New America Ed Central. Retrieved from http://dev-edcentral.pantheon.io/building-immigrants-strengths-improve-childrens-educations

Yoshikawa, H., & Kholoptseva, J. (2013). *Unauthorized immigrant parents and their children's development.* Washington, DC: Migration Policy Institute.

Yu, B. (2013). Issues in bilingualism and heritage language maintenance: Perspectives of minority-language mothers of children with autism spectrum disorders. *American Journal of Speech and Language Pathology, 22,* 10–24.

Zehler, A. M., Fleischman, H. L., Hopstock, P. J., Stephenson, T. G., Pendzick, M. L., & Sapru, S. (2003). *Descriptive study of services to LEP students and LEP students with disabilities* (Contract No. ED-00-CO-0089). Policy report submitted to U.S. Department of Education (OELA).

Zepeda, M., Castro, D. C., & Cronin, S. (2011). Preparing early childhood teachers to work with young dual language learners. *Child Development Perspectives, 5*(1), 10–14.

Zimmerman, I. L., Steiner, V. G., & Pond, R. E. (2012). *Preschool Language Scales-5* (Spanish) (PLS-5 Spanish). Bloomington, MN: Pearson.

Zucker, T. A., Cabell, S. Q., Solari, E. J., & Landry, S. H. (2010). *Developing talkers: Pre-K curricular supplement to promote oral language.* Houston, TX: University of Texas Health Science Center at Houston.

Zucker, T. A., Solari, E. J., Landry, S. H., & Swank, P. R. (2013). Effects of a brief tiered language intervention for prekindergartners at risk. *Early Education and Development, 24*(3), 366–392.

Appendix 9A

Language Exposure Evaluation Report (LEER)

Child's name: _____ Today's date: _____

About Your Child

1. What is your relationship to the child?
   - ❑ Mother
   - ❑ Father
   - ❑ Grandparent
   - ❑ Other relative
   - ❑ Foster parent
   - ❑ Other—*Please describe:* _____

2. Write in what languages are spoken in your home?
   _____

3. What languages do <u>you</u> use when you talk to your child? *(Check one)*
   - ❑ English   ❑ Home language   ❑ Both

4. What languages do <u>other people at home</u> use with your child? *(Check one)*
   - ❑ English   ❑ Home language   ❑ Both

5. What languages does <u>your child</u> use when talking at home? *(Check one)*
   - ❑ English   ❑ Home language   ❑ Both

6. With what language is your child <u>most comfortable</u> now? *(Check one)*
   - ❑ English   ❑ Home language   ❑ Both

7. From the ages of 0 to 1 year, was English, your home language, or both spoken to your child at home?
   - ❑ English   ❑ Home language   ❑ Both

Current Language Use

We are interested in how much English and home language your child hears and speaks. First, think about weekdays (Monday–Friday) and then think about weekends (Saturday and Sunday).

8. **Monday–Friday**   What languages does your child HEAR?

Morning routine (awake to 9 am)	Early afternoon (9 am to 1 pm)	Mid-afternoon (1 pm to 4 pm)	Evening (4 pm to bedtime)
❑ Home language	❑ Home language	❑ Home language	❑ Home language
❑ English	❑ English	❑ English	❑ English
❑ Both	❑ Both	❑ Both	❑ Both

9. **Saturday and Sunday**   What languages does your child HEAR?

Morning routine (awake to 9 am)	Early afternoon (9 am to 1 pm)	Mid-afternoon (1 pm to 4 pm)	Evening (4 pm to bedtime)
❑ Home language	❑ Home language	❑ Home language	❑ Home language
❑ English	❑ English	❑ English	❑ English
❑ Both	❑ Both	❑ Both	❑ Both

10. **Monday–Friday**   What languages does your child SPEAK?

Morning routine (awake to 9 am)	Early afternoon (9 am to 1 pm)	Mid-afternoon (1 pm to 4 pm)	Evening (4 pm to bedtime)
❑ Home language	❑ Home language	❑ Home language	❑ Home language
❑ English	❑ English	❑ English	❑ English
❑ Both	❑ Both	❑ Both	❑ Both

(continued)

Appendix 9A *(continued)*

11. **<u>Saturday and Sunday</u>** What languages does your child SPEAK?

Morning routine *(awake to 9 am)*	*Early afternoon* *(9 am to 1 pm)*	*Mid-afternoon* *(1 pm to 4 pm)*	*Evening* *(4 pm to bedtime)*
❏ Home language	❏ Home language	❏ Home language	❏ Home language
❏ English	❏ English	❏ English	❏ English
❏ Both	❏ Both	❏ Both	❏ Both

<u>About You and Your Family</u>

12. What is the highest level of education that you have completed? *(Check one)*?
    - ❏ 6th grade or less
    - ❏ Less than 12th grade
    - ❏ GED
    - ❏ High school diploma
    - ❏ Some education after high school/vocational program
    - ❏ Associate degree (AA)
    - ❏ College degree (BA/BS)
    - ❏ Graduate/Professional degree

13. What is the country of each parent's birth? *(fill in for all applicable guardians)*
    Mother: _____ Father: _____ Other guardian: _____

14. How many years has each lived in the United States? *(fill in for all applicable guardians)*
    Mother: _____ Father: _____ Other guardian: _____

# 10

Meeting the Needs of Young Children With Disabilities in a Blended ECE and ECSE Multi-Tiered System of Support

Robin Miller Young, Lynette K. Chandler, and Judith J. Carta

Nathan participated in a case study evaluation (CSE) with his parents, Michael and Tanya, when he was 2 years old to determine if he met eligibility criteria for a disability due to delays in communication and socialization skills. When parents and evaluation team members met and shared information that had been gathered, they agreed that Nathan met the criteria as a child with a developmental delay and they developed an individualized family service plan (IFSP). The IFSP specified the speech and developmental therapy services Nathan and his family would receive through early intervention (EI) services (Individuals with Disabilities Education Improvement Act [IDEA] of 2004), to help him achieve targeted functional communication and prosocial goals.

Three months before Nathan's third birthday, Michael and Tanya and their EI service coordinator met with their local school district's EI transition coordinator to discuss Nathan's progress toward achieving his goals as well as his strengths and needs. Although Nathan was making progress in goal achievement, they decided that he might be eligible for early childhood special education (ECSE) services at age 3 (IDEA Part B—school-based services) in order to help him achieve educational goals, so Nathan and his parents participated in a CSE conducted by the local school district's early childhood staff members. Team members gathered information on his progress in EI services, observed him at home with family members, reviewed checklists completed by family members, and engaged Nathan and his family in an arena-style, play-based assessment conducted at the preschool. Based on all of the information gathered, the school staff and parents agreed that Nathan met the developmental delay eligibility criteria. Working together, they wrote an IEP (individualized education program) that included educational goals and objectives, and related services, such as speech therapy, to support his attainment of the educational objectives. The early childhood team recommended enrolling Nathan in a blended ECE (early childhood education)/ECSE preschool classroom, staffed by an ECE/ECSE licensed teacher and operated in a multi-tiered system of support (MTSS). Michael and Tanya looked at each other and decided they needed to learn more about blended practices and an MTSS for meeting Nathan's needs.

INTRODUCTION

Preschool-age children who have disabilities and their families should expect that the ECSE services they receive will lead to significant progress on individualized goals and within the general education curriculum (*Endrew v. Douglas County School District*, 2017). To ensure that individuals make progress, IDEA (1997; 2004) describes the requirements and responsibilities of states in providing supports and services to students with disabilities and their families. Through IDEA, each child has an IEP written by an IEP team that includes educators, support personnel, and the child's parents. The IEP team is expected to write ambitious goals; delineate progress-monitoring procedures; document the type of classroom setting(s) the child will attend (general and/or special education classroom); identify special education and related services such as speech, occupational, and physical therapy that will be provided for the child; and identify where those services will be provided (e.g., within the general classroom or other special education settings). The IEP team also documents the child's access to the general education curriculum, and if the child is not enrolled a general education classroom, the IEP must document how the child will have opportunities to interact with peers who do not have disabilities.

The manner in which school districts meet all the provisions of IDEA varies. In some school districts, ECSE services are provided with limited regard for access to the general education curriculum, participation in educational settings and situations that include peers from the community, and supports that would allow a child to engage successfully in his or her neighborhood school. Other more progressive school districts have conceptualized their schools as places where all children can grow and thrive. These school districts offer blended or inclusive programs that include children with and without disabilities, and they ensure that all children have access to the general education curriculum and receive the supports and services needed to make progress within the general education curriculum and toward achieving individualized goals. These school districts also employ MTSS as an additional approach for identifying and meeting the needs of all children.

The MTSS general education initiative is a "whole-school, data-driven, prevention-based framework for improving learning outcomes for every student through a layered continuum of evidence-based practices and systems" (Colorado Department of Education, 2015, p. 1). MTSS and IDEA have many things in common. They both use assessment data to identify student strengths and needs; they both engage in team-based and data-based decision making to identify learning goals; and they both implement strategies to address goals. At the preschool level, IDEA and MTSS both provide services to promote achievement of early academic and functional outcomes for young children (Division for Early Childhood [DEC],

National Association for the Education of Young Children [NAEYC], & the National Head Start Association [NHSA], 2013), and both may be implemented in inclusive/ blended or stand-alone special education settings.

This chapter will focus on the implementation of MTSS and IDEA in inclusive or blended classroom settings as these settings are supported by IDEA and are considered recommended practices by several national early childhood organizations (e.g., DEC, NAEYC, Head Start). The blended practices model strives to provide individualized instruction, access to the general education curriculum, and caregiving of young children from diverse cultural and linguistic backgrounds and diverse abilities using theories and practices from ECE/ECSE (Grisham-Brown, Hemmeter, & Pretti-Frontczak, 2017).

In this chapter, we describe the MTSS and blended practices initiatives as desirable, inter-related, and interdependent schooling models for educating all children, including those who have or are at-risk of developing disabilities. We provide guidance for integrating an MTSS framework with blended curricular, instructional, environmental, and assessment practices while at the same time providing ECSE services for children with disabilities. The chapter concludes with debunked myths regarding MTSS for young children with disabilities and essential resources to support further efforts to integrate these education system initiatives to benefit all young children.

SYSTEM INITIATIVES AND CULTURAL SHIFTS TO SUPPORT YOUNG CHILDREN WITH DISABILITIES

This section will discuss the general education initiative to identify and meet the needs of all students (grades K–12), beginning with Response to Intervention (RtI), which was a forerunner to the MTSS initiative. The section also discusses the blended practices model and how MTSS and IDEA services can be provided within blended settings.

Response to Intervention

The National Association of State Directors of Special Education (NASDSE) defined RtI as a "practice of providing high quality instruction and interventions matched to student need, monitoring progress frequently to make decisions about changes in instruction or goals and applying student response data to important educational decisions" (Kurns & Tilly, 2007, p. 1). NASDSE grounded the RtI initiative on the following core principles: 1) educators can effectively teach all children, 2) intervention should occur early when the first signs of learning difficulties occur, 3) decisions on how to educate children should be based on children's performance data, 4) assessment data should be collected to match different decision-making purposes, 5) interventions should be matched to student needs, and 6) research-based and scientifically validated assessment processes and interventions should be used to the greatest extent possible (Batsche et al., 2005).

In response to the growing interest in and development of RtI models and practices, members of the ECE and ECSE fields started examining this K–12 general education framework to determine if the innovation might be appropriate for young children, including those with and without disabilities (Buysse, Winton, & Zimmerman, 2007; VanDerHeyden, Snyder, & Hojnoski, 2006; Young,

Shields, & Chandler, 2011). Also, the federal government funded the Center for Response to Intervention in Early Childhood (CRTIEC) to conduct research and provide resources on RtI applied to the education of young children (see the Resources section at the end of the chapter for more information about CRTIEC).

In time, leaders in the fields of ECE and ECSE called for consensus on the RtI framework's applicability for young children, so the Division for Early Childhood (DEC) and the National Association for the Education of Young Children (NAEYC) partnered with the National Head Start Association (NHSA) and published *Frameworks for Response to Intervention in Early Childhood: Description and Implications* (DEC, NAEYC, & NHSA, 2013). The following core aspects of the RtI approaches were acknowledged to be aligned with recommended practices in early learning programs:

- Specification of a multi-tiered system of supports
- Early provision of support or intentional teaching/caregiving with sufficient intensity to promote positive outcomes and prevent later problems
- Use of child data to inform teaching and responsive caregiving practices
- Use of research-based, scientifically validated practices to the maximum extent possible (DEC *et al.*, 2013, p. 3)

In 2014, DEC updated and revised its recommended practices (RPs) to "provide guidance to practitioners and families about the most effective ways to improve the learning outcomes and promote the development of young children, birth through five years of age, who have or are at-risk for developmental delays or disabilities" (DEC, 2014, p. 1). The DEC RPs are divided into seven topic areas: leadership, environment, family, instruction, interaction, teaming and collaboration, and transition. The practices within these topic areas are congruent with the core principles of RtI identified by NASDE (Batsche et al., 2005) and the RtI practices described in the *Frameworks for Response to Intervention* position statement (DEC *et al.*, 2013), and they provide guidance for using the RtI framework to work with and support children who are at risk or have disabilities.

A number of experts and scholars have identified similarities between RtI and IDEA philosophies and practices. For example, Brown, Knopf, Conroy, Googe, and Greer (2013) compared and contrasted IDEA services (ECSE) for young children with disabilities to components of the RtI model. They distilled five common shared elements between the RtI framework and IDEA services for young children with disabilities:

1. Preference for services in general education settings to the greatest extent possible
2. Problem-solving methods for development and implementation of educational and instructional services and supports
3. Individualization of educational and instructional services and supports
4. Measurement of progress toward specified goals or objectives to maximize children's learning and development
5. Employment of research- or evidence-based practices (Brown et al., 2013, p. 345)

The RtI framework and IDEA requirements and services work together in blended classroom settings to provide children with disabilities access to the general education curriculum, opportunities to interact with peers who do not have disabilities, and individualized instruction and services to meet general curriculum and individualized (IEP) goals (Carta, McElhattan, & Guerrero, 2016; Chandler, Young, & Ulezi, 2011).

Multi-Tiered Systems of Support Framework

As the initial K–12 RtI models were being customized and implemented in local settings, reform leaders examined the processes of consensus-building around benefits for system participants and stakeholders, changing infrastructures systemwide to operationalize RtI core principles and implementing new decision-making and supportive practices within a systems approach. As a result of the change process examination, reform leaders revised the original RtI model and shifted its focus. The revised framework emphasizes a systems approach to providing a continuum of supports arranged from least to most intensive across tiers to meet children's and families' needs (Walker & Shinn, 2010). As this shift was taking place in the K–12 field, leaders within ECE and ECSE education decided that the design and activation of an MTSS framework is a natural "next step" in system-development efforts to help young children with and without disabilities achieve early academic and functional outcomes.

The MTSS framework is a systemwide initiative that includes system components and processes that interact with one another and are interrelated and interdependent (Castillo, 2014), with the goal of ensuring that all learners are educated well. The framework components include 1) a high-quality core curricular and instructional program; 2) the provision of interventions and supports of various intensities matched with student needs; 3) a data-based decision-making process; and 4) a strengths-based, problem-solving focus in the decision-making process conducted with teams in a collaborative manner (Castillo, 2014). MTSS retains the RtI framework components with two notable conceptual shifts. First, MTSS utilizes a system-level perspective to design and deliver services to children and families. That is, decisions on who will be served, what interventions will be used, how participant progress will be monitored (i.e., components), how to create and sustain a supportive culture, how teams will function, and how the program will be held accountable for reaching goals (i.e., processes) are coordinated from the classrooms, through schools/programs, upward through district-, regional-, and sometimes national-level organizational structures (e.g., Head Start). Second, one of the primary objectives of the MTSS system is promotion of targeted learning outcomes and prevention of learning difficulties for all children. The term MTSS is now regularly used in place of RtI to highlight the focus on system-level practices and the focus on early identification and prevention. The ECE and ECSE fields have embraced this expanded scope, and several researchers and organizations have recommended adoption of the system-level MTSS framework for providing effective and efficient education services for young children with a focus on achievement of developmental and educational outcomes (Buysse & Peisner-Feinberg, 2013; Carta et al., 2016; National Association of School Psychologists [NASP], 2015).

Blended Practices Models for Educating Young Children With Disabilities

Delivering educational services for young children with disabilities in settings with typically developing children has been supported by federal programs as well as early childhood professional organizations for more than 30 years (McLean, Sandall, & Smith, 2016). In 2009, DEC and NAEYC collaboratively developed a joint position paper that defined some of the key features of inclusion in the following statement:

> Early childhood inclusion embodies the values, policies, and practices that support the right of every infant and young child and his or her family, regardless of ability, to participate in a broad range of activities and contexts as full members of families, communities, and society. The desired results of inclusive experiences for children with and without disabilities and their families include a sense of belonging and membership, positive social relationships and friendships, and development and learning to reach their full potential. The defining features of inclusion that can be used to identify high quality early childhood programs and services are access, participation, and supports. (DEC & NAEYC, 2009, p. 2)

Inclusion is "an expected practice measured through federal and state accountability and performance standards" (Pretti-Frontczak, Grisham-Brown, & Sullivan, 2014, p. v). Just like RtI evolved into MTSS, inclusion at the early childhood level is evolving into a blended practices model. The blended model has the potential to promote strong skill development in young children with and without identified disabilities, a worthwhile goal for every community.

The blended practices model builds on inclusion by combining "beliefs, values, traditions, practices, and even funds from multiple disciplines, sources, and perspectives to maximize our efforts in serving all young children" (Pretti-Frontczak et al., 2014, p. v). The blended concept sets the stage for meeting all children's needs by employing the following practices: 1) all children share the classroom environment and have access to classroom activities and materials, 2) educators use a variety of instructional strategies to promote participation in classroom activities and routines and a sense of belonging among children, and 3) educators use differentiated instruction to support children with diverse abilities (DEC, 2007).

Blended programs are defined by these quality components (Grisham-Brown et al., 2017; Grisham-Brown, Pretti-Frontczak, Bachman, Gannon, & Mitchell, 2014; Pretti-Frontczak et al., 2014):

1. The program serves diverse children and families. (Diversity is celebrated and expected within blended programs. Children and families may vary in terms of ability, culture, language, socio-economic status, family make-up, and so forth.)

2. The program employs educators and other staff who are trained in both ECE and early intervention/ECSE, who can work with and support all children and their families.

3. The program combines fiscal, human, and program resources to address the diverse needs of all children.

4. The program blends philosophies and recommended practices from a number of disciplines across assessment and progress monitoring, curriculum, activities and routines, and teaching strategies to promote learning and development for all children.

In a blended practices model, the schools, classrooms, programs, and community events are designed *proactively* to build on strengths of all the children and families to promote successful acquisition of targeted goals, benchmarks, and milestones. This proactive model meets the needs of all children using advance knowledge of their strengths and needs and engages families of children with and without disabilities from the outset in designing an educational program that will meet the needs of all children.

The blended practices model promotes the development of new and innovative program options. In some inclusion programs, combining ECE with ECSE has been accomplished using a strictly additive model (1 + 1 = 2), whereas blended programs include ECE and ECSE multiplied by an X factor, representing the synergistic, fluid, boundaryless, and transdisciplinary interaction of these two interrelated and interdependent systems (wherein 1 + 1 times X is greater than 2). The result is a program option that allows for the planning and execution of incredibly proactive, creative, flexible, responsive, and innovative services. With a blended model, a greater number of curricular, instructional, environmental, and assessment options, and other system components and processes, can be combined in flexible ways to better build on strengths and address areas of concern.

The blended practices model is ideally suited to meet the needs of all young children, including those who are at risk and those with disabilities. Blended programs usually employ a dually licensed ECE/ECSE teacher who brings knowledge of 1) developmentally appropriate practice and specific instructional strategies to promote development for children at risk and with disabilities (e.g., strategies identified in the 2014 DEC *Recommended Practices* document), 2) child-initiated or emergent curriculum, 3) knowledge of an assessment-for-decision-making paradigm that includes frequent progress monitoring for quick curricular and instructional adjustments, and 4) knowledge of how to collaborate with and support staff partners (e.g., physical therapist, speech-language pathologist [SLP], behavior specialist) and family members.

In blended classroom settings, early childhood and other staff members are responsible for administering the general education curriculum as well as implementing both MTSS and IDEA services. Table 10.1 provides a brief overview of the similarities and differences across IDEA and MTSS. It is important that teachers, administrators, and related services staff are familiar with the IDEA rules and regulations related to identifying and providing services to children with disabilities and to understand the similarities and unique features of IDEA and MTSS. It also is important that administrators, in collaboration with program staff, support and integrate IDEA and MTSS within the blended classroom. Chandler and her colleagues (2008) provided examples of how a general education curriculum science activity, delivered in a blended classroom setting that included children without disabilities, children identified as at risk, and children with disabilities and IEPs, was adapted to meet the needs of all children using differentiated instruction and scaffolding for all children (Tier 1, MTSS). They also provide examples of how the teacher was able to address specific IEP goals and make adaptations for students with disabilities during this activity as described in the following list:

- A child with fine motor delays writes the results of his or her science experiment using pencils with foam grips to improve grasping and writes on large sheets of paper that are placed on a clipboard to hold them stationary.

Table 10.1. Similarities and differences across the Individuals with Disabilities Education Act (2004) and multi-tiered systems of support

	IDEA requirements	MTSS
Target population	Children from 0 to 21 with disabilities	Children from K to 21. May be used with children from birth to five as well.
Focus	Provide a free and appropriate public education (FAPE) that includes services and supports to meet the child's academic, functional, and developmental needs.	Provide early intervening strategies to address a selected number of targeted skills/behavior (e.g., early literacy).
Eligibility assessment/evaluation	Programs conduct a case study evaluation (CSE) of academic achievement and functional performance. The CSE includes technically adequate formal assessments, observation, interview, family input, records review, and progress monitoring. Data from MTSS may be used in some cases.	Universal screening is used to identify children at risk or with delays in specific areas (e.g., math, early literacy).
Eligibility criteria	Two criteria must be met: identification of one or more of the disabilities identified by the IDEA and documentation that the disability adversely affects the student's educational performance.	Eligibility for more intensive intervention (provided through tiers) is determined by the program (e.g., child scores at or below the 25th percentile).
Child goals	The individualized education program (IEP) details the child's FAPE. The IEP includes annual goals to address academic achievement and functional skills for each academic area and functional performance skill affected by the student's disability.	Goals to address specific needs identified through universal screening are developed by the class or program team.
Supports and services	Special education and related services, supplementary aids and services, linguistic and cultural accommodations, and supports for teachers that 1) address IEP goals and 2) enable the child to participate and make progress in the general education curriculum are documented on the IEP.	Tiered levels of instruction with increasing intensity of support are aligned with the general education curriculum and targeted skills. Intervention strategies to address the child's needs are developed by the program.
Location of services	The IEP team identifies the least restrictive environment (LRE) in which services will be provided. Services to address IEP goals may be provided in or outside of the early childhood classroom (e.g., services provided in a resource room or therapy room). Services may be provided in a variety of settings including public school-based programs, Head Start programs, and community child care.	MTSS may be implemented in a variety of settings, including public school-based programs, Head Start programs, and community child care settings.
Interventions, teaching practices	Scientifically based instructional practices are used to the extent possible.	Recommended practice is to use scientifically based instructional practices to the extent possible.
Family involvement	Family concerns must be considered during assessment and when developing the IEP. Document the type and frequency of communication used to share progress with family.	Involve families as appropriate.

Table 10.1. *(continued)*

	IDEA requirements	MTSS
Progress-monitoring assessment/ evaluation	The frequency of progress monitoring, progress-monitoring strategies, and evaluation criteria for IEP goals must be documented on the IEP. A formal review of progress is documented during an annual IEP meeting. For children from 3 to 5 years old, program staff complete the Early Childhood Outcomes (or other outcomes assessment) upon program entry and program exit.	Teams determine the frequency of and strategies for monitoring progress on targeted goals.
Personnel	Special educators, therapists, and other related service staff (e.g., occupational therapist, physical therapist, speech-language pathologist, behavior specialist), general educators (as appropriate depending on LRE), and families	Classroom teacher and family members. Recommended practice is to also include, as appropriate, special educators and related service staff.
Transition	For young children, programs follow specific procedures to facilitate the transition from early intervention to school-based special education services.	Programs may share information about the child's performance on universal screening measures and progress in tiered instruction when a child transitions to a new program.

Key: CSE, case study evaluation; FAPE, free and appropriate public education; IEP, individualized education program; LRE, least restrictive environment; MTSS, multi-tiered systems of support.
Individuals with Disabilities Education Improvement Act (IDEA) of 2004, PL 108–446, 20 U.S.C. §§ 1400 *et seq*

- A child who is nonverbal makes predictions about the experiment by holding up a Yes or No card or presses the Yes or No button on an augmentative communication device that says "yes" or "no" when pressed.
- A child with an IEP goal to initiate and respond to peers and who has cognitive delays helps another child show a plate of mixed ingredients to other children and then is paired with a peer partner when conducting the experiment in the science center. Together they document the results of the experiment.
- A child works on early math skills and letter identification skills by counting the number of Y (yes) and N (no) marks on the experiment results form.
- The teacher varies the type of questions he or she poses and the type of answer he or she requests to allow children with diverse communication and linguistic abilities participate. For example, he or she 1) asks one child for only yes–no answers and another for two-word answers, 2) provides two choices (e.g., "Big bubbles or little bubbles?") versus open-ended questions (e.g., "What size are the bubbles?" or "What just happened?"), and 3) asks questions and accepts answers in a child's native language.
- A child with an IEP goal to listen to and follow directions works with an adult as he or she conducts his or her own experiment. The adult provides 1- to 2-step directions and provides other forms of scaffolding assistance, such as questioning, prompting, and modeling as needed.
- A child who has visually impairments (with low vision) uses multiple senses to identify if there are bubbles by getting close to, touching, and listening for

bubbles after the two items are mixed. The teacher also works with this child before the activity to explain the concept of bubbles and to give him or her experience looking at, feeling, and hearing bubbles. The individual prediction sheet that this child uses to record the results of the experiment has words and pictures written with high contrast between the words or pictures (e.g., very dark black) and paper (e.g., white) in order to make use of the child's functional vision.

- The teacher provides a set of sequenced picture cues that indicate the steps to be followed in completing the individual experiment for a child with autism who has problems following multistep verbal instructions.

- A child who is learning English also uses picture cues that include words written in English and in the child's native language. The teaching assistant also answers questions and provides assistance using the child's native language as needed. The child's experiment recording sheet also is written in English and the child's native language so that the child's family can review the activity with the child at home.

- A child with cognitive delays who is not yet writing or copying words draws pictures of the results of his or her experiment and then describes to the teacher what he or she has drawn. The teacher then writes the words under the pictures.

- The SLP provides a child with expressive language delays opportunities to use his or her expressive and sequencing skills by asking the child simple questions about his or her experiment, such as "What do you need to do first, second, and so forth?" or "Are there bubbles?" and then waits for an answer. If the child does not answer, the SLP models the answer and asks the child to repeat the answer.

Each of these adaptations would allow children with varying abilities and needs to participate in the science experiment activity and to practice early language and literacy skills and/or other identified skills (Chandler et al., 2008).

In summary, the DEC and several researchers and authors recommend that programs move beyond inclusion to the adoption of blended programs and practices (e.g., Grisham-Brown et al., 2017; Grisham-Brown & Pretti-Frontczak, 2011; Pretti-Frontczak et al., 2014). Blended programs are ideally suited for integration with IDEA requirements and the MTSS framework in serving children of diverse abilities. Program staff members employ blended approaches related to assessment, classroom design, instructional strategies, individualized practices, interacting with children, supporting and working with families, and teaming and collaboration that are compatible with the MTSS framework. Blended programs also rely on "a strong leadership team, a commitment to data-driven decision-making, the formation of collaborative partnerships, and ongoing and sustained professional development" (Pretti-Frontczak et al., 2014, p. vi) that are ideally matched to the system-level emphasis of the MTSS framework. Early childhood programs and schools that are merging blended practices into an MTSS framework are starting to share their journeys so that others can learn from their successes and challenges. Young and colleagues (2008) described one such journey, including the 10 steps an early childhood program's instructional leadership team can take to embed blended practices within an MTSS framework to improve early literacy and language outcomes for all children, including those who are at risk of delays and disabilities and those who have identified delays and disabilities, between the preschool and kindergarten years.

Central to making these initiatives the "norm" across all ECE/ECSE programs is training and support at preservice and in-service levels. Blended training should prepare educators, administrators, and other professionals and staff to work together as they develop and provide programs that meet the needs of all children and their families. Professional development should address system-level supports identified by Leiber and her colleagues (2002): shared philosophy, shared instructional strategies and supports, administrative support, collaboration, and positive relationships with families. Preservice training should provide shared on-site experiences in which teacher education candidates from various disciplines work together and with staff in blended classrooms. Finally, administrators must be prepared to provide the types of supports that lead to high-quality, effective blended programs (e.g., time for planning, professional development, coaching and mentoring, managing fiscal and other resources, and evaluation) (Chandler et al., 2011).

Meeting the Needs of Young Children With and Without Disabilities Through the MTSS Framework in Blended Settings

In early education programs throughout the United States, young children with and without disabilities and their families are benefiting from their participation in MTSS with a blended practices model. The following examples describe some of the most common experiences of these children and their families and were written to highlight the following: 1) the point of entry into the MTSS framework and blended practices, nature of the eligibility determination process, and development of the IEP; and 2) various aspects of the MTSS framework, IDEA regulations when required, and blended practices model.

Example 1 This example describes how Nathan received IDEA services and participated in MTSS within a blended preschool classroom. The child named Nathan in this chapter's opening vignette received early intervention services through IDEA (Part C) and was transitioning to preschool. Prior to his entry to preschool, Nathan participated in a CSE to determine eligibility for ECSE services through IDEA (Part B); he did not have to "fail" earlier interventions to be identified as a child with a disability [IDEA and MTSS]. Also, the evaluation included "one-point-in-time" (arena-style, play-based assessment) and "growth-over-time" (EI progress rates) data sources, aligned with preferred assessment practices (DEC, 2009; NASP, 2015) [IDEA and MTSS] to determine that he was eligible for special education services through IDEA.

Nathan's IEP, developed by school staff and his parents, included goals and objectives that could be best met in a blended ECE classroom with a teacher who was licensed in ECE and ECSE. His teacher provided highly individualized and embedded instruction to address the goals on his IEP throughout the daily sessions and monitored his progress frequently in order to make needed changes to ensure his success [IDEA]. The SLP also provided small-group therapy services within the classroom's physical environment and daily routine. She did this by bringing together Nathan and two randomly chosen classmates without IEPs and engaging all of them in a variety of developmentally appropriate activities judiciously chosen to promote attainment of Nathan's IEP goals. She also collaborated with Nathan's teacher to design strategies that the teacher could use throughout the day to promote Nathan's communication skills. Nathan (and his peers) also participated in universal screening on key skills and tiered interventions as needed [MTSS].

The cyclical process of gathering regular assessment data to gauge progress on IEP objectives and the general education curriculum targets, then providing ECE and ECSE instruction in a flexible and fluid manner, in a blended setting with same-age peers, using post-instruction data for making plans for the next instructional targets, also represents a likely scenario of blended services/practices. The latter part of this illustration is also presented in a vignette at the chapter's conclusion to complete the story of Nathan's family's experience.

Example 2   This example illustrates how a child enrolled in a blended classroom came to receive IDEA services. Sofia was enrolled by her parents in a community preschool at age 3. On the first day, the ECE/ECSE teacher and classroom teammates were immediately concerned that Sofia, a native English speaker, did not demonstrate the socialization or communication skills expected for her age. In addition, she did not engage in joint referencing of objects (i.e., looking at a toy across the table and then looking to an adult and back to the toy so both the child and adult could attend to the object at the same time), and she only used play materials in a repetitive and stereotypical manner. By the end of the first week, the team asked the parents to meet with them. In that meeting, the classroom team members and Sophia's parents shared strengths and concerns about Sofia's overall developmental progress. The teacher proposed that a CSE be conducted to determine a profile of Sofia's developmental status ("one point in time") and rates of progress ("growth-over-time"), so that Sofia's parents and the classroom team could make sound educational decisions on Sofia's behalf, including whether she was eligible to receive ECSE services through IDEA. Specifically, Sofia's parents and her classroom team members jointly determined what components would be included in the CSE by deciding in which domains there was already enough information to make informed educational decisions, in which domains additional data were needed, and how additional information would be gathered. Sofia's parents gave written consent for the evaluation to take place, and everyone agreed to complete their assessment responsibilities within the next 30 days. While the CSE was being completed, Sofia continued to have opportunities to participate in the general education curriculum with peers who were typically developing. Her teacher also provided highly scaffolded instruction to enhance her success in daily play and instructional activities and interactions [MTSS]. After the assessment activities were completed, the parents and classroom team members reviewed all the data and decided that Sofia met the criteria as a child with a disability. Then they developed an IEP for her, and they decided to enroll her in an ECSE self-contained class in the same building so that she could obtain more intensive IDEA services. She also participated in a twice-a-week music and movement activity with the classmates from her original classroom. During her preschool years, her classroom team members, including her parents, met regularly and employed the steps of the problem-solving process (see Figure 4.1 in Chapter 4) [MTSS]. This data-based, decision-making process was employed to ensure that she received supports of the appropriate intensity to meet her rapidly improving proficiencies across the developmental domains. Specifically, Sofia moved through the early childhood program's tiered instructional model, with supports of decreasing intensity, as the team determined how to best meet her needs. Overall, she moved from Tier 3 to Tier 1 services, defined by changing curricular, instructional, and environmental variables, and she was eventually reenrolled in a blended ECE/ECSE classroom (a less intensive programming option) [IDEA] before transitioning from preschool to an inclusive kindergarten classroom, so she received the general education and special education services for which she was eligible that also met her needs [MTSS].

Example 3   In this example we follow a 4-year-old child named Nishra who is attending an early childhood inclusive/blended education program operated by local school districts as a community preschool. She started as a learner who was "typically developing," and her parents paid tuition for her enrollment in the blended program. Once the school year started, a standardized universal speech articulation screening process was completed for all students, and Nishra, a native English speaker, did not meet proficiency criteria for producing four age-appropriate sounds. At the conclusion of a parent–teacher conference, the team decided to have Nishra play a sound development game at center time on Mondays, Wednesdays, and Fridays. With this intervention, she had adult and peer models of correct sounds, and she was asked to make targeted sounds 30 times each day. This intervention resulted in Nishra having 120 total sound production trials per intervention day (4 sounds × 30 opportunities to make sounds = 120 trials), which worked out to be 360 sound production trials per week (120 trials × 3 days = 360 total targeted sounds per week). The team characterized this as a Tier 3 intervention, given the highly individualized plan and its intensity; the remainder of her programming was the core, Tier 1 [MTSS]. Nishra's teacher tallied her proficiency on targeted sounds. To obtain a more comprehensive view of Nishra's strengths and needs, the team asked Nishra's parents and teacher to complete developmental questionnaires.

In 15 days, the team reconvened and examined the data. Treatment integrity was high, Nishra's attendance had been perfect, and she attempted all the sounds she was asked to make during the Tier 3 sound game intervention. Her performance level was still far below a proficiency level, so the team discussed what the components that would be included in the CSE by deciding in which domains there was already enough information to make informed educational decisions, in which domains additional data were needed, and how additional information would be gathered. Parent and teacher ratings on the developmental questionnaire were well within the average range for her age, and a review of classroom work samples indicated that Nishra was making adequate progress in the general education curriculum. So, the team (including Nishra's parents) decided to do a "speech and language" only evaluation that met federal and state requirements including "one-point-in-time" and "growth-over-time" data sources [IDEA]. Until the evaluation was completed, Nishra still received Tier 3 intervention to enhance her speech sound production skills [MTSS]. After evaluation, the team convened and agreed that Nishra met the IDEA eligibility criteria as a child with a speech or language impairment. She remained in her current early childhood placement and received speech therapy as an ECSE service. However, in this community-based program, tuition-paying students received speech therapy outside of the classroom, before or after the preschool experience. Like other ECSE IDEA services, speech therapy was provided free of charge to the parents. Ongoing data-based decision making by her classroom team and parents supported Nishra in generalizing her emerging articulation skills in natural conversation opportunities with peers and adults in classroom activities.

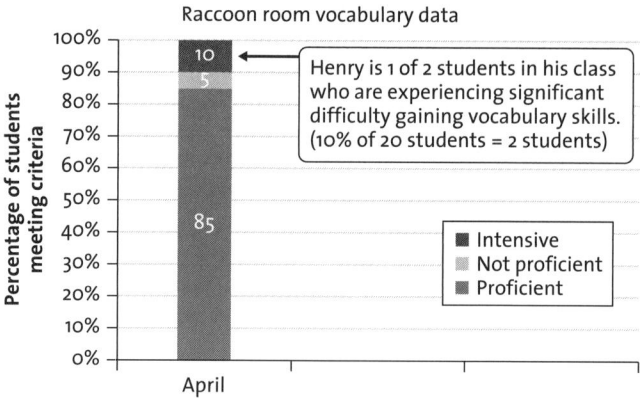

Figure 10.1. Henry's performance on a universal screener.

Example 4 This illustration describes 1) how a classroom team and a child's family used the MTSS framework and the blended practices model to match instructional intensity to the child's needs and 2) how tiered instruction moved from least intensive (Tier 1 only) to most intensive (Tiers 2 and 3) general education supports, and back to least intensive (Tier 1 only) without the need for a CSE [MTSS only, no IDEA]. This scenario is also presented as Video 5 in this book's accompanying video series. A class of 4-year-old children received core curricular, instructional, and environmental practices. Evidence from several different data sources converged on the finding that most children's vocabulary needs were being met; however, a small group of children, including a boy named Henry, were going to need additional support to close the word gap with their peers (see Figure 10.1 for a graph of classwide performance on a universal screening measure), so the ECE/ECSE teacher taught the children targeted skills during a small-group activity to boost their word knowledge in a standard protocol, evidence-based vocabulary development intervention (Tier 2) during center time of the day. After a period of intervention, Henry was still not making sufficient gains, so a team meeting was held with his family.

Using the data-based, collaborative decision-making process, the school staff and family designed an individualized plan for Henry that included providing him with one-to-one teacher-directed instruction using the same packaged intervention that had been used in Tier 2. This packaged program was used as the basis for a Tier 3 intervention because while Henry had been responding to the Tier 2 instructional strategy that was a correct match for his needs, the team felt he would make better progress if the instructional strategy was made more powerful. Henry needed adult models exclusively as children's models could not be relied on to be accurate and to be delivered quickly. He also need more frequent and individual opportunities to respond rather than frequent choral responses and occasional individual opportunities to respond, which he had experienced in Tier 2. Finally, a one-to-one instructional intervention would provide more scaffolded support to help him respond correctly. The family also offered to support him with specific strategies at home. Henry's progress in the Tier 3 intervention was

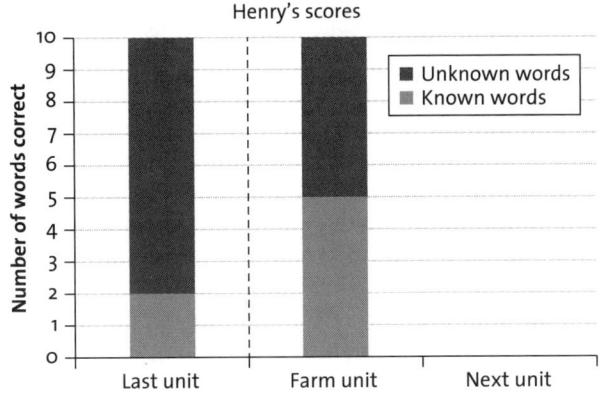

Figure 10.2. Henry's data following Tier 2 instruction.

monitored frequently. In addition, he participated in ongoing universal screening and progress monitoring related to the general education curriculum, in natural settings with his peers, and at home. Figure 10.2 illustrates Henry's progress in the multi-week, inter-disciplinary instructional unit on farming that was the basis for core (Tier 1) instruction for the whole class. The data were gathered when the unit concluded, which occurred about mid-way in Henry's Tier 3 experience.

He had made greater progress in the farming unit than he had in the prior unit, designated as "last unit" on the graph. However, the goal was for Henry to demonstrate 80% proficiency, which translated to knowing 8/10 instructional unit target words, and he only demonstrated proficiency on 5/10 words. As a result, the team members strengthened implementation fidelity and continued the intervention through the beginning of the "next unit" provided as part of core instruction. Over time, as Henry made progress on multiple indicators of his expanding vocabulary knowledge, he was moved back to the Tier 2 intervention. Gradually, Henry no longer needed additional vocabulary intervention, and the tiered instructional supports were discontinued. By the time of the kindergarten transition meeting, he had been demonstrating word knowledge proficiency for several months, and he was participating successfully in the core preschool curriculum without Tier 2 or Tier 3 support. The classroom staff and family felt confident he had closed the word gap with his peers and was ready to engage successfully in the kindergarten program.

Example 5   This final illustration is based on a scenario described previously (Hojnoski, Missall, & Young, 2016). The mother of a preschooler, who was not enrolled in any formal early care and education program, called the school district's preschool office and requested that her son Keaton participate in a preschool screening. The mother indicated that her sister suggested the screening because the sister provides care for the child while the mother is at work. The sister was concerned that Keaton seemed slower than the other children in her care to follow directions and sustain interest in storybook reading. Keaton passed the developmental screening. However, he did qualify as a child who was at risk of developing delays or disabilities based on family-related factors, so he was enrolled with funds from the state pre-K at-risk grant in the community preschool program operated by the district as an MTSS and blended program. Over the course of 18 months, his ECE/ECSE teacher and team, including his mother, monitored his progress on universal screening measures known to be indicators of later school success (e.g., IGDIs 1.0 Picture Naming Fluency [PNF] and Preschool Numeracy Indicators [PNIs], a forerunner of the myIGDIs Early Numeracy Assessment) and rubric ratings of student work samples in a portfolio system.

Over time, Keaton's team used the four-step problem-solving process described in Chapter 4 to attempt to improve his performance of targeted early academic skills [MTSS]. After small-group and large-group explicit instruction with significant scaffolding had been provided (e.g., Tier 2 for both early language and literacy and numeracy) with high fidelity for several months of regular attendance, his performance on a variety of measures related to early math and vocabulary was still discrepant from national and local norms in "one-point-in-time" analyses (e.g., PNIs 1:1 correspondence score of 5 when school's 25th percentile score was 14) and in "growth-over-time" (e.g., IGDIs 1.0 PNF score dropped from 20 to 15), so the team members arrived at consensus to conduct a CSE when it seemed that he might need more intensive and individually designed supports and services. Consequently, the team determined that Keaton was eligible for ECSE as a child who met the developmental delay criteria [IDEA]. He received ECSE IDEA services within the blended ECE/ECSE classroom and also continued to participate in the general education curriculum and the MTSS framework through the end of his preschool experience. He transitioned into an inclusive/blended kindergarten program [IDEA], where he continued to receive special education services and participated in the MTSS framework employed at the elementary level in his school district.

Myths and Truths About the MTSS Framework, Children With Disabilities, and Blended Practices

Often, one of the biggest challenges to system-reform efforts lies in the myths that develop about various aspects of the reform as a result of incomplete information or misconceptions about how the practices of the reform should be implemented. A number of papers have described some of these myths and misconceptions about RtI and early education that relate to this discussion of MTSS and blended practices (DEC *et al.*, 2013; Greenwood et al. 2011; Young & Chandler, 2013). Addressing some of the myths regarding an MTSS framework and blended practices model for young children with disabilities may help build consensus regarding the appropriateness and benefits of the initiatives and help keep the initiatives moving forward.

1. MYTH: Children with disabilities and IEPs cannot participate in MTSS.

TRUTH: While children with identified disabilities should receive special education and related services related to their annual goals as documented on their IEPs, these services should not prevent them from participating in MTSS. Every child regardless of IEP status has strengths and needs that vary across different developmental domains, preacademic areas, and specific skill areas (Grisham-Brown et al., 2014). Some of a child's needs may be addressed through the IEP;

however, other needs may not be identified for intensive special education services. For example, a child with disabilities and an IEP may have delays in expressive communication and receive special education services to address IEP goals in the language and communication domain. However, universal screening that is part of MTSS may identify that child as at risk in early math skills. That child with an IEP might then receive Tier 2 services to address early math skills (i.e., the child's early math skills did not warrant inclusion of annual goals on the IEP). That child also may have strengths in social interaction, self-care skills, and motor skills and receive Tier 1 programming and continue receiving this Tier 1 core support as long as he or she demonstrates growth rates in these areas that fall within the expected range for typically developing children.

2. MYTH: MTSS is intended to replace ECSE. If a school district has adopted MTSS, then children cannot be referred for or receive ECSE.

TRUTH: IDEA is a federal statute that provides procedural safeguards to protect children's and parents' rights with respect to special education and related services. Children who meet IDEA, state, and local education agency (LEA) criteria for a "disability" and are determined eligible for special education and related services must have individualized goals and receive ECSE services as documented on the IEP. The two systems work together to provide appropriate and required services and supports to all children in a program.

3. MYTH: A child must experience MTSS and fail supports provided at each tier prior to being referred for an evaluation to determine eligibility for special education and related services.

TRUTH: The federal Office of Special Education Programs (OSEP) is very clear that MTSS may not be used to delay referral, evaluation, or the provision of special education and related services. A recent memo from OSEP on April 29, 2016, further clarifies,

> that states and local education agencies (LEAs) have an obligation under the Individuals with Disabilities Education Act (IDEA) to ensure that evaluations of all children suspected of having a disability, including evaluations of 3-, 4-, or 5-year-old children enrolled in preschool programs, are not delayed or denied because of implementation of a Response to Intervention (RtI) strategy." (Early Childhood Technical Assistance Center [ECTA], n.d.)

Although it is possible to use information and data on progress for a child who participated in MTSS and was subsequently referred for special education evaluation, participation in MTSS may not replace or delay the comprehensive CSE.

4. MYTH: Children with disabilities should only be served in the most intensive tier.

TRUTH: Many people assume that children who have disabilities and receive special education services, who are then identified as at-risk through universal screening, will automatically receive instruction at the most intensive level (e.g., Tier 3). However, it is the assessment of the child's performance, team-based problem-solving, and progress-monitoring data that determines whether a child would benefit from more intensive instruction at Tiers 2 or 3. Disability alone does not determine the intensity of instruction. MTSS is designed to be a fluid process with movement into and out of specific levels of tiered instruction over time.

Children with disabilities may begin to receive more intensive services at Tier 2 or 3, and movement between the tiers will be based on their response to intervention within a tier.

5. MYTH: MTSS cannot be used in a self-contained special education class in which all children have disabilities and IEPs.

TRUTH: The use of MTSS is not restricted to blended or inclusive classroom settings. It can be a very effective process for providing services in self-contained classrooms as well. Just as in blended classrooms, children in self-contained classrooms present a range of strengths and needs that can be addressed through tiered instruction. For example, some children may benefit from small-group or individualized instruction in early writing skills whereas others may make sufficient progress by participation in the core curriculum, Tier 1. Also, the self-contained class may include children who can participate successfully in a core physical development curriculum (e.g., physical education, motor time activities) or a core social-emotional curriculum. Likewise, universal assessment can help teachers understand the range of skills in identified areas or domains, or it may pinpoint areas to change within the core curriculum.

CONCLUSION

One hand represents the interdependent components and processes of the MTSS school system framework designed to achieve schooling success for all students. The other hand represents a blended practices model that calls on educators to blend the best of knowledge bases for children with disabilities (e.g., IDEA and DEC recommended practices) with that of the knowledge base for children who do not have disabilities, to enhance the growth and development of all children. Since these initiatives target changing an entire system, as opposed to changing one isolated practice, they call for a ramping up of the system culture that will embrace and provide meaningful scaffolds to support the changing infrastructure and processes. Core human service organizational values embraced by the ECE/ECSE community such as family-centered practices, person-first language, respect for diversity, empowered teams, trustworthiness, transparent communication, and equity and social justice will bring the two hands together so the promises of equity, parity, and achievement of essential outcomes for all children can be applauded and celebrated.

Placement in the ECE/ECSE blended class allowed Nathan to receive highly directed teacher instruction [ECSE] in just one classroom, specific to his IEP objectives, and opportunities to practice and develop skill fluency with peers while also participating in the general education curriculum (Tier 1) of that same classroom. When the district adopted an initiative to improve children's social-emotional skills, and a Tier 2 packaged program was offered to the preschool staff, his teacher offered to pilot it and participated in training to implement the intervention with fidelity. Nathan participated in the Tier 2 packaged prosocial skill development intervention in the blended setting, receiving instruction with his peers as well as opportunities to practice and improve his social skills. Some of his classmates have become playmates, and they have had successful playdates outside of the school setting. Nathan also continued to receive speech therapy as an IDEA "related service" necessary for him to achieve the educational goals on his IEP. The classroom SLP integrated therapeutic activities into heterogeneous peer play groups to address Nathan's IEP objectives and also provided one-to-one therapy based on her ongoing assessment of his progress. Nathan's progress on early language and literacy measures were monitored three times a year, when all the children participated in the school's universal monitoring procedures. This allowed his teacher to monitor progress on tasks that were shown to be predictive of later reading success, as well as his specific goals and objectives. Michael and Tanya met with the classroom team regularly to review Nathan's progress on the universal progress-monitoring measures, as well as his individual goals and objectives. Tanya said she was glad Nathan started right away in a blended class, and in collaboration with his classroom team they could decide to change his level of intervention and supports so that he continued to have an individualized program that met his needs. Michael and Tanya walked out of the annual review meeting held after Nathan had been enrolled in the early childhood blended program for a year with smiles on their faces. They were excited about the growth they expected Nathan to make before the next conference!

RESOURCES

Center for Response to Intervention in Early Childhood (CRTIEC). http://www.crtiec.dept.ku.edu. This is a web site with resources derived from CRTIEC, a research and development center funded from 2008 to 2014 by the Institute for Education Science, National Center for Special Education Research to develop measures and interventions for advancing tiered models to support early literacy and language in young children.

Division for Early Childhood (DEC), National Association for the Education of Young Children (NAEYC), & National Head Start Association (NHSA). (2013). *Frameworks for Response to Intervention in early childhood: Description and implications*. Missoula, MT: Author. Retrieved from http://www.dec-sped.org/position-statements

Early Childhood Technical Assistance Center (ECTAC). http://ectacenter.org. The ECTAC is funded by OSEP to improve state early intervention and ECSE systems and enhance the outcomes of these programs for young children and their families.

Kaiser, A.P., & Hemmeter, M. L. (Eds.). (2014). Special issue on the Center on Response to Intervention in Early Childhood: Developing evidence-based tools for a multi-tier approach to preschool language and early literacy instruction. *Journal of Early Intervention, 36*(4), 243–245.

RTI Action Network: A Program of the National Center for Learning Disabilities. http://www.rtinetwork.org/pre-k. Pre-K resources include seven blog entries, a "Virtual School" video of an inclusive/blended early childhood education program, and various essays on RTI/MTSS for young children.

U.S. Department of Education. https://www2.ed.gov/policy/speced/guid/early learning/joint-statement-full-text.pdf. Policy statement on inclusion of children with disabilities in early childhood programs.

REFERENCES

Batsche, G., Elliott, J., Graden, J. L., Grimes, J., Kovaleski, J. F., . . . Tilly III, W. D. (2005). *Response to Intervention: Policy considerations and implementation.* Alexandria, VA: NASDSE.

Brown, W. H., Knopf, H. T., Conroy, M. A., Googe, H. S., & Greer, F. (2013). Preschool inclusion and Response to Intervention for children with disabilities. In V. Buysse & E. Peisner-Feinberg (Eds.), *Handbook of Response to Intervention in early childhood* (pp. 339–353). Baltimore, MD: Paul H. Brookes Publishing Co.

Buysse, V., & Peisner-Feinberg, E. (2013). Response to Intervention: Conceptual foundations for the early childhood field. In V. Buysse & E. Peisner-Feinberg (Eds.), *Handbook of Response to Intervention in early childhood* (pp. 3–23). Baltimore, MD: Paul H. Brookes Publishing Co.

Buysse, V., Winton, P., & Zimmerman, T. (Eds.). (2007). RtI goes to pre-k: An early intervening system called recognition and response. *Early Development, 11,* 6–10.

Carta, J. J., McElhattan, T., & Guerrero, G. (2016). The application of Response to Intervention to young children with identified disabilities. In B. Reichow, B. A. Boyd, E. E. Barton, & S. L. Odom (Eds.), *Handbook of early childhood special education* (pp. 163–178). Cham, Switzerland: Springer International Publishing.

Castillo, J. M. (2014). Best practices in program evaluation in a model of Response to Intervention/multi-tiered system of supports. In P. L. Harrison & A. Thomas (Eds.), *Best practices in school psychology: Foundations* (pp. 329–342). Bethesda, MD: NASP.

Chandler, L. K., Young, R. M., Shields, L., Ash, J., Bauman, Butts, J., . . . Summers, D. (2008). Promoting early literacy skills within daily activities and routines in preschool classrooms. *Young Exceptional Children, 11*(2), 2–16.

Chandler, L. K., Young, R. M., & Ulezi, N. C. (2011). Early childhood special education methods and practices for preschool-aged children and their families. In C. Groark, S. M. Eidelman, L. Kaczmarek, & S. Maude (Eds.), *Early childhood intervention: Shaping the future for children with special needs and their families: Volume 2; Proven and promising practices* (pp. 39–75). Santa Barbara, CA: ABC–CLIO, Praeger.

Colorado Department of Education. (2015, May). *Colorado Multi-Tiered System of Support (MTSS).* Retrieved March 27, 2017, from https://www.cde.state.co.us/mtss/whatismtss

Division for Early Childhood (DEC). (2007). *Promoting positive outcomes for children with disabilities: Recommendations for assessment, curriculum, and program evaluation.* Missoula, MT: DEC. Retrieved from http://www.dec-sped.org/position-statements

Division for Early Childhood (DEC). (2009). *DEC concept paper: Developmental delay as an eligibility category.* Missoula, MT: Author. Retrieved from http://www.dec-sped.org/position-statements

Division for Early Childhood (DEC). (2014). *DEC recommended practices in early intervention/early childhood special education.* Retrieved from http://www.dec-sped.org/recommendedpractices

Division for Early Childhood (DEC) & National Association for the Education of Young Children (NAEYC). (2009). *Early childhood inclusion: A joint position statement of the Division for Early Childhood (DEC) and the National Association for the Education of Young Children (NAEYC).* Retrieved from http://www.dec-sped.org/position-statements

Division for Early Childhood (DEC), National Association for the Education of Young Children (NAEYC), & National Head Start Association (NHSA). (2013). *Frameworks for Response to Intervention in early childhood: Description and implications.* Missoula, MT: Author. Retrieved from http://www.dec-sped.org/position-statements

Early Childhood Technical Assistance Center (ECTA). (n.d.). *Response to Intervention in early childhood.* Retrieved from http://ectacenter.org/topics/RTI/RTI.asp

Endrew F. v. Douglas County School Dist. RE-1, 580 U.S., No. 15-827 (March 22, 2017).

Greenwood, C. R., Bradfield, T., Kaminski, R., Linas, M., Carta, J. J., & Nylander, D. (2011). The Response to Intervention (RTI) approach in early childhood. *Focus on Exceptional Children, 43*(9), 1–22.

Grisham-Brown, J., Hemmeter, M. L., & Pretti-Frontczak, K. (2017). *Blended practices for teaching young children in inclusive settings* (2nd ed.). Baltimore, MD: Paul H. Brookes Publishing Co.

Grisham-Brown, J., & Pretti-Frontczak, K. (2011). *Assessing young children in inclusive settings: The blended practices approach*. Baltimore, MD: Paul H. Brookes Publishing Co.

Grisham-Brown, J., Pretti-Frontczak, K., Bachman, A., Gannon, C., & Mitchell, D. (2014). Delivering individualized instruction during ongoing classroom activities and routines: Three success stories (pp. 97–110). In K. Pretti-Frontczak, J. Grisham-Brown, & L. Sullivan (Eds.), *Blending practices for all children* (Young Exceptional Children Monograph Series No. 16). Los Angeles, CA: DEC.

Hojnoski, R. L., Missall, K. M., & Young, R. M. (2016). Defining and measuring early academic development to promote student outcomes. In A. Garro (Ed.), *Early childhood assessment in school and clinical child psychology* (pp. 51–72). New York, NY: Springer.

Individuals with Disabilities Education Act Amendments (IDEA) of 1997, PL 105-17, 20 U.S.C. §§ 1400 *et seq.*

Individuals with Disabilities Education Improvement Act (IDEA) of 2004, PL 108-446, 20 U.S.C. §§ 1400 *et seq.*

Kurns, S., & Tilly, D. W. (2007). *Response to Intervention blueprints: School building level edition*. Alexandria, VA: National Association of State Directors of Special Education.

Leiber, J., Wolery, R. A., Horn, E., Tschantz, J., Beckman, P. J., & Hanson, M. J. (2002). Collaborative relationships among adults in inclusive preschool programs. In S.L. Odom (Ed.), *Widening the circle: Including children with disabilities in preschool programs* (pp. 81–97). New York, NY: Teachers College Press.

McLean, M., Sandall, S.R., & Smith, B.J. (2016). A history of early childhood special education. In B. Reichow, B.A. Boyd, E. E. Barton, & S. L. Odom (Eds.), *Handbook of early childhood special education* (pp. 3–19). Switzerland: Springer International Publishing.

National Association of School Psychologists. (2015). *Early childhood services: Promoting positive outcomes for young children* (Position statement). Bethesda, MD: Author.

Pretti-Frontczak, K., Grisham-Brown, J., & Sullivan, L. (2014). Message from the editors: Combining beliefs, values, traditions, and practices to best serve all young children. In K. Pretti-Frontczak, J. Grisham-Brown, & L. Sullivan (Eds.), *Blending practices for all children* (Young Exceptional Children Monograph Series No. 16) (pp. v–viii). Los Angeles, CA: Division for Early Childhood of the Council for Exceptional Children.

VanDerHeyden, A. M., Snyder, P., & Hojnoski, R.L. (Eds.). (2006). Special series: Integrating frameworks from early childhood intervention and school psychology to accelerate growth for all young children. *School Psychology Review, 35*(4).

Walker, H. M., & Shinn, M. R. (2010). Systemic, evidence-based approaches for promoting positive student outcomes within a multitier framework: Moving from efficacy to effectiveness. In M. R. Shinn & H. M. Walker (Eds.), *Interventions for achievement and behavior problems in a three-tiered model including RTI* (pp. 1–26). Bethesda, MD: National Association of School Psychologists (NASP).

Young, R. M., & Chandler, L. K. (2013, February). *Leading RTI in EC/preschool initiatives: The rationale and promising models*. Invited half-day workshop for the National Association of School Psychologists (NASP) annual conference, Seattle, WA.

Young, R. M., Chandler, L. K., Shields, L., Laubenstein, P., Butts, J., & Black, K. (2008, May/June). Project ELI: Improving early literacy outcomes: An early literacy and language initiative that words. *Principal*, 14–20.

Young, R. M., Shields, L., & Chandler, L. K. (2011). The emerging early childhood (EC) RtI movement: Promoting early schooling successes for three- to five-year-olds. [Monograph Lucky 21 #4]. *Response to Intervention (RtI): 21 questions and answers; just what is RtI?* (pp. 12–16). Warner Robins, GA: CASE.

11

Scaling Up Multi-Tiered Systems of Support

Lise Fox, Barbara J. Smith, and Deanna Pearce Law

In a meeting of state administrators in early education (i.e., Head Start collaboration director, IDEA 619 program administrator, director of the Office of Early Learning, and their staff), the discussion focused on national and state data on preschool suspension and growing concerns from programs about children with challenging behavior. Staff from the Office of Early Learning presented information they had gathered about options for addressing these concerns that might be implemented across all early learning programs in the state. The group was most interested in an approach that offered multi-tiered systems of supports (MTSS) that was focused on promoting the development of the social and emotional skills in the state's early learning standards and was designed to build the capacity of classroom practitioners (versus training specialists) to deliver services. The committee of state administrators reviewed information about the Pyramid Model for promoting the social and emotional competence of infants and young children (Fox, Dunlap, Hemmeter, Joseph, & Strain, 2003) and decided to explore how they might provide leadership in supporting programs in their implementation of the model. In the exploration process, the committee discussed making sure that 1) the Pyramid Model is an effective approach and would address their needs and 2) they had the capacity and readiness for implementation. The committee identified several questions that they needed to answer before making their decision to implement the Pyramid Model. The committee contacted the Pyramid Model developers to confirm that the Pyramid Model would provide the evidence-based practices and processes needed for an MTSS and asked about what would be involved in the state implementation process. The committee wanted to identify the nature and time line of activities that might be involved in implementation and understand the resources that were required. They also wanted more information about the classroom and program data systems that would be used for screening, progress monitoring, and implementation fidelity. The committee wanted to make sure that the data systems were comprehensive, would work well within their programs, and would fit with systems that programs were currently using.

The widespread implementation of MTSS is a complex process that involves the development of fiscal, policy, professional development, leadership, and organizational infrastructures at the program and state levels that support implementation fidelity and sustainability. In this chapter, we describe how the developers of the Pyramid Model (Fox, Dunlap, et al., 2003; Hemmeter, Ostrosky, & Fox, 2006) have used implementation science (IS) to establish and scale-up the Pyramid Model within several states (Dunlap, Smith, Fox, & Blase, 2014). This example of statewide implementation of the Pyramid Model is an illustration to others who aim to scale-up MTSS frameworks addressing other essential dimensions of early care and education programs and schools.

IS describes the critical processes or implementation frameworks involved in implementing practices that research has demonstrated to be effective and worth replicating (Blase, Van Dyke, & Fixsen, 2013; Fixsen, Naoom, Blase, Friedman, & Wallace, 2005; see Chapter 3). The Pyramid Model state and program capacity-building approach takes into consideration these implementation frameworks that are necessary for success at a state system level as well as within local programs. Historically, the field of early childhood has lacked a collective framework and vernacular to investigate the critical components necessary for successful implementation of programs (Metz, Naoom, Halle, & Bartley, 2015). Fortunately, IS provides guidance surrounding how to scale-up effective programs and practices using five Active Implementation Frameworks (AIFs). These AIFs are described in more detail in Chapter 3 and include the following: 1) usable innovation, 2) stages, 3) teams, 4) drivers, and 5) improvement cycles. Development of the Pyramid Model as an evidence-based approach for meeting young children's social and emotional competence as described in Chapter 7 meets the criteria as a usable intervention. Though the remaining four frameworks are evident in the Pyramid Model implementation and scale-up work described in this chapter, emphasis will be placed on the integral roles of the AIF stages and drivers frameworks (Fixsen et al., 2005) in state-level work. These frameworks are briefly described to guide discussion in this chapter.

IMPLEMENTATION SCIENCE FRAMEWORKS USED IN PYRAMID MODEL SCALE-UP

IS explains effective implementation as occurring over time and in discernable stages or phases (Fixsen et al., 2005; Meyers, Durlak, & Wandersman, 2012). As described in Chapter 3—the dynamic and iterative processes involved in implementation—stages might not occur linearly, although they are generally sequential and include 1) Exploration, 2) Installation, 3) Initial Implementation, and 4) Full Implementation (Fixsen et al., 2005). The second framework evident in the Pyramid Model work is the concept of Implementation Drivers, which are described as the engine of change that occurs within the stages (Fixsen et al., 2005). These drivers are described as 1) competency drivers, 2) leadership drivers, and 3) organizational drivers. The implementation drivers provide the core components of the infrastructure required to support practice as well as organizational and systems change (Metz & Bartley, 2012). Competency drivers represent the actions required to improve and sustain practitioners' and supervisors' ability to implement an evidence-based practice and include the selection of staff, training, coaching, and performance assessment. Leadership drivers include adaptive and technical skills as well as the knowledge and resources to lead the changes needed for the adoption of the evidence-based practice. Organizational drivers reflect systems intervention or change, facilitative or supportive administration, and data systems that support decision making.

Implementation frameworks (e.g., stages and drivers) guide the installation of evidence-based practices at the program level and, if successfully implemented and scaled-up statewide, are also implemented at the state level. Each level (state, program) is comprised of its own system of implementation drivers and stages. Actions at one level influence and are influenced by actions at the other level and together these system conditions generate patterns of systemwide behavior, or system dynamics (Hargreaves, 2010). Metz and Bartley (2012) described a cascading logic model linking implementation at each system level and the specific activities required to support service delivery, relationships between levels, implementation strategies, and desired outcomes. In Figure 11.1, a cascading logic model illustrates the implementation links involved in systems implementation of the Pyramid Model.

The strategies among levels need to be aligned and coordinated, and achievement of outcomes at one level is necessary for success at the next level. Thus, to ensure optimal implementation, alignment across levels is necessary to build a supporting infrastructure. This is the statewide implementation and scale-up approach used with the Pyramid Model. For instance, given the importance of multi-level systems and its impact on implementation outcomes, organizational drivers, specifically data collection for decision making, provide a basis from which to understand the required structures at each system level (Fixsen, Blase, Naoom, & Duda, 2015; Fixsen et al. 2005; Metz & Bartley, 2012). The implementation of data-based decision

	Population (Who)	Intervention strategies and measures (What)	Intervention outcomes
Technical Assistance for Practice and System Change	Young children	Pyramid Model (fidelity measure)	Improved social-emotional outcomes
	Populations (Who)	Organizational and systems change strategies (How)	Change-related outcomes
	Practitioners, teachers, staff, and supervisors	Provision of skillful, timely training; coaching; and performance assessments in supportive administrative environments	Competent implementation of the Pyramid Model (fidelity measure)
	Personnel in early childhood professional development collaboratives, agency staff, regional staff	Agreements with technical assistance providers and program developers. Training and coaching for trainers, master cadre, and coaches. Release time for supervisors/coaches to learn to coach. Installation of fidelity monitoring and outcome data systems.	Skillful, timely training; coaching; and performance assessments in supportive administrative environments

Figure 11.1. A cascade of outcomes to strategies to outcomes. Source: Blasé et al., 2010.

making requires a functional data system that can optimize decision making by providing fidelity data and outcome data at the program level (Fixsen et al., 2005; Fixsen et al., 2015). These data are also shared with the state to assist in policy and resource planning as well as to document efficacy. From a multi-level systems perspective, it is important that these data systems communicate between levels to ensure that evidence can be used at all levels to improve services and promote data-driven policy decisions (Metz & Bartley, 2012). Systemic issues and barriers at the program level need to be communicated to and resolved at the state level (Fixsen et al., 2015). Resources, regulations, and systems supports at each level need to be aligned to support implementation (Layzer, 2013; Metz & Bartley, 2012). Given the complexity of widespread scale-up of MTSS within the field of early childhood education, we offer our experiences with the Pyramid Model to promote greater understanding of how multi-level implementation may operate.

The Pyramid Model (Fox, Dunlap, et al., 2003) was developed to provide a framework for the implementation of evidence-based practices to promote the social-emotional competence of all children, and offer effective intervention for children who have challenging behavior. The framework was developed by researchers affiliated with two federally funded training and technical assistance projects (i.e., Center on the Social and Emotional Foundations for Early Learning, Technical Assistance Center on Social and Emotional Interventions for Young Children[1]) that examined the research literature to identify the evidence-based practices that could be aligned to a promotion, prevention, and intervention model and used as an MTSS by early care and education programs (Hemmeter et al., 2006; Hemmeter, Fox, & Snyder, 2013). The centers operated for about 12 years. Faculty involved in the training and technical assistance centers developed training materials, data decision-making tools, and family engagement materials that could be used by programs for implementation of the framework.

The focus of the two centers changed as a result of lessons learned in the first 4 years of developing the Pyramid Model and providing training nationwide using training materials developed to assist personnel in using the evidence-based practices contained in the Pyramid Model framework. Moreover, the developers of the Pyramid Model were influenced by their experiences with the implementation and sustainability shortcomings of large-scale training efforts and an evolving literature on IS indicating that training alone seldom results in lasting improvement in practice at the teacher/provider level. Therefore, the focus became state and program system capacity building to ensure that the necessary training, technical assistance, leadership, data use, and coaching support is available to providers to promote fidelity of practice use as well as sustainability of use.

Developers of the Pyramid Model provided training and technical assistance on the implementation, sustainability, and scale-up of the Pyramid Model to state leadership teams, program leadership teams, trainers, coaches, and practitioners. The critical structures that are described in this chapter were developed through

---

[1]The Center on the Social and Emotional Foundations for Early Learning was funded by the Office of Head Start and Child Care Bureau of the Administration on Children, Youth, and Families of the U.S. Department of Health and Human Services (grant number 90YD0119), and the Technical Assistance Center on Social Emotional Interventions for Young Children was funded by the U.S. Department of Education, Office of Special Education Programs (H326B070002).

our engagement with states and programs and continual reflection on how to refine the approach that was used to guide implementation and scale-up. What is presented in this chapter is the approach that evolved over time and was informed by IS and the challenges and successes of states and programs engaged in bringing the Pyramid Model to scale. Examples from states that have implemented the critical elements in different ways with robust results are provided in textboxes throughout the chapter.

A key component of the national Pyramid Model centers' work was concentrated on building internal state competence in order to develop capacity to sustain Pyramid Model practices. Fox and Hemmeter (2014) reported that states have scaled-up and sustained the Pyramid Model work approximately 3–8 years after formal technical assistance by the Pyramid Model developers ended. For example, statewide implementation has resulted in a sustainable system of professional development and external coaching for programwide implementation in Colorado, California, Iowa, Wisconsin, and Minnesota. Elements that support sustainability in these and other states (Pennsylvania, Nebraska, New Jersey, Maryland) include state data systems, continuous programs of professional development including online training modules, the training of coaches, and the integration of the Pyramid Model within quality rating systems and higher education coursework.

Dunlap and colleagues (2014) provided a roadmap to statewide implementation of the Pyramid Model (see link in the list of Resources at the end of the chapter). The Pyramid Model approach outlined the importance of the stages and drivers of implementation. The authors expressed that success is more likely to occur if coordinators and implementers understand and use the stages of implementation to engage in specific activities. Within each stage, it is recommended that the planners attend to short- and long-term goals to ensure fidelity of practices. The roadmap also included a description of major structures that can be viewed as teams of people engaging in and supporting implementation. The structures included 1) a state leadership team to guide the statewide implementation, 2) program leadership teams to guide program implementation, and 3) a master cadre (MC) of training and technical assistance (T/TA) experts who are often regionally based and recruited by the state leadership team to support the program leadership teams. Thus, the multi-level teams (state, MC, and programs) adhere to the implementation stages recommended by the National Implementation Research Network (NIRN) and also follow similar components delineated under NIRN's implementation drivers. For instance, at the program level, program leadership teams invest in staff training and professional development, identify and deploy resources for coaching, focus on data collection and use, and facilitate support for children with the most challenging behaviors. At the state level, the state leadership team establishes the training and technical assistance policies and resources to support the programs and the MC. Thus, from a multi-level implementation lens, the level of detail, communication, and coordination evident within each team and between teams is necessary to achieve success (Dunlap et al., 2014). Ultimately, achievement at the state level will impact achievement at the local level and vice versa.

Just as IS research has highlighted the importance of thinking beyond a singular program's fidelity outcomes, the Pyramid Model state and program capacity-building approach illustrates the importance of systemwide infrastructure elements necessary for full implementation, scale-up, and sustainability. The Pyramid Model operates within multiple levels and linked teams and takes into consideration many aspects of organizational infrastructure, stage-based activities, and readiness components embedded within active implementation frameworks necessary for successful implementation and sustainability.

PYRAMID MODEL CRITICAL STRUCTURES FOR STATE IMPLEMENTATION AND SCALE-UP

There are four critical structures of the Pyramid Model statewide implementation and scale-up approach (Dunlap et al., 2014) that we have used successfully and that we recommend as states consider the implementation of the Pyramid Model. The structures are described in more detail in the following sections, including what the activities and outcomes are during each implementation stage and how they relate to IS elements. These critical structures are

1. *State leadership team (SLT)*: A cross-agency team of individuals representing key agencies and stakeholders related to early education. Typically, these agencies include the state education agency, state public preschool programs, IDEA preschool and infant toddler services, state child care and Head Start, state professional development providers, families, and other early childhood services such as early childhood mental health. The purpose of this team is to guide the implementation, scale-up, and sustainability of the Pyramid Model statewide.

2. *Master cadre (MC)*: The SLT establishes a cadre of experts to provide external coaching, training, and technical assistance to local programs engaged in implementing, scaling up, and sustaining the Pyramid Model.

3. *Demonstration sites*: The SLT selects programs to serve as demonstrators of high fidelity, programwide implementation of the Pyramid Model. The sites partner with the SLT to provide efficacy data and to allow visitations and tours for interested people and programs, and in return the SLT provides ongoing support and visibility of the program.

4. *Data-based decision making*: The SLT, MC, and demonstration sites engage in data-based decision making to ensure that the Pyramid Model practices are implemented with fidelity; that systems are in place to support implementation, scale-up, and sustainability; and that child outcomes are positive.

Figure 11.2 shows the four critical structures of the PM statewide approach in relation to the IS drivers. Each structure is described in detail below along with the activities and outcomes related to IS stages, drivers, and other features.

STATE LEADERSHIP TEAM: GUIDING THE STATEWIDE EFFORT

The SLT is a group of cross-agency leaders committed to the statewide, high-fidelity implementation; scale-up; and sustainability of the Pyramid Model. We recommend that the team be comprised of decision makers (mid-level) from state agencies engaged in early care and education. Thus, the SLT membership might include state education agency early childhood education programs such as public preschool and Title I, IDEA preschool services; IDEA Infant Toddler services; state child care; Head Start; early childhood mental health services; higher education and other professional development services; families; and other stakeholders as appropriate. As we

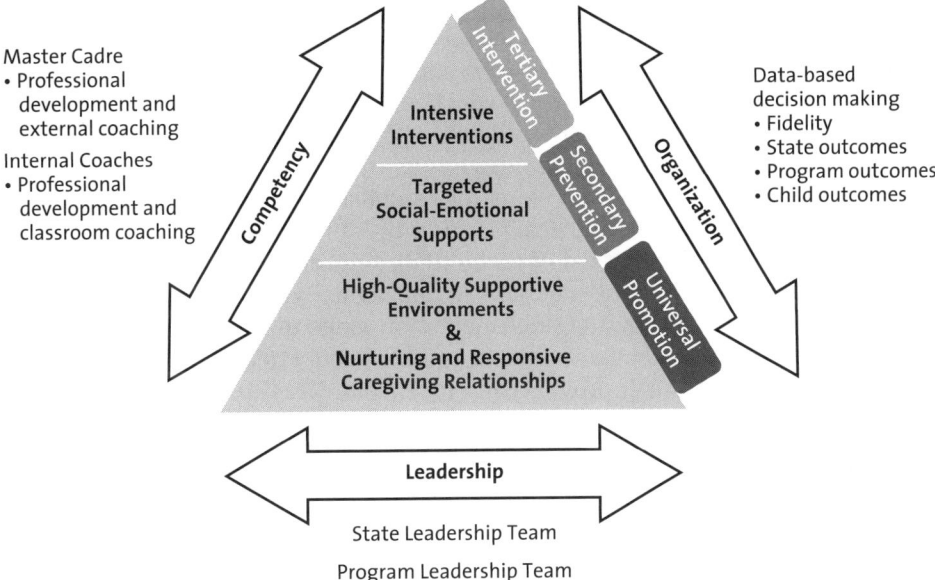

Figure 11.2. Pyramid Model state implementation structures and drivers.

have supported SLTs, we have recommended that teams use a set of effective team strategies that were developed over time by center faculty to ensure that teams can work efficiently and effectively as they move through the implementation stages. For instance, effective team strategies include practices related to group decision making, action-oriented meeting logistics, and team rules such as limiting membership to no more than 15 people and not allowing team members to send representatives to meetings in their place. Additional effective team strategies include the following:

1. Form a team.
2. Use collaborative decision making.
3. Write a vision statement.
4. Adopt team ground rules/norms.
5. Use a meeting agenda, meeting summary, and meeting evaluation format that facilitates a well-organized meeting.
6. Develop an action plan.

Exploration and Installation Stages

During the exploration and installation stage, a convener or group of interested people gather others to determine if they are willing to work together as an SLT to implement the Pyramid Model statewide. During these early stages, the SLT is formed and as a group establishes 1) a written vision statement to guide their work and to ensure that all team members are committed to the same goal; 2) a set of operating ground rules guided by the strategies and materials described above such as committing to a multi-year effort (planning through sustaining and scale-up), to meet monthly, to make decisions collaboratively based on data, and to share resources; and 3) an initial self-assessment on use of the Pyramid Model State Benchmarks of Quality (BoQ) (Smith, Dunlap, & Blase, 2015), which is an instrument to guide the development of the system of support for programs implementing the Pyramid Model.

The BoQ is an essential tool for teams to use as they identify current resources for implementation and develop plans for establishing the activities and drivers needed for implementation and scale-up (see link in Resources at the end of the chapter). The BoQ is comprised of the activities needed for a professional development system necessary for programs to adopt the Pyramid Model with fidelity. Each activity is defined by the implementation stage during which it is accomplished. Once the initial self-assessment is completed, the SLT prioritizes actions to be taken and tracks their progress.

The BoQ is organized by the following categories of activities:

1. *State leadership team*: Items in this section are used to assess current capacity and needed action steps related to membership, logistics, action planning, coordination and staffing, funding, communication and visibility, and authority and visibility.

2. *Family involvement*: Items in this section guide the SLT to address family participation, communication, feedback, and representation.

3. *Pyramid Model sites*: In this section of the BoQ, teams address action items related to establishing demonstration programs, implementation communities, and expansion sites. This section describes the activities that the SLT will engage in during all implementation stages to support the implementation of the Pyramid Model in early adopting sites, communities, demonstration programs, and scale-up or expansion sites. It includes activities such as recruitment and selection of sites (e.g., leadership teams, internal coaches), data collection, and use.

4. *Professional development*: This section of the BoQ outlines the activities of the SLT related to recruitment, selection, and support of the MC of training and technical assistance providers who will support the demonstration sites. It also details the action needed to ensure the sustainability and scale-up of these experts as the state adds expansion sites while providing scaled-back support to ongoing programs.

5. *Evaluation/data-based decision making*: This set of activities describes the work of the SLT in ensuring that data are collected and used by MC and programs as well as the SLT. Data tools include MC contact logs, the state benchmarks of quality, and programwide benchmarks of quality (see link in Resources at the end of the chapter) to track progress and guide systems development; the Teaching Pyramid Observation Tool (TPOT; Hemmeter et al., 2014); and The Pyramid Infant Toddler Observation Scale (TPITOS; Bigelow, Carta, Irvin, & Hemmeter, in press) to measure the implementation of Pyramid Model practices and child outcome measures. In this section of the BoQ, the SLT is guided to prepare an annual evaluation report to describe implementation progress; the impact of implementation on child, provider, and program outcomes; and the outcomes related to professional development

efforts. The evaluation report is used by the SLT for their progress monitoring and planning as well as to provide a public report on outcomes that is used to gain continued political and resource investment in Pyramid Model implementation.

Implementation Stages

During the initial and full implementation stages, the SLT engages in the actions described in the BoQ related to creating the systems and supports to programs that will result in implementation of the Pyramid Model with fidelity. These activities are associated with selection of demonstration sites, selection of and ensuring the MC is functioning effectively to provide external coaching for program leadership teams, and that communication with programs is resulting in information and data the SLT can use to improve and expand services and supports. For instance, regular communication with program leadership teams will provide the SLT with information on resources and procedures they need. Programs will share their data with the SLT indicating time and effort for practitioners to reach fidelity, as well as child outcomes. The key activity of the implementation stages for the SLT is to refine procedures and supports based on the feedback of these early adopters to ensure adequate support and to design effective scale-up.

Scaling Up and Sustaining

The SLT work associated with scale-up and sustainability is not a "stage" as it is woven throughout the BoQ to ensure that the SLT members are considering long-term goals and actions to support sustaining high fidelity in programs while scaling up or expanding to new programs. As programs reach program-wide high-fidelity implementation (as indicated in their data), the support of the external coach will be maintained on a less frequent schedule (e.g., visits from monthly to quarterly). Maintaining the external coach support is needed to prevent loss of fidelity due to staff turnover, changes in program focus, and other typical program occurrences. The SLT will need to recruit more training and technical assistance professionals who can provide external coaching (i.e., MC) as more programs are brought into the initiative. The SLT needs to plan for the budgetary and staffing implications of this expansion. The BoQ contains items and guidance related to scale-up and sustainability, such as suggesting that all SLT action plans and objectives contain sections on sustainability and scale-up and describing activities specific to increasing the number of settings using the Pyramid Model with the goal of achieving statewide, high-fidelity implementation over time. In addition, the BoQ suggests identifying resources, fiscal as well as personnel, for at least 3 years, and the SLT has a process in place for team membership succession within their own agencies (replacing themselves) that ensures continued commitment and understanding and progress of SLT work. IS leadership, organizational, and competency drivers are evident throughout the work of the SLT. The SLT provides the leadership statewide, provides a vision of high-fidelity implementation, establishes the collection and regular use of data for decision making, and establishes the competency resources needed to support program-level implementation (training, technical assistance, and guidance around on-site coaching).

> Colorado and Minnesota established SLTs that have evolved over time and are still active after nearly a decade for Colorado and 6 years for Minnesota. Colorado's SLT has a dual focus of advancing both the Pyramid Model and inclusion practices. Colorado Pyramid Model efforts were driven not only by early training by center faculty on the practices, but more importantly the establishment of a state-funded training and technical assistance center, the Colorado Center for Social Emotional Competence and Inclusion, the Pyramid Plus Center. This dual focus was a direct result of two national efforts, the Pyramid Model training by the centers, and the SpecialQuest initiative focused on expanding early childhood inclusion. The Minnesota team focused directly on embedding implementation science and related elements in their work to implement and scale the Pyramid Model.

MASTER CADRE: TRAINING AND SUPPORTING IMPLEMENTATION

The MC of training and technical assistance professionals is established to meet statewide professional development and implementation support needs. These professionals might be regionally based or work within existing technical assistance or educational resource center networks. The purpose of the MC is to provide external coaching, training, and ongoing technical assistance to programs on programwide implementation. The activities of the MC include training and supporting the program leadership team, training and supporting internal coaches, assisting programs in the use of data for decision making, training and supporting behavior specialists in the provision of intensive individualized interventions, and assisting local programs in the design and implementation of continuous professional development.

Exploration and Installation Stages

During the Exploration and Installation stages, the SLT selects the MC. The SLT examines current resources and determines who will serve in this role, how many are needed, where they will be located geographically, and what fiscal resources will be used. This selection is accomplished in various ways depending on the state, including repurposing an existing T/TA system of professionals or creating a new group of T/TA professionals through an application process. The cross-agency nature of the SLT lends itself to establishing T/TA support from multiple systems to address the needs of particular early childhood programs.

> When Minnesota began their statewide initiative for Pyramid Model implementation, they already had an early childhood T/TA system in place. The Minnesota Centers of Excellence for Young Children with Disabilities is a statewide professional development system that is regionally based to provide support to local school districts through the services of professional development facilitators (PDFs). The Minnesota SLT identified selected PDFs to become the MC for the Pyramid Model. They were trained in Pyramid Model practices and in the strategies needed to provide

> technical assistance to local program leadership teams in implementing the Pyramid Model. The PDFs attend program leadership team meetings, assist the program coach in implementing practice-based coaching (Snyder, Hemmeter, & Fox, 2015), and collect and use data for making decisions. The PDFs report to the SLT on progress, challenges, and needs of programs to ensure high-fidelity implementation, sustainability, and scale-up plans.
>
> Colorado established the Pyramid Plus Center. The Pyramid Plus Center staff initially served as the MC to establish demonstration programs. Then, the center developed a system of certifying trainers and coaches that are community-based and provide the T/TA to local programs. In addition, Pyramid Plus has developed a community implementation process that includes Pyramid Plus staff supporting a leadership team at the community level and training and certifying trainers and coaches for that community. This community implementation process results in the community having a local MC capacity that can support the development of local implementation sites and use of data for improvement.

Implementation Stages

Once the SLT has selected the MC, the MC begins the provision of their training and external coaching to programs. These training events are extensive (see list in the section titled Exploration and Installation Stages on page 227) and address the multiple components needed to establish the infrastructure and practices for an MTSS, including training in the implementation process, coaching, classroom practices, tiered interventions, and data-based decision making. As the program begins implementation, the MC meets with the program leadership team regularly (i.e., monthly) and guides the team in establishing the leadership, organizational, and competency drivers needed for programwide implementation.

The MC understands not only the Pyramid Model practices and the approaches related to ensuring high-fidelity implementation but also key IS practices and conveys these to the program leadership team so that they understand that the effort will be a multi-year one and that they are building a system that supports high-fidelity use of Pyramid Model practices. The MC helps the program leadership team use the programwide Benchmarks of Quality as well as other data tools that guide their decisions over time about program improvement, training and support of personnel, and child outcomes. The MC also assists the leadership team in the development of program policies, including how and when to use tertiary tier supports.

Scaling Up and Sustaining

The MC is the hub of the SLT sustainability and scale-up plans. The MC continues to provide external coaching to new programs that become implementation sites and offers training and collaboration opportunities that support the initial implementation of new programs and the more sophisticated needs of programs that have moved into sustainability. For example, MC members might offer training to leadership teams in the sustainability stage related to addressing staff turnover, new data systems, or innovations that might be used within the framework (e.g., Tier 2 or Tier 3 intervention packages, new screening tools). MC members might also convene forums in which teams share their successes and implementation strategies with other teams within the state. In addition, veteran MC members provide mentorship to new MC members who join their ranks as implementation is scaled-up to new programs. Finally, as the state and programs scale-up and move into sustainability, the MC will play a pivotal role in informing the SLT about the needs and progress of local programs as the SLT continues to provide implementation supports.

> Between 2010 and 2015, Minnesota grew from 10 to 37 MC members. Colorado has certified 115 trainers and coaches since 2010, and 24 have gone through re-certification (needed every 3 years).

PROGRAMWIDE DEMONSTRATION SITES

Demonstration sites that showcase how the Pyramid Model is implemented programwide (i.e., in all classrooms and across all practitioners) are essential to the state scale-up effort. Demonstration sites are used to quickly establish the usefulness and value of the innovation and identify the infrastructure supports necessary for expanding its use (Fixsen, Blase, Horner, Sims, & Sugai, 2013). In addition, a demonstration site can offer others interested in the implementation of the program a place to learn more about how the Pyramid Model is used as an MTSS within local programs, including understanding the implementation supports that are in place and the outcomes that have been influenced by the model.

A demonstration site is guided by a program leadership team that guides local implementation (Fox & Hemmeter, 2009; Fox, Lentini, & Binder, 2013). In early care and education, a program might vary considerably in the number and configuration of classrooms. For example, a small community early childhood program might become a demonstration site and be guided by an on-site leadership team that ensures implementation across the program's six classrooms, or a school district might serve as a demonstration site with guidance from a district leadership team that has oversight of implementation within 50 public early childhood classrooms.

Demonstration sites might begin their work as an implementation site and evolve to demonstration status by achieving a designation that is tied to a determination of implementation fidelity and willingness to serve as a model. On the other hand, demonstration sites might be specifically recruited and mentored to achieve demonstration status. The demonstration site's program leadership team is guided by a member of the MC who serves as an external coach to the leadership team. The membership of the leadership team includes a program administrator who can commit to implementing systemic change and dedicating resources, practitioners who offer unique perspectives about classroom implementation, the program personnel who will provide classroom coaching, and the program personnel who guide the development of individualized behavior support plans for children with needs for intensive intervention. The role of the external coach (i.e., MC member) is to serve as a guide to the leadership team as the team develops and executes an implementation plan that addresses staff buy-in, family engagement, programwide expectations, staff supports, professional development including coaching, and the use of data for decision making.

Demonstration sites provide information that is pivotal for statewide scale-up by communicating to the SLT their experiences in striving toward high fidelity of implementation and sharing data on implementation and outcomes. This information is used by the SLT as they design the supports that will be provided to future implementation sites. In addition, information from the demonstration sites is used to build the political will and investment of key stakeholders in statewide scale-up.

Exploration and Installation Stages

In the planning and implementation stage of Pyramid Model scale-up, the SLT determines how demonstration sites will be recruited and identified. States select a limited number of programs for their initial cohort of demonstration sites so that they can devote sufficient resources to ensure that demonstration sites will be successful in achieving implementation fidelity. Demonstration sites are provided with substantial training from the MC that includes the following:

1. Training to practitioners on the implementation of Pyramid Model practices
2. Training to the program leadership team on how to establish and support an infrastructure for achieving and maintaining implementation fidelity
3. Training in data tools and systems that are used for data decision making related to child, teacher, and program support
4. Training in practice-based coaching that is used to guide implementation fidelity by practitioners
5. Training of behavior support personnel who guide the development of individualized interventions for children with social-emotional delays or persistent challenging behavior

The initial installation requires a substantial investment in training delivery and the continuous support of the program leadership team as they begin initial installation. See the textbox for an illustration from Wisconsin related to the recruitment and support of sites as they begin implementation.

In Wisconsin, programs were recruited to complete an application to become a demonstration site. Programs were provided with web-based information on programwide implementation and the readiness criteria that a program should consider prior to submitting an application. The program submitted an application that clearly stated the program's commitment and listed the members of the program leadership team along with a signature from each member. Applications were reviewed and programs were selected using a scoring rubric that supports the selection of programs that are most "ready" to be successful. Selected programs were matched to an external coach (MC member), and the team attended an implementation academy to learn the process of implementation and developing their initial implementation plan. This process was used to establish the initial demonstration sites and continues to be used to establish implementation sites as the state engages in expansion and scale-up activities.

Implementation Stages

The implementation stage begins as initial training is completed and the program leadership team guides program staff in their use of the Pyramid Model practices. The MC continues to support the program leadership team as they meet monthly to address the implementation plan, promote family engagement, address practitioner implementation in the classroom, plan for professional development and coaching support, and use data for decision making, both related to improving implementation fidelity on the program and classroom level and to the use of effective interventions to address children's needs for social, emotional, and behavioral support.

The program leadership team provides the SLT with data on their implementation fidelity and the outcomes that result from implementation. As the program continues to improve in their implementation fidelity across classrooms and has developed a strong infrastructure of support for programwide implementation, the program shares its experiences with other programs by hosting tours of their program, providing conference presentations, disseminating reports that highlight their implementation story and outcomes, and sharing their experiences with key policymakers and other stakeholders that are important to the statewide scale-up effort.

> In Colorado, the Bal Swan Children's Center was one of the four programs that were designated demonstration sites for Pyramid Plus Center's implementation. Bal Swan is a private community early education program that provides services to 350 children, including offering full inclusion to children with special needs. Bal Swan received technical assistance and training over a 3-year period to move from initial implementation to demonstrating full implementation fidelity. As a state demonstration site, Bal Swan hosts tours, provides training to other programs, participates in conference presentations and webinars, and has been featured in news stories to gain visibility and investment in the model.

Scaling Up and Sustaining

Scale-up and sustainability refers to the scale-up across the state and the scale-up locally across classrooms or centers. States might seek to establish multiple demonstration sites so that each community has access to a demonstration or strategically develop additional demonstration sites within different types of programs to portray how the model works within child care, Head Start, and public preschool programs.

At the program level, sustainability is a critical concern. It is important that the implementation of the Pyramid Model as an MTSS is not seen as a one-shot project or innovation that is time-limited. The goal is to integrate the approach as the way that the program operates and the approach that is used to meet the social, emotional, and behavioral support needs of every child in the program. At this stage, the demonstration site is not dependent on external resources (e.g., an external coach or MC member) to support their continued implementation fidelity and has developed internal capacity to address turnover in personnel, changes in leadership, and improvements in the use of data systems; to establish procedures and policies; and to provide internal supports for professional development.

> The Southeast Kansas Community Action Program (SEK–CAP) Head Start has been implementing the Pyramid Model since 2001. The program provides services to about 1,200 children ages 0–5 and their families through Head Start classrooms and Early Head Start home-visiting services in 12 counties in Southeast Kansas. The program continuously improves their implementation of the model and has fully institutionalized the approach within all aspects of the program. Sustainability strategies that are evident in the program include use of Pyramid Model practices in job descriptions; use of the Pyramid Model with all services provided by the agency, including home visiting and prenatal education; data collection and data-based decision making, including an examination of implementation fidelity, intervention fidelity, and outcome monitoring; providing all new staff with an orientation to the model and professional development on Pyramid Model practices including coaching support; providing family training on Pyramid Model practices through individualized services and group training opportunities; and engaging the program in continuous improvement in the implementation of strategies to become more efficient and proficient with implementation.

CONCLUSION

In this chapter, we described how states and programs have successfully implemented, scaled-up, and sustained the implementation of the Pyramid Model as an MTSS for promoting young children's social and emotional competence and addressing challenging behavior. Although our focus was on statewide implementation and scale-up, we believe that the critical structures needed for statewide implementation are relevant to implementation within a school district or regional program with multiple sites (e.g., Head Start grantee). Similar to the state implementation, program-level implementation will require a leadership team that provides oversight, funding, and support for implementation and sustainability; an external coach or coaches who can provide training and technical assistance to establish the innovation; the development of high-fidelity demonstration sites or classrooms; and the use of data for decision making in all aspects from the classroom level to the leadership team. As we have worked with programs and states, we have learned that implementation must include the following considerations:

1. Establishing an SLT with members who can influence policies and program decisions and commit resources is critical to sustainability and scale-up. A key factor related to sustainability is the integration of the Pyramid Model into policies that might be developed within states related to program quality rating systems, career ladders for training personnel, professional development systems including classroom coaching, polices related to child discipline and the prevention of preschool suspension, and the structure of supports that will be provided to children within programs.

2. The SLT must have funding associated with the work of the team and the coordination of all aspects of implementation. Funding must be dedicated to staff who coordinate the SLT and support the MC, and funds must be dedicated to the MC so that there is a sustainable system for ongoing professional development.

States have found resources through realigning existing resources as well as gaining new resources through raising awareness of the outcomes of implementing the Pyramid Model.

3. An important strategy for sustainability and continued investment in the program is to share the successes of implementation. This might occur in a variety of ways, including meetings or webinars to share success stories, reports on program outcomes, using social media to promote high-fidelity programs, and hosting a policy summit to discuss the value and need of the Pyramid Model to children's outcomes. SLT should publish an annual evaluation report that provides key stakeholders and potential supporters with data on the critical features and key outcomes.

> Pyramid Model implementation sites throughout the state of Minnesota come together in the spring of each year to celebrate scale-up and sustainability of the Pyramid Model. Each site is given the opportunity to showcase celebrations of their work at the local level by presenting a poster session, presenting a PowerPoint presentation demonstrating core features of progress their team has made in the last year, and/or presenting video footage of what implementation looks like at their site level. Implementation retreats typically include statewide updates on Pyramid Model scale-up, local site presentations, poster sessions, and networking opportunities based on role at the site level (e.g., internal coaches, administrators, behavior specialists, practitioners). In Pennsylvania, there is a process for recognizing programs for implementing the Pyramid Model with fidelity at Tier 1, Tiers 1 and 2, or all three tiers. Programs receive a banner to post in their building when they are first recognized and a dated badge to add to the banner in each subsequent year that they maintain fidelity. The banners and badges are awarded at an annual Implementers' Forum in the spring.

4. One of the most challenging aspects of implementation is the provision of coaching to practitioners so that they can implement Pyramid Model practices and interventions with fidelity. Although classroom coaching is resource intensive, its value can't be overstated. We have learned that classroom coaching of the practitioner is essential for implementation success. We have also learned that program leadership teams are able to develop creative and sustainable ways to allocate coaching resources and use technology or a variety of coaching delivery arrangements (e.g., reciprocal peer coaching, group coaching) to provide coaching to classroom practitioners.

5. The use of data for decision making is not an intuitive process for teams, programs, and practitioners. We have learned that the use of data-based decision-making tools has to be taught and supported until teams and practitioners become fluent in their use, including how to review a data summary, identify a problem or aspect to address, and develop an action plan in response to the data. Support for data-based decision making has to be provided at the classroom, program, and state implementation team levels.

The early childhood administrators decided to pursue Pyramid Model implementation and braid in funding for professional development and technical assistance that were within the budgets of each agency (e.g., Head Start, child care, public preschool, special education). They formed a state cross-agency team to develop their plan for installation and the support to programs for implementation. At the end of 2 years, the SLT has partnered with 3–5 programs who wanted to be early implementers of the Pyramid Model. Together they have established an MC of professionals who provides external coaching to the program leadership teams; implemented practice-based coaching to assist teachers in using the Pyramid Model practices with fidelity; and gathered and used data to make decisions about teaching, coaching, child outcomes, and systems to promote social-emotional competence, teach social skills, and address challenging behavior. The SLT has selected a second cohort of programs for expansion while maintaining support to the initial set of programs. Additional MCs are recruited and trained so that initial and new programs receive their support. The state has a written 5-year scale-up plan outlining how many programs will be recruited each year, how many new MCs will be recruited and the resources needed to support the expansion.

RESOURCES

Technical Assistance Center on Social Emotional Intervention for Young Children. http://www.challengingbehavior.org. Materials for implementation include state implementation descriptions and resources, program implementation descriptions and resources, issue briefs, coaching and data decision-making resources, materials for families, and materials related to intervention practices.

The Center on the Social and Emotional Foundations for Early Learning. http://csefel.vanderbilt.edu. Resources include professional development training modules, summaries of evidence-based practices, and the state collaborative planning toolkit.

Division for Early Childhood (DEC), National Association for the Education of Young Children (NAEYC), & National Head Start Association (NHSA). (2013). *Frameworks for Response to Intervention in early childhood: Description and implications*. Missoula, MT: Author. Retrieved from http://www.dec-sped.org/position-statements

Dunlap, G., Smith, B. J., Fox, L., & Blase, K. (2014). *Road map to statewide implementation of the Pyramid Model. Roadmap to effective intervention practices #6*. Tampa: University of South Florida, Technical Assistance Center on Social Emotional Intervention for Young Children. This document provides a guide to the steps needed for implementing widespread use of the Pyramid Model.

Smith, B. J., Dunlap, G., & Blase, K. (2015, May). *Implementing the Pyramid Model state-wide: State Benchmarks of Quality*. http://challengingbehavior.fmhi.usf.edu/communities/state_docs/TACSEI%20State%20Benchmarks5.28.15.pdf. The statewide BoQ tool is used by the state leadership team to identify current implementation status of the state system, plan implementation activities, and measure implementation progress.

Fox, L., Veguilla, M., & Perez Binder, D. (2014). *Data decision-making and program-wide implementation of the Pyramid Model. Roadmap to effective intervention practices #7.* Tampa: University of South Florida, Technical Assistance Center on Social Emotional Intervention for Young Children. Retrieved from https://files.eric.ed.gov/fulltext/ED577844.pdf. This guide provides programs with a description of the data tools that are used in Pyramid Model implementation and guidance on how to use the data for decision making.

Fox, L., Hemmeter, M. L., Jack, S., & Binder, D. P. (2017). *Early childhood program-wide PBS Benchmarks of Quality, version 2.0.* http://challengingbehavior.cbcs.usf.edu/docs/BoQ_EarlyChildhood_Program-Wide.pdf. The Early Childhood Program-Wide Benchmarks of Quality are used by program leadership teams to examine the critical elements needed for programwide implementation and the indicators or benchmarks needed to achieve those elements

The National Implementation Research Network's Active Implementation Hub. http://implementation.fpg.unc.edu. The NIRN Active Implementation Hub provides brief training modules, tools, and informational resources related to IS and scaling up.

Pyramid Plus. (2015, September). *Pyramid Plus: The Colorado Center for Social Emotional Competence and Inclusion 2014-2015 Annual Report.* Retrieved from http://www.pyramidplus.org/sites/default/files/2016-08/PPAnnual%20Report%202015_0.pdf. The Pyramid Plus annual report provides an example of how states might summarize their implementation efforts and outcomes for community stakeholders.

REFERENCES

Bigelow, K., Carta, J., Irvin, D., & Hemmeter, M. L. (in press). *The Pyramid Infant Toddler Observation Scale (TPITOS), Research Edition.* Baltimore, MD: Paul H. Brookes Publishing Co.

Blase, K. (2012). *Technical assistance as the bridge from science to service.* Presentation at the 2012 Inclusion Conference, Chapel Hill, NC.

Blase, K., Van Dyke, M., & Fixsen, D. (2013). *Stages of implementation analysis: Where are we?"* Chapel Hill: FPG Child Development Institute, University of North Carolina at Chapel Hill.

Dunlap, G., Smith, B. J., Fox, L., & Blase, K. (2014). *Road map to statewide implementation of the Pyramid Model. Roadmap to effective intervention practices #6.* Tampa: University of South Florida, Technical Assistance Center on Social Emotional Intervention for Young Children.

Fixsen, D., Blase, K., Horner, R., Sims, B., & Sugai, G. (2013). *Scaling Up Brief, No. 3.* Chapel Hill: State Implementation and Scaling-up of Evidence-based Practices Center, FPG Child Development Institute: University of North Carolina Chapel Hill. Retrieved from https://implementation.fpg.unc.edu/sites/implementation.fpg.unc.edu/files/NIRN-ImplementationDriversAssessingBestPractices.pdf

Fixsen, D., Blase, K., Naoom, S., & Duda, M. (2015). Implementation drivers: Assessing best practices. Chapel Hill: University of North Carolina at Chapel Hill, FPG Child Development Institute, National Implementation Science Network.

Fixsen, D. L., Naoom, S. F., Blase, K. A., Friedman, R. M., & Wallace, F. (2005). *Implementation research: A synthesis of the literature.* Tampa: University of South Florida, Louis de la Parte Florida Mental Health Institute, National Implementation Research Network.

Fox, L., Dunlap, G., Hemmeter, M. L., Joseph, G. E., & Strain, P. S. (2003). The Teaching Pyramid: A model for supporting social competence and preventing challenging behavior in young children. *Young Children, 58*(4), 48–52.

Fox, L., & Hemmeter, M. L. (2009). A program-wide model for supporting social emotional development and addressing challenging behavior in early childhood settings. In W. Sailor, G. Dunlap, G. Sugai, & R. Horner (Eds.), *Handbook of positive behavior support* (pp. 177–202). New York, NY: Springer.

Fox, L., & Hemmeter, L. (2014). Implementing positive behavioral intervention and support: The evidence-base of the pyramid model for supporting social emotional competence in infants and young children. *Pyramid Model Consortium.* Retrieved from http://www.pyramidmodel.org/wp-content/uploads/2016/11/implementing_positive_behavioral_intervention_and_support.pdf

Fox, L., Lentini, R., & Binder, D. P. (2013). Promoting the social-emotional competence of all children: Implementing the Pyramid Model program-wide. *Young Exceptional Children Monograph Series No. 15,* 1–13.

Hargreaves, M. (2010). *Evaluating system change: A planning guide.* Cambridge, MA: Mathematica Policy Research.

Hemmeter, M. L., Fox, L., & Snyder, P. (2013). A tiered model for promoting social-emotional competence and addressing challenging behavior. In V. Buysse & E. Peisner-Feinberg (Eds.), *Handbook of Response to Intervention in early childhood* (pp. 85–101). Baltimore, MD: Paul H. Brookes Publishing Co.

Hemmeter, M. L., Fox, L., & Snyder, P. (2014). *Teaching Pyramid Observation Tool–Research edition* [manual]. Baltimore, MD: Paul H. Brookes Publishing Co.

Hemmeter, M. L., Ostrosky, M., & Fox, L. (2006). Social and emotional foundations for early learning: A conceptual model for intervention. *School Psychology Review, 35,* 583–601.

Layzer, C. (2013). Using implementation science to support replication, scale-up, and ongoing monitoring. In T. Halle, A. Metz, & I. Martinez-Beck (Eds.), *Applying implementation science in early childhood programs and systems* (pp. 227–237). Baltimore, MD: Paul H. Brookes Publishing Co.

Metz, A., & Bartley, L. (2012). Active implementation frameworks for program success: How to use implementation science to improve outcomes for children. *Zero to Three, 32*(4), 11–18.

Metz, A., Naoom, S. F., Halle, T., & Bartley, L. (2015). *An integrated stage-based framework for implementation of early childhood programs and systems* (OPRE Research Brief OPRE 201548). Washington, DC: Office of Planning, Research and Evaluation, Administration for Children and Families, U.S. Department of Health and Human Services.

Meyers, D. C., Durlak, J. A., & Wandersman, A. (2012). The quality implementation framework: A synthesis of critical steps in the implementation process. *American Journal of Community Psychology, 50 (3–4),* 462–480. doi:10.1007/s10464-012-9522-x

Smith, B. J., Dunlap, G., Blase, K. (2015). Implementing the Pyramid Model state-wide: State benchmarks of quality. Technical Assistance Center on Social Emotional Intervention for Young Children Department of Child and Family Studies. Tampa: University of South Florida.

Snyder, P., Hemmeter, M. L., & Fox, L. (2015). Supporting implementation of evidence-based practices through practice-based coaching. *Topics in Early Childhood Special Education, 35,* 133–143. Retrieved from http://challengingbehavior.fmhi.usf.edu/do/resources/documents/roadmap_6

12
Engaging Families in Multi-Tiered Systems of Support

Lisa L. Knoche and Susan M. Sheridan

Ms. Cassandra is a first-year early childhood educator (ECE) in a preschool program that is located within an elementary school. Zain is a 4-year-old student in Ms. Cassandra's class. He is in his second year in the preschool classroom but his first year with Ms. Cassandra. Latrice is Zain's mother; she works full time and is a single parent. Since the beginning of the year, Ms. Cassandra has found Zain's behaviors in the classroom to be challenging. He has difficulty paying attention and is disruptive during group activities. In addition, Ms. Cassandra is worried about his limited vocabulary. Ms. Cassandra is using an evidence-based early literacy curriculum and collects data on all children's vocabulary development weekly using a progress-monitoring tool. Zain consistently scores very low; she has seen limited progress in the first 3 months of the academic year. She has tried to incorporate more vocabulary instruction during small-group time, but Zain rarely stays engaged through the group time. Ms. Cassandra has been working to actively recognize when Zain is on task during group time and reward his behavior, but she is uncertain of the strategies Latrice uses at home. Although Ms. Cassandra has contact with Latrice each day when she drops Zain off at school, their interactions are rushed and they rarely exchange more than a "good morning." In this school, parents have a very short window of time to bring children to the classroom at the beginning of the day; they are expected to leave quickly so that class activity can begin. Ms. Cassandra sends notes home to inform Latrice of Zain's behavior, but she has not had a chance to share Zain's vocabulary data or discuss the behavior plan that she has been trying out in the classroom. Ms. Cassandra will have a parent–teacher conference with Latrice within the next month and wants to take full advantage of the time with Latrice but is unsure how this visit will go. How can Ms. Cassandra partner with Latrice to support Zain's classroom engagement and vocabulary development?

INTRODUCTION

Ecological theory considers child development within the context of interacting systems (including the child, peers, adults, learning environments, community agencies, and policies) that influence and are influenced by one another (Bronfenbrenner,

1977). This serves as the foundation for a partnership orientation in early childhood education. Specific to multi-tiered systems of support (MTSS), the relationships that occur *within* primary settings (e.g., home, school), and relationships *between* primary systems and settings (i.e., the interface between family and school systems) influence child development and learning in significant ways. Consistencies in positive stimulation across caregiving systems (i.e., family and school) and positive relationships among parents and ECEs (e.g., early childhood teachers and specialists) may encourage positive development for those showing early signs of educational risk (Jung, 2010; Turnbull, Blue-Banning, Turbiville, & Park, 1999).

The two most important developmental systems to influence young children are families and schools. Family is the primary system and, because it is generally a lifelong resource, the most important. Very few educational interventions have produced results with such consistently positive, significant, and stable effects over time, geographic context, developmental level, and subject areas as parent support and participation (Jeynes, 2003, 2005; Nye, Turner, & Schwartz, 2006). Given these important associations, the role of families in the education of young children must be carefully considered.

This chapter highlights the important ways that early education programs can engage families in each aspect of MTSS and details strategies that programs can use to create partnerships with families to engage in problem-solving efforts through sharing of information, goals, and responsibilities. We address how to set a foundation for partnerships in Tier 1 and discuss how programs and families can engage in more frequent collaborative efforts and problem-solving activities as a means of supporting children's learning and promoting their competence as needed. The roles of all key stakeholders, including ECEs, as well as agency administrators and other staff in leadership roles are considered.

What Is Family Engagement?

Both parent–child and parent–ECE relationships play an essential role in young children's learning and are key components of active family engagement. These relationships early in a child's life create a system of meaningful support that facilitates child growth and development. Family engagement is conceptualized as behaviors that connect with and support children or others in their environment in ways that are interactive, purposeful, and directed toward meaningful learning and affective outcomes. Family engagement includes interactions and provision of experiences that nurture children and promote children's autonomy and learning. Thus, family engagement is viewed as a more general concept than traditional parent/family involvement, which is often more narrowly understood as school- or home-based activities that are supportive of school efforts and/or children's performance in school. In this chapter, we have opted to use the term "family" engagement to recognize that there are a multiplicity of adults (e.g., grandparents, aunts, cousins, siblings), in addition to parents, who are actively involved in caregiving responsibilities and educational decision making.

Parent–Child Relationships Among the earliest influences on children's learning and development are those that occur in the home setting, within the context of parent–child interactions (*parent* refers to any adult who is serving in a primary caregiving role). Children's early environmental and relational experiences in the home setting constitute the "curriculum of the home" and are related to language and cognitive skills (e.g., Chazan-Cohen et al., 2009; Hood, Conlon, & Andrews, 2008; Raikes et al., 2006), school readiness (e.g., Espinosa, 2002; Pan, Rowe, Singer & Snow, 2005; Weigel, Martin, & Bennett, 2006a), and academic success (e.g., Foster, Lambert, Abbott-Shim, McCarty, & Franze, 2005; Weigel, Martin, & Bennett, 2006a, 2006b) across the toddler, preschool, and primary grades. Parental warmth and sensitivity during interactions with their child support child security and exploration (Chazan-Cohen et al., 2009; Shonkoff & Phillips, 2000) and cognitive growth (El Nokali, Bachman, & Votruba-Drzal, 2010; Pungello, Iruka, Dotterer, Mills-Koonce, & Reznick, 2009). When parents engage in activities that support a child's autonomy, they promote child language and social outcomes and encourage the development of skills essential to a child's success in school (Clark & Ladd, 2000; Grolnick & Farkas, 2002; McNamara, Selig, & Hawley, 2010). In addition, active and meaningful parental participation in language- and literacy-related activities have been reported as important in facilitating optimal school readiness and success (El Nokali et al., 2010; Pan et al., 2005). Parental efforts to enhance the learning and literacy environment at home through rich verbal exposure, joint book reading, and provision of print materials are positively related to preschool children's emergent literacy skills (Sénéchal, 2006; Weigel et al., 2006a).

Family–School Partnerships   Consistent with ecological theory, the educational experience for young children can also be enhanced through means that create connections among primary socializing systems, through the establishment and maintenance of *family–school partnerships*. In a family–school partnership approach, families and school professionals cooperate, coordinate, and collaborate to enhance opportunities and success for children in the social, emotional, behavioral, and academic domains (Christenson & Sheridan, 2001). Family–school partnership models focus on creating a constructive relationship to promote positive social-emotional, behavioral, academic, and developmental trajectories in children and youth, emphasizing the reciprocal influence and shared responsibility for educating and socializing children (Christenson & Sheridan, 2001). In partnership models, emphasis is placed on the co-construction of goals and priorities for children's learning, mutual contributions around information sharing and decision making, sharing in the responsibility for child progress, and joint monitoring of goal attainment (Fantuzzo, Tighe, & Childs, 2000; Sheridan & Kratochwill, 2008). Parents and ECEs each bring their individual understanding of the child and their knowledge of the child's behavior to share with one another and together identify areas of need and patterns of behavior occurring across settings. Everyone involved is an equally responsible partner with vital information to contribute to the co-creation of plans for promoting the child's learning and development. When parents and ECEs partner to create consistency across settings, young children experience greater improvements in executive functioning, early language and literacy, behavior, and social development (Rickards, Walstab, Wright-Rossi, Simpson, & Reddihough, 2007; Sheridan, Knoche, Edwards, Bovaird, & Kupzyk, 2010; Sheridan, Ryoo, Garbacz, Kunz, & Chumney, 2013; Sheridan et al., 2014). Quality parent–ECE relationships strive to create continuity across settings. Significant to the implementation of MTSS, consistency across home and other settings encourages higher rates of learning, compared to inconsistent stimulation across settings (Crosnoe, Leventhal, Wirth, Pierce, & Pianta, 2010).

Where Do Families "Fit" Within Multi-Tiered Systems of Support?

Given the significant and primary role of families in promoting young children's development, their involvement in MTSS is critical. Family engagement takes place along a continuum, from earliest system development through full system implementation. The National Center for Learning Disabilities' *The Roadmap to Pre-K RTI* (Coleman, Roth, & West, 2009) specifies that developing opportunities for family involvement in MTSS begins with their involvement in the early implementation efforts. This includes encouraging families to participate in planning for the MTSS model to be used, sharing information with families, and allowing them to have a role in evaluating the success of the effort. For example, the Colorado Department of Education includes MTSS Family, School and Community Partnering as an essential component of MTSS implementation (https://www.cde.state.co.us/mtss/fscp). This framework encourages implementation of the six partnership standards established by the National PTA (https://www.pta.org/nationalstandards), which are 1) welcoming families into the community of the school so they are valued and connected to each other, 2) maintaining effective, regular two-way communication, 3) supporting school success through ongoing collaboration between home and school, 4) empowering families to be advocates for their children, 5) ensuring equal power between home and school in decision making, and 6) establishing community collaborations and connections (National PTA, n.d.). This MTSS family, school, and community partnering framework provides indicators (e.g., "gold standard," acceptable, unacceptable) of successful implementation of the six national PTA partnership standards so as to promote careful monitoring and improvement of practices in service of child learning. Following the implementation of an MTSS within an educational setting, families continue to have a central role to play irrespective of which tier of support the child is experiencing.

Reflecting on Engagement A strong family engagement philosophy, including one that values family–school partnership and recognizes the critical role of families in supporting their young children's development is foundational to an MTSS. The philosophy is characterized by effective communication, a recognition of the importance of family engagement and family values, cultural awareness and sensitivity, and open invitations to parents. The Self-Assessment of Family Engagement Practices (Sjuts & Sheridan, 2011) can be used by early childhood programs as a needs assessment to determine thoughts and universal practices regarding family engagement (see Appendix 12A). Respondents can include multiple key stakeholders within early childhood programs and is particularly useful when completed by classroom staff to reflect on their own practices.

Opportunities for Engagement Generally, there are multiple opportunities for family engagement within early childhood programs. These opportunities for parent engagement are characterized by varying levels of individualization. Regardless of the package of supports being offered to the child within the MTSS based on their progress on developmental tasks, the family continues to have an opportunity to engage at multiple levels of the program; see Figure 12.1. Next, we define the opportunities for engagement and then specify how they interact within an MTSS.

One opportunity for engagement includes *universal*, programmatic opportunities that are offered to all children and families in group settings where

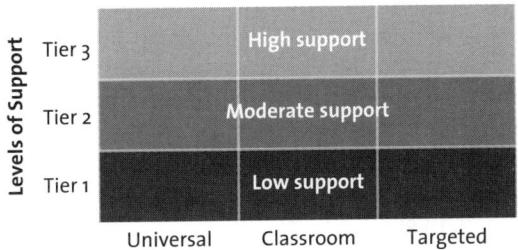

Figure 12.1. Opportunities for parent engagement within an MTSS.

individualization is limited. Although they may provide an opportunity for one-to-one interactions, the planning and implementation are intended to address the needs of a large group and are offered simultaneously to all families and children within a program. Universal events might include centerwide family events, backpack programs, or opportunities for program governance. A second, increasingly individualized opportunity for engagement occurs at the level of the *classroom*. Classroom-level opportunities for engagement and partnership involve children and families within a specific program or classroom. Parent meetings or a family classroom volunteer are examples of opportunities at the classroom level. Finally, the *targeted* opportunities are those that are most individualized. Targeted opportunities are tailored to a single child/family and ECE, although offered to all families within a program, the experience is individualized for each child and family. Targeted opportunities include parent–ECE conferences, home visits, and more.

In addition, within each of these opportunities, the experiences for families can be characterized as *structured* or *unstructured*. Structured interactions are those that are scheduled and regularly part of planned program activities. Structured interactions might include opportunities such as home visits, parent–ECE conferences, and parent meetings. Unstructured interactions are more informal in nature and include opportunities such as drop-off and pick-up, telephone calls, e-mails, texts, newsletters, and other home communications. All of these opportunities create mechanisms for connecting with all families within an MTSS and promoting family engagement and should be carefully considered by programs and professionals.

Within an MTSS framework, children's needs determine the level of intensity of instructional support that is required to promote their educational success. This means that the educational supports that children receive will vary within an MTSS framework, but the opportunities for family engagement remain consistent across families. For some children, instructional supports offered at the universal level of instruction will be sufficient to meet their needs; other children will receive more individualized supports. The families of these children, irrespective of the supports the children are receiving in the classroom, will each have universal (e.g., family night), classroom (e.g., parent meetings), and targeted (e.g., parent–teacher conferences) opportunities for engagement with the early childhood program. Ideally, the supports therein will be differentiated based on child need. All families should be provided opportunities at all levels to engage with the early childhood program; however, as children progress through the MTSS, the experiences of the family at each level will be individualized and unique based on specific needs (see Figure 12.1). That is, if a child is participating in intensive instructional supports, the family will likely be involved in targeted engagement opportunities. However, planning must also take into account the unique experiences of that family during other parent engagement opportunities (e.g. universal, programwide events). Similarly, the family of a child who is succeeding with the universal instructional supports offered in the classroom will also participate in targeted family engagement opportunities, and their experience can be tailored according to child need. In summary, family engagement practices are relevant for all children and families in an early childhood program and their unique needs and experiences must be considered in planning and implementation.

STRATEGIES AND PRACTICES TO SUPPORT FAMILY ENGAGEMENT WITHIN MTSS

A number of strategies have been developed to strengthen parental responsiveness, support parental confidence, and encourage parents to actively participate in educational decision making as a partner (Ferguson, Jordan, & Baldwin, 2010; Garbacz, Herman, Thompson, & Reinke, 2017; Lochman et al., 2017). Although many of these strategies have been developed for families of students in the elementary grades, the evidence-based Getting-Ready strategies have been used to effectively promote the development of young children via parent–ECE partnerships and parent–child relationships (Knoche et al., 2012; Sheridan et al., 2010; Sheridan, Knoche, Kupzyk, Edwards, & Marvin, 2011; Sheridan et al., 2014).

Getting-Ready Strategies

The Getting-Ready intervention strategies combine triadic practices (McCollum & Yates, 1994) with collaborative processes (Sheridan & Kratochwill, 2008). The strategies are individualized, responsive, and applied uniquely with families in a dynamic process. Strategies include those intended to strengthen relationships (i.e., between parents and their child, and between parents and their child's ECE), as well as those intended to build parents' competencies. To encourage child learning and developmental goal attainment, parents need to have the requisite skills to engage in meaningful exchanges with their child. The Getting-Ready family engagement strategies are fully defined in Table 12.1.

The Getting-Ready strategies can be used by educators at all tiers of a multi-tier system as well as during universal, classroom, and individualized parent engagement opportunities, including in structured and unstructured interactions with families. Furthermore, they can be used by anyone who interacts with families including ECEs, administrators, and other service providers. Specific examples of strategy use are provided in Table 12.2; these examples are intended to illustrate strategy use by varied users but are not exhaustive.

Collaborative Interactions Between Families and Early Childhood Educators   Collaborative interactions between families and ECEs represent a structured process wherein ECEs work cooperatively with parents to help children accomplish mutually determined developmental goals. While these interactions are appropriate and have utility for all families and children in early childhood programs, they may have

Table 12.1. Getting-Ready family engagement strategies and definitions

	Strategies to strengthen relationships
Communicate openly and clearly	Parents and early childhood educators (ECEs) are fully engaged in a two-way exchange in which each participant's (parent and ECE) input is valued and parents' input is elicited via questions that require embellishment (versus "yes" or "no" answers), and checks for understanding are frequent.
Establish parent–child interaction	Elements of the environment are intentionally and actively arranged or rearranged to increase the probability of developmentally matched, mutually enjoyable parent–child interaction.
Affirm parent competencies	Parents' strengths are identified, recognized, and built upon. The ECE may affirm any behavior he or she sees or evidence of parents' efforts that suggest the parent is focused on the child, engaged meaningfully with the child, and working on improving his or her own or the child's skills.
Make mutual, joint decisions	Parents and ECEs have conversations as co-equal participants and agree on goals, priorities, strategies, or plans regarding the child's learning and development. Collaborative, back-and-forth exchanges between parents and providers are priorities, and strategies are selected and incorporated into natural settings at home and in the early learning setting.
	Strategies to build competencies
Focus attention on the child's strengths	Parents' attention is oriented toward their child's specific developmental strengths and needs as an opportunity to help parents understand their child's development in terms of what is typical and what may be important to monitor.
Share information and resources	This is the act of asking about or labeling, interpreting, or explaining the developmental significance of the child's observed emotional, cognitive, linguistic, or motor abilities; providing information about developmental milestones and behaviors or skill levels that need some extra support; and explaining resources available from which to receive that support.
Use observations and data	Objective information about the child, including the child's skill levels and progress toward developmental goals, is discussed. Information is gleaned from parents' and ECEs' observations of the child as well as other means, such as assessment data.
Model and suggest	*Model* the use of a learning strategy with a child while the parent observes and then invite the parent to use the strategy in the moment, during that parent–child–ECE interaction. *Suggest* the use of explicit statements to the parent about behaviors to support the child's development and parent–child interactions, offering the parent ideas about how to interact with his or her child during the interaction or in the future.

particular benefit for children with specific and individualized needs. Through the process, family members and ECEs engage jointly in two-way communication as they share observations, concerns, and perspectives on a child's learning and developmental status; make plans and decisions in support of learning opportunities and outcomes; and ensure that mechanisms for checking in, monitoring progress, and modifying plans are in place. Each participant (i.e., parent, family members, ECE) is considered an expert in the collaborative interaction since each has important perspectives on the child from unique vantage points across home and school.

Table 12.2. Examples of select Getting-Ready strategy use across educational users

	Principal/administrator	Early childhood educator
Strengthen relationships	As an educational leader, administrators can support policies that invite *open communication* with families, including opportunities for them to provide meaningful input into programmatic practices that affect children and families, including a comfortable forum for sharing their observations and concerns. Administrators can also *affirm competencies* at universal levels to recognize the role of families in their children's education.	During a home visit, a parent was reading with her child. The Early childhood educator (ECE) commented and *affirmed the parent's competencies*: "When you point to the print while you read, just like you are doing now, you are showing Zain that print has meaning. That is an excellent strategy you are using to build his skills as a future reader." In a parent–ECE conference, the ECE brings up the different strategies at school that seem to be working for the child, who is an active learner. The parent states that the child doesn't like sitting down and that he has to be interested in something in order to stay with it. The ECE and parent agree that strategies to increase the child's persistence should include his interests and allow him to be active. One activity they *mutually decided* would be fun is to have the child drive his cars (a favorite toy, as reported by the parent) around the shapes of the letters they are working on.
Build competencies	During programwide staff meetings, the building administrator *focuses attention* on family strengths observed during parent–ECE conferences and discusses how these capacities will benefit young children. Staff are encouraged to implement strengths-based efforts with children and families. In the parent steering committee, the principal shares data gathered from observations to guide decisions about MTSS.	At pick-up, the ECE *focuses attention on child strengths* despite having a challenging day when she takes time to say to the parent, "Zain puts his coat on all by himself now at school, and if I help him get the zipper started, he can pull it up and then put on his hat. He needs help getting all the fingers into his gloves correctly, but he can put mittens on all by himself," before discussing concerns. While discussing strategies about letter formation during a parent–ECE conference, the ECE offers to *model* how they make "rainbow letters" at school, thinking that this might be something the parent would like to do at home with the child. The ECE engages with the child in letter tracing; the ECE and child take turns tracing the letter with different color crayons. The ECE then hands a crayon to the parent and suggests, "Here, how about if you and Zain write the next rainbow letter together."

Free and open sharing of ideas, values, and priorities is central to the collaborative process. These characteristics of collaboration contribute to a shared sense of ownership, wherein the input of both parents and ECEs is respected, valued, and utilized.

Collaborative interactions are intended to create continuity across a child's home and early childhood classroom environments. This means that experiences across both home and school are planned and coordinated with each other in an effort to encourage a child's learning and development. Parents and ECEs each bring information about their respective relationships and environments, which is vital to the co-creation of effective, meaningful, and appropriate plans for promoting the child's learning and development.

Collaborative interactions promote mutual interest and investment between parents and ECEs, resulting in a sense of shared responsibility for a child's learning and healthy development. Within the context of home visits, parent–ECE conferences, or similar structured opportunities, collaborative interactions allow for mindful and intentional exchanges between the adults who are most concerned with a child's progress. Using a collaborative process in these professional settings, parents and ECEs are given tools to work together to establish targeted goals for young children, co-create optimal learning conditions to support children as they achieve important goals across domains, and monitor their ongoing growth and development. An important product that emerges from collaborative home–school interactions is the construction of a home–school plan (see Appendix 12B).

Table 12.3 presents the steps of the collaborative interaction process. The first step involves sharing observations and strengths, wherein parents and ECEs share their observations of the child's present skill levels across developmental domains. They talk about the child's strengths and the child's learning needs and identify how the child manifests those strengths and skills at home and school. Second, ECEs and parents mutually set a goal as related to a particular domain. Through a discussion of observations, assessments, and other information sources, the parent and ECE arrive at a mutual decision about the level of performance desired for the child that will move the child closer to achieving the desired goal. The third step in the collaborative process is creating action steps. Based on their observations of the child's current level of performance related to the goal, and through a discussion of what is feasible and appropriate in each respective setting, parents and the ECE jointly determine the actions that will be needed to help the child achieve the goal. This often includes creating broadened opportunities and

Table 12.3. Structure for collaborative interactions

Steps	Description of steps of collaborative interaction process
Share observations of child strengths	Parents and early childhood educators (ECEs) share their observations of the child's present skill levels across developmental domains. Parents and ECEs talk about the child's strengths and the child's learning needs. Both strengths and needs are discussed.
Set goal	A specific target skill or child level of performance is established by parent and ECE. Goal is objective, measurable, and attainable by the child.
Decide on steps	Based on their observations of the child's current level of performance related to the target, parents and the ECE jointly determine the next steps needed to help the child achieve the goal. Action steps and a reasonable time line are set, and plans for communicating between home and school are agreed upon.
Share ideas/develop plan for home and school	Parents and ECEs talk about the opportunities at home and at school for the child to practice the steps, and strategies that could be put into place at home and at school to support the child's learning. Together, parents and ECEs develop and agree upon steps that will be followed at home and school to help the child work toward achieving the goal.
Monitor and modify	The ongoing process of observing and recording the child's progress in relationship to the target goal, both at school and at home. The repeated monitoring of child performance in relation to the target goal allows for modifications to be made as necessary and facilitate appropriate individualized attention.

experiences for the child to learn or practice a skill at home and school, benchmarks that will document the child's progress, and a determination of appropriate time lines. A home–school plan is then developed that specifies the strategies to be implemented and practiced with the child at home and at the early childhood setting to support goal attainment (see Home–School Plan, Appendix 12B). The final step in the formal collaborative interaction process requires ECEs and parents to continuously monitor and evaluate the child's progress toward his or her goal and modify strategies as needed. At this stage, goals can be reconsidered or set anew, plan steps and strategies can be adjusted or revised, or other decisions can be made to support both the child and the parent–ECE partnership.

Although the steps constituting collaborative interactions in structured parent–ECE situations are sequential and build upon one another, the process is best practiced in a flexible manner. Indeed, it is most effective when it builds on the strengths and current status of the child, is reflexive and responsive to a child's progress and growth, and is attentive to what is acceptable and feasible within the natural home and early childhood settings. As with other opportunities for family engagement, Getting-Ready strategies (Table 12.1) are infused in all aspects of collaborative interactions.

What Supports Do Early Childhood Professionals Need to Effectively Engage with Families?

Effective and intentional engagement with parents in a multi-tier system requires support and planning. Effective support must include reflection on current practices related to family engagement. The Self-Assessment of Family Engagement Practices (Sjuts & Sheridan, 2011; Appendix 12A) is a tool that, when used, allows professionals to reflect on communication practices, beliefs about family engagement, respect for family values and practices, cultural awareness, and methods of inviting parents into the setting. All key stakeholders involved in early childhood programming are encouraged to reflect on practices and beliefs. Active participation from all levels that interact with families is essential. Key stakeholders (e.g., administrators, office personnel, health professionals, special educators, ECEs) each have specific responsibilities in regard to children and families that afford them unique opportunities to create experiences and engage families. The collective reflections from the group of varied stakeholders on current program practices related to family engagement will most accurately reveal the climate that is experienced by families. In addition, efforts to ask families about their direct experiences are also highly valuable.

It is through action plans that family engagement practices within an MTSS will be strengthened and maintained. Following reflection, key stakeholders independently and collectively generate proposed targets and plans to support effective communication practices, encourage positive beliefs about family engagement, demonstrate respect for family values and practices as well as cultural awareness, and consider the methods being used to invite parents into the setting. As previously discussed, there are universal, classroom, and individual opportunities for family engagement. Action plans must include steps for each of these opportunities and consider the experiences of families and their children who are receiving varying levels of instructional support within the MTSS.

CONCLUSION

Family engagement is a key aspect of consideration for MTSS of early childhood program settings. Consistencies in positive stimulation across caregiving systems (i.e., family and school) and positive relationships among parents and ECEs are significant for young children, particularly those at educational risk (Jung, 2010; Turnbull et al., 1999). Furthermore, parent support and participation in educational interventions have consistently been associated with significant and stable effects for children (Jeynes, 2003, 2005; Nye et al., 2006). Family engagement includes a focus on and support for the parent–child relationship as well as parent–educator partnerships. Within an MTSS, a strong and positive universal philosophy of family engagement is needed to promote child competence and educational success. While family engagement strategies might be particularly salient for families of children who are receiving more intensive instructional supports, the supports that are offered must be built upon a strong universal program of family engagement practices. The family engagement practices are relevant for all families in an early childhood program. Furthermore, all stakeholders in ECE programs have a role to play in promoting family engagement; the Getting-Ready strategies are one approach that can be integrated across universal, classroom, and targeted opportunities to support engagement. Intentional planning, implementation, and reflection are required to effectively implement family engagement practices within an MTSS.

Ms. Cassandra approached her principal supervisor, Mrs. Jeffries, about her desire to plan for her meeting with Latrice. Mrs. Jeffries encouraged her to reflect on her current practices with families. Ms. Cassandra specifically thought about her communication practices with families, and she realized that she communicated comfortably with families of children who were excelling in the classroom or were on target; when children were struggling, she was not effectively communicating her concerns with families. Her school was implementing an MTSS, and this provided an opportunity to think about the needs of each child and family. She realized that open communication and mutual decision making would be very important for her conference with Latrice about Zain's progress to proceed smoothly. She also wanted to have data to share during the conference and thought about Zain's specific strengths that she could share with Latrice in addition to her concerns. Ms. Cassandra used the format for collaborative interactions during her conference with Latrice. Latrice actively participated, and they jointly established a plan to work on shared vocabulary at home and school. They agreed to check in two times each week on Zain's progress and agreed to e-mail or text if they could not talk in person during drop-off.

In addition, Ms. Cassandra's request for information on parent engagement encouraged Mrs. Jeffries to use a staff meeting to reflect on universal parent engagement practices for the program. The staff realized the limited drop-off time was preventing effective communication between parents and teachers. Mrs. Jeffries and the staff expanded the drop-off window each morning to allow more time for teacher–family communication and information exchange and support a strong universal program of parent engagement.

RESOURCES

Colorado Department of Education. (n.d.). *Multi-tiered family, school, and community partnering.* Available from https://www.cde.state.co.us/mtss/fscp

Division for Early Childhood (DEC), National Association for the Education of Young Children (NAEYC), & National Head Start Association (NHSA). (2013). *Frameworks for Response to Intervention in early childhood: Description and implications.* Missoula, MT: Author. Retrieved from http://www.dec-sped.org/position-statements

Keyser, J. (2006). *From parents to partners: Building a family centered early childhood program.* St. Paul, MN: Redleaf Press.

National PTA. (n.d.). *National standards for family–school partnerships.* Available from http://www.pta.org/nationalstandards

Sheridan, S. M., & Kratochwill, T. R. (2008). *Conjoint behavioral consultation: Promoting family–school connections and interventions.* New York, NY: Springer.

REFERENCES

Bronfenbrenner, U. (1977). Toward an experimental ecology of human development. *American Psychologist, 32,* 515–531.

Chazan-Cohen, R., Raikes, H., Brooks-Gunn, J., Ayoub, C., Pan, B. A., Kisker, E. E., . . . Fuligni, A. S. (2009). Low-income children's school readiness: Parent contributions over the first five years. *Early Education and Development, 20,* 958–977.

Christenson, S. L., & Sheridan, S. M. (2001). *Schools and families: Creating essential connections for learning.* New York, NY: Guilford Press.

Clark, K. E., & Ladd, G. W. (2000). Connectedness and autonomy support in parent–child relationships: Links to children's socioemotional orientation and peer relationships. *Developmental Psychology, 36,* 485–498.

Coleman, M. R., Roth, F. P., & West, T. (2009). *RoadMap to PreK RTI: Applying response to intervention in preschool settings.* New York, NY: National Center for Learning Disabilities.

Crosnoe, R., Leventhal, T., Wirth, R. J., Pierce, K. M., & Pianta, R. C. (2010). Family socioeconomic status and consistent environmental stimulation in early childhood. *Child Development, 81,* 972–987. doi:10.1111/j.1467-8624.2010.01446.x

El Nokali, N., Bachman, H. J., & Votruba-Drzal, E. (2010). Parent involvement and children's academic achievement and social development in elementary school. *Child Development, 81,* 988–1005.

Espinosa, L. M. (2002). The connections between social-emotional development and literacy. *Kauffman Early Education Exchange, 1,* 31–44.

Fantuzzo, J., Tighe, E., & Childs, S. (2000). Family involvement questionnaire: A multivariate assessment of family participation in early childhood education. *Journal of Educational Psychology, 92*(2), 367–376.

Ferguson, C., Jordan, C., & Baldwin, M. (2010). *Working systematically in action: Engaging family and community.* Austin, TX: SEDL.

Foster, M. A., Lambert, R., Abbott-Shinn, M., McCarty, F., & Franze, S. (2005). A model of home learning environment and social risk factors in relation to children's emergent literacy and social outcomes. *Early Childhood Research Quarterly, 20,* 13–36.

Garbacz, S. A., Herman, K. C., Thompson, A. M., & Reinke, W. M. (2017). Family engagement in education and intervention: Implementation and evaluation to maximize family, school, and student outcomes. *Journal of School Psychology, 62,* 1–10. https://doi.org/10.1016/j.jsp.2017.04.002

Grolnick, W. S., & Farkas, M. (2002). Parenting and the development of children's self-regulation. In M. H. Bornstein (Ed.), *Handbook of parenting, Volume 5: Practical issues in parenting* (pp. 89–110). Mahwah, NJ: Erlbaum.

Hood, M., Conlon, E., & Andrews, G. (2008). Preschool home literacy practices and children's literacy development: A longitudinal analysis. *Journal of Educational Psychology, 100,* 252–271.

Jeynes, W. H. (2003). A meta-analysis the effects of parental involvement on minority children's academic achievement. *Education and Urban Society, 35*(2), 202–218.

Jeynes, W. H. (2005). A meta-analysis of the relation of parental involvement to urban elementary school student academic achievement. *Urban Education, 40*(3), 237–269.

Jung, L. A. (2010). Identifying families' supports and resources. In R. A. McWilliam (Ed.), *Working with families of young children with special needs* (pp. 9–26). New York, NY: Guilford Press.

Knoche, L., Sheridan, S., Clarke, B., Edwards, C., Marvin, C., Cline, K., & Kupzyk, K. (2012). Getting Ready: Results of a randomized trial of a relationship-focused intervention on parent engagement in rural Early Head Start. *Infant Mental Health Journal, 33,* 439–458.

Lochman, J. E., Boxmeyer, C. L., Jones, S., Qu, L., Ewoldsen, D., & Nelson, W. M. (2017). Testing the feasibility of a briefer school-based preventive intervention with aggressive children: A hybrid intervention with face-to-face and internet components. *Journal of School Psychology, 62,* 33–50. https://doi.org/10.1016/j.jsp.2017.03.010

McCollum, J. A., & Yates, T. J. (1994). Dyad as focus, triad as means: A family-centered approach to supporting parent–child interactions. *Infants and Young Children, 6,* 54–63.

McNamara, K. A., Selig, J. P., & Hawley, P. H. (2010). A typological approach to the study of parenting: Associations between maternal parenting patterns and child behaviour and social reception. *Early Child Development and Care, 180,* 1185–1202.

Nye, C., Turner, H., & Schwartz, J. (2006). Approaches to parent involvement for improving the academic performance of elementary school-age children: A systematic review. *Campbell Systematic Reviews, 2*(4), 1–46.

Pan, B. A., Rowe, M. L., Singer, J. D., & Snow, C. E. (2005). Maternal correlates of growth in toddler vocabulary production in low-income families. *Child Development, 76,* 763–782.

National PTA. (n.d.) *National standards for family–school partnerships*. Retrieved from https://www.pta.org/nationalstandards

Pungello, L., Iruka, I., Dotterer, A. M., Mills-Koonce, R., & Reznick, S. (2009). The effects of income, race, and sensitive and harsh parenting on receptive and expressive language development in early childhood. *Developmental Psychology, 45,* 544–557.

Raikes, H., Alexander Pan, B., Luze, G., Tamis-LeMonda, C. S., Brooks-Gunn, J., & Constantine, J. (2006). Mother–child bookreading in low-income families: Correlates and outcomes during the first three years of life. *Child Development, 77,* 924–953.

Rickards, A. L., Walstab, J. E., Wright-Rossi, R. A., Simpson, J., & Reddihough, D. S. (2007). A randomized, controlled trial of a home-based intervention program for children with autism and developmental delay. *Journal of Developmental & Behavioral Pediatrics, 28,* 308–316.

Sénéchal, M. (2006). Testing the home literacy model: Parent involvement in kindergarten is differentially related to grade 4 reading comprehension, fluency, spelling, and reading for pleasure. *Scientific Studies of Reading, 10*(1), 59–87.

Sheridan, S. M., Knoche, L. L., Edwards, C. P., Bovaird, J. A., & Kupzyk, K. A. (2010). Parent engagement and school readiness: Effects of the Getting Ready intervention on preschool children's social-emotional competencies. *Early Education and Development, 21,* 125–156.

Sheridan, S. M., Knoche, L. L., Kupzyk, K. A., Edwards, C. P., & Marvin, C.A. (2011). A randomized trial examining the effects of parent engagement on early language and literacy: The Getting Ready intervention. *Journal of School Psychology, 49,* 361–383. doi:10.1016/j.jsp.2011.03.00.

Sheridan, S. M., & Kratochwill, T. (2008). *Conjoint behavioral consultation: Promoting family-school connections and interventions*. New York, NY: Springer.

Sheridan, S. M., Ryoo, J. H., Garbacz, S. A., Kunz, G. M., & Chumney, F. L. (2013). The efficacy of conjoint behavioral consultation on parents and children in the home setting: Results of a randomized controlled trial. *Journal of School Psychology, 51,* 717–733.

Sheridan, S. M., Knoche, L. L., Edwards, C. P., Clarke, B. L., Kim, E. M., & Kupzyk, K. A. (2014). Efficacy of the Getting Ready intervention and the role of parental depression. *Early Education and Development, 25,* 1–24.

Shonkoff, J. P., & Phillips, D. (2000). *From neurons to neighborhoods: The science of early childhood development.* Washington, DC: National Academies Press.

Sjuts, T. M., & Sheridan, S. M. (2011). *Self-Assessment of Parent Engagement Practices (SPEP).* Unpublished instrument, Nebraska Center for Research on Children, Youth, Families and Schools, University of Nebraska-Lincoln, Lincoln, NE.

Turnbull, A. P., Blue-Banning, M., Turbiville, V., & Park, J. (1999). From parent education to partnership education: A call for a transformed focus. *Topics in Early Childhood Special Education, 19,* 164–171.

Weigel, D. J., Martin, S. S., & Bennett, K. K. (2006a). Contributions of the home literacy environment to preschool-aged children's emerging literacy and language skills. *Early Child Development and Care, 176,* 357–378.

Weigel, D. J., Martin, S. S., & Bennett, K. K. (2006b). Mothers' literacy beliefs: Connections with the home literacy environment and pre-school children's literacy development. *Journal of Early Childhood Literacy, 6,* 191–211.

Appendix 12A

Self-Assessment of Family Engagement Practices

The self-evaluation measure serves as a needs assessment to determine thoughts and practices regarding family engagement. This tool is not evaluative; rather, its purpose is to facilitate self-reflection on current practices. For each item, please choose the number that best reflects how well you currently achieve the following partnership objectives and strategies. Use your ratings to begin a process to identify your program's strengths, areas for improvement, priorities, and specific plans to strengthen family–school partnerships. Consider using areas of strength (4s and 5s) to target areas in need of improvement (1s and 2s).

How well do you/does your staff demonstrate the following:	Very poorly	Poorly	Okay	Pretty well	Very well
Communication					
1. Make validating statements regarding parents' efforts and strengths (e.g., skills, knowledge, resources).	1	2	3	4	5
2. Provide parents with developmental and other information that helps them make decisions about their children.	1	2	3	4	5
3. Provide examples or demonstrations for parents.	1	2	3	4	5
4. Engage parents in frequent and open two-way information sharing.	1	2	3	4	5
5. Work with parents to set mutual goals for their child's development.	1	2	3	4	5
6. Ask parents about their efforts to meet child and family goals, including successes and difficulties.	1	2	3	4	5
7. Communicate with parents about the academic, behavior, and social performance of their child.	1	2	3	4	5
8. Give parents adequate information about curriculum; provide parents with daily information about what their children do in the classroom.	1	2	3	4	5
9. Convey (in a sincere manner) admiration and/or recognition to the family regarding what they have accomplished to date.	1	2	3	4	5
10. Comment to the parents about the strengths, accomplishments, or positive aspects of the child.	1	2	3	4	5
11. Allow and encourage parents to ask questions about staff practices.	1	2	3	4	5
12. Encourage parents to tell you what the child is doing at home and what parents are working on at home.	1	2	3	4	5
13. Help families feel they can make a positive difference in their children's lives.	1	2	3	4	5
Belief about family engagement					
14. Acknowledge parents' role in helping their child learn; communicate to parents they are important in their child's education.	1	2	3	4	5
15. Incorporate family strengths and resources in the supports offered.	1	2	3	4	5
16. Consider parents as co-teachers regarding their child's education.	1	2	3	4	5
17. Demonstrate attitudes that reflect the belief that all families have strengths that can be utilized to assist their child.	1	2	3	4	5
18. Work together with parents to generate options for intervention strategies.	1	2	3	4	5
19. Convey the message that parents are experts concerning their own children.	1	2	3	4	5
20. Break barriers to participation by providing child care, language translation, written information in home language, home visiting, etc.	1	2	3	4	5

(continued)

The development of this self-evaluation form was supported by a grant awarded to Susan Sheridan, Lisa Knoche, and Judy Carta (Grant #R324A090075) by the Institute of Education Sciences. Permission is granted for its use in program development and planning purposes; please do not duplicate in a public forum without permission from Lisa Knoche at lknoche2@unl.edu. Copyright © Nebraska Center for Research on Children, Youth, Families and Schools / cyfs.unl.edu

How well do you/does your staff demonstrate the following:	Very poorly	Poorly	Okay	Pretty well	Very well
Family values and practices					
21. Communicate with families in their preferred format.	1	2	3	4	5
22. Provide materials that incorporate family interests.	1	2	3	4	5
23. Provide reading materials at the parents' reading level.	1	2	3	4	5
24. Offer parents opportunities to problem-solve and make joint decisions both staff and parents are comfortable with.	1	2	3	4	5
25. Ask the family about their observations, opinions, or beliefs regarding their child's development or potential before offering your own.	1	2	3	4	5
26. Convey a sense of respect and acceptance of parents' opinions, feelings, priorities, lifestyle, etc., even if in conflict with your own.	1	2	3	4	5
27. Listen to parents and provide the minimum amount of structure (e.g., questions) necessary for parents to provide information.	1	2	3	4	5
28. Offer opinions and recommendations regarding the child's needs and interventions in a way that allows parents to disagree without feeling guilty or in conflict.	1	2	3	4	5
Cultural awareness and sensitivity					
29. Communicate and provide materials in the families' native language.	1	2	3	4	5
30. Use activities that incorporate different types of families (single-parent, grandparent guardians) reflective of those in classroom.	1	2	3	4	5
31. Have an understanding of, are open to, and respect the culture and value system of families you serve.	1	2	3	4	5
32. Make special efforts to reach families from all racial, cultural, and language groups.	1	2	3	4	5
Invitation to parents					
33. Frequently invite parents to participate in their child's learning at home and at school.	1	2	3	4	5
34. Provide opportunities for parents to actively participate in classroom activities.	1	2	3	4	5
35. Make parents feel comfortable being in the classroom (e.g., wanted, useful, belong there).	1	2	3	4	5
36. Provide materials that are family friendly and include information and instructions that help families expand on the school curriculum.	1	2	3	4	5
37. Provide parents with avenues to explore learning with their children in the school environment.	1	2	3	4	5

Notes:

The development of this self-evaluation form was supported by a grant awarded to Susan Sheridan, Lisa Knoche, and Judy Carta (Grant #R324A090075) by the Institute of Education Sciences. Permission is granted for its use in program development and planning purposes; please do not duplicate in a public forum without permission from Lisa Knoche at lknoche2@unl.edu. Copyright © Nebraska Center for Research on Children, Youth, Families and Schools / cyfs.unl.edu

Appendix 12B

HOME–SCHOOL PLAN

Child's name: _____   Date: _____

Goal:

At *home* we will . . .	As partners at *home* and *school* we will . . .	At *school* we will . . .

Notes and observations:

The development of this self-evaluation form was supported by a grant awarded to Susan Sheridan, Lisa Knoche, and Judy Carta (Grant #R324A090075) by the Institute of Education Sciences. Permission is granted for its use in program development and planning purposes; please do not duplicate in a public forum without permission from Lisa Knoche at lknoche2@unl.edu. Copyright © Nebraska Center for Research on Children, Youth, Families and Schools / cyfs.unl.edu

Multi-Tiered Systems of Support for Young Children: Driving Change in Early Education by Judith J. Carta and Robin Miller Young.
Copyright © 2019 by Paul H. Brookes Publishing Co., Inc. All rights reserved.

13

The Path Forward for Multi-Tiered Systems of Support in Early Education

Scott R. McConnell

Three professionals find themselves sitting together on a plane, delayed at departure, and waiting on the tarmac. Jo is the state Department of Education Part B coordinator responsible for design, support, and evaluation of early childhood special education (ECSE) services. Pat is director of early childhood services for one of the largest local education agencies in that state, responsible for management of school readiness and Head Start programs (the district is a grantee). Although Pat is not directly responsible for ECSE, she has close relations with the special education director and is committed to inclusion in all classrooms. Jaime is a teacher and team leader in a comprehensive early childhood center operated by a different district; Jaime's program houses six classrooms with a braided funding base, bringing together money and requirements (and children) from school readiness, ECSE, Head Start, and child care programs.

Pat notices that Jo, sitting in the middle seat, is reading the introductory chapter of a book on multi-tiered systems of support (MTSS; see Chapter 1). Pat mentions to Jo that she, too, has been learning about MTSS but isn't sure it fits well with all the other demands of her program. She is concerned, however, that her teachers know relatively little about different evidence-based practices and they have relatively little experience providing different interventions to some, but not all, of their students.

Jaime chimes in, noting that MTSS has been a frequent topic of recent conversations, as teachers look for better ways to serve all of their children, particularly as the diversity of their students expands. Although some of her classrooms include children with and

---

Support for preparation of this chapter was provided in part by the Institute of Education Sciences, U.S. Department of Education, through Grant R305A160034, *Expanding Individual Growth and Development Indicators of Language and Early Literacy for Universal Screening in Multi-Tiered Systems of Support with Three-Year-Olds* to the University of Minnesota. The opinions expressed are those of the authors and do not represent views of the Institute or the U.S. Department of Education.

Scott McConnell and colleagues developed assessment tools and related resources known as *Individual Growth & Development Indicators*, described here. This intellectual property has been licensed by the University of Minnesota to Early Learning Labs, Inc., and the authors and University have equity and/or royalty interests in Early Learning Labs, Inc. These relationships have been reviewed and are being managed by the University of Minnesota in accordance with its conflict of interest policies.

without disabilities, most of her staff's time is devoted to either direct services for children with individualized education programs (IEPs) or consultation to teachers of these children. How would they justify spending time on issues beyond those required in a student's IEP?

As the plane finally starts its taxi to head for their destination, Pat, Jo, and Jaime find themselves in conversation about core features, promises, and challenges of MTSS in early childhood . . . and wondering what the future of this approach might be.

CURRENT FEATURES OF MULTI-TIERED SYSTEMS OF SUPPORT THAT SHAPE ITS FUTURE

Reading policy briefs and research reports published between 2009 and 2016 (Buysse & Peisner-Feinberg, 2009; Carta et al., 2016; Coleman, Roth, & West, 2009; Linas, Carta, & Greenwood, 2010), one quickly concludes that MTSS, including Response to Intervention and other tiered interventions, are becoming increasingly common in early childhood programs. As the chapters in this book clearly demonstrate, policy, research, and practice have developed to a point where one can reflect on experiences to date, review current program implementation efforts, and anticipate activities tomorrow in the continued development of assessment and prevention/early intervention systems designed to better differentiate services for young children and families, and in turn improve outcomes *and* the efficiency with which they are attained.

Like other innovations in education, multi-tiered systems of support (or MTSS) will probably emerge in degrees and over time, with variations across programs, communities, and service delivery models. Such variation is both an asset, allowing future implementers to discern features that produce benefits and those that impede progress, and a challenge, particularly as evaluation of implementation efforts lags or produces varied results. For these reasons and others, now may be a fruitful time to consider factors that may propel or inhibit implementation of MTSS in early childhood, as well as those factors that may shape the ways it evolves over time.

CONTEXTUAL FEATURES OF EARLY EDUCATION AFFECTING MULTI-TIERED SYSTEMS OF SUPPORT

Laws, regulations, and the ongoing evolution of early education in the United States, or formal educational programs for children who are not yet old enough to enroll in kindergarten, are changing the face of programs by expanding the numbers and populations of children served, changing the ways children are served, and calling on education professionals to teach these children in new and more efficacious ways. Changes to the legal context of early education—changes that have occurred recently, and those very likely to arrive in the years ahead—both accelerate and potentially impede the need for MTSS in early education.

Legislative and Regulatory Variables

Arguably, the largest recent changes in services for preschool children are due to increased integration, alignment, and coherence in historically separate funding and regulatory programs at the federal level. Regulatory frameworks, discretionary funding programs, and directed research in three separate federal agencies—early childhood special education (administered federally by the Office of Special Education Programs in the Department of Education), Head Start (administered by the Office of Head Start, Administration for Children and Families, U.S. Department of Human Services), and child care (administered by the Office of Child Care, also within the Administration for Children and Families, U.S. Department of Human Services)—have examined, considered, incentivized, and (increasingly) pushed for greater programmatic integration and more seamless delivery of services both to improve individual channels of service (e.g., increasing inclusion for children with disabilities in Head Start classrooms and child care programs) and to better leverage sizable investments in early education.

Preschool for All (PSA), an initiative launched toward the end of President Obama's administration (https://www.acf.hhs.gov/ecd/preschool-for-all), lifted these initiatives to a new level of organization and visibility. PSA was designed to improve quality and expand access to early education for low- and moderate-income children by blending federal child care and Head Start money, leveraging state and local funds, and formalizing service delivery requirements. Although not explicitly requiring or encouraging MTSS in early education, PSA requires program features (e.g., regular and outcome-aligned assessment, rigorous curricula, trained workforce, ongoing program evaluation) that make implementation of these systems more likely.

Enabling legislation for these and other federal programs will likely continue to contribute to these changes. The Every Student Succeeds Act (ESSA), signed in 2015 and reauthorizing the Elementary and Secondary Education Act governing much of the broad outline of public education in the United States, both expands and more formally integrates early education programs into educational programming (First Five Years Fund, n.d.). Current federal law governing special education, the Individuals with Disabilities Education Improvement Act (IDEA) of 2004 (PL 108-446) similarly creates positive pressure; services to young children with disabilities are expected (at a minimum) to be provided in a least restrictive environment or settings (including inclusive settings), to assist children in accessing the general education curriculum, and to report outcomes indexed against general education standards for children served in preschool programs.

Complementary activities are occurring in many states and local communities. This is most clear in efforts to create publicly funded preschool programs. A number of states (including Georgia, Oklahoma, Florida, and New Jersey) have established statewide programs to provide classroom-based experiences for 4-year-olds (and, in some cases, younger children) that seek to both expand access and improve quality of early education programs (see Diffey, Parker, & Atchison, 2017). Similarly, several cities (perhaps most notably, New York City) are taking similar strides creating preschool programs that are intended, eventually, to provide educational opportunities for children before they begin kindergarten. These programs are generally similar in a stated intent of reducing later problems in academic achievement, and in reducing or eliminating disparities in educational achievement and attainment for different groups of children.

To date, these initiatives vary in several important ways. First, some programs are universal (providing access to all children who are age-eligible) and others are targeted (typically with eligibility determined by common risk factors like low family income, teen parents, or neighborhood of residence). Second, some state and local early education expansion efforts are located primarily in local educational agencies (or school districts), others leverage the private marketplace of early childhood providers, and some rely on a mixed delivery model of public and private early education programs. Generally, all of these efforts have some requirements for assessment, selected curricula, and staff qualifications, but fairly substantial variation exists across (and sometimes within) different jurisdictions. Finally, many of these efforts set the stage for thinking about increased coordination and alignment of services vertically across ages (i.e., how does early education support later school success?) and horizontally across funding and programmatic imperatives (how are services coordinated across, for instance, Head Start and child care programs?).

While these legislative and regulatory variables do not yet explicitly mandate MTSS in early education, a strong argument can be made that they set the table for such innovation. However, few of these programs are designed in ways that might assure high and uniform attainment of school readiness objectives. This variation from intention (at least part of the rationale for virtually all these programs is to promote school readiness and reduce the achievement gap) will prove challenging. As a result, one can reasonably expect efforts to integrate across needs-based systems (e.g., special education, Head Start, child care) while at the same time seeking better, and in many cases similar, outcomes for different groups of children. This goal, improved and similar outcomes for diverse groups of children, is perfectly consistent with expected outcomes of MTSS; as a result, both opportunities and requirements to implement features of MTSS in early education would be logical developments.

Social Variables

A variety of rather broad social, structural, and programmatic factors will likely affect the short- and medium-term development of MTSS in early education. While identifying and weighing these variables may be more art than science, several may warrant our attention, including increased interest in improving outcomes in early education, the ways in which early education is an increasingly important element of multidimensional initiatives, and a growing interest in differentiating services in ways that increase equity in outcomes.

Increased Interest in Improving Outcomes in Early Education   The final decades of the 20th century and early years of the 21st century produced substantial knowledge regarding ways that children's development prior to kindergarten entry contributes substantially to later achievement and success (Neuman & Dickinson, 2011; Shonkoff & Phillips, 2000; Snow, Burns, & Griffin, 1998). This knowledge has changed our core assumptions about the importance of early care and education (Pianta, Cox, & Snow, 2007) and has increased attention to systematic and reliable methods for helping young children learn and acquire essential skills and competencies (Division for Early Childhood, 2014). Although educators and advocates for young children are still not in full agreement, there is a clear and growing trend toward intentional efforts to increase young children's skills and competencies before kindergarten entry.

This focus on outcomes in preschool is not simple nor narrowly focused; although priority is often placed on language and early reading, most licensing bodies still define the desired outcomes in early childhood (those expected prior to kindergarten entry) across multiple domains, including language, early literacy, early numeracy and science, social-emotional competence, approaches to learning, art, self-care, and adaptive skills (National Association for the Education of Young Children & National Association of Early Childhood Specialists in State Departments of Education, 2002). In short, as the culture continues to evolve, one part of that evolution appears to be that preschoolers should be able to do more across this variety of developmental domains.

Early Childhood Care and Education as Part of Broader Community Development Efforts   Growth in civic support for early care and education in recent years has been driven, in part, by economic analyses that indicate both that expenditures for preschool programs return substantial returns on public investment (Heckman, 2006) and, as a result, contribute to a more skilled workforce and more robust state and national economies (Grunewald & Rolnick, 2003). Leaders in business and industry have joined with educators, politicians, and others to advocate for expanded preschool programming. One result has been an increasing awareness of, and attention to, services for young children and their families. This is apparent in efforts to better integrate resources and cohere outcomes in early education and child care through quality rating and improvement systems (Scott-Little & Maxwell, 2015), the central role and importance of early care and education in comprehensive individual and community development programs like the Obama Administration's Promise Neighborhoods (Komro, Flay, Biglan, & Promise Neighborhoods Research Consortium, 2011) and in more educationally focused interventions that are discussed later in this chapter.

Social Impact Bonds and Other Performance-Based Funding Mechanisms   Early education has joined other social and behavioral intervention systems by increasingly adopting performance-based funding mechanisms focused on both input and outcome variables. In addition to increasing requirements from federal, state, and local regulations for specific quality features, including seasonal assessments and use of data in instructional planning, these requirements are increasingly being paired with tiered reimbursement and funding models where early education programs receive additional funds for implementing important practices (Tout, Zaslow, Halle, & Forry, 2009).

More recently, the federal government and some philanthropic organizations have introduced differential funding based on the results that programs attain (Warner, 2013). These "pay for success" models focus specifically on the outcomes that programs obtain, typically indexed directly to both improving proportions of students achieving certain thresholds (e.g., school readiness) and for reducing disparities in children served by the program. Some pay for success models recruit private investments, at times from large and well-known investment banks and equity funds, to fund social impact bonds, with investors receiving returns on investments based on improved outcomes, and expected cost savings, from effective programs (Meehan, 2013).

These and other factors that both require effective practices and incent improved outcomes may not require MTSS models but certainly create fertile bases for their selection and implementation. MTSS is expected to improve outcomes within and across groups and to do so in efficient ways. As a result, MTSS becomes a key to meeting and achieving increasing expectations for early education.

Early Childhood Services as Part of the Move Toward Targeted Universalism Third, MTSS in early education is a resource to reduce disparities and increase equity. Like other tiered intervention approaches, these efforts rest on the principle of *targeted universalism* (Powell, 2008; Skocpol, 1991). Targeted universalism rejects the idea that equitable or equivalent outcomes can be produced by providing common or functionally equivalent resources for individuals (or groups) who differ in their need for instruction or support. Rather, to produce results that are similar across individuals or groups with different needs, resources must be differentially allocated based on those needs.

In early education, MTSS is one way to operationalize targeted universalism. Children at risk for later achievement problems, and particularly those already demonstrating a need for additional intervention to meet preschool developmental goals and expectations, should be provided supplemental instruction or intervention at levels needed to close gaps as soon as possible. MTSS does this with procedures that identify children who may benefit from supplemental intervention, interventions that grow in intensity and resource based on need, and protocols to frequently assess progress to continuously refine the nature and intensity of intervention.

Early Education Variables

Within the world of early education, another set of factors helps to shape the future of MTSS. Perhaps most significant has been the recent and rapid growth in evidence-based practices for assessing and teaching preschool children (Diamond, Justice, Siegler, & Snyder, 2013; Division for Early Childhood, 2014; Greenwood, Carta, & McConnell, 2011). These advances in both reliability and scope of practices for teaching a variety of skills to young children are essential to delivering the promise of early education as a preventive and compensatory effort, helping children meet developmental goals and establish solid foundations for later learning and accomplishment. This growing array of evidence-based practices becomes the foundation for improvements across tiers of intervention in MTSS (see Chapters 5, 6, and 8 for examples).

Closely paralleling these improvements in assessment and intervention, early education program developers and other behavioral scientists are learning important strategies for bringing effective practices to scale, ensuring broad application that balances adherence to essential features with adaptations that tailor interventions for local conditions (see Chapters 3 and 11). Together, accelerating research and development of evidence-based practices and methods for deploying these practices across situations and settings creates the resources needed to improve outcomes for all children.

Changes in preservice and in-service training also contribute to ongoing evolution of early education in ways that affect MTSS implementation. At the preservice level, at least two recent developments are noteworthy. First, an increasing number of teacher training programs are adopting integrated or comprehensive approaches to preparing students in early education and ECSE (Lim & Able-Boone, 2005). These programs provide joint classes and programming, integrated practicum or student teaching assignments, and explicit attention to practices for serving children with a variety of needs. As these programs also adapt to help future teachers meet requirements for practice after graduation—requirements that include assessment and intervention services aligned with or embedded in MTSS—preservice training will expand the base of professionals prepared for, and expecting to use, assessment and differentiated intervention in their classrooms.

But what about professionals already in practice? Again, a growing ecosystem of resources, from innovative research on training and professional development to state- and building-level leadership models that support and help implement ongoing professional development (see Chapters 2 and 11), to exciting innovations in real-time and asynchronous technology support for teachers in classrooms (Coogle, Rahn, & Ottley, 2015) are expanding and improving the core features needed for MTSS at classroom, program, and state or district levels.

GOING OUT ON A LIMB: FUTURE CHALLENGES AND OPPORTUNITIES

While predictions about the future are indeed difficult to make, the time to prepare for that future is now. Future implementation of MTSS will undoubtedly face headwinds of resistance and development but also tailwinds of purpose and positive experience. The following section covers some of these possible challenges and opportunities.

Challenges to Broad Adoption and Continued Development of MTSS

At least two challenges may restrict broad adoption and continued development of MTSS in the years ahead. First, underlying principles and widely adopted standards of scope and reach of early education—the audience to be served, and the outcomes this service is expected to produce—may be at odds with broad-scale adoption. Second, the current segmented or fractured nature of services to preschool children, including those developing typically and those with special needs, may restrict development and deployment of MTSS.

Conceptual Challenges of Scope and Reach   Early education has a long and rich history of innovation and success. However, while some can argue that its foundational roots are in the compensatory efforts of long-ago pioneers like Maria Montessori and Simon Binet or more recent leaders like Bettye Caldwell, David Weikert, or Craig Ramey, the imperative to intentionally design, teach, and assess preschool children has been challenged (see also Carta, Atwater, Schwartz, & McConnell, 1993). Significant numbers of early educators working in the United States today have adopted an approach to early education that emphasizes child-directed behavior and play, broad and less reliable approaches to describing child performance, and a general reluctance or active resistance to intentional and specific approaches to setting goals; assessing status and progress; or providing instruction, intervention, and experience that help children achieve specific goals. This reluctance or resistance can impede efforts to implement essential elements of MTSS in early education.

Effects on Assessment for Identification and Progress Monitoring   Direct assessment of child skills, at one time or repeatedly, is controversial in many quarters. At times, program leaders and practitioners resist on-demand assessments (those in which children are asked to respond to specific questions or assessment tasks, often in structured adult-directed activities). Sometimes, specific program compliance requirements call for assessment measures that are "authentic and observationally based." These words are poorly defined terms that are typically interpreted as requiring avoidance of structured, adult-directed, or on-demand assessments. Finally, assessment systems are at times required to be comprehensive across an array of developmental domains that may or may not be the object of intervention and future social and academic success.

Taken together, these concerns or preferences about assessment can lead to measurement systems that are cumbersome and expensive, and lacking in important psychometric features. More troubling, these concerns or preferences are sometimes based on little or no attention to research and evaluation; instead, broad beliefs about the nature and causes of children's development trump scientific developments. This would not be troubling if the resulting practices happened to have positive features. However, this seems to be too seldom true; instead, some jurisdictions and programs favor practices that are expensive, lack features of psychometric rigor and, through their implementation, crowd-out practices that would better serve efforts to improve outcomes for all children. Favoring these practices crowds out, and even inhibits, development of engaging, focused, and purposeful assessments that both meet rigorous quality standards and efficiently provide teachers and others information they can use to inform and improve intervention.

Effects on Intervention at All Three Tiers of Service   Some contemporary conceptual models have similar consequences for intervention elements of MTSS. Although an argument can be made that resistance to intentional and effective intervention has declined (especially as noted in position papers and advocacy of professional organizations and requirements for scientifically based curricula within state or local education agency program requirements), controversy or disagreement remains. There may be less controversy about the importance of intentional and intensive intervention for children with greater need, including children eligible for Tier 2 or Tier 3 services in MTSS, or children receiving special education services (Division for Early Childhood, Council for Exceptional Children, National Association for the Education of Young Children, & National Head Start Association, 2014). However, discourse about more highly specified or more structured instructional interactions at Tier 1 still occasions hesitation or rejection by early educators or their program managers (Carlsson-Paige, 2008).

Overall Effect on MTSS   Can MTSS be efficacious in programs that avoid systematic assessment and intentional and at times adult-directed intervention? Currently, there is very little evidence and no strong arguments to suggest this. Rather, the current state of knowledge in assessment (Greenwood et al., 2011) and intervention (Diamond et al., 2013) suggests that reliable effects require a relatively high degree of specification and some simple to moderate level of structure and fidelity. Without question, the procedures associated with assessment and intervention should be acceptable to teachers, program managers, parents, and others. Furthermore, to be effective and implemented, these assessment and instructional procedures must be engaging, and even enjoyable, to the children receiving them.

However, standards for acceptability are not absolute, and demonstrations that intentional assessment and intervention can both produce good outcomes and be implemented in ways that are joyful and efficient may be needed to shift underlying conceptual beliefs of some early educators. This is an obligation not only for researchers and program developers but also for program leaders and champions of high-quality service; together, these groups can and should continue their efforts to expand, adopt, and support effective practices.

Ongoing Development of Unified Services for Early Education This chapter earlier discussed changes in laws and regulations governing early education at the federal level, and complementary activities at state and local levels of program operation. Although promising, in practice many children still live in areas where early education services are siloed, highly fractured across agencies, and far from universal in reach.

This lack of universal access creates the first challenge for implementing MTSS in early education. Educators have no confidence that a high-quality Tier 1 experience is offered to all children; indeed, it cannot yet be conceptualized what this universal curriculum would be for children spending substantial portions of time at home or in unlicensed child care or licensed child care or Head Start or preschool; the conclusion is only that they might well be different. Furthermore, one of the core principles of MTSS is the idea that *all* children will be periodically screened and that *any* children who might benefit will be provided higher-intensity Tier 2 or Tier 3 services. This is relatively straightforward, for instance, in MTSS systems for reading in elementary grades; second graders can be screened in all second-grade classrooms. The analog for 4-year-olds, however, is not clear; there is not one system, or even a small and known number of systems, for receiving universal screening and provision of supplemental services.

The population of children enrolled in known early education programs (e.g., preschool programs provided by local school districts or their partners, Head Start agencies, large child care centers licensed by states) is also changing. Historically in the United States, publicly funded early education services have more typically been provided to children considered at risk for later challenges in achievement and success in school (e.g., children in poverty, those whose parents speak languages other than English, those with disabilities). While the logic and results of these targeted efforts have clear merit, often the criteria associated with eligibility are correlated with factors that might suggest the need for Tier 2 or Tier 3 services. As a result, expected results of MTSS screening assessments (e.g., assumptions that 80% of children are benefiting from Tier 1 service, 15% might require Tier 2 service, and 5% are likely to require Tier 3 service) may not be met. Adaptations to assessment and programming across all tiers in programs like these are essential. While these adaptations may need to be very local in scope (reflecting population, goals, and resources of an individual program) or reflect research and development that is not yet available, possibilities include increased dosages of intervention (e.g., full-day, full-year programming), improvements in Tier 1 services, or more radical transformations that provide the care, intensity, and ongoing monitoring for all children that is sometimes associated with only Tier 2 or Tier 3 services.

Finally, as a unified early education system continues to evolve, individual children may encounter a significant variation in both the array and quality of services as a function of characteristics of their family and where they live. Rigor and quality of assessment, intervention, and staffing in early education continue to make significant improvements, but significant variability still exists. This variability provides a challenging context for implementation of high-quality MTSS services.

Limits on the Speed of Innovation and Implementation   Like any rapidly evolving system, early education in early decades of the 21st century is characterized by rapid and sometimes chaotic revision. Conceptual foundations, legal authority, programming options, staff qualifications, and an array of other variables change in related and unrelated ways. Standards for judging progress at systems and community levels are similarly dynamic. Given this dynamic and multi-dimensional context, it may be very difficult to discern systematic development and iterative improvement. However, careful, systematic, and continuous efforts to develop and refine systems like MTSS are essential; as a result, advocates need to persist, to work hard, and to engage others in discussions that yield increased understanding, agreement, and joint effort.

Promising Factors Driving Adoption and Continued Development of MTSS

While challenges may seem daunting, their effects are blunted by an array of important promises and recent developments that will contribute to ongoing development of MTSS in early education. First, among these is a strong and growing civic commitment to supporting the development of preschool-age children. In an era of tremendous political acrimony both in legislatures and communities, it is noteworthy that support for expanding and improving early education crosses most political spectrums and only appears to grow over time (e.g., Wong, 2015). At the federal level, support for Head Start and ongoing evolution of child care appear to be solid, and expansion of access continues to receive priority. States and local communities have passed constitutional amendments to expand early education (Hartle & Ghazvini, 2014) and have established new programs and funding streams to increase program options. This commitment to making a difference in the developmental course of young children, and to doing so in ways that support school and lifelong success, provides a solid foundation and important engine for continued development of MTSS and other features of early education. This social and civic commitment is buttressed by the growing body of research on the importance of early development for later achievement and success (e.g., Shonkoff & Phillips, 2000) and on assessment and intervention procedures that can contribute to this development (e.g., Buysse & Peisner-Feinberg, 2013; Diamond et al., 2013; Dickinson & Neuman, 2006; Neuman & Dickinson, 2001, 2011; Snow et al., 1998).

Growing political, social, and civic commitment is directly supported by the growing cadre of teachers, administrators, researchers, and policymakers who are driving ongoing innovation and improvement. The authors of chapters included in this book, and many others, are part of a burgeoning group committed to better integrating parents and communities; extending their reach to children who speak other languages and those with disabilities; and expanding their efforts to review, evaluate, and work to improve program services at the level of individual children, local programs, districts, and states.

Educators, program specialists, program/school leaders, and others are learning quickly how to shorten the interval between research findings and broad-scale, high-fidelity implementation of effective practices. Implementation Science (Cook

& Odom, 2013; Fixsen, Naoom, Blase, Friedman, & Wallace, 2005; see Chapter 3) is detailing ways that researchers should design and evaluate procedures; administrators and advocates should prepare the ground for implementation; and service systems should roll out new practices and refine these practices over time.

MTSS for young children also becomes more viable as program elements in early education and its K–12 counterpart continue to align and integrate. Although a great deal more alignment and integration is possible, substantial progress has already been made. Funding and program options link together seemingly separate efforts like Head Start, ECSE, early education, and child care. States and local districts examine ways to better align age-3-to-grade-3 curriculum and instruction (see Daily, 2014). Integrated data systems create mechanisms for increasing coordination and efficiency of services across program boundaries (e.g., Data Quality Campaign & Early Childhood Data Collective, 2016). Each of these developments brings a broader array of assessment and intervention options together in one system and sets the ground for MTSS implementation.

Educators, program specialists, program/school leaders, and others also are witnessing attention to increasing quality in all sectors of early education and care. As noted, many funding programs now require not only scientifically based curricula but also outcome assessments that are aligned with or predictive of early elementary achievement. While variability in both the form and function of these requirements continues, and while resources for using this information to drive toward program improvement are still emerging, this press to improve outcomes associated with early education is a clear incentive—and perhaps even a necessary condition—for implementation of MTSS.

CONCLUSION

The chapters of this book make clear that MTSS is not a single, easy-to-define "thing," but rather an elegant and dynamic process for observing children's development and for providing timely and effective supports to contribute to this development when needed. MTSS is a mechanism for bringing targeted universalism to early education and to improving outcomes for all children in the most efficient ways possible.

MTSS is not a free-standing solution but rather a set of principles (and, in many instances, practices) that have strong potential to improve efficacy *and* efficiency of early education. To achieve this promise will likely require ongoing collaboration of parents, practitioners, program managers, policymakers, higher education trainers, researchers, and others. It will require clear, strong, and enduring efforts to prompt and support implementation. And it will require commitment and effort to conduct continuous review and improvement of efforts over time. MTSS is a good idea, and there are some very promising demonstrations of that value. Now is the time to bring those ideas to scale.

The plane has finally reached its destination and is taxiing to the gate for passengers to exit. Pat, Jo, and Jaime have spent the entire flight talking, laughing, arguing, and planning. They have noticed how they share very similar goals: They want all children to succeed, they think early education can be an instrumental part of ensuring that success, and they think it can be done in ways that are both fun and efficient. However, they also see how their respective roles in that effort are quite different, but directly linked to the efforts of their seatmates. They notice strong evidence for some assessment and intervention practices, some promising or sensible plans for other components of service, and many areas where a great deal more information is needed. They agree that making MTSS work will require commitment, reliance on the best and most rigorous procedures they can find, and ongoing effort to develop, evaluate, and refine what they each do to make it work.

Jo, the state's Part B ECSE coordinator, sees clearly that leadership is needed at the state level in various ways. First, it is important to clearly describe the ways in which special education and MTSS support, align, and complement one another both in services to children with disabilities and in preventing the need for future special education services. Leadership will also be needed in coordination with other state-level administrators with the goal of crafting a shared mission and coordinated activities that support (and do not impede) implementation efforts. There may also be opportunities to provide professional development to ECSE staff interested in consulting with public and other community-based programs on design, implementation, and ongoing support of MTSS for both behavior and early academic skills.

Pat sees a complementary, but quite different, set of leadership opportunities. In particular, guiding programs to adopt both a culture and commitment to differentiated and effective services, and providing material, training, and other supports to help implement these changes, is critical. There also will be opportunities to determine and increase alignment with other early childhood services in the area, continuing to expand their emerging commitment to inclusive and comprehensive services for all preschool children. It is also important to find ways to take advantage of training, professional development, and other resources the state can provide and to use these resources wisely as the program comes to scale.

Jaime is perhaps most excited. As an early educator, Jaime and her colleagues have a great commitment to serving all children—but they are sometimes uncertain about how to do so. MTSS seems to have specific, actionable ways of doing so but will require a big change in both how the teachers define their jobs and how they spend their time. Jaime thinks about ways to build and support new practices and wonders if embedded professional development opportunities such as coaching and Professional Learning Communities ([PLCs] Dufour et al., 2010) may be important ingredients in this new effort.

As they deplane, now with new and strong collegial connections, they commit to meeting again soon; to recruiting colleagues to join them; and to beginning review, planning, and implementation. They agree: There is promise, but there is also hard work ahead.

RESOURCES

The BUILD Initiative. http://www.buildinitiative.org. The BUILD Initiative supports state leaders' efforts to develop a comprehensive early childhood system tailored to the needs of their state's young children and families. This systems building approach helps children thrive, while carefully using private and public resources.

Center for Response to Intervention in Early Childhood (CRTIEC). http://www.crtiec.dept.ku.edu. This is a web site with resources derived from CRTIEC, a research and development center funded from 2008 to 2014 by the Institute of Education Sciences, National Center for Special Education Research to develop measures and interventions for advancing tiered models to support early literacy and language in young children.

Diamond, K. E., Justice, L. M., Siegler, R. S., & Snyder, P. A. (2013). *Synthesis of IES research on early intervention and early childhood education* (NCSER 2013-3001). Retrieved from http://ies.ed.gov/ncser/pubs/20133001/pdf/20133001.pdf

Division for Early Childhood (DEC), National Association for the Education of Young Children (NAEYC), & National Head Start Association (NHSA). (2013). *Frameworks for Response to Intervention in early childhood: Description and implications*. Missoula, MT: Author. Retrieved from http://www.dec-sped.org/position-statements

Greenwood, C. R., Carta, J. J., & McConnell, S. (2011). Advances in measurement for universal screening and individual progress monitoring of young children. *Journal of Early Intervention, 33*(4), 254–267. https://doi.org/10.1177/1053815111428467

REFERENCES

Buysse, V. & Peisner-Feinberg, E. (2009). Recognition and Response (R & R): Implementation sites in Florida and Maryland. In M. R. Coleman, F. P. Roth, & T. West (Eds.), Roadmap to pre-K RTI: Applying response to intervention in preschool settings (pp. 9-10). New York, NY: National Center for Learning Disabilities. Retrieved from http://www.rtinetwork.org/images/roadmaptoprekrti.pdf

Buysse, V., & Peisner-Feinberg, E. (Eds.). (2013). *Handbook of Response to Intervention in early childhood*. Baltimore, MD: Paul H. Brookes Publishing Co.

Carlsson-Paige, N. (2008). Reclaiming play: Helping children learn and thrive in school. *Exchange: The Early Childhood Leaders' Magazine since 1978, 180,* 44–48.

Carta, J. J., Atwater, J. B., Schwartz, I. S., & McConnell, S. R. (1993). Developmentally appropriate practices and early child special education: A reaction to Johnson and McChesney Johnson. *Topics in Early Childhood Special Education, 13*(3), 243–254.

Carta, J. J., Greenwood, C. R., Goldstein, H., McConnell, S. R., Kaminski, R., Bradfield, T. A., ... Atwater, J. (2016). Advances in multi-tiered systems of support for prekindergarten children: Lessons learned from 5 years of research and development from the Center for Response to Intervention in Early Childhood. In S. R. Jimerson, M. K. Burns, & A. M. VanDerHeyden (Eds.), *Handbook of Response to Intervention* (pp. 587–606). New York, NY: Springer. Retrieved from http://link.springer.com/chapter/10.1007/978-1-4899-7568-3_33

Coleman, M. R., Roth, F. P., & West, T. (Eds.). (2009). *Roadmap to Pre-K RTI: Applying Response to Intervention in preschool settings*. New York, NY: National Center for Learning Disabilities.

Coogle, C. G., Rahn, N. L., & Ottley, J. R. (2015). Pre-service teacher use of communication strategies upon receiving immediate feedback. *Early Childhood Research Quarterly, 32,* 105–115. https://doi.org/10.1016/j.ecresq.2015.03.003

Cook, B. G., & Odom, S. L. (2013). Evidence-based practices and implementation science in special education. *Exceptional Children, 79*(2), 135–144.

Daily, S. (2014, October). *Initiatives from preschool to third grade: A policymaker's guide* (Unpublished manuscript). Denver, CO: Education Commission of the States. Retrieved from http://www.ecs.org/docs/early-learning-primer.pdf

Data Quality Campaign & Early Childhood Data Collective. (2016). *Roadmap for early childhood and K–12 data linkages: Key focus areas to ensure quality implementation* (Unpublished manuscript). Bethesda, MD.: Early Childhood Data Collaborative. Retrieved from http://www.ecedata.org/publications/roadmap-early-childhood

Diamond, K. E., Justice, L. M., Siegler, R. S., & Snyder, P. A. (2013). *Synthesis of IES research on early intervention and early childhood education* (NCSER 2013-3001). Retrieved from http://ies.ed.gov/ncser/pubs/20133001/pdf/20133001.pdf

Dickinson, D. K., & Neuman, S. B. (Eds.). (2006). *Handbook of early literacy research* (Vol. 2). New York, NY: Guilford Press.

Diffey, L., Parker, E., & Atchison, B. (2017, January). *State pre-k funding 2016–17 fiscal year: Trends and opportunities.* Retrieved from http://www.ecs.org/ec-content/uploads/State-Pre-K-Funding-2016-17-Fiscal-Year-Trends-and-opportunities-1.pdf

Division for Early Childhood. (2014). *DEC recommended practices in early intervention/early childhood special education 2014.* Arlington, VA: Author. Retrieved from http://www.dec-sped.org/recommendedpractices

Division for Early Childhood, Council for Exceptional Children, National Association for the Education of Young Children, & National Head Start Association. (2014). Frameworks for Response to Intervention in early childhood. *Communication Disorders Quarterly, 35*(2), 108–119.

Dufour, R., Dufour, R., Eaker, R., & Many, T. (2010). *Learning by Doing: A Handbook for Professional Learning Communities at Work* (2nd ed.). Bloomington, IN: Solution Tree Press.

Elementary and Secondary Education Act of 1965, PL 89-10, 20 U.S.C. §§ 241 *et seq.*

ESSA (2015). Every Student Succeeds Act of 2015, PL 114-95, §§ 114 Stat. 1177.

First Five Years Fund. (n.d.). *Analysis: Early learning provisions of the Every Student Succeeds Act.* Retrieved from http://ffyf.org/resources/eceinessa2015

Fixsen, D. L., Naoom, S. F., Blase, K. A., Friedman, R. M., & Wallace, F. (2005). *Implementation research: A synthesis of the literature.* (FMHI Publication #231). Tampa: University of South Florida, Louis de la Parte Florida Mental Health Institute, The National Implementation Network.

Greenwood, C. R., Carta, J. J., & McConnell, S. (2011). Advances in measurement for universal screening and individual progress monitoring of young children. *Journal of Early Intervention, 33*(4), 254–267. https://doi.org/10.1177/1053815111428467

Grunewald, R., & Rolnick, A. (2003, December). Early childhood development: Economic development with a high public return. *The Region, 17*(4), 6–12.

Hartle, L., & Ghazvini, A. S. (2014). Florida's voluntary universal prekindergarten: A citizen's initiative meets political and policy realities. In *World Class Initiatives and Practices in Early Education* (pp. 33–52). New York, NY: Springer.

Heckman, J. J. (2006). Skill formation and the economics of investing in disadvantaged children. *Science, 312*(5782), 1900–1902. https://doi.org/10.1126/science.1128898.

Individuals with Disabilities Education Improvement Act of 2004, PL 108-446, 20 U.S.C. §§ 1400 *et seq.*

Komro, K. A., Flay, B. R., Biglan, A., & Promise Neighborhoods Research Consortium. (2011). Creating nurturing environments: A science-based framework for promoting child health and development within high-poverty neighborhoods. *Clinical Child and Family Psychology Review, 14*, 111–134. https://doi.org/10.1007/s10567-011-0095-2

Lim, C.-I., & Able-Boone, H. (2005). Diversity competencies within early childhood teacher preparation: Innovative practices and future directions. *Journal of Early Childhood Teacher Education, 26*(3), 225–238. https://doi.org/10.1080/10901020500369803

Linas, M., Carta, J. J., & Greenwood, C. R. (2010). *2nd annual taking a snapshot of early childhood Response to Intervention (RTI) across the USA.* Retrieved from http://www.crtiec.org/aboutcrtiec/documents/CRTIECUSSurveySnapShotNationalReporMethodst2010.pdf

Meehan, S. (2013). Pre-K program attracts investors out for returns. *Education Week, 32*(1), 18–19.

National Association for the Education of Young Children & National Association of Early Childhood Specialists in State Departments of Education. (2002). *Early learning standards: Creating the conditions for success.* Washington, DC: National Association for the Education of Young Children.

Neuman, S. B., & Dickinson, D. K. (Eds.). (2001). *Handbook of early literacy research* (Vol. 1). New York, NY: Guilford Press.

Neuman, S. B., & Dickinson, D. K. (Eds.). (2011). *Handbook of early literacy research* (Vol. 3). New York, NY: Guilford Press.

Pianta, R. C., Cox, M. J., & Snow, K. L. (Eds.). (2007). *School readiness and the transition to kindergarten in the era of accountability.* Baltimore, MD: Paul H. Brookes Publishing Co.

Powell, J. A. (2008). Post-racialism or targeted universalism. *Denver University Law Review, 86,* 785.

Scott-Little, C., & Maxwell, K. (2015). Improving systems of learning through the use of child standards and assessments. In *Rising to the challenge: Building effective systems for young children and families, a BUILD E-Book* (pp. 28–31). Boston, MA: BUILD Initiative. Retrieved from http://www.buildinitiative.org/Portals/0/Uploads/Documents/E-BookChapter6ImprovingSystemsofLearningThroughtheUseofChildStandardsandAssessments.pdf

Shonkoff, J. P., & Phillips, D. (2000). *From neurons to neighborhoods: The science of early childhood development.* Washington, DC: National Academies Press.

Skocpol, T. (1991). Targeting within universalism: Politically viable policies to combat poverty in the United States. In C. Jencks & P. Peterson (Eds.), *The urban underclass* (pp. 411–436). Washington, DC: The Brookings Institution.

Snow, C. E., Burns, M. S., & Griffin, P. (Eds.). (1998). *Preventing reading difficulties in young children.* Washington, DC: National Academies Press.

Tout, K., Zaslow, M., Halle, T. G., & Forry, N. (2009). *Issues for the next decade of Quality Rating and Improvement Systems* (OPRE Issue Brief #3 No. 2009–14). Washington, DC: Child Trends. Retrieved from https://www.researchgate.net/profile/Tamara_Halle/publication/237267473_Issues_for_the_Next_DecaDe_of_QualIty_ratINg_aND_ImprovemeNt_systems/links/0c960535d6f0e415fe000000.pdf

Warner, M. E. (2013). Private finance for public goods: Social impact bonds. *Journal of Economic Policy Reform, 16*(4), 303–319. https://doi.org/10.1080/17487870.2013.835727

Wong, A. (2015, October). The bipartisan appeal of Pre-K. *The Atlantic.* Retrieved from https://www.theatlantic.com/education/archive/2015/10/pre-k-vs-college/412048

Index

References to tables, figures, and notes are indicated with a *t*, *f*, and *n*, respectively.

Academic year data-collection and decision-making calendar, 33*f*
Accountability
 exploration, 69
 in leadership practices, 20–21
Achievement gap, 1
 Instructional Support, Tier 3, 159
 multi-tiered systems of support (MTSS) future, 258
Active Implementation Frameworks (AIFs)
 Implementation Science (IS) and, 41–59, 49*f*, 50*f*, 56*f*, 57*f*, 63, 69
Activity matrix, in Social-emotional outcomes, Tier 2, 140–141, 141*f*, 145, 148
Administration
 Behavior Incident Report and, 136, 137*f*
 facilitative, 54*f*, 55
 Obama Administration's Promise Neighborhoods, 257
Administrative leadership team (LEAD team)
 for targeted outcomes collaboration, 25–26, 27*f*
Administrative support and resources, in multi-tiered systems of support (MTSS), 11
Ages & Stages Questionnaires®: Social-Emotional, Second Edition, 136
Alphabet knowledge skills, 118*f*, 119*f*, 120*f*, 122*t*
 in Literacy and Language, Tier 2, 117
Alphabet progress, 118*f*, 119*f*, 120*f*
 in Literacy and Language, Tier 2, 117–119
Assessment
 of critical skills, 101
 definition of, 74
 fidelity, 54*t*, 55
 of Individualized education programs (IEPs), 33*f*
 of Individuals with Disabilities Education Improvement Act (IDEA) of 2004 (PL 108-446), 16
 by Instructional Leadership Team (ILT), 32
 Instructional support, Tier 3, 157–158, 158*f*
 intervention and, 77–78, 79*f*
 in leadership practices, 25, 32, 33*f*
 in multi-tiered systems of support (MTSS) future, 258, 260, 263
 practical performance, 47
 purpose of, 74
 Self-Assessment of Family Engagement Practices, 238, 249–250, 250*n*
 in usable innovation selection, 47
Authority, *see* Implementation Teams

Bal Swan Children's Center, scaling up in, 228
Battelle Developmental Inventory-2, Spanish Screening, 176*t*
Behavior incident report, 136, 137*f*, 138
Behavior rating scales, in Social-emotional outcomes, Tier 2, 136, 137*f*, 148
Behaviors, 80
 family engagement and, 235, 237
 target skills and data on, 81–82, 82*f*
Benchmarks
 in Literacy and Language, 84, 84*f*, 85*f*, 86
 as static scores, 83–84
 see also Pyramid Model State Benchmarks of Quality (BoQ)
Bilingual advantages, of dual language learners (DLLs), 172
Bilingual Input/Output Survey, 180
Burmese language, dual language learners and, 171, 185–186

Center for Response to Intervention in Early Childhood (CRTIEC)
 disabilities in blended ECE-ECSE MTSS and, 196
 in Literacy and Language, Tier 1, 98–100

269

Center on the Social and Emotional Foundations for Early Learning, 218, 218n
Classroom Code for Interactive Recording of Children's Literacy Environments (CIRCLE), 100
Classroom-level analysis, 88
Coaching, 47–48, 54, 54t
  practice-based coaching (PBC), 105–106, 146
  in scaling up, 221f, 226–227
Code-focused skills, in Literacy and Language, Tier 2, 116–117
Collaboration
  in multi-tiered systems of support (MTSS) future, 263
  within stakeholders, 57
Collaborative for Academic, Social, and Emotional Learning (CASEL), 132
Colorado, scaling up in, 224, 228
Communication, 22, 26
  in exploration, 64
  family engagement and, 241–242, 241t, 242t, 245
  in full implementation, 67
  for initial implementation, 66
  of Instructional Leadership Team (ILT), 33
  in leadership practices, 33
  in Self-Assessment of Family Engagement Practices, 249–250, 250n
Communication cycle, 56–57, 56f, 57f
Competency drivers, 54, 54f
  in scaling up, 216–217
Connect4Learning, in Social-emotional outcomes, Tier 2, 133–134
The Creative Curriculum, in Social-emotional outcomes, Tier 2, 133–134
Curricular factors, 77f

Data
  academic year data-collection and decision-making calendar, 33f
  class-level, 12
  disabilities in blended ECE-ECSE MTSS and, 206, 206f
  on target skills or behaviors, 81–82, 82f
Data-based decision making, 33f, 54f, 55–56
  comparisons in
    intraindividual and interindividual, 87
    scores across time in, 84–87, 84f, 85f
    static scores in, 83–84
  levels of, 88, 92
  scaling up and, 217–218, 220, 221f, 222–223
Data-based problem solving, 7, 12, 45–46

Decision making, 7
  academic year calendar for, 33f
  in disabilities in blended ECE-ECSE MTSS, 204–205, 208
  family engagement and, 241t, 243, 243t, 245
  for installation, 65
  in Social-emotional outcomes, Tier 2, 146
Developing Talkers/Hablemos Junto, 183, 185
Developmental Indicators for the Assessment of Learning Spanish, 176t
Developmentally appropriate practices (DAPs), 24
Disabilities in blended ECE-ECSE MTSS
  blended practice model in, 198–199
  Center for Response to Intervention in Early Childhood (CRTIEC) and, 196
  developmental delays and, 193–194, 207–208
  Division for Early Childhood (DEC), 196, 198, 202
  early intervention (EI) services, 193
  eligibility of, 200t, 203
  example 1: same-age peers, 203–204
  example 2: decreasing intensity, 204–205
  example 3: speech impairment, 205
  example 4: vocabulary, 206–207, 206f, 207f
  example 5: developmental delay, 207–208
  family and, 193–194, 204
  framework for, 197
  general education curriculum and, 194, 199, 204–205, 210
  inclusion and, 198
  inclusive/blended classrooms and, 194–195, 198–199, 200t–201t, 201–203
  individualized education programs (IEPs), 193–194, 199, 201–204, 208–211
  individualized family service plan (IFSP), 193
  individuals with Disabilities Education Improvement Act (IDEA) of 2004 (PL 108-446) and, 194–197, 199, 200t–201t, 205, 209–211
  innovation and, 199
  myths and truths
    individualized education programs (IEPs) and, 208–209
    intensity, 209–210
  National Association for the Education of Young Children (NAEYC) and, 196, 198
  National Head Start Association (NHSA), 196
  Office of Special Education Programs (OSEP) and, 209
  proactive model in, 199

progress monitoring of, 201t, 211
Response to Intervention (RtI) and, 195–197
school districts and, 194
self-contained classrooms and, 210
system initiatives and cultural shifts about, 195–210, 200t–201t, 206f, 207f
universal screening data on vocabulary and, 206, 206f
Distal measures, 165–166
Diversity
of dual language learners (DLLs), 172, 174–175, 176t–177t
multi-tiered systems of support (MTSS) future and, 253
Division for Early Childhood (DEC), 11
disabilities in blended ECE-ECSE MTSS and, 196, 198, 202
leadership practices for, 23
Dual language learners (DLLs)
assessment of
cultural and social contexts, 174–175, 176t–177t
dialects and, 174–175, 176t–177t
home language in, 175, 177t, 179
informality in, 179
interlocutor sensitivity in, 175, 178
interpreter support of, 178
Istation ISIP Early Reading (Mathes) in Spanish, 175, 177t, 179
measurement approaches in, 178–179
norms and, 176t–177t
screening and progress-monitoring measures, 174–175, 176t–177t, 178
Spanish Individual Growth and Development Indicators, 175, 177t
standards of practice in, 178
universal screening, 173–174
bilingual advantages of, 172
challenges of, 172
description of, 172
diversity of, 172, 174–175, 176t–177t
home-language surveys, 179–180, 191f–192f
Language Exposure Evaluation Report (LEER) for, 180, 191f–192f
languages spoken, 191f–192f
need and, 172, 185–186
poverty and, 172
Tier 1, 184–185
English-language instruction adaptation, 180–181
families' interventions, 182
home-language instruction, 180, 185
language-bridging techniques, 181
supplemental small-group language and literacy instruction, 181
visual and graphic cues, real objects in, 181, 185–186

Tier 2, 173
curriculum for, 182
Developing Talkers/Hablemos Junto, 183, 185
Get Ready to Read, 183
Puentos de Cuentos, 183
Read It Again Dual Language, 182
Read It Again-PreK!, 182
Story Champs, 183
Tier 3, 173
candidates for, 184
differentiation difficulty, 183–184
indications for use, 183
strategies for, 184
Vocabulary Oral Language and Academic Readiness (VOLAR), 184
tiered instruction for, 179–180

Early childhood education (ECE)
challenges in, 1
multi-tiered systems of support (MTSS) in, 7–11
Early Childhood Leadership Team (ECLT) Implementation Science (IS) and, 41–42
Early childhood special education (ECSE)
in targeted outcomes collaboration, 27f–28f
Early childhood system, 18
Early intervention (EI) services, in disabilities in blended ECE-ECSE MTSS, 193
Early learning program, delays and disabilities in, 19–20
Ecological theory, family engagement and, 235–236
Elementary and Secondary Education Act, in multi-tiered systems of support (MTSS) future, 255
Eligibility
of disabilities in blended ECE-ECSE MTSS, 200t, 203
multi-tiered systems of support (MTSS) future and, 261
in problem-solving model, 82f
Embedding
in Instructional support, Tier 3, 165f
in Social-emotional outcomes, Tier 2, 142
Emotions, see Social-emotional outcomes
Engagement, 86f, 87
in intervention development and implementation, 90–91
see also Family engagement
English language learners (ELLs), 23
Evaluation
of Response to intervention (RtI), 7
in scaling up, 230

Every Student Succeeds Act (ESSA) of 2015 (PL 114-95), 11
  in multi-tiered systems of support (MTSS) future, 255
Evidence-based practices (EBPs)
  effectiveness of, 4
  in intervention design, 3
  in Literacy and Language, Tier 1, 102–103
  in Literacy and Language, Tier 2, 126
  in multi-tiered systems of support (MTSS), 4, 10
  multi-tiered systems of support (MTSS) future and, 258, 260
Exemplary Model of Early Reading Growth and Excellence (EMERGE), 121, 122t
Explicit instruction
  Instructional support, Tier 3, and, 160, 166
  for Literacy and Language, Tier 1, 102–103
  for Literacy and Language, Tier 2, 121
  in Tune-Up Checklist, 111t
Exploration
  capacity in, 71
  communication in, 64
  data analysis in, 63–64, 70
  decision making in, 64
  in family engagement, 237
  Implementation Teams formation in, 63, 69
  meeting frequency in, 64
  readiness in, 63, 71
  resources in, 63–64, 70
  target selection in, 70
  time and, 50, 50f, 63–64, 69–71
Exploration and installation stages
  in Pyramid Model State Benchmarks of Quality (BoQ), 221–223
  in scaling up, 221–225, 221f, 227

Facilitative administration, 54f, 55
Families
  cultural awareness and sensitivity, 250
  disabilities in blended ECE-ECSE MTSS and, 193–194, 204
  dual language learners (DLLs) and, 182, 192f
  leadership practices and, 25
  multi-tiered systems of support (MTSS) and, 7
  Social-emotional outcomes, Tier 2 and, 137f, 145, 147
  values and practices, 250
Family engagement
  action plans about, 244
  behaviors and, 235, 237
  child social outcomes and, 237
  classroom opportunities for, 239, 239f
  communication and, 241–242, 241t, 242t, 245
  competency affirmation and, 242t
  consistency from, 237, 245
  description of, 236–237
  family-school partnership, 237
  Getting-Ready intervention strategies, 240
    collaborative interactions, 243t, 244
    competencies building, 241t, 242t
    decision making, 241t, 243, 243t, 245
    definitions and strategies in, 241t
    Home-School Plan, 243–244, 243t, 251f
    model and suggest in, 241t, 242t
    monitor and modify, 243t
    relationships building, 241t, 242t, 245
    structure for, 243–244, 243t
  language and literacy and, 237
  parent-child relationship, 236–237
  professional support for, 244, 249–250
  The Roadmap to Pre-K RTI, 238
  Self-Assessment of Family Engagement Practices, 238, 249–250, 250n
  shared responsibility with, 243, 245
  stakeholders and, 244, 249–250
  structured opportunities for, 239, 244
  targeted opportunities for, 239–240, 239f, 244
  universal opportunities for, 238–240, 239f, 244
  unstructured opportunities for, 239
Federal support, 10–11
Feedback, for guided practice, 102–103
Feedback loops, 64, 67
  for initial implementation, 65–66
  practice-policy, 56–57, 57f
Fidelity assessment, 54t, 55
Forest Friends, in Literacy and Language, Tier 2, 123
From Neurons to Neighborhoods: The Science of Early Childhood Development, 132
Full implementation, 50f, 51
  communication in, 67
  decision making in, 67
  enhancements for, 66
  improvement cycles for, 66
  infrastructure for, 66
  practitioner competency improvement for, 66
Funding, in multi-tiered systems of support (MTSS) future, 254–255, 257–258

General education curriculum, in disabilities in blended ECE-ECSE MTSS and, 194, 199, 204–205, 210

Goals, 19–20
  in targeted outcomes collaboration, 28, 30, 31t–32t
Guided practice, 102–103

Head Start, 2, 20
  multi-tiered systems of support (MTSS) future and, 253, 255–256
  National Head Start Association (NHSA), 11, 196
  Southeast Kansas Community Action Program Head Start, 229
Head Start Early Learning Outcomes Framework: Ages Birth to Five, 132
Home language
  disabilities in blended ECE-ECSE MTSS and, 202
  in dual language learners (DLLs), 175, 177t, 179
Home-School Plan, 251f, 251n

IDEA, see Individuals with Disabilities Education Improvement Act (IDEA) of 2004 (PL 108-446)
IDEAS (identify, define, explain, ask, say it again), 103–104, 106
Implementation drivers, 53–55, 54f
  in scaling up, 216–217
Implementation fidelity, 78
  in Instructional support, Tier 3, 162, 163f
  in Literacy and Language, Tier 1, 103–104, 106, 111t
  in Literacy and Language, Tier 2, 125–126
  in multi-tiered systems of support (MTSS), 4–5
  in scaling up, 217f, 228, 231
Implementation "how"
  Implementation Teams in, 44, 49f, 50f, 52–53, 59, 63, 69
  improvement cycle for, 49f, 50f, 55–57, 56f, 57f, 59
  MTSS in Early Childhood (EC): Stages of Implementation Analysis, 51–52, 68, 69t–71t
  Stage-Based Active Implementation Planning Tool, 51, 63, 63t–67t
  support in, 44, 49f, 50f, 53–55, 54f, 59
Implementation integrity, 78, 79f, 80
Implementation Science (IS), 12, 18
  Active Implementation Frameworks (AIFs) and, 41
    implementation "how" in, 44, 48–57, 49f, 50f, 56f, 57f, 63, 69
    stakeholders in, 42, 57–58
    usable innovation selection in, 44–48, 59
  definition of, 42–43, 43f

Early Childhood Leadership Team (ECLT) and, 41–42
  effective implementation of, 42, 42f
  Instructional Leadership Team (ILT) and, 30, 42
  leadership development and, 24, 30
  Literacy and Language, Tier 2 and, 125
  multi-tiered systems of support (MTSS) future and, 262–263
  scaling up and, 216–220, 217f, 218n
Implementation Teams
  description of, 52
  in implementation "how," 44, 49f, 50f, 52–53, 59, 63, 69
  role of, 52–53
Improvement cycle
  for implementation "how," 49f, 50f, 55–57, 56f, 57f, 59
  practice-policy communication cycle in, 56–57, 56f, 57f
Incredible Years Classroom Dinosaur Curriculum, in Social-emotional outcomes, Tier 2, 133–134
Individual Conflict of Interest policy, 113n
Individual Growth and Development Indicators (IGDIs)
  in data-based decision making, 85–86, 85f
  in Literacy and Language practices, Tier 1, 105, Tier 2, 120
  multi-tiered systems of support (MTSS) future and, 253n
  Spanish Individual Growth and Development Indicators, 175, 177t
Individualized education programs (IEPs), 8
  assessment of, 33f
  Blended ECE and ECSE and, 193–194, 208–211
  disabilities in blended ECE-ECSE MTSS and, 193–194, 199, 201–202, 208–211
  in Instructional support, Tier 3, 153
  multi-tiered systems of support (MTSS) future and, 253–254
Individualized family service plan (IFSP)
  disabilities in blended ECE-ECSE MTSS and, 193
Individualized Growth and Development Indicators of Early Literacy (IGDIs-EL)
  in data-based decision making, 88–89, 91
  in Literacy and Language, Tier 2, 117, 120
Individuals with Disabilities Education Improvement Act (IDEA) of 2004 (PL 108-446), 11
  assessment of, 16
  disabilities in blended ECE-ECSE MTSS and, 194–197, 199, 200t–201t, 205, 209–211
  multi-tiered systems of support (MTSS) future and, 255

Individual-student-level analysis
  intervention development and
    implementation, 90–91
Infrastructures, 45
  in full implementation, 66
  for initial implementation, 65
  for installation, 64–65
  in scaling up, 218–219
Initial implementation
  communication for, 66
  decision making for, 66
  improvement cycles for, 65
  infrastructure for, 65
  meeting frequency for, 65
  time and, 50f, 51, 65–66
  troubleshooting for, 65
Installation
  decision making for, 65
  infrastructure for, 64–65
  team competencies for, 64
Institute of Educational Sciences (IES), 161
Instructional Leadership Team (ILT)
  assessment choice by, 32
  communication protocols of, 33
  consensus for, 15–16
  core curriculum deployment by, 32
  essential functions for, 46
  expectations of, 30
  Implementation Science (IS) and, 30
  for Literacy and Language, 73
  outcomes statement from, 30
  partnerships development by, 34
  planning time of, 30, 32
  Professional Learning Community groups (PLCs) of, 15
  for targeted outcomes collaboration, 26, 27f–28f, 28, 29f, 30, 31t–32t, 32–34
  teaching strategies implementation by, 32–33
Instructional support, Tier 3
  description of, 155
  dual language learners (DLL) in, 153
  effect sizes from, 154–155
  facts on
    effectiveness, 156
    implementation, 155
    necessity, 154–155
  implementation
    assessment framework, 157–158, 158f
    challenges of, 154
    child behavior, 163f, 167
    embedded intervention in, 165f
    feasibility, 162, 165
    fidelity, 162, 163f
    identification, 157–159, 158f
    Instructional support, Tier 1 and, 156–157, 159, 166
    Instructional support, Tier 2 and, 155–157, 159, 166
    need for, 156–157
    progress monitoring, 158–159, 158f, 165–167
    resources, 154, 165
    scaffolding, 164–165
    small-group instruction, 164–165, 165f
    variables, 162
  individualized education program (IEPs) in, 153
  intervention features
    achievement gap, 159
    explicit instruction, 160, 166
    guided practice, 160
    individualized instruction, 161–162
    lesson structure, 160
    Reading Ready Early Literacy Intervention (RRELI), 160–162, 163f, 165, 165f
    systematic instruction, 160
  measures, 157
  multiple needs in, 154
  phonological awareness (PA) in, 153, 167
  Positive Behavioral Interventions and Support (PBIS), 155
  problem behaviors and, 156–157
  special education and, 157
Intense support, 6, 6f
  in disabilities in blended ECE-ECSE MTSS, 209–210
Intentional instructional strategies, 10
Intervention
  individualized education program (IEPs) for, 8
Intervention design
  evidence-based practice (EBPs) in, 3
  of multi-tiered systems of support (MTSS), 3
  Response to Intervention (RtI) in, 3–4
Intervention plan development and implementation, 7
Intervention support group (ISG), 148

Jungle Friends, in Literacy and Language, Tier 2, 123

Language
  My-IGDI for, 9
Language Challenge (LC)
  in Tune-Up Checklist, 111t
Language Exposure Evaluation Report (LEER)
  for dual language learners (DLLs), 180, 191f–192f
Leadership, shared, 7

Index

Leadership drivers, 54*f*
   in scaling up, 217
Leadership drivers, in data-based decision making, 55
Leadership institutes, 24
Leadership practices
   accountability in, 20–21
   assessment choices, 32, 33*f*
   communication protocols, 33
   core curriculum deployment, 32
   environment creation, 33
   introduction on, 16–18, 17*f*
   in multi-tiered systems of support (MTSS) future, 264
   organizational culture and, 21–22
   partnerships crafting, 34
   in preparation, 22–25
      Competency 1: Pre-K-Grade 3 learning continuum, 24
      Competency 2: Developmentally appropriate practices (DAPs), 24
      Competency 3: Personalized blended learning environment, 25
      Competency 4: Multiple assessment measures, 25
      Competency 5: Professional capacity building, 25
      Competency 6: Family and community learning hub, 25
   professional development (PD) and, 34
   staff and, 21–22
   strengths-based problem solving, 34
   system components and processes, 16–18, 17*f*
   system's focus and, 18–19
   targeted outcomes collaboration, 25–26, 27*f*–28*f*, 29*f*, 30, 31*t*–32*t*, 33*t*, 34–35
   teaching strategies implementation, 32–33
   vertical system hierarchy, 16, 17*f*
   videos on, 17–18
Learning Experiences and Alternative Program (LEAP), 141
Legislative variables, in multi-tiered systems of support (MTSS) future, 254–256
Letters, sounds and, 118*f*, 119*f*, 120*f*
Literacy and Language
   benchmarks in, 84, 84*f*, 85*f*, 86
   at elementary level, 73
   Instructional Leadership Team (ILT) for, 73
   interventions for, 9–10, 86, 86*f*, 90–91
   problem identification in, 88–89, 92
Literacy and Language, Tier 1
   Center for Response to Intervention in Early Childhood (CRTIEC) in, 98–100
   critical skills for, 101
   current state of
      active engagement, 100–101
      instructional support, 99–100
   curriculum for, 97
   explicit instruction for, 102–103
   high-quality implementation support, 105–106
   IDEAS (identify, define, explain, ask, say it again) for, 103–104, 106
   literacy and Language, Tier 2 and, 126–127
   "mid-course corrections" for, 104
   obstacles
      curriculum content, 101–102
      evidence-based practices (EBPs), 102–103
      measures for, 105
      universal screening and progress monitoring, 104–107
   phonological awareness (PA) in, 106–107
   resources for, 102
   steps for, 98–99
   systematic review in, 103
   Teacher Literacy Focus (TLF) in, 99–100
   Tune-Up Checklist for, 103, 111*t*
Literacy and Language, Tier 2
   assessment
      alphabet knowledge skills, 117, 118*f*, 119*f*, 120*f*, 122*t*
      alphabet progress, 117–119, 118*f*, 119*f*, 120*f*
      code-focused skills, 116–117
      measures for, 117, 118*f*, 119*f*, 120, 120*f*
      oral Language skills, 116
      for prevention, 114
      progress monitoring, 117, 118*f*, 119*f*, 120, 120*f*, 127–128, 207, 207*f*
      universal screenings, 116–117, 206
   candidates for, 113–114
   curriculum for, 116
   definition of, 114
   early skills in, 114–116
   explicit instruction for, 121
   getting started with implementation in, 126–127
   intervention in, 126–128
   instructional approaches for, 120–124
      EMERGE in, 121, 122*t*
      problem-solving approach in, 121
      standard treatment protocols in, 121–125, 122*t*
   literacy and Language, Tier 1 and, 126–127
   print knowing in, 114, 122*t*, 123
   professional development, 124–127
      evidence-based practices (EBPs) in, 126

Literacy Express Curriculum, in Dual language learners (DLLs), 181
Local education agency (LEA), 209
Local norms, in static scores, 83
Loyola University of Chicago, principal preparation at, 23

Master cadre (MC)
   in scaling up, 220, 221*f*, 224–226, 229
Mathematics, 78, 79*f*
Minnesota Centers of Excellence for Young Children with Disabilities, scaling up at, 224–226, 230
Motivation
   Behavior Incident Report and, 136, 137*f*, 138
   leadership practices and, 22
   Social-emotional outcomes, Tier 2, and, 139–140, 139*f*
MTSS in Early Childhood (EC): Stages of Implementation Analysis, 51–52, 68, 69*t*–71*t*
Multiple assessment measures, in leadership practices, 25
Multi-tiered systems of support (MTSS)
   administrative support and resources, 11
   benefits of, 15
   core components of, 2
     data-based problem solving and decision making, 7
     evidence-based practices (EBPs) and intervention practices, 4
     family, school, and community partnering, 7
     implementation fidelity, 4–5
     layered support continuum, 5–6, 6*f*
     shared leadership, 7
     universal screening and progress monitoring, 5
   core principles of, 3
   description of, 3–7
   in early childhood education, 7–11
   evidence-based practice (EBPs), 4, 10
   federal and state support in, 10–11
   identification in, 1–2
   implementation challenges of, 10–11
   intervention design of, 3
   problem solving in, 2
   Pyramid Model in, 8–9
   screening in, 8
   trained workforce lack in, 10
Multi-tiered systems of support (MTSS) future
   adoption and development challenges
     all three tiers of service effects, 260
     eligibility, 261
     evidence-based practices (EBPs), 260
     innovation and implementation speed limits, 262
     overall effect, 260–261
     scope and reach concepts, 259
     unified services ongoing development, 261–262
   adoption and development opportunities, 262–263
   alignment in, 263
   collaboration in, 263–264
   contextual features and, 254–259
     assessment, 258
     evidence-based practices (EBPs), 258
     outcomes improvement, 256–257
     "pay for success" and, 257
     preservice and in-service training, 258–259
     professional development, 259
     social impact bonds and other funding mechanisms, 257–258
     targeted universalism, 258
   current features and, 254
   early education variables, 258–259
   Elementary and Secondary Education Act in, 255
   Every Student Succeeds Act (ESSA), 255
   Head Start and, 253, 255–256
   Implementation Science (IS) and, 262–263
   Individual Growth & Development Indicators and, 253*n*
   individualized education programs (IEPs) and, 253–254
   Individuals with Disabilities Education Improvement Act (IDEA) of 2004 (PL 108-446) and, 255
   legislative and regulatory variables, 254–256
   Office of Special Education Programs (OSEP) and, 255
   outcome assessments in, 263
   Preschool for All (PSA) and, 255
   Professional Learning Community groups (PLCs) in, 264
   publicly funded preschool programs, 255–256
   universal screening and, 261
My-IGDI, for language, 9

National Association for the Education of Young Children (NAEYC), 11
   disabilities in blended ECE-ECSE MTSS and, 196, 198
   initiative of, 23
National Association of Elementary School Principals (NAESP)
   competencies of, 24
   on leadership practices, 22–23

The National Center for Learning
    Disabilities, The Roadmap to Pre-K
    RTI from, 238
National Center on Quality Teaching and
    Learning (NCQTL), 102, 106
National Governors' Association (NGA)
    on preservice, 23
National Head Start Association (NHSA), 11
    disabilities in blended ECE-ECSE MTSS
    and, 196
National Implementation Research
    Network (NIRN), 48, 218, 219
National PTA, family engagement and, 238
National Research Council, target skills or
    behaviors from, 80–81

Obama Administration's Promise
    Neighborhoods, multi-tiered systems
    of support (MTSS) future and, 257
Office of Special Education Programs
    (OSEP), 132
    disabilities in blended CSE-CSSE MTSS
    and, 209
    multi-tiered systems of support (MTSS)
    future and, 255
Oral language skills, 116
Organizational culture
    leadership practices and, 21–22
    Targeted outcomes collaboration and,
    26, 34–35
Organizational drivers, 54f
    in scaling up, 217
Organizational drivers, in data-based
    decision making, 55
Outcomes interpretation
    usable innovation selection and, 48
    see also Social-emotional outcomes

PAth to Literacy, 113n, 122–123, 122t
PATHS Preschool, in Social-emotional
    outcomes, Tier 2, 133–134
Pennsylvania, scaling up in, 230
Personalized blended learning
    environment, 25
Phonological awareness (PA)
    in Instructional support, Tier 3, 153, 167
    in Literacy and Language, Tier 1, 106–107
    in Literacy and Language, Tier 2, 123
Picture Naming Fluency (PNF), 84f, 85f, 89
    in data-based decision making, 85–86
PL 108-446, see Individuals with
    Disabilities Education Improvement
    Act (IDEA) of 2004
Plan evaluation
    problem solving, 91
    in problem-solving model, 75f, 80

Positive Behavioral Interventions and
    Support (PBIS), 20
    in Instructional support, Tier 3, 155
Practical performance assessments, 47
Practice-based coaching (PBC), 46
    in Literacy and Language, Tier 1, 105–106
Practice–policy feedback loops, in data-
    based decision making, 56–57, 57f
Preschool Curriculum Evaluation
    Research Initiative, 102
Preschool Early Literacy Indicator (PELI),
    105, 117, 120
Preschool for All (PSA)
    in multi-tiered systems of support
    (MTSS) future, 255
Preservice
    multi-tiered systems of support (MTSS)
    future and, 258–259
    National Governors' Association (NGA)
    on, 23
Principals, see National Association of
    Elementary School Principals
    (NAESP)
Print knowing, in Literacy and Language,
    Tier 2, 114–115, 122t, 123
Problem behaviors, Instructional support,
    Tier 3 and, 156–157
Problem solving
    data-based, 7, 12, 45–46
    in disabilities in blended CSE-ECSE and
    MTSS, 208
    intervention development and
    implementation, 90–91
    in multi-tiered systems of support
    (MTSS), 2
    plan evaluation and, 91
    problem analysis and, 89–90
    problem identification and, 84f, 88–89, 92
    Recognition and Response Model in, 9
    social, 133f, 141f
Problem-solving model
    data collection in, 75–76, 91
    intervention development and
    implementation in, 75f, 77–78, 79f,
    91–92
    plan evaluation in, 75f, 80
    problem identification in, 75–76, 75f
    target skills or behaviors
        data on, 81–82, 82f
        domain- or skill-specific screening of, 82f
        intervention development in, 82f
        selection of, 80–81
    Treatment Integrity Checklist for, 79f
Professional capacity building, 25
Professional development (PD)
    Implementation Science (IS) and, 125
    from Instructional Leadership Team
    (ILT), 34

Professional development (PD)—*continued*
  leadership practices and, 34
  Literacy and Language, Tier 2, 124–127
  multi-tiered systems of support (MTSS) future and, 259
  Pyramid Model State Benchmarks of Quality (BoQ) and, 222
Professional Learning Community groups (PLCs)
  developmentally appropriate practice (DAPs) in, 24
  of Instructional Leadership Team (ILT), 15
  in multi-tiered systems of support (MTSS) future, 264
  for targeted outcomes collaboration, 27*f*–28*f*, 28, 30, 31*t*–32*t*, 35
Program-level data, 12, 88–90
Program-level implementation, in scaling up, 229
Progress monitoring
  of disabilities in blended ECE-ECSE MTSS, 201*t*, 211
  of dual language learners (DLLs), 174–175, 176*t*–177*t*, 178
  of Instructional support, Tier 3, 158–159, 158*f*, 165–167
  of Literacy and Language, Tier 1, 104–107
  of multi-tiered systems of support (MTSS), 5
  multi-tiered systems of support (MTSS) future and, 260
  of Social-emotional outcomes, Tier 2, 131, 143–145, 143*f*, 144*f*, 147–148
Promoting Alternative Thinking Strategies (PATHS)
  in leadership practices, 31*t*–32*t*, 33*f*
Proximal measures, 165–166
Pyramid Infant Toddler Observation Scale (TPITOS), 222
Pyramid Model
  in multi-tiered systems of support (MTSS), 8–9
  Social-emotional outcomes, Tier 2, and, 134–135, 134*f*
Pyramid Model State Benchmarks of Quality (BoQ)
  exploration and installation stage, 221–223
  implementation stage and, 225
  professional development and, 222
  scaling up and sustainability, 223
Pyramid Plus Center, 225, 228

Read It Again Pre-K! (RIA)
  in Literacy and Language, Tier 1, 122*t*, 123

Reading Ready Early Literacy Intervention (RRELI)
  in Instructional support, Tier 3, 160–162, 163*f*, 165, 165*f*
Recognition and Response Model, 9
Recognition and Response-Dual Language Learner (R&R-DLL)
  in Dual language learners (DLLs), 173
Regulatory variables, in multi-tiered systems of support (MTSS) future, 254–256
Resources
  in exploration, 63–64, 70
  Instructional support, Tier 3, and, 154, 165
  for Literacy and Language, Tier 1, 102
  in multi-tiered systems of support (MTSS), 11
  videos, 12
Response to Intervention (RtI)
  adoption of, 18
  disabilities in blended ECE-ECSE MTSS and, 195–197
  evaluation of, 7
  in Intervention design, 3–4
  The Roadmap to Pre-K RTI, 238
  support tiers for, 5–6, 6*f*

The Roadmap to Pre-K RTI, 238

Scaling up
  coaching, 221*f*
  master cadre (MC), 220, 221*f*, 231
    exploration and installation stages, 224–225
    implementation stages, 225
    sustainability, 225–226, 229
  programwide demonstration sites, 220
    annual evaluation reports, 230
    coaching, 221*f*, 226–227
    cross-agency team for, 231
    implementation fidelity, 217*f*, 228, 231
    implementation stages, 226–228
    leadership team of, 226
    success stories about, 230
    sustainability, 227–228, 230
  Pyramid Model, 215
    cascading logic model, 217, 217*f*
    Center on the Social and Emotional Foundations for Early Learning, 218, 218*n*
    competency drivers in, 216–217
    data-based decision making, 217–218, 220, 221*f*, 222–223
    evidence-based practices (EBPs) in, 217
    exploration and installation stage, 221–223, 221*f*

fidelity measures, 217f
Implementation Drivers in, 216–217
Implementation Science (IS) frameworks, 216–220, 217f, 218n
implementation stages, 223
infrastructure, 218–219
intervention, 217f, 221f
leadership drivers in, 217
Minnesota Centers of Excellence for Young Children with Disabilities, 224–226, 230
National Implementation Research Network (NIRN), 218
organizational drivers in, 217
professional development facilitators (PDFs), 224–225
program-level implementation of, 229
purpose of, 218
Pyramid Infant Toddler Observation Scale (TPITOS), 222
Pyramid Model State Benchmarks of Quality (BoQ), 221–223, 225
Southeast Kansas Community Action Program (SEK–CAP) Head Start, 229
state implementation critical structures, 220
state leadership team (SLT), 220–224, 221f, 227, 229–231
statewide implementation stages, 218
sustainability and, 223
Teaching Pyramid Observation Tool (TPOT), 222
Technical Assistance Center on Social and Emotional Interventions for Young Children, 218, 218n
training and technical assistance (T/TA) experts, 219, 224–225
Second Step, in Social-emotional outcomes, Tier 2, 133–134
Selection, 54, 54t
of target skills or behaviors, 80–81
Self-assessment, 101
Self-Assessment of Family Engagement Practices, 238, 249–250, 250n
Self-concept, positive, 133f
Self-regulation, 1
Single-case design, 86–87, 86f
Skill growth rates, 87
Social-contextual factors, 77f
Social-emotional outcomes, 1
in multi-tiered systems of support (MTSS) future, 215
Social-emotional outcomes, Tier 1, 135
Social-emotional outcomes, Tier 2
children in need identification, 131, 138
behavior rating scales, 136, 137f, 148
screening tools for, 136
teacher observation, 136
competency areas and skills in, 132–133, 133f
families and, 137f, 145, 147
frameworks for, 132
instruction individualization
additional adult and peer support, 141–142
embedding, 142
frequency count in, 143–144, 144f
increased practice opportunities, 140–142, 141f, 145–146
initiations and challenging playground behavior, 144, 144f
intensive progress monitoring, 131, 143–145, 143f, 144f, 147–148
prompting, 141–142, 145
rating scale in, 143–144, 143f
rehearsal opportunities in, 141
skills task analysis, 140
taking turns, 140, 142
instructional supports
effective instruction characteristics, 138–140, 139f
new skills motivational incentives, 139–140, 139f
instructional supports steps
implementation and outcomes monitoring, 145–147
instructional approaches selection, 145
instructional decision making, 146
Social-emotional outcomes, Tier 1, and, 135
teacher support, 146–147
tiered models promotion in
curricula in, 133–134, 146
leadership team in, 135–136
prevention in, 133–134, 134f
Pyramid Model in, 134–135, 134f
Sounds, letters and, 118f, 119f, 120f
Southeast Kansas Community Action Program Head Start (SEK-CAP), scaling up in, 229
Spanish Individual Growth and Development Indicators, 175, 177t
Spanish language, see Dual language learners (DLLs)
Specific, Measurable, Attainable, Results-oriented, and Time-bound (SMART)
in targeted outcomes collaboration, 28, 30, 31t–32t
Stage-Based Active Implementation Planning Tool, 51, 63, 63t–67t
Stakeholders, 20
collaboration within, 57
examples of, 21
family engagement and, 244, 249–250
in Implementation Science (IS), 42, 57–58
practitioner competency building by, 58
support of, 57–58

Standard operating procedures (SOP), 29*f*
State leadership team (SLT)
   master cadre (MC) and, 229
   in scaling up, 220–224, 221*f*, 227, 229–231
State support, 10–11, 264
Story Champs, 122*t*, 123–124
Story Friends™, in Literacy and Language, Tier 2, 113*n*, 122*t*, 123–124, 127
Supplemental support, 6, 6*f*
System change, 19, 34–35
System components and processes, 16–17, 17*f*
Systematic review, 103
Systems intervention, in data-based decision making, 55

Taking turns, in Social-emotional outcomes, Tier 2, 140, 142
Target skills or behaviors
   data on, 81–82, 82*f*
   selection of, 80–81
Targeted outcomes collaboration, 33*t*
   administrative leadership team (LEAD team) for, 25–26, 27*f*
   Instructional Leadership Team (ILT) for, 26, 27*f*–28*f*, 28, 29*f*, 30, 31*t*–32*t*, 32–34
   organizational culture and, 26, 34–35
   Professional Learning Community groups (PLCs) for, 27*f*–28*f*, 28, 30, 31*t*–32*t*, 35
   Specific, Measurable, Attainable, Results-oriented, and Time-bound (SMART) in, 28, 30, 31*t*–32*t*
Teacher Literacy Focus (TLF)
   in Literacy and Language, Tier 1, 99–100
Teaching Pyramid Observation Tool (TPOT), 222
Technical Assistance Center on Social Emotional Interventions for Young Children, in scaling up, 218, 218*n*
Time
   exploration and, 50, 50*f*, 63–64, 69–71
   in implementation "how," 44, 48–52, 49*f*, 50*f*, 59, 63–67, 69–71
   initial implementation and, 50*f*, 51, 65–66
   of Instructional Leadership Team (ILT), 30, 32
   in Instructional support, Tier 3, 164
   scores across, 84–87, 84*f*, 85*f*
   Specific, Measurable, Attainable, Results-oriented, and Time-bound (SMART) in, 28, 30, 31*t*–32*t*
Training, 54, 54*t*
Training and technical assistance (T/TA) experts
   in scaling up, 219, 224–225
Tune-Up Checklist, for Literacy and Language, Tier 1, 103, 111*t*

Universal screening
   benchmarks in, 84, 84*f*, 85*f*, 86
   of dual language learners (DLLs), 173–174
Universal screening and progress monitoring
   of Literacy and Language, Tier 1, 104–107
   of multi-tiered systems of support (MTSS), 5
Universal screening data on vocabulary, Disabilities in blended ECE-ECSE MTSS and, 206, 206*f*
Usable innovation selection, 44, 59
   evidence-based practices (EBPs) in, 45–48
   hiring, training, coaching, and performance assessment in, 47–48
   operational definitions in, 46–47
   outcomes interpretation and, 48
   practical performance assessments in, 47

Values, 101
Videos, 12
Vignettes
   on disabilities in blended ECE-ECSE MTSS, 193–194, 210–211
   on dual language learners (DLLs), 171, 185–186
   on family engagement, 235, 245
   on Implementation Science (IS), 41–42, 59
   on Instructional support, Tier 3, 153–154, 166–167
   on leadership practices, 15–16, 35
   on Literacy and Language, Tier 1, 97–98, 106–107
   on Literacy and Language, Tier 2, 113, 116, 127–128
   on multi-tiered systems of support (MTSS) future, 253–254
   on Problem-solving model, 73–74, 90, 92
   on scaling up, 215, 231
   on Social-emotional outcomes, Tier 2, 131, 145–148
Visual impairments, 201–202
Vocabulary
   disabilities in blended ECE-ECSE MTSS and, 206–207, 206*f*, 207*f*
   family engagement and, 235
Vocabulary Oral Language and Academic Readiness (VOLAR), 184

What Works Clearinghouse, 102